DATE DUE

			PRINTED IN U.S.A.

Handbook
~ of ~
Radio Publicity
&
Promotion

3rd Edition

Jack MacDonald
Curtis R. Holsopple

TAB **TAB BOOKS**
Blue Ridge Summit, PA

THIRD EDITION
FIRST PRINTING

© 1970 and 1991 by **TAB BOOKS**
TAB BOOKS is a division of McGraw-Hill, Inc.

Library of Congress Cataloging-in-Publication Data

MacDonald, Jack.
   Handbook of radio publicity and promotion / by Jack MacDonald and Curtis R. Holsopple.—3rd ed.
     p.   cm.
   ISBN 0-8306-3390-1
   1. Radio advertising.   I. Holsopple, Curtis R.   II. Title.
HF6146.R3M173   1990
659.14'2—dc20   90-34850
                                                      CIP

TAB BOOKS offers software for sale. For information and a catalog, please contact TAB Software Department, Blue Ridge Summit, PA 17294-0850.

Questions regarding the content of this book should be addressed to:

   Reader Inquiry Branch
   TAB BOOKS
   Blue Ridge Summit, PA 17294-0214

Acquisitions Editor: Kim Tabor
Editing and Design: Joanne M. Slike
Typesetting: Terry Hite
Proofreading: Linda King

Contents

SECTION 3
Outside Stunts

SECTION 4
Fun Promotions

SECTION 5
Community Boosters

SECTION 6
Promotions for Every Month

SECTION 7
Station Anniversary Promotions

SECTION 8
Merchants' Milestones

SECTION 9

On-Air Themes

SECTION 10

Quickie Humor Material

SECTION 11

Station Identification

SECTION 12

Station Promos

Preface

EVERYONE'S CREATIVE BATTERY RUNS LOW AT SOME POINT. IF YOU want to jump-start your radio station's promotion efforts, this is the book for you. This third edition of the *Handbook of Radio Promotion and Publicity* is heavily revised, updated, and rearranged. The original edition's goal was to gather together as many useful radio promotion ideas as possible. This third edition brings that original work up to date, and does it with a much-improved layout for easy access to information.

The original manuscript for *The Handbook of Radio Promotion and Publicity* was prepared by Jack MacDonald, a West Coast-based writer with many connections in Hollywood. Besides his movietown career interests, Mac-Donald's original book demonstrated his boundless imagination, loony sense of humor, and a tireless ability to assemble a staggering collection of idea-starters on every aspect of radio promotions.

After MacDonald's death in the early 1980s, *The Handbook of Radio Publicity and Promotion* continued to be popular with radio stations needing this unique resource. But the English language, the North American culture, and radio station formats have all evolved and progressed since the late 1950s when the book had its beginnings.

TAB Books saw that this book deserved a renewed lease on life. A rewrite was undertaken, and it turned out to be a massive job. Here are the features of this third edition:

- An all-new opening chapter defines and establishes the need for radio promotions, explaining how these promotions can benefit the station, its listeners, and its community. Section 1 lays out ethical, legal, and procedural guidelines for radio promotions, and methods for effective print promotional materials to augment the on-air product.

- Heavily revised formatting makes this edition much more readable than the original volume. Much-improved consistency and economy in writing style makes individual promotions easier to understand and use. On-air scripts are now rendered in all-caps, separating script material from the book's narrative body text.

- Promotions have been modified, added, and deleted to bring the book in line with today's real-world radio station circumstances. Certainly the role of women in broadcasting has expanded and changed in three decades of evolution.

- The patterns of shopping for consumer goods have shifted away from the downtown business district through the neighborhood shopping center to the huge suburban malls. Now, revitalized downtown shopping districts are popular again, but they borrow heavily from the unified approach of the malls. These shifts all affect how on-location promotions must be handled, and the third edition of this book reflects this.

Revising this book has been a joyous romp through American nostalgia of the mid- to late twentieth century. Some promotions from the first edition were irretrievable, though. Several had to do with women's hats, and women just don't wear hats like they used to. In other cases, word choice has changed radically—businessmen are now business leaders, and increasingly more of them are women. In the 60s we talked about "modern conveniences." Now they are a given in high-tech living. And the "office girls" of the early 60s don't "man" the phones anymore, but the office staff *covers* the phones better than ever. Our language, and our attitudes, have changed.

Is this book complete? No, although we've tried. Is up to date? No way—the target is moving too fast. Can you use everything we have included here? Impossible. As thick as this book is, it's just a starting point—actually, it's a broad collection of starting points. We think there is something in here for everyone, from major market stations to local peanut whistles, and every conceivable kind of radio station in between.

You may even read one of our promotions and say, "Hey, they stole my idea!" Sorry, but everything in this book has probably been tried (with variations) many dozens of times across the country. You're free to experiment and innovate with what you find here. In fact, you'd *better* innovate because your circumstances are probably unique anyway.

Radio is a part of the cultural landscape around the world. Here's to those pioneers and daredevils who try these promotions and others—they're a breath of fresh air to the medium.

CURTIS R. HOLSOPPLE
Harrisonburg, Virginia

Introduction

RADIO BROADCASTING HAS GONE HAND-IN-HAND WITH PROMOTION FROM the medium's very birth. Yet if you read any history of broadcasting or talk to any pioneer who survives from that era, you will find a common thread—early radio formats in North America were mostly music and lecture programming that lacked the commercialism we see today. But to say that early broadcast radio was entirely noncommercial is false.

Early broadcasting was supported largely by commercial companies, such as manufacturers of electrical appliances. While the earliest radio programs were usually culturally uplifting, the existence of the radio station and its programming assured the sponsoring store or manufacturer that their wireless receivers would sell at a brisk pace.

Why did department stores find noncommercial and culturally uplifting programming so worthwhile? Clearly, radio broadcasting was a marketing tool, a means of promotion and publicity. (Noncommercial, huh? Not for a minute!)

Today we take radio and television for granted. The medium of electronic communication is as common as indoor plumbing. Yet in the first two decades of the twentieth century, radio (and indoor plumbing) was a bit of a novelty. From its very birth, it made an ideal attention-getter.

1.1   THE UNDERLYING REASONS FOR PROMOTIONS

This *Handbook of Radio Publicity and Promotion* is a resource to help your radio station put its best foot forward. Mostly, its a collection of bright ideas that have been tried and that have worked. Let's take a moment to look at the underlying reasoning behind good radio promotions.

Why Promote Your Station?

Many years have passed since radio was a toddler taking its first wobbling steps. But the idea of using the medium as an avenue of promotion and publicity has only grown stronger with age. Radio stations have always felt the need to promote themselves. Commercial and noncommercial stations alike can't resist using a variety of means to ensure that someone out there is listening.

Radio promotion and publicity—that's what this book is all about. This isn't a scholarly narrative. It's just a collection of bright ideas from the school of hard knocks. Given your own unique circumstances coupled with your own creative inspiration, these ideas can help make your station succeed.

You've probably already heard of or used some of the ideas presented in this book. No matter what kind of stunt, program, contest, gimmick, or attention-getter we've found and collected here, two underlying principles have been at work:

- Maintain the audience you have.
- Broaden your potential audience.

Promotions Should Work for You

We're presenting ideas in this book. We expect you to argue with, adapt from, dismantle, and rebuild anything you use. Although a copyright exists for this book as a whole, you are free (even expected!) to use the suggestions and action plans found here.

Be Appealing to Your Audience

No matter how many listeners you have, your true audience is just one person. Anything you do on your station has the potential of drawing that individual in closer, or causing that person to reach out and turn your station off. You might, for instance, run a contest that is open only to a restricted segment of your audience. If you do that, try to arrange things so that the ineligible listeners will still enjoy listening from the sidelines. Keep everyone involved in some way.

Here are some additional tips:

- Tie your station in with the community. Be personal and likable. Look for ways to boost civic pride. In doing so, you will cement your station's importance as a contributor to community life.
- It may sound a little selfish, but you should avoid entangling yourselves into joint promotions involving other radio stations. If you are trying to establish your station as a community leader, avoid placing your reputation in the hands of other stations that may see things differently.
- Don't load down your contests with complicated rules. If you can't explain the promotion within the confines of a single 60-second promo, you've got a problem. In fact, try to keep the explanation down to 30 seconds or less.
- Simpler promotions are more likely to showcase your station as a good friend to have around. Overly elaborate promotions may overshadow the station by absorbing too much airtime, or by frustrating the listeners.

A Seven-Point Checklist

Good radio promotions should embody the seven points listed below. If you devise some kind of publicity stunt for your station that is lacking more than one of these, give it a hard look before proceeding.

1. Keep it simple and understandable.
2. Keep it brief and snappy.
3. Keep it open, accessible, and appealing to the audience.
4. Don't overwhelm your on-air programming with the promotion it is supposed to showcase.
5. Employ built-in elements of suspense, using teasers to build interest.
6. Design your contests so that the winners must be listening to win. (Remember, you're working at building your audience.)
7. Have fun. Be an entertaining friend to your listeners. Keep it fun for your staff as well.

Achieving "Spread"

Effective promotions have something called "spread"—a natural chain reaction where the promotion reaches a listener directly and that listener tells a friend about it. The nonlistener checks in to see what all the excitement is about and the promotion grows—it "spreads."

Just as your station's commercials sell a sponsor's product or service, your promotional efforts sell your station. The listeners must remember *you* as a standout. Even in a small-market situation, your station's signal is only one of many available to the listeners. You must make your station's identity stand tall in the listener's mind. Sell your call letters. Sell your dial location. Sell your station's logo (or slogan). Sell your format. Make sure they know you and know how to find your station again later.

Obviously, radio promotions help lock-in listeners. Your contests and stunts make sure that listeners don't want to miss anything. And while they're waiting for the secret song or the chance to be caller number seven, they hear your programming, your music, your news, and your commercials.

A close tie-in to running audience-building contests is to tell commercial sponsors what you're up to. Selling commercial time adjacent to contest segments boosts the value of that commercial's audience penetration. Your station can charge more for the commercial adjacencies, and the sponsor can reasonably expect more bang for his buck as more listeners hear the commercials.

1.2 HANDLING THE MECHANICS

Now that we've dealt with the philosophical background, let's dig into the mechanics of radio promotions.

Ways to Get Entries

There are several ways to get people to enter your contests. If you don't think this stage through in advance, you'll dig yourself a huge hole full of problems and never climb out.

1. **Mail entries.** "Just keep those cards and letters coming, folks." It's a well-worn cliche, but our advice is to go for the cards and discourage the letters in most cases. Cards are easier to handle, since there's no envelope to open and they stack and file easily. If you're insisting on one entry per person, just file the cards alphabetically for an instant check.

2. **Telephone entries.** "Caller number three gets a chance at the big prize." This is a nice gimmick, since members of the public get a chance to have direct interaction with station staff—maybe even the idolized DJ. That builds rapport with the audience, and that, in turn, builds audience numbers.

   But telephone entries require special handling or they can really bog down your DJ in a hurry. Define for the audience how telephone entries will be handled. Perhaps you'll have a special telephone number dedicated exclusively to contest call-ins. Often you will only accept calls during a certain time period. You may use the "caller number five" trick to ward off people with speed-dialing telephones who might hog the show.

   Have contest entry forms ready in the control room so that the DJ has a handy place to write down the contestant's name, address, phone number, and other pertinent information. And if your station does a high volume in phone-ins, you'd better have some office help on duty to help take the calls.

3. **In-person entries at sponsoring merchants.** A strong selling point for potential sponsors is that you will bring customers into their stores. Sure, "no purchase is necessary to enter," but the merchants know that getting people to come to the store won't hurt anything either.

   Having the sponsoring merchant handle the collection of entry forms relieves the station staff of this clerical task. Seeing the traffic first-hand also shows the sponsor the value of advertising on your station.

4. **Automatic entry into additional contests.** If you do several small- and medium-size promotions during the year, have all of those entries dumped into a big bin for a grand-prize drawing once a year. (See the "Year-Long Promotion" outlined in section 2 of this book).

5. **Having air personalities present in the stores to accept entries.** If your station is like most, it is small, crowded, somewhat messy, and not well-suited to casual visits from the public. But fix up your air personalities with

a remote console in a store window or the central area of a shopping mall, and you have a dandy way for your staff to meet the public.

Doing broadcast remotes is an ideal way to get listeners involved in your station and to help them build loyalty to your place on the dial. Increased listener loyalty means higher ratings, which means higher ad rates, which means increased success for your station.

Keeping Track of Entries

It's your contest, so structure things to keep it easy on yourself.

1. **Use standard-sized forms.** As mentioned before, written entries should usually be restricted to postcards. Make it clear in your contest rules that nonstandard entries will be tossed in the dumpster. If you mix mail entries with phone-in entries, have the phone-in entry forms made out of postcard stock so they are handled and filed the same way.

2. **Date stamping breaks ties**. If you think you'll need to break ties in the contest you're running, maybe you should date- and time-stamp each postcard or phone entry as it is received. Sure, "the entry with the earliest postmark wins," but sometimes you can't read the blurry blotch inscribed by the folks at the post office. Date stamping entries upon receipt provides a backup system.

3. **Be ready to store the entries**. Have suitable storage and/or filing space ready before the entries arrive. If you're doing a contest worth running, you'll be up to your gizzard in postcards in short order. Have the big rotating drum built in advance, if that's how you're going to store the entries. Or if you must have organized filing, get those file cabinets set up. And be a stickler for security! You don't want anyone getting the idea that they can rig this system!

1.3   PROMOTIONS NEED A REASON FOR EXISTING

Anyone can open a book full of ideas about promotions, randomly pick out a plan, and try to make it work. Your station will get far more benefit, however, if you take some time to list your station's strong points and areas that need improving.

If yours is the only station in the county and you still aren't making it into the top five in ratings, concentrate your contest on whatever dayparts are your strongest. Meanwhile, you'd better do some survey work and find out what listeners prefer.

What NOT to Do

Don't base your next contest on a weak facet of your station. If your station's news offerings are second-rate (or worse), don't try to build ratings with a promotion that pays listeners for news tips—they aren't listening to you for news, and news-tip promotion will flop, just proving how poor your performance is.

Instead, give your news department a hard look and make needed changes. Then, promote the socks off of your own upgraded efforts to give listeners first-rate news coverage.

Motivated Promotions

In general, promotions work best when there is some natural motivation for having one. Specific promotions work best at certain times of the year and also may integrate best with the programming for specific dayparts.

Obviously, your station's underlying reason for having a promotion is to build listenership. Similarly, sponsors want to participate in promotions when they can see an obvious payoff through increased business traffic. Your promotion must be good for both you and your sponsor, or it will be a losing proposition.

Your listeners, however, must perceive the promotion as a goodwill gesture. Your promotion must have some kind of reward for the listeners, even those who don't participate actively in your contest or event. From the listeners' viewpoint, your promotion should represent your station's effort to reach out and get acquainted. Likewise, the sponsoring agencies and businesses should be using promotions to extend a warm welcome to your listeners.

Your promotions may always have a "what's in this for me" element for all concerned, but don't forget to have fun doing them. If at all possible, your promotions should make all participants get better acquainted, learn something useful about each other, and still have some laughs.

Through carefully-crafted promotions, your station can actually make the community a better place. Who knows? You may develop some community activity that will turn into a popular tourist attraction. Or your joint efforts with a local charity could make life better for a lot of people.

You don't always have to be the driving force behind a given promotion. Check with the Chamber of Commerce, the local Scouting offices, large churches, and other civic organizations. You'll discover ample public events that you can cover for their news and human interest value. That alone will make more folks want to listen to your station—exactly the focus of any good promotion.

1.4 GETTING IT ON THE AIR

Here are some helpful hints that, at first blush, seem trivial. But don't you dare overlook the small stuff, or big problems can develop.

Using Phone Calls on the Air

If you have listeners calling in or if you place calls for broadcast, remember to get permission before putting a caller on the air. You're trampling on federal regulations and a potential lawsuit from the caller if you get sloppy about this one.

Live calls on the air can get scary if someone from the lunatic fringe is on the line. Make sure your station is equipped with some kind of time-delay device permitting you to bleep out offensive remarks before they actually get on the air. In addition, a high-quality phone connection is essential. Both the feed from the phone line into the board and the return audio from the studio to the caller must be as clean as possible. Your station's engineer and general manager must be committed to this issue of quality, or any phone participation situations will be clear as mud.

The connection to the phone line and operation of the "bleep-out" system must be simple and reliable. Don't make your DJs go through physical contortions and mental gymnastics or your air quality will suffer through avoidable foul-ups.

Promote Your Promotions

Wouldn't it be dull if you threw a party and nobody came? That could happen if you don't invite anyone. When making plans for an upcoming promotion, make sure your listeners find out. Build anticipation and be distinctive in identifying the promotion.

Spend some time working out a snappy (and pronounceable) name for the event. Dig through the production library for just the right jingles, musical stings, or sound effects. If your event depends heavily on printed matter, get a good artist to help with all graphic design matters.

If your promotion involves live remotes, have large posters prepared professionally. Don't settle for the receptionist's teenage daughter hand-lettering things on poster board with felt markers. And a big banner run out on someone's computer with a poorly-inked dot-matrix printer isn't much better. Get the posters done professionally.

Build a Unified Identity Package

The on-air promos that tell of an upcoming promotion should include distinctive music, sounds effects, or slogans that will carry through the entire promotion. The current promotion's theme or slogan should be worked into the station ID announcements. All of your air personalities should talk it up. Repetition and consistency are both important.

The promotion should also be consistently identified with your station. Get your station's call letters, frequency, and verbal logo worked into all promotion elements, including the name of the promotion. That means always referring to your "Backyard Barbecue Contest" as the "WZZZ Backyard Barbecue Contest" or the "Z-93 Backyard Barbecue Contest." If you do any advertising on TV or in the newspaper, your printed image should embody the same phrases and concepts as the on-air promos.

SOME GENERAL PRECAUTIONS   1.5

The main focus of promotion and publicity is to help improve images and impressions—to build positive relationships. Your station seeks wider acceptance among listeners. Your sponsors want more and happier customers. The listeners want to feel that the radio station and its sponsors are sensitive and responsive to their needs.

The last thing you need, therefore, is for a promotion to fall apart. Worse yet is the promotion that boomerangs and causes hard feelings. And the ultimate disaster would be some kind of stunt that ends in accidental damage, personal injury, or death.

Involve Others

Hopefully, your worst flops will go relatively unnoticed by anyone but the general manager and the station's accountant. To head off disaster at any level, take time to plan and get others involved in the planning stage. Brainstorming and arguing may seem like time-wasters, but they're much better for you and your station than mopping up after a fiasco.

Plan for Print Pieces Early

Many print shops and copy centers can handle routine photocopying in an hour or a day, but don't think you can get posters, banners, and specially designed handouts that quickly. You'd better bargain on a month's lead-time as the very minimum, and up to three months to be safe.

Props and Facilities

Once you know how your promotion will be conducted, get going on construction or acquisition of any displays, filing cabinets, entry card mixing bins, or other special props. Likewise, get your chief engineer in on the planning stages from the start, anticipating whether you'll need extra cart machines and carts, special hookups or remote lines, or additional telephone equipment.

Long-Range Planning

Your station's sales department should have a long-range strategy for upcoming promotions so that they can line up appropriate sponsors well in advance. A one-year master plan is the bare minimum, and a two-year plan is better. This allows your sales reps to get your station's promotions worked into the sponsor's own budgeting and promotion plans. And this will defuse the sponsor's excuse of "I don't have any budget for prizes and extra sponsorships this year."

1.6   AD-LIB ETIQUETTE

Today's radio is fast-paced (even if the station's sound calls for a laid-back approach). Often, your on-air personalities are ad-libbing rather than working from an established and approved script. Even so, you should uphold some standards of conduct about the way your DJs portray themselves, their station, its activities, and its sponsors.

On-Air Comments about Promotions

Having fun with your promotions is important—even essential. Your audience, sponsors, and staff should all find the promotions you run to be attractive and entertaining. Having fun motivates involvement.

Making fun, however, is a different matter. Belittling or putting down a person, business, product, or service can be a turnoff for your audience. Make sure that all aspects of your promotions are appropriate for your station and your market. Don't embarrass your air staff with promotions that are too dumb to believe. Insist that your air staff not make critical remarks on the air if a promotion idea doesn't seem right to them. (Problem-spotting should have been solicited far in advance at staff meetings when the promotion is first proposed.)

It follows logically, then, that plugs for prizes and the merchants supplying them should be positive. There is room for humor and light-heartedness, but don't allow your air staff to get out-of-hand while "shooting from the lip."

On-Air Comments about Other Staffers

In this handbook we offer several promotions built on the premise of a rivalry between two air personalities. We think that this can be healthy and interesting, whether you contrive the rivalry or whether you build upon built-in tensions or differences in style found among the staff.

The hardest-hitting humor material presented in this book is mild, however, compared to what we're hearing on the radio today. You'll have to be the judge of what your staff and audience is willing to tolerate, but our recommendation is to keep things friendly between your on-air personalities. Good, clean challenges and "gentlemen's bets" are fun for everyone. Nasty put-downs and verbal slams don't make for good radio.

We find it equally tiresome to hear a male DJ making sexually slanted remarks every time the female newscaster comes into the control room to give the headlines and a weather update. Come on, guys, let the women be newscasters. Let them be people. Don't cheapen the news or newscasters by treating female announcers like call girls who happen to be able to read.

We like the back-and-forth banter between laid-back DJs and equally informal newscasters. That is "personality radio" at its best and we shed no tears for the lost "voice of doom" approach to newscasting.

WHAT DJs SHOULDN'T HAVE TO DO   1.7

We'd like to knock down a commonly held myth in radio: the combo operator can run the whole radio station alone. Well, balderdash.

Sure, most small- and medium-market stations employ staff persons who carry a variety of responsibilities. Yet we've seen so many stations carry versatility to its illogical extreme—making the on-air DJ slave away alone in the control room *and* write and produce spots in the production studio *and* reload the automation system for the sister station *and* empty the waste baskets *and* answer the phone *and* meet lobby visitors *and* clear the news wire *and* warm-over local news copy for the next newscast, all at the same time.

At what point does dead air, missed spots, up-cut network feeds, and confused announcing style become too high a price to pay for getting one person to do six jobs for half-pay? If your station's on-air product sounds slapped-together, don't bother doing promotions to improve listenership. If your commercials sound like they were written and recorded in five minutes, don't bother approaching your sponsors for freebies to give away during the next big contest. Promotions aren't going to help when the underlying programming quality is poor.

Here are a few simple guidelines to help your station perform at its best:

1. **Keep air personalities on the air.** DJs and newscasters are primarily there to keep the on-air product going. Don't force them to become distracted from that all-important task.

2. **Don't let phone-ins take over.** While listeners enjoy calling in and talking directly with the on-air DJ, the air staff must be instructed to keep this aspect of the operation secondary to the on-air product. Teach them to tell persistent callers, "Sorry, I really have to tend to business. Bye!" Then, hang up the phone—gently.

3. **Have operators on duty.** When planning for a heavy influx of calls associated with on-air promotions that solicit immediate telephoned responses, schedule additional support staff to answer all calls and screen them. Transferring calls to the control room should be held to a minimum.

4. **Don't make the on-air DJ play receptionist.** If you are collecting soda cans, dried-up Christmas trees, or entry blanks, have a receptionist present to handle the chores in the lobby. Besides, for the safety and security of your building and staff, the unlocked doors should not be left unattended during nonbusiness hours. It's a good idea to have all doors wired so that a "door open" light flashes in the control room anytime a door is opened.

5. **Be careful with money.** Don't make your air staff solely responsible for collection of money. It's hazardous to have a person working alone with cash. Talk to a local bank or armored car company about secure ways of handling large sums of cash, such as those collected during charity fundraisers. Keep money secure in locked collection boxes that cannot be carried away by unauthorized persons. This puts temptation beyond the reach of anyone, and lets potential thieves know that you are not going to be an easy target.

1.8   PRINTED MATERIALS

You don't play scratchy records and muffled tapes. You don't use announcers with severe speech impediments. So why settle for a rotten image in print?

Your Graphic Image Counts

If you take pride in your station's on-air sound (and you should), then brag about it! Get in touch with the local photo studio and have some good pictures taken. Have a local typesetting shop typeset each person's name and airshift or job title to mount inside a picture frame with the photo. These should be hung in the lobby to greet all visitors.

Those studio photos won't go to waste grinning at the front door. Have some 5-×-7 black-and-white prints made. These can be used in many of ways:

- in newspaper ads promoting the station
- in flyers that include biographical information about each DJ
- in producing press passes for your news crew and sportscasters

Don't skimp on the typesetting either. Worn-out felt pens and cardboard may be enough for plugging church bake sales, but that treatment just doesn't put your professional staff in the best light. Some photocopy shops and most typesetters can help you design attractive posters.

Lead Time Is Required

You know about lead time—it's the time needed to take a sponsor's vague request for "some kind of commercial" and turn it into an effective spot. Radio salespeople like to brag about going from concept to commercial in a couple of hours, but you know that this is the exception, not the rule. Similarly, when you want a print piece to support your latest radio promotion, don't expect to slap it together at the last minute.

Yes, the local copy-quick center can zap out 100 photocopies in 60 minutes or your money back. But the successful design, layout and proofreading of a brochure can require from two to eight weeks. Let's assume you need pre-printed entry blanks and want to hand out publicity photos and biographies on all of your air personalities. Here's how to allow for time to let the creative juices flow:

Week 1

- Have a staff meeting to plan for future promotions, select specific plans, kick around ideas, and identify potential problems.
- Identify special needs: photos, telephone lines, props, remote equipment, and so forth.

Week 2

- Make final decisions about name of promotion and any related catchphrases.
- Photographer takes necessary pictures, sends them off for processing.
- Begin scriptwriting for promos and formats.
- Contact design shop/typesetter to schedule promotional flyer production.
- Sales staff contacts potential sponsors with details about the promotion.

Week 3

- Sales staff brings in script outlines for spots related to promotion.
- Station rep goes to design shop with copies of promo scripts and proofs from photo session—this gives the design shop "inspirational material" for designing flyers, brochures, and posters.

Week 4

- Write scripts for spots based on sales staff input from sponsors.
- Inspect/correct/approve drafts of print pieces.
- Select photos to be used.
- Schedule ad space in local newspaper; make sure ads are coordinated with work done by design shop so a unified graphic image is presented.

Week 5

- Put first round of promos on the air teasing upcoming promotion.
- Lay out and approve ads for the paper.
- Send print pieces to the printer.
- Record spots related to promotion and submit them to sponsors for approval.

Week 6

- Put second round of promos on the air detailing upcoming promotion.
- Print pieces come back from the printer.
- Ads begin running in the newspaper.

Week 7—Contingencies

- Design shop was booked up; layout stage delayed several days.
- Photos all looked lousy; had to reshoot and photographer isn't available till next Tuesday.
- Morning man got bronchitis; production of promos and spots delayed since the contest revolves around him.
- Entry blanks not back from the printer yet; factory rep says the ink won't dry and there's nothing we can do but wait.
- Airplane crashes at 115 N. Main Street the day before the promotion starts; major prize was plane fare for two to the Virgin Islands; major sponsor (travel agent) decides timing isn't the best and wants contest held off a week.

There you are: two months of hard work just to get to the starting line. Check this timetable with any print shop and you'll probably be told that it's too short if anything. And don't laugh too hard at Week 7—that's all real-world stuff that broadcasters and print-media people face routinely.

About Those Bios and Photos

If your DJs have a loyal following (and we hope they do), they'll get fan mail. Requests for autographed pictures and biographical information are a part of the deal. You can meet this demand with prepared materials that won't break the bank.

- **The Photos**. Most fans want the picture of their favorite DJ or newscaster "in the environment." So hire a good photographer to take action shots in the studio. Special lighting may be needed, but try for the picture that feels spontaneous. When these are printed, have a professional print shop duplicate the photos as *halftones* on an offset press. Don't sink the king's ransom into having hundreds of 8×10 glossy photos produced at the local camera shop.

- **The Biography**. Keep this stuff simple and readable. Fans like to know your air staff's birthdays, personal tastes, hobbies, favorite books, places they've lived, and so on. Stay away from lengthy text and philosophical meanderings.

- **The Autographs**. Don't preprint or rubber stamp the DJ's signature. Autographs are a personal touch and must be done by hand—in person, if possible, while the fan watches.

MEDIA RELATIONS   1.9

It's a good idea to stay on cordial, cooperative terms with the other media outlets in your market. You'll need their help sometime.

Developing Friendships

Many of the promotions in this book require supporting advertising in the local newspaper. Other promotional stunts are ripe for human-interest news coverage, especially if something visually interesting is happening.

Whether you need paid advertising space or news coverage, it's best to cultivate your station's relationship with the staff at the local paper. Invite the publisher, editor, and department supervisors out to your station for a mid-morning tour and then take them out to lunch.

During the station tour, tell the newspaper staff about your operation and its need for newspaper coverage. Then, during lunch, turn the tables and ask your guests to talk about life down at the *Daily Bugle*.

Even if the tour-and-lunch approach has already been done, it doesn't hurt to do it again at least once every year or two. Surely your station's facilities have been updated in some way, and your staff may have turned over a bit. The same will be true at the newspaper.

On another occasion, give the same treatment to the news and feature-production staff from the local TV stations. If you're in a large enough market to have local independent teleproduction facilities, get them in on the deal, but don't let the group get too large. The whole idea is to build relationships in a noncompetitive environment.

Have Fun Together

Some of the rivalry-based promotions found in this book may lend themselves to developing exhibition sports teams; the "Waves" versus the "Pages." Contact your local parks and recreation department, and you may find a variety of city-league sports teams in operation.

If your station is too small to field a full team, consider ganging up with other radio and TV stations on a joint team. If your group is still too small, consider getting the local newspapers and print shops in on the deal, and call your team "Media Mix."

Professional Relationships

Part of the reason for the socializing just mentioned lies in developing trust and understanding—two necessary elements in a good working relationship. Your staff needs to understand the needs and methods of the other media people, and it'll do them good to see how you operate.

When the time comes to place your station's ad in the local paper, contact the *Daily Bugle's* advertising manager plenty early. Set up an appointment to go over and work on the ad. Then don't be late or forget about the appointment.

In like manner, if your station does something newsworthy, you'll want to be on the good side of the assignment editor. Nothing beats the public relations boost of getting your station and staff in a large human-interest photo with an extended caption.

Give these editors and managers plenty of notice in writing, and follow it up with personal phone calls to confirm that they know you exist.

1.10   USING THIS BOOK

If you're the typical reader, you've already nosed around in this book, sneaking a peek at some of the promotions. We hope you'll take some time to read this opening section carefully; it'll enhance your ability to use this book.

In each promotion, we've tried to outline the basic procedures in the "How It Works" section. Then we've gone on to elaborate on details and variations. In many cases we've suggested appropriate prizes. In some cases, on-air copy has been provided.

If you look at a specific promotion that appeals to you, but feel that you don't have quite enough information to use it, take some time to read through several other promotions. You may find additional suggestions that you can translate back into the first stunt to make it a winner.

Introducing WZZZ Centerville

For the sake of having a generic radio station to talk about, we have used the call sign WZZZ and the city of Centerville in most cases. Where a frequency is needed, we often used 460—obviously not inside the AM broadcast band, but usable as an example.

Stations often use "logos" or slogans instead of the call letters. In the case of our example, the uninspired logo of "Z-46" comes to mind. Surely yours is better.

Whether yours is an AM-daytimer peanut whistle, a 100-watt noncommercial FM, a medium-market 24-hour operation, or a metropolitan ratings leader, you'll find plenty of ideas in this book that can help your station.

Remember: keep it simple, and have fun!

SECTION

2

Contests for All Occasions

PEOPLE LOVE A CHALLENGE. THERE'S A STRONG APPEAL TO CONQUERING some obstacle or "showing your stuff" in some way. Contests sponsored by radio stations come in every format imaginable. The common thread in all of them, however, is the "thrill of victory," big or small. Toss in some attractive prizes from your sponsors, and the audience will tune you in for sure.

2.1   YEAR-LONG PROMOTIONS

Throughout the year you normally run a number of various contests. The Year-Long Promotion involves a contest that continues all year. It culminates in the selection of a winner sometime in the oh-so-slow period early in January.

How It Works

Every entry in every contest you conduct all year is automatically entered in this big contest. In fact, this is the only way for a listener to enter the big contest. The more regular contests a person participates in, the more chances he or she will have to win the big prize.

It's as simple as that: Every piece of contest mail received over the entire 12-month period goes into the big hopper. The audience excitement over this promotion will grow progressively over the year. Your hold over that audience will grow with it.

When to Start

Start this year-long promotion immediately after New Year's so that it will have the full 12-month span in which to operate. Or, if you normally need a boost in September, start it then. The point is, pick your weakest month as a starting point so that next year your station will get a real boost as a result of this promotion.

The Prize

In the prize area the possibilities are almost unlimited. You have this going: You have the entire year in which to plug the grand prize, so there is almost no prize that cannot be yours for the asking. The year-long promotion will more than compensate your sponsor(s) who put up the grand prize.

There are a number of prize possibilities open to you in a promotion of this type:

1. Duplicate the prizes given away in every other contest for the year.

2. A major travel prize ranging from two weeks in Europe or Hawaii to a round-the-world tour.

3. A major merchandise prize. You can go about as far as you want in this direction, from giving away a boat and trailer to attaching a new automobile to the trailer to giving a person a new car every year for three to five years. (That last idea isn't so far-fetched; the car is leased from a dealer and the winner must turn in the old one each year to get the next new one.)

On-Air Promos

Tag these plugs for your year-long contest onto every promo for your regular contests:

* * * *

"DON'T FORGET—WHEN YOU ENTER THIS CONTEST YOU AUTOMATICALLY ENTER WZZZ'S GREAT GLOBE-TROTTER CONTEST WITH A CHANCE TO WIN A ROUND-THE-WORLD TRIP FOR TWO.

* * * *

YOUR POSTCARD ENTRY IN THIS CONTEST AUTOMATICALLY GIVES YOU ANOTHER CHANCE TO BECOME WZZZ'S GLOBE-TROTTER AND WIN A ROUND-THE-WORLD TRIP FOR TWO.

* * * *

Air separate promos on the year-long contest as well. Be sure to change them periodically to keep them fresh. The whole idea behind this promotion is to give you a continuing hold over a growing audience, so you have to maintain your enthusiasm for the promotion if audience excitement is to build.

After about six months your air personalities will probably feel as though they will become ill if they have to utter another word about your year-long contest. This is just about the time when this promotion will really be getting into high gear, so don't let up.

Publicity

Get posters into the windows of the company that is donating your prize. Working with your prize source, develop some printed inserts to be included with the sponsor's monthly billing statements. At the conclusion of the contest, you should end up with a mountain of mail good for local and national publicity pictures. If you decide to give away duplicate prizes, these should be put on continuous display, either at your station or some other central location.

The Drawing Gimmick: Measuring the Mail

The selection of the winner should be as spectacular as the contest itself. Here, too, you have a lot going for you because of the nature of the promotion. You have the natural hook to spice up that dull period following the holidays. One way you can pick your winner is with a measure-the-mail drawing.

Suppose the prize is one of the trips suggested. Get an authoritative estimate of how many miles of mail you have if the letters and postcards are laid end-to-end. Then have slips or cards made, one for each one-tenth of a mile of the entire distance. Get a local or national celebrity to draw out the mileage card for you. This gives you how many miles of mail you have to put down to get a winner.

Let's say it is 28 and $3/10$ miles. In an open area adjacent to your station (preferably) or in some other public spot (inside a gym or armory, of course, if there is snow on the ground), you mark two lines either $1/10$, $1/20$, or $1/40$ of a mile apart. Heap up all the mail at this area and invite the public to watch the fun. Keep the whole operation in full public view so there can be no claim that you have rigged the contest.

Initially, you can use your DJs. They start lining up mail end-to-end between the two lines. When they have laid down 10 or 20 rows, scoop up that mail and put it aside. When they have put down, say, 23 miles of mail, start doing cut-ins from your studio, picking up random names from the mail as it is being put down. Arrange for some unimpeachable person or persons to handle the final phase. They are brought in at about the 27-mile mark and they put down the remainder of the mail.

Also, at this point, you will want to cover the proceedings continuously, and the name on each piece of mail put down from here on should be publicly announced. The suspense really builds, doesn't it? Your winner, of course, is the person whose letter or postcard touches the line at the 28 and $3/10$ mail-mile mark. This same technique can also be used even if your prize is something other than a trip.

Basically, this is a very simple promotion—and one that can build a continuing and loyal audience for you. One word of warning: the potency of this promotion will grow as the months pass, so do not become discouraged if it seems somewhat slow in catching on. Stay with it; you will end up with one of the most high-powered stunts ever seen in your market.

Perk Up Your Year-Long Promotion

If you started in January, by summer you should have accumulated thousands of entries in the Year-Long Promotion. Here are a couple of fresh ways to give it an extra push and your DJs something more to talk about.

Bonus

Each day one of your DJs goes to the great mound of entries in the Year-Long Promotion and at random draws a card from one of your earlier contests. He reads the name of that person on the air and invites the person to call within two minutes to win a special bonus: probably a popular album or CD.

If the person calls, your DJ has many things to talk about, all helping push your Prize of the Year Contest. For instance, he may ask how many of the WZZZ contests the person has entered besides the one on the card or what the person will do if he wins the Prize of the Year.

You may decide to do this bonus bit on a fairly regular basis, or you may continue it on a complete random basis for as long as you wish—with the bonus coming as a surprise feature with fanfare anytime during your broadcast day.

Caution: Make sure your DJs make it clear that the cards drawn for the bonus bit are put back in the stack for the Prize of the Year drawing. Otherwise, you may have some worried listeners.

Count the Mail Contest

Another way to hype your Year-Long Promotion is to run a "Count the Mail Contest." This is a separate contest for a smaller prize in which listeners are asked to estimate the number of pieces of mail received by the station.

You can make a shortie out of this and simply have the closest estimate win. Or you can stretch it out until someone hits the exact figure. In the latter case you can give clues: the number of pounds of mail you have received; the number of mail sacks you have, and so on. You might even put all of the cards and letters on display in your lobby or in some other public place.

Year-Long Promotion—On-Air Copy

(Tag for regular promotion spots)

REMEMBER, YOUR ENTRIES IN (name of current promotion) ALSO QUALIFY YOU FOR THE WZZZ PRIZE OF THE YEAR DRAWING IN JANUARY.

* * * *

HERE'S A BONUS . . . YOUR ENTRIES IN (name of current promotion) GO INTO THE

GIANT HOPPER FOR THE WZZZ PRIZE OF THE YEAR DRAWING NEXT JANU-ARY. EVERY ENTRY IN THIS CONTEST IS AUTOMATICALLY HELD OVER FOR THIS GIANT CONTEST. SO, ENTER EVERY WZZZ CONTEST—ALL YEAR LONG.

* * * *

THROUGHOUT THE YEAR ALL ENTRIES IN THE MANY WONDERFUL WZZZ CONTESTS ARE SAVED FOR THE WZZZ PRIZE OF THE YEAR DRAWING TO BE HELD NEXT JANUARY. THE WINNER OF THIS YEAR-LONG CONTEST WILL RECEIVE A DUPLICATE OF EACH PRIZE AWARDED IN ALL OF THE WZZZ CON-TESTS FOR THE YEAR. THE MORE ENTRIES YOU HAVE IN THE REGULAR WZZZ CONTESTS, THE BETTER YOUR CHANCE OF WINNING THE WZZZ PRIZE OF THE YEAR. SO ENTER OFTEN—AND ENTER 'EM ALL.

* * * *

Get a big metal corn crib or some other metallic container to put all contest mail in. This becomes known as "Big Bin." Throughout the year, in connection with promo spots, you use a gong-effect to indicate how full Big Bin is getting. Like this:

Sound: (great resounding gong)

Anncr: THAT'S "BIG BIN"—THE GIGANTIC CONTAINER INTO WHICH ALL OF THE WZZZ CONTEST ENTRIES FROM THROUGHOUT THE YEAR ARE PLACED. THEY ARE HELD THERE FOR THE WZZZ PRIZE OF THE YEAR DRAWING TO BE HELD NEXT JANUARY. THE PRIZE WILL BE A DUPLICATE OF EVERY OTHER PRIZE AWARDED IN WZZZ CON-TESTS DURING THE ENTIRE YEAR. BIG BIN IS NEARLY EMPTY NOW—BUT BY NEXT JANUARY IT WILL BE FILLED WITH THE THOU-SANDS OF ENTRIES RECEIVED DURING THE YEAR. THE MORE OF THESE ENTRIES THAT BEAR YOUR NAME, THE BETTER YOUR CHANCES TO WIN THE WZZZ PRIZE OF THE YEAR.

Sound: (repeat gong)

(as the year progresses and Big Bin fills, deaden the gong sound accordingly.)

* * * *

YOU'VE STILL GOT FROM JUNE TO JANUARY TO ENTER WZZZ'S FABULOUS YEAR-LONG CONTEST FOR A (prize). THOUSANDS HAVE ENTERED—EVERY-

BODY STILL CAN. EVERY ENTRY IN ANY WZZZ CONTEST OR PROMOTION THROUGHOUT THE YEAR QUALIFIES FOR THE PRIZE OF THE YEAR DRAWING IN JANUARY. THE MORE YOU ENTER, THE BETTER YOUR CHANCES.

* * * *

WZZZ'S YEAR-LONG PRIZE OF THE YEAR CONTEST IS HALF OVER, AND WE'VE GOT MOUNTAINS OF MAIL. HAVE YOU ENTERED YET? THE PRIZE IS A (name it). ANY ENTRY IN ANY WZZZ CONTEST OR PROMOTION THROUGHOUT THE YEAR IS SAVED FOR THIS FABULOUS DRAWING IN JANUARY. WE'LL GET BIGGER STUDIOS IF WE MUST TO STORE THE MAIL, SO ENTER TODAY—ENTER THEM ALL.

* * * *

ENTRIES IN WZZZ'S YEAR-LONG PRIZE OF THE YEAR DRAWING HAVE BEEN COMING IN AT THE RATE OF _____ THOUSAND PER MONTH. WE EXPECT THIS TO DOUBLE WITH THE WONDERFUL ARRAY OF CONTESTS AND PROMOTIONS WZZZ HAS PLANNED FOR THIS SUMMER AND FALL. ENTER ALL OF THEM, EACH ENTRY IS ANOTHER CHANCE FOR WZZZ'S PRIZE OF THE YEAR—A DUPLICATE OF EACH AND EVERY WZZZ PRIZE AWARDED THROUGHOUT THE YEAR. THE DRAWING WILL BE HELD IN JANUARY, YOU'VE GOT _____ MONTHS TO GO.

THE GOOD NEIGHBOR GAME   2.2

This is a contest promotion, but the prizes are very minor. As a continuing promotion, The Good Neighbor Game should be good for six weeks. If you keep it spiced up with gimmicks and add in some additional twists as you go along, you can probably extend it over the three-month period. As always, the things you add into these promotions should be local and timely. It is impossible to overstress the value of localizing everything you do.

How It Works

You can assign this promotion to one of your DJs—or you can use it on several different shows. There are advantages in each; after considering the situation in your own market, you will have to decide which way is best for you.

Once again, this is a very simple promotion. (Remember, in section 1 we said that if you could not explain all of the details of a promotion such as this within 30 seconds, your promotion was too complicated.) The disc jockey using the promotion places calls each day (or one of the receptionists in your office places them for him). He can place one call a show or one call an hour. Any more than one an hour would be too much. About an hour before the call is placed, the DJ announces that he will be calling a family named "Smith" or "Jones" or "Culligan" within your listening area. He urges all listeners to be a good neighbor and call anyone they know by that name and tell him to tune to WZZZ because he may win a prize.

The DJ continues to plug the name throughout the hour. Then, just before the call is placed, the DJ announces a "Word that Wins" or a "Phrase that Pays." The call is placed and if the person called can give the word or phrase, he wins the prize. That's all there is to it.

The Prize

The prizes given away in this promotion need not be anything big. There are better ways to give away CDs or albums, so we suggest you do not use them with this promotion.

Sales Possibilities

The Good Neighbor Game is a promotion that is certainly a saleable package; you would do well to have it sponsored. If you do, the sponsor will probably want to provide the prizes.

Setting Up Audience Interest

You will be adapting this promotion to your local situation, so the on-air copy that we suggest is rather general. Remember to use an occasional out-of-town phone call and plug the fact that you do. Set up a standard format for the original announcement of the name for the day. And have your DJs use running plugs like:

IF YOUR NAME IS SMITH, WE MAY BE CALLING YOU IN JUST EIGHT MINUTES.

The Good Neighbor Game—On-Air Copy

IT'S TIME TO PLAY THE WZZZ GOOD NEIGHBOR GAME AGAIN . . . AND THE NAME FOR THIS HOUR IS—"SMITH." IN JUST ONE HOUR I'M GOING TO PLACE A PHONE CALL TO SOMEONE NAMED "SMITH." IF THE PERSON WHO ANSWERS CAN TELL ME THE "WORD THAT WINS," WE'LL SEND HIM A VALU-ABLE PRIZE (identify prize). IF YOU KNOW SOMEONE NAMED "SMITH," YOU CAN BE A WZZZ GOOD NEIGHBOR BY CALLING HIM AND TELLING HIM TO STAY TUNED TO WZZZ—RADIO 460—FOR THE "WORD THAT WINS." THE NAME FOR THIS HOUR AGAIN IS "SMITH."

* * * *

WZZZ INVITES YOU TO BE A WZZZ GOOD NEIGHBOR. WE'RE PLAYING THE WZZZ GOOD NEIGHBOR GAME AGAIN, AND SOMEONE NAMED "JOHNSON" IS GOING TO HAVE A CHANCE TO WIN A (identify prize). ONE HOUR FROM NOW WE'LL PLACE A TELEPHONE CALL TO SOMEONE NAMED "JOHNSON." IF WHOEVER ANSWERS THE PHONE CALL TELLS ME THE "WORD THAT WINS," THEY'LL RECEIVE A (identify prize). YOU CAN BE A WZZZ GOOD NEIGHBOR BY CALLING THE "JOHNSONS" YOU KNOW AND TELLING THEM TO STAY TUNED TO WZZZ RADIO 460. WE WILL ANNOUNCE THE "WORD THAT WINS" IN ONE HOUR—ON WZZZ—YOUR GOOD NEIGHBOR FOR BETTER LISTENING.

* * * *

THE NAME IS—BROWN!

* * * *

THE GAME IS—WZZZ'S GOOD NEIGHBOR GAME!

* * * *

IN JUST ONE HOUR WE'LL BE CALLING SOMEONE NAMED "BROWN" AND ASKING HIM TO IDENTIFY THE "WORD THAT WINS" FOR A VALUABLE PRIZE. YOU CAN BE A WZZZ GOOD NEIGHBOR BY CALLING ANYONE YOU KNOW NAMED "BROWN" AND TELLING HIM TO STAY TUNED TO WZZZ FOR THE "WORD THAT WINS," WHICH I'LL ANNOUNCE BEFORE MAKING THE CALL. WZZZ—YOUR GOOD NEIGHBOR AT THE RADIO 460 SPOT ON YOUR DIAL.

* * * *

YOU CAN BE A WZZZ GOOD NEIGHBOR JUST BY MAKING A TELEPHONE CALL AND DOING A FRIEND A FAVOR. HERE'S HOW. IN JUST ONE HOUR I'M GOING TO PLACE A CALL TO SOMEONE IN THE WZZZ LISTENING AREA NAMED "FRANKLIN." THAT NAME AGAIN—"FRANKLIN." IF THE PERSON WHO ANSWERS THAT CALL CAN TELL ME THE "WORD THAT WINS," HE'LL WIN (identify prize). YOU CAN BE A WZZZ GOOD NEIGHBOR BY CALLING THE FOLKS YOU KNOW NAMED "FRANKLIN" AND TELLING THEM TO STAY TUNED TO WZZZ FOR THE "WORD THAT WINS." FRANKLIN IS THE NAME— AND WE'LL BE CALLING WITHIN THE HOUR.

* * * *

YOU'RE TUNED TO WZZZ—RADIO 460—WHERE YOU CAN PLAY THE WZZZ GOOD NEIGHBOR GAME WITH US EVERY MORNING ON THE LATE MORNING SHOW. WZZZ—RADIO 460—YOUR GOOD-LISTENING NEIGHBOR.

2.3   THE RIDING MAN

This is a giveaway contest that you can have a lot of fun with. Because it is basically an outside promotion, wait until late enough in the year to be reasonably assured of good weather.

How It Works

Motorcycles, motor scooters, and mopeds are very popular in this country. This whole promotion is built around such a vehicle. At least one type is undoubtedly being sold in your city. The Vespa and the Lambretta companies, both of Italy, have particularly aggressive sales programs. The Cushman motor scooter people of Lincoln, Nebraska are quite active, too, in the motor scooter field. Honda, Suzuki, Kawasaki, and Yamaha are the big names in the motorcycle business.

Through your local dealer make arrangements to get a machine to use as a giveaway prize. Be sure you tie this in with a sale of some airtime to the dealer. The contest consists of filling up the tank with gas and having one of your disc jockeys ride it over a prescribed course until it runs out of gas. Listeners are asked to send in estimates as to where they think he will run out of gas. The person who comes closest wins the machine.

A motor scooter will run about 100 miles on a tank of gas. The course you lay out for the DJ to follow should be, if possible, a fairly simple rectangle that can be described easily on the air. It could run, say, from your station to City Hall and back. If you want your contest to run for 20 days, select a course that is five miles long and have the DJ make one circuit a day. On the final day he will ride until the motor scooter runs out of gas.

If you only want to go 10 days, have the DJ make two circuits a day—or one circuit around a 10-mile course. Be sure to tell listeners to state the specific point of stopping in their entries: for example, "Twenty-seven feet south of the corner of Main and Cedar Streets."

Some Added Twists

Have some maps of the course printed. Listeners can use these as entry forms by marking where they think the scooter will stop. Have the maps available at your station or at the scooter dealer's. This helps in your sales pitch to the dealer if you can build traffic for the dealer by having entrants go into the store to get a map. However, this will definitely cut down on the response you get to the contest. Be sure that the dealer puts signs in his store plugging the contest.

You will probably do best with this promotion if you have your morning DJ ride the scooter. That way you can have him out on the street riding between noon and 1:00 P.M. when there are the most people on the streets.

Be sure that the fuel valve on the scooter is set so that all of the gas, including the reserve tank, will be used up during the run. Also, whenever practical, have your mobile news car follow the DJ and do remote reports on his progress.

As suggested before, on the final day of your contest have the DJ ride until he runs out of gas. In many towns there are motor scooter clubs. The dealer can tell you if there is one in your town. If there is, get them out as a group on the final day to follow your DJ as he rides around town.

Make a big production of measuring the spot where the scooter finally stops. Cover it live, if possible. Get the police into the act and have them do the official measuring for you.

To get some added fun out of the contest while it is running, make arrangements for your DJ to stop at one or more spots for a coffee break each day while he is out riding.

The Riding Man—Expanded

If you wish to expand this promotion into a really major contest, here is a way to do it: Line up a big prize that has some mobility to it. For instance, a boat with trailer. Make sure that each day this prize is parked at a different spot on the course your DJ follows. If he ends up stopping in the same block as the boat, the winner gets that prize, as well as the motor scooter. The chances of someone winning the boat are, actually, pretty slim. But the *possibility* of winning it can add a lot of excitement to the contest.

The Riding Man—On-Air Copy

YOU CAN WIN THE VESPA MOTOR SCOOTER IN WZZZ'S RIDING MAN CONTEST. _____ WILL BE DRIVING AROUND THE STREETS OF CENTERVILLE. WATCH FOR HIM. HE'LL BE RIDING HIS VESPA EVERY DAY BETWEEN NOON AND 1:00 P.M.—NORTH FROM THE WZZZ STUDIOS ON MAIN STREET TO THE CITY HALL, EAST ON CEDAR, SOUTH AGAIN ON MAPLE, AND THEN WEST ON VINE BACK TO WZZZ. THE WZZZ RIDING MAN STARTS ON MONDAY—AND HE'LL BE RIDING EVERY DAY UNTIL HE RUNS OUT OF GAS. JUST TELL US ON A POSTCARD EXACTLY WHERE YOU THINK HE WILL RUN OUT OF GAS—AND YOU MAY WIN THIS BEAUTIFUL VESPA MOTOR SCOOTER FROM

THE CENTERVILLE CYCLE SHOP, 611 MAIN STREET. WATCH FOR THE WZZZ RIDING MAN—AND GET YOUR POSTCARD ENTRY IN THE MAIL. JUST TELL US WHERE—HOW MANY FEET FROM WHAT INTERSECTION—YOU THINK _____ WILL RUN OUT OF GAS. THAT'S ALL THERE IS TO IT.

* * * *

WZZZ'S RIDING MAN, _____, IS ON THE STREETS OF CENTERVILLE EVERY DAY BETWEEN NOON AND 1:00 P.M. DRIVING HIS VESPA MOTOR SCOOTER FROM THE CENTERVILLE CYCLE SHOP, 611 MAIN STREET. YOU CAN WIN THE VESPA JUST BY TELLING US ON A POSTCARD EXACTLY WHERE YOU THINK _____ WILL RUN OUT OF GAS. STAY TUNED. IN JUST TEN MINUTES, WE'LL TELL YOU THE ROUTE WZZZ'S RIDING MAN FOLLOWS IN HIS DAILY RIDE.

* * * *

READY NOW, BECAUSE HERE IS THE ROUTE WZZZ'S RIDING MAN, _____, FOLLOWS EVERY DAY AS HE DRIVES HIS VESPA MOTOR SCOOTER AROUND CENTERVILLE . . . NORTH ON MAIN STREET FROM THE WZZZ STUDIOS TO THE CITY HALL . . . EAST ON CEDAR . . . SOUTH ON MAPLE . . . AND THEN WEST ON VINE BACK TO WZZZ. TELL US ON A POST-CARD EXACTLY HOW MANY FEET FROM WHAT INTERSECTION YOU THINK _____ WILL RUN OUT OF GAS—AND YOU MAY WIN THIS BEAUTI-FUL VESPA MOTOR SCOOTER FROM THE CENTERVILLE CYCLE SHOP, 611 MAIN STREET.

* * * *

WZZZ'S RIDING MAN, _____, HAS NOW DRIVEN _____ MILES ON HIS VESPA MOTOR SCOOTER. HE'LL KEEP GOING UNTIL HE RUNS OUT OF GAS. AND WHEN HE DOES, SOMEONE WILL WIN THE VESPA MOTOR SCOOTER. IT MAY BE YOU. JUST SEND US A POSTCARD STATING EXACTLY WHERE YOU THINK _____ WILL RUN OUT OF GAS. THE WZZZ RID-ING MAN IS ON THE STREETS OF CENTERVILLE EVERY DAY BETWEEN NOON AND 1:00 P.M. WATCH FOR HIM. AND STAY TUNED—BECAUSE IN JUST TWELVE MINUTES WE'LL GIVE YOU THE EXACT COURSE HE FOLLOWS AS HE RIDES.

2.4   JOIN THE JET SET

This is a spectacular contest and should be one of the biggest things that you do during the year. We suggest that you run it over a fairly extended period of time and that you promote it heavily on the air. Considerable effort should be put into the production of your spots to make this sound as exciting as possible.

How It Works

Offer your listeners a chance to win this exciting prize: a round-trip for two to one of the 10 most glamorous cities in the world. And all they have to do is listen to your station to be a winner.

Three times each hour, 18 hours a day, you air the sound of a jet airplane over a record that is playing. The first person to call in after hearing the jet sound joins the Jet Set and becomes eligible to be the grand-prize winner. Each eligible person is mailed a Jet Set ticket that looks like an airline ticket and contains the rules of the contest and a number.

Sell It

If you want to tie in sponsors to this contest, handle it this way: Have the numbered Jet Set tickets available to the public at your sponsors' places of business. There, contestants fill out a portion of the numbered ticket and drop it in a box. The stubs are then turned in to the station and filed numerically. Then, on the air you announce a sequence of numbers (for instance, 700 to 799) and the first person holding any number within that range becomes a finalist.

The Cities

These cities are good ones to consider using: Tokyo, London, Cancún, Paris, Rome, Madrid, Honolulu, Lisbon, and Buenos Aires. And, certainly, you will want to talk up all of the interesting things about these cities on the air.

The Prizes

Because of the intensive promotion you will be giving this contest on the air, you should not have any great difficulty trading it out with an airline. As you know, you will probably have to deal with a foreign flag airline. The grand prize need not include anything more than transportation, but you can include hotel and a lot of other frills if you want.

Also, you should consider giving out a fairly large number of lesser prizes. It is not necessary, but it will add a lot to the promotion. These should be given out on both a daily and a weekly basis, with everyone entered having a chance at them.

Timing

As mentioned, this contest should run over a considerable period of time. We suggest starting it on May 1 and running it through June 15—a 46-day contest period—then announcing your grand-prize winner about three days later. Try to get some prominent figure to do the final drawing for you.

Agency and Sponsor Tie-In

You should also give serious consideration to running a concurrent agency time-buyer and contest sponsor along with your "Join the Jet Set" contest. The prize here need not be a trip to one of the foreign cities, but it certainly can be a prize sent to the winners from one of the foreign cities.

Make It Big

This is a big contest with a big prize—and it will sound even bigger on the air because, while you will be awarding a trip to only one city, you will be talking about 10 different cities in the world. So everything you can do to make it sound as big as it is will be to your advantage. As mentioned before, the production of your on-air spots should be well worked out. Everyone on the air should be involved completely. And all stops should be pulled out to gain outside publicity and exposure.

2.5   THE KITE CONTEST

When was the last time you flew a kite? You probably asked yourself why you didn't do it more often. Here's a way to plug in to that appealing pastime.

How It Works

It will probably not be practical for you to stage this contest near your studios because of wires and other obstructions. Put it on in the high school or college athletic field. If there are bluffs in your area, this may be the ideal site for the Kite Contest. You will do best to schedule this one for a Saturday morning or afternoon. (Check with the Weather Bureau to find out which time of the day the winds are most favorable for kite flying).

The only requirement for entering the event is that each kite must have your call letters and frequency on it somewhere.

Categories

Break the contest up into various categories:

1. The largest flyable kite
2. The smallest flyable kite
3. The most attractively decorated kite
4. The most unusual kite
5. The highest flying kite
6. The best tricks performed with a kite
7. The kite with the longest tail that will fly

All of these categories can be divided up into male and female groups, as well as into various age groups.

Promoting the Kite Contest

In promoting the event, you can have your DJs fly kites in the vicinity of your station (if it is safe!). You can even have one of your DJs construct a huge man-carrying kite that he will try out at the Kite Contest. You should be able to get some good publicity on the latter. Check around for some advice and support from local hang glider enthusiasts. Powered ultralight aircraft owners may also get into the act of helping publicize your contest.

A Word to the Doubters

There are going to be those among you who believe that kite flying is only for little kids. We suggest you go to the park some breezy spring day and see for yourself that it actually is a sport that attracts all age groups. Then you might go to the store, buy a kite, and give it a try yourself. We did it not too long ago and had more fun and laughs than with anything we had done in months. The point is there is a great deal of appeal in a stunt such as this and you will probably be surprised at the turnout you will get.

Prizes

Take along stacks of those 45 records that are cluttering up your library (or, these days, mini CDs) and give them out to everyone who participates. You can keep it in the music vein and give away albums or CDs to the winners in the various categories. Or you can arrange for some other type prize. Do not strive for major prizes to give away in connection with this promotion. The prizes are incidental to the fun of the contest itself.

On-Air Copy

(For several days, transcribed voice comes on with no comment from DJ)

Voice: GO FLY A KITE!

* * * *

(Next, for a couple of days)

Voice: WZZZ INVITES EVERYONE TO GO FLY A KITE!

* * * *

(Then, follow with this)

Voice: WZZZ INVITES EVERYONE TO GO FLY A KITE—IN THE WZZZ KITE CONTEST. THAT'S RIGHT . . . WE WANT EVERYONE TO GO FLY A KITE AT THE HIGH SCHOOL MEMORIAL STADIUM ON SATURDAY, MARCH TWENTY-SIXTH. TAKE-OFF TIME IS TEN O'CLOCK IN THE MORNING. STAY TUNED FOR DETAILS ON WZZZ.

* * * *

(Then, into straight copy)

CALLING ALL KITES. WZZZ IS CALLING ALL KITES—TO THE WZZZ KITE CONTEST. AND HERE'S THE CHANCE FOR KITE FANS OF ALL AGES TO JOIN THE WZZZ DISC JOCKEYS IN THEIR SECOND CHILDHOOD . . . WITH A CHANCE TO BE UP IN THE AIR FOR PRIZES. WZZZ INVITES EVERYONE TO GO FLY A KITE ON SATURDAY, MARCH TWENTY-SIXTH, STARTING AT TEN O'CLOCK IN THE MORNING AT THE HIGH SCHOOL MEMORIAL STADIUM. THIS CONTEST ISN'T JUST FOR YOUNGSTERS—IT'S FOR KITE-FLYING FANS OF ALL AGES, BOTH MEN AND WOMEN. AND THERE'S NO LIMIT TO THE IMAGINATION YOU PUT INTO BUILDING YOUR KITE. THE ONLY REQUIRE-MENT TO ENTER IS THAT YOUR KITE MUST HAVE "WZZZ 460" OR "Z-46" PAINTED ON IT SOMEPLACE. YES, GO FLY A KITE—AT THE WZZZ KITE CON-TEST. LOTS OF PRIZES FOR EVERYONE.

2.6 WZZZ ESP

The almost occult nature of extrasensory perception makes it a subject that seems to fascinate almost everyone. Many people accept the thought that such a thing as ESP exists, that everyone has it to one extent or another, and that there are certain people who are good at it. One of the things that you have going for you in this promotion is that many people feel that they have ESP to a very marked degree. You probably think you, yourself, are gifted in this area—and maybe you are.

How It Works

The promotion works like this: After announcing the event, listeners are asked to send in postcards with their names and phone numbers. These are placed in a drum or some other container and are drawn once an hour or once per show for use with the promotion.

The DJ on the air holds a picture of some object. The picture remains the same throughout the promotion. The DJ announces that he will concentrate on the picture for a period of 10 seconds. After doing so, he says he will select a postcard and place a phone call after his next record. The call is actually placed while the record is playing to save time and to be sure of getting an answer. The person called is asked to identify the object and, if he or she identifies it correctly, the winner gets whatever the object is. In the case of a wrong answer, the DJ announces what that answer was. You will create a lot more suspense if you stay with this sequence of events.

Air Approach

Your air approach to this promotion should be reasonably serious in keeping with the subject. This is a fun promotion, yes. But not a ha-ha-type fun. If you allow your DJs to make bad jokes about the subject, you will destroy completely the effectiveness of the promotion.

Care in Selecting the Item

You can use a picture of almost anything. Do not try to get too tricky in choosing something. If you decide on, say, a wristwatch, do not make it necessary for the winner to identify it as an electronic watch with two time zones and three alarms. Simply identifying it as a wristwatch is enough. If the picture is of a box of facial tissue, the prize can be a year's supply of facial tissue.

On-Air Copy—WZZZ ESP

Following is some suggested on-air copy for use with this promotion. You will probably want to record these promos in advance so you can use an echo or filter to add on an eerie effect.

Anncr 1:   (Echo) E − S − P

Anncr 2: EXTRASENSORY PERCEPTION

Anncr 1: (Echo) E−S−P   ON   W−Z−Z−Z

Anncr 2: STAY TUNED FOR DETAILS

Anncr 1: (Echo) E−S−P

Anncr 2: RESEARCH HAS DETERMINED THAT SOME PEOPLE POSSESS POWERS BEYOND THE SCOPE OF THE NORMAL RANGE OF HUMAN SENSES.

Anncr 1: (Echo) EXTRASENSORY PERCEPTION

Anncr 2: ARE YOU ONE OF THESE PEOPLE WITH THE SPECIAL AWARENESS KNOWN AS EXTRASENSORY PERCEPTION? IF SO—STAY TUNED FOR . . .

Anncr 1: (Echo) E−S−P   ON   W−Z−Z−Z

* * * *

(Background voice in monotone calling cards at random sequence.)

ACE OF DIAMONDS . . . THREE OF SPADES . . . TWO OF DIAMONDS . . . NINE OF CLUBS . . . . (Under for:) FOR YEARS RESEARCHERS HAVE TESTED THE UNIQUE ABILITY OF SOME PEOPLE TO COMMUNICATE BY MEANS OTHER THAN THE NORMAL SENSES. THIS ABILITY IS KNOWN AS EXTRASENSORY PERCEPTION . . . E−S−P. NOW, YOU CAN TAKE PART IN A TEST OF ESP TO BE CONDUCTED RIGHT HERE ON RADIO WZZZ. TAKE PART IN THE WZZZ EXTRASENSORY PERCEPTION TEST. WIN THE WZZZ MYSTERY PRIZE. SEND US A POSTCARD WITH YOUR NAME AND PHONE NUMBER. THAT'S ALL—JUST A POSTCARD WITH YOUR NAME AND PHONE NUMBER. AND STAY TUNED TO WZZZ FOR FURTHER DETAILS ON THE WZZZ EXTRASENSORY PERCEPTION TEST.

(Monotone card calling up to conclusion.)

* * * *

Anncr 1: E−S−P (Echo)

Anncr 2: EXTRASENSORY PERCEPTION

Anncr 1: (Echo) E−S−P   ON   W−Z−Z−Z

Anncr 2: EXTRASENSORY PERCEPTION ON WZZZ. THAT'S RIGHT . . . THERE'S ESP ON WZZZ . . . AND YOU CAN BE A PART OF WZZZ'S TEST OF EXTRASENSORY PERCEPTION JUST BY SENDING US A POSTCARD WITH YOUR NAME AND PHONE NUMBER. RIGHT HERE IN THE WZZZ STUDIOS WE HAVE A PICTURE OF THE WZZZ MYS-TERY PRIZE. TO CONDUCT THE WZZZ EXTRASENSORY PERCEP-TION TEST, AIR PERSONALITIES WILL CONCENTRATE ON THE PRIZE PICTURE FOR TEN SECONDS. THEN, WE WILL PLACE A CALL TO A LISTENER WHO HAS SENT IN A POSTCARD. IF THE PER-SON CALLED CAN CORRECTLY IDENTIFY THE WZZZ MYSTERY PRIZE, HE OR SHE WINS WHATEVER IT IS. TO BE ELIGIBLE TO RECEIVE A CALL IN THE WZZZ ESP TEST, JUST SEND A POSTCARD TO ESP AT WZZZ. 100 MAIN STREET, CENTERVILLE.

Anncr 1: (Echo) E–S–P ON W–Z–Z–Z

EXPANDED ESP PROMOTION   2.7

In expanding this promotion, the basic format is similar, while the method of handling the details, the prize structure, and the general scope of the contest is varied. This time out we are talking about a major promotion with major prizes; you should place a larger amount of emphasis on the promotion.

Again, all listeners who feel they possess the power of extrasensory per-ception are asked to send in a postcard with their names and phone numbers in order to participate. These postcards are handled in a similar manner to pick the person to be called.

Variations

This time, instead of a single picture and a single prize, assemble as large a group of prizes as possible. Included in this group of prizes should be a number of things of real value. The size of your top prizes will be determined by the size of your market. Along with these, arrange for as many smaller prizes as you can. Since a relatively small number of the prizes will actually be given away, you will not be in over your head as far as cash outlay or trade-out time.

A picture of each prize is placed in an envelope and these are placed in a special container for use when the contest is run on the air. Each of the enve-lopes is numbered and placed in the container in a consecutive order for ease of use and handling. On each envelope is typed a word-clue and a phrase-clue. The use of the clues is given later in the discussion of this promotion.

How It Works

After the phone call has been put through, the person called is asked to select the number of the prize for which he wishes to try. When he has selected a number, that envelope is pulled out. (Once an envelope has been pulled, it should not be returned to the game until the following day. Also, the numbers on the envelopes should be changed each day. And, when an envelope is used and the prize missed, the clues should be changed before it is put back into the game.)

Each prize envelope actually contains three similar prizes. The contest participants can win the top prize in the envelope by guessing it correctly without the aid of any clues. He can win the middle-range prize by guessing it correctly with the help of the word-clue. He can win the low-end prize by guessing it correctly with the help of both the word- and the phrase-clues. For instance, if the prize to be guessed is a watch, the top prize would be a $100 watch, the middle prize a $30 watch, and the low-end prize a $12 watch. If the prize in a particular envelope is steak from a local meat market, the top prize could be 20 pounds of steak, the middle prize 7 pounds and the low-end prize 3 pounds of steak.

After the person called has selected the numbered envelope, the DJ asks whether he wishes to try for the top prize, the middle prize, or the small prize. If, say, the person says he wishes to go for the small prize, the disc jockey then concentrates on the picture for a period of 10 seconds to transmit, through ESP, the identity of the item. Then, he gives the word-clue and the phrase-clue. The person playing the game then has 10 seconds in which to make his guess. If he misses, the DJ tells him what the prize was that he failed to win. You will probably wish to award small consolation prizes such as theater tickets or something similar to people who fail to win the larger prizes.

Sponsor Tie-In

To help you arrange for prizes to provide a good sponsor tie-in and to give your promotion an additional twist, here is a suggestion: Have prize lists made available at the places of business of sponsors who provide prizes. This will create store traffic for them. And it will give you an excellent plus for your promotion. In addition to a listing of the prizes, the sheet should also contain the details of the contest, along with the rules for participating.

In Conclusion

Handled properly, this promotion can create a great deal of excitement in your area. As stated before, the subject matter holds a real fascination for many people. When you have winners, be sure to publicize the fact on the air. It may be possible for you to arrange to work with a local psychologist who is an expert in the field of extrasensory perception to give additional authority and significance to your promotion.

"WHO SAID THAT?" 2.8

This is a big contest with a built-in listener hook to keep those dials set on your frequency and the ears listening attentively.

How It Works

Air the voices of famous people of the past and present and invite listeners to identify them. Use a different "voice" each day, Monday through Friday. The public sends in postcards at the end of the week and identifies as many of the "voices" as possible. One winning card is selected from all of the entries by a random drawing. The size of the prize the winner receives is determined by the number of correct answers he or she has made.

The regular contest spots with the "voices" should be run once every two hours. In addition, on the alternate hours you will want to run some clues as to the identity of the "voice." These are important. Remember, when a person hears a voice on the air, he will seldom be 100 percent certain of who it is and will want to listen for the additional clues. Be sure you stagger the times when you run the "voices" as well as the clues.

How Long to Run

Actually, this contest can be continued for a considerable period of time. After you have been running the original format for four or five weeks, you may even want to vary it by basing it on people currently in the news.

Production

Considerable work should go into the production of the spots for "Who Said That?". We suggest a fairly strong echo effect on the opening. Also, wherever possible, try to have several different voice cuts from each of the mystery "voices" you are using. In each series of five "voices" for a given week, two of them should be quite easy, one should be a little harder, one should be relatively hard and one should be musical.

Source Material

Many public libraries have a large supply of material upon which you can draw for the "voices." Also, as mentioned above, you should have one "voice" each week be musical, with the material you use coming from song cuts.

Newspaper Ads

If you can manage it, use newspaper ads to call attention to your contest. After the opening ad, run ads with pictures of the "voices" you used in the contest the previous week.

Sell It

This is an excellent promotion to sell, too. Offer your potential sponsor these incentives: Printed forms that he can hand out containing 100 names of prominent people, among which will be the actual "voices" you will be using; also, a large board for display at the sponsor's place of business that has the names and pictures of all of the previous "voices" you have used. You will add to this weekly.

Prizes

As mentioned before, your winner will be selected by a drawing from among all of the entries. The size of the prize will be determined by the number of correct answers he or she has. Thus, if you want to use cash for your prize, the winner can receive $100 for each correct name and a total of $600 if he or she has all five correct. Or you can use merchandise prizes. If so, you should associate a given prize with a given "voice" on a specific day. This will make it easier to trade-out the prizes. You can offer the merchandise prizes, plus a cash prize if the winner has all five "voices" right.

Since you are going to have only one prize per week, in order to keep up the interest of the public, you should offer an overall prize, too. It works like this: In addition to being in the running for the weekly prize, each entry with five correct answers is placed in a special barrel for a drawing for the overall prize to be conducted at the conclusion of the contest.

2.9   THE MIGHTY FOUR-SIXTY

This is a very simple word-making contest. We are not going to try to pass it off as anything startling or original. It is not. It is, however, one of the most remarkable mail-pull contests in the book. We cannot really explain why a contest of this nature consistently pulls the kind of results it does. Perhaps it is because the effort required to enter is, to a large degree, mechanical. Or maybe it is because of a basic fascination with words that most people have. What we do know is that this contest works, and works amazingly well. That is why we have included it here.

How It Works

Pick a promotional slogan, such as "The Mighty Four-Sixty." Offer a prize to the person who can make the most words out of the letters in the slogan. That is all there is to it. But you had better set up an efficient way of handling the mail because you are going to be deluged with entries.

Rules

You may wish to include some additional rules, but whatever you do, start with these:

1. All entries must be postmarked by a certain date—probably a week and one-half to two weeks after the contest starts.
2. Only words found in *Webster's Collegiate Dictionary* will qualify. If you fail to include this rule, you are going to buy yourself about a 10-year supply of headaches.
3. Each letter in the slogan can be used only once in each word the contestant makes. There are three "t's" in the slogan, so words with up to three "t's" are allowed. There is only one "m," so words with more than one "m," will be disallowed.
4. No foreign words will be allowed.
5. No proper names will be allowed.
6. The number of words the contestant has made must be written and circled beneath the return address on the outside of the envelope.

When the Mail Comes In

Select the 10 or 15 letters with the highest number of words indicated on the outside of the envelope; do not even bother to open them. Then have two people go through the entries separately as a double-check. As each new batch of mail comes in, look for numbers higher than those you have already set aside. Put those in your pile of possible winners and remove the lower numbers. This way you will always have a stack of the highest 10 or 15 numbers. In all probability, you will only have to check one or two entries against the dictionary to get your winner.

Clues

Put a listener hook into this contest by working out a list of 100 or more fairly obscure words that can be made from the slogan. Promote the fact that your DJs will be announcing these at a rate of up to four an hour. When the disc jockey announces a word, be sure he spells it out twice.

The Prize

The prize can be almost anything you select. You may wish to have more than one prize. Actually, the prize is far from being the most important thing in this contest. People will enter simply because they enjoy the challenge of making words out of the letters you provide.

The Slogan

We suggest that the slogan you use feature your frequency rather than your call letters. Perhaps you can come up with one that uses both. The slogan should have a maximum of 15 to 20 letters in it. One thing to make sure of: Your slogan must have enough vowels in it to give it a high word-making potential.

The Mighty Four-Sixty—On-Air Copy

THE MIGHTY FOUR-SIXTY . . . THE FOUR WORDS THAT SPELL LISTENING PLEASURE THE YEAR AROUND CAN NOW SPELL A WONDERFUL PRIZE OF _____ FOR YOU IN WZZZ'S "MIGHTY FOUR-SIXTY" WORD-MAKING CONTEST. HOW MANY RECOGNIZED ENGLISH WORDS CAN YOU MAKE FROM THE LETTERS IN THIS GOOD-LISTENING PHRASE: "THE MIGHTY FOUR-SIXTY." TRY IT. IT'S FUN. FOR INSTANCE, THERE'S ME, BE, MY, TRY, TIE, SIGH, GUY—TO NAME JUST A FEW. ENTER THE MIGHTY FOUR-SIXTY WORD-MAKING CONTEST. IT CAN MEAN A MIGHTY _____ FOR YOU.

* * * *

THE MIGHTY FOUR-SIXTY . . . HOW MANY RECOGNIZED ENGLISH WORDS CAN YOU MAKE USING THE 18 LETTERS IN THIS GOOD-LISTENING PHRASE— "THE MIGHTY FOUR-SIXTY." YOUR WORD TOTAL CAN SPELL A GRAND PRIZE OF _____. STAY TUNED TO THE MIGHTY FOUR-SIXTY—WZZZ—FOR DETAILS.

* * * *

"THE MIGHTY FOUR-SIXTY" CAN ADD UP TO _____ IN WZZZ'S "THE MIGHTY FOUR-SIXTY" WORD-MAKING CONTEST. STAY TUNED TO THE MIGHTY FOUR-SIXTY—WZZZ FOR DETAILS.

* * * *

FOUGHT . . . F—O—U—G—H—T . . . THAT'S JUST ONE OF THE WORDS YOU CAN SPELL WITH THE LETTERS IN THE GOOD-LISTENING PHRASE "THE

MIGHTY FOUR-SIXTY." HOW MANY OTHERS CAN YOU COMPOSE FOR WZZZ'S "THE MIGHTY FOUR-SIXTY" WORD-MAKING CONTEST?? STAY TUNED FOR DETAILS.

* * * *

HOW'S YOUR LIST OF WORDS COMING ALONG FOR WZZZ'S "THE MIGHTY FOUR-SIXTY" WORD-MAKING CONTEST? HERE'S A HELP . . . ROUTE . . . R−O−U−T−E . . . THAT'S JUST ONE OF THE WORDS THAT QUALIFY. REMEMBER, ALL WORDS MUST APPEAR IN *WEBSTER'S COLLEGIATE DICTIONARY*. STAY TUNED TO WZZZ—THE MIGHTY FOUR-SIXTY—FOR MORE TIPS ON WINNING WORDS.

* * * *

HOW'S YOUR WORD SENSE? HERE'S A CHANCE TO TEST IT IN WZZZ'S "THE MIGHTY FOUR-SIXTY" WORD-MAKING CONTEST. HOW MANY RECOGNIZED ENGLISH WORDS CAN YOU COMPOSE USING ONLY THE LETTERS CONTAINED IN THIS FOUR-WORD PHRASE—"THE MIGHTY FOUR-SIXTY." THAT'S THE CHALLENGE. TEST YOUR WORD SENSE. ALL WORDS MUST APPEAR IN *WEBSTER'S COLLEGIATE DICTIONARY* TO QUALIFY. USE THE LETTERS ONLY AS OFTEN AS THEY APPEAR IN THE PHRASE WHEN MAKING ANY GIVEN WORD. IT'S LOTS OF FUN. IT'S WZZZ'S "THE MIGHTY FOUR-SIXTY" WORD-MAKING CONTEST.

WHAT DOES WIBL (KER) REALLY MEAN? 2.10

This promotion is included in the contest section of this book mainly because you will be giving away some prizes to listeners who submit entries judged to be the best. But, actually, it is a fun promotion that provides the basis for some clever on-air material, audience involvement, and some cute newspaper ads.

How It Works

Announce on the air that you are conducting a contest to find out what your call letters really mean. Listeners are invited to submit word combinations that incorporate your call letters, along with a story in which the slogan is the tag line.

The winning entries will be used on the air—and, possibly, in newspaper ads.

Example

Suppose your call letters are KER. A possible story would be:

> A traveling group of entertainers from the United States is working in North Africa. They are captured by a band of murderous Bedouins. The sheik declares that he is going to kill all of them until one of the group named Roberta starts singing for him. He likes her voice and tells her that, as long as she keeps on singing, the group will stay alive. At which all of the other members of the group shout at her: "Keep Entertaining, Roberta!"

Some other possibilities using the same call letters might be:

"Keep Everything, Roger."

"Katie Eloped, Right?"

"Karl Enjoys Running"

"Kindly Express Regrets."

Or, suppose that your call letters are WIBL. Here are some possible lines:

"When Igor Bit Louis."

"Why, Is Bill Leaving?"

"Who Is Boris Lupinsky?"

"Willy Is Batting Last."

"What Is Barney Losing?"

Prizes

The natural prizes for a contest such as this are radios. You can have the winning slogans silk-screened on each of the radios for the winners.

Newspaper Ads

As mentioned, a promotion such as this provides the basis for a very cute series of newspaper ads. Get a local cartoonist to do a sketch with each of the call letter slogans that you plan to use. Of course, include the story that goes with each. The headline for all ads should be "What Does KER Really Mean?"

2.11   WHAT DO YOU KNOW?

This is a good contest to use on your 6:00 to 9:00 A.M. show. It is the time-honored trivia quiz, and it is very simple and easy to handle.

How It Works

Once an hour or once each morning between 7:40 and 8:20 A.M., your morning personality announces that he or she is going to play "What Do You Know?" The DJ asks a question and the first person to call in with the right answer wins. If this one strikes you as being rather thin, remember, we have said that the simplest promotions are almost always the best ones. Besides, there are some added advantages here, so read on.

The Questions

Virtually all of the questions used should pertain to local trivia: How long is Main Street? What was the name of the first baby born in Centerville after it became a town? In what year was the Smith Building completed? How deep is Snyder's Lake? What is the height of the tallest hill in town? How many inches of snow fell on Centerville in the winter of 1978?

If at all practical, have your morning DJ work out his or her own questions. This is one of the added advantages we mentioned. In this way he or she will become, through the research necessary to dig out the questions, an authority on local history and folklore. And this fact will add immeasurably to his value as an air personality.

Occasionally, but only occasionally, throw in a gimmick question such as: When did the last streetcar run on Maple Street? Answer: No streetcar has ever run on Maple Street.

The Prize

The best prize for a contest of this nature is a CD or record album. Your distributor will be glad to provide albums for the plugs. The best idea is to give away the same album for a whole week. You may wish to vary this, say, during the United Way campaign or Community Chest drive, by having the prize be a $5 contribution to the charity in the winner's name.

This is not the sort of contest from which you are going to get a tremendous response. But thousands of listeners will be playing the game along with you even though they never bother to call in. It is a good, basic, uncomplicated contest.

What Do You Know?—On-Air Copy

WHAT DO YOU KNOW? THAT'S THE QUESTION (morning DJ) ASKS EVERY MORNING WHEN HE GREETS YOU WITH THE HAPPY SOUND OF WZZZ RADIO FROM 6:00 TO 9:00 A.M. "WHAT DO YOU KNOW?" IS THE QUESTION-AND-

ANSWER GAME IN WHICH YOUR LOCAL KNOWLEDGE CAN WIN YOU A RECORD ALBUM. (Morning DJ) PLAYS BOTH "WHAT DO YOU KNOW?" AND HAPPY MUSIC EVERY WEEKDAY MORNING FROM 6:00 TO 9:00 ON WZZZ— RADIO 460.

* * * *

WHETHER YOUR LOCAL KNOWLEDGE IS GOOD OR BAD . . . YOU'LL FIND IT FUN TO PLAY "WHAT DO YOU KNOW?"—THE HAPPY QUESTION-AND-ANSWER GAME WITH (morning DJ). EVERY MORNING BETWEEN 6:00 AND 9:00 ON WZZZ. (Morning DJ) ASKS QUESTIONS BASED ON LOCAL FACTS AND HIS-TORY. THE RIGHT ANSWER WINS SOMEONE A NEW RECORD ALBUM OR CD. AND EVERY LISTENER ADDS TO HIS STORE OF KNOWLEDGE ABOUT CENTER-VILLE'S COLORFUL PAST. PLAY "WHAT DO YOU KNOW?" EVERY MORNING WITH (morning DJ). THAT'S ON WZZZ—RADIO 460—WHERE MORE PEOPLE HAVE FOUND THEY LIKE THE SOUND.

* * * *

"WHAT DO YOU KNOW?" TUNE TO WZZZ WEEKDAY MORNINGS AND FIND OUT WHAT YOU DO KNOW WHEN (morning DJ) PLAYS THIS HAPPY QUESTION-AND-ANSWER GAME BETWEEN 6:00 AND 9:00 A.M. (Morning DJ) HAS A QUES-TION EVERY MORNING—AND IF YOU'VE GOT THE ANSWER, YOU MAY WIN A NEW CD OR RECORD ALBUM. ENJOY THE HAPPY SOUND—AND PLAY "WHAT DO YOU KNOW?" WITH (morning DJ) WEEKDAY MORNINGS ON WZZZ—RADIO 460.

* * * *

(Morning DJ) ASKS "WHAT DO YOU KNOW?" EVERY WEEKDAY MORNING BETWEEN 6:00 AND 9:00 A.M. ON WZZZ. TUNE IN AND TELL HIM.

* * * *

DO YOU KNOW WHO? WHAT? WHERE? WHY? HOW? . . . "WHAT DO YOU KNOW?"—THAT'S THE GAME WZZZ'S POPULAR (morning DJ) PLAYS EVERY MORNING BETWEEN 6:00 AND 9:00 A.M. "WHAT DO YOU KNOW?" (Morning DJ) GIVES AWAY CDS OR RECORD ALBUMS EACH DAY IN THIS HAPPY GAME OF QUESTION-AND-ANSWER. AND YOU CAN BE A WINNER. SO, BE IN TUNE WITH THE TIME. LISTEN TO (morning DJ)—THE WZZZ WAKE-UP MAN. MEET

HIM RIGHT HERE AT THE RADIO 460 SPOT ON YOUR DIAL MONDAY THROUGH
SATURDAY FROM 6:00 TO 9:00 A.M.

* * * *

WANT TO WAKE UP HAPPY? WELL, THE BIGGEST CLICK ON THE CLOCK
RADIO CIRCUIT IS THE (morning DJ) SHOW—MORNINGS 6:00 TO 9:00 ON WZZZ.
SO, SET THAT CLOCK RADIO AT THE RADIO 460 SPOT—AND WAKE UP WITH
(morning DJ). YES, (morning DJ)—"MR. CENTERVILLE" HIMSELF—MAKES
MORNING A HAPPY TIME . . . WITH THE FIRST WORD IN NEWS—THE LAST
WORD IN MUSIC. AND EVERY MORNING, (morning DJ) PLAYS "WHAT DO YOU
KNOW?"—THE EXCITING QUESTION-AND-ANSWER GAME. PLAY "WHAT DO
YOU KNOW?". YOU CAN WIN ONE OF THE COMPACT DISCS (morning DJ) GIVES
AWAY EACH DAY. JOIN THE HAPPY THRONG WHO WAKE UP WITH (morning
DJ)—MORNINGS ON WZZZ.

BOOTY BOTTLES

2.12

Here is a good promotion for the late spring and summer period. In most areas,
by late May people are starting to spend more and more time outside. There is a
change in the listening pattern as you move through the period when the schools
are letting out. Because of the outside elements involved, this is a good one to
help you swing through this period.

How It Works

Go to a pharmaceutical supply house in your area and buy a quantity of plastic
bottles about 5 inches high that have fairly wide mouths. The supply house will
be able to tell you how to get your message printed on the bottles. The message
should be something like: "BOOTY BOTTLE Radio WZZZ—The Mighty
460."

Put passes to baseball games, passes to movie theaters, slips of paper
redeemable for records either at your station or at a record store, and other
prizes into the booty bottles. This is a good chance for you to help out your
local baseball team, so include lots of tickets and, perhaps in a few of the bottles, season passes to the ball games.

The booty bottles are then hidden all over your listening area. The bottles
can be hidden almost anywhere. Broadcast regular clues as to the location of
the booty bottles. The clues should be fairly specific.

Major Contest

If you wish to expand this promotion into a major contest, here's how to do it: In addition to the booty bottles mentioned above, set up another group. There should be one for each day you plan to run the promotion. If the promotion is to run three weeks, then the special group will number 15, 18, or 21, depending on whether you plan to run the contest five, six or seven days a week. Into these bottles you will put slips of paper marked from 1 to 21. Be sure to initial or code the slips so you can positively identify them.

Each of these special bottles is hidden on the day (or the night before) it is to be used. On the first day of the promotion, if bottle number one is turned in before midnight, the finder wins a special prize. On the second day, bottle number two is put out, and so on. (Do not hide the bottles in advance because someone will find one of the higher numbers and hold it to win a big prize.)

At about 7:10 on your morning show, the DJ spins a carnival wheel, which will come to rest on the name of one of the presidents. Then, if the booty bottle for that day is turned in before midnight, the finder receives a picture of that president—as it appears on paper currency, of course.

If the bottle is turned in at any later date, the finder receives five dollars or some other prize. The presidents and the bills they appear on are: $5 — Lincoln; $10 — Hamilton; $20 — Jackson; $50 — Grant; $100 — Franklin; $1,000 — Cleveland; $5,000 — Madison; and $10,000 — Chase. Throughout the day broadcast a whole series of clues as to the location of the booty bottle that wins the bigger prize.

Booty Bottle—On-Air Copy

LOOK FOR THE WZZZ BOOTY BOTTLES HIDDEN THROUGHOUT CENTERVILLE. BOOTY CONSISTS OF VALUABLE THEATER TICKETS, PASSES, AND COUPONS REDEEMABLE FOR RECORDS, TICKETS TO THE BASEBALL GAMES, AND A LOT OF OTHER VALUABLE PRIZES. THERE MAY BE BOOTY IN A BOTTLE ON YOUR DOORSTEP . . . HERE'S A CLUE:

* * * *

BOOTY BOTTLES ARE ALL AROUND . . . THAT'S RIGHT—WZZZ BOOTY BOTTLES ARE HIDDEN ABOUT CENTERVILLE. THEY CONTAIN PRIZES FOR THE FINDERS . . . AND FINDERS KEEPERS. KEEP A LOOKOUT—BOOTY BOTTLES ARE ABOUT. WZZZ BOOTY BOTTLES. STAY TUNED FOR CLUES THAT CAN LEAD YOU TO THE BOOTY.

* * * *

WZZZ HAS PUT BOOTY IN BOTTLES . . . WZZZ BOOTY BOTTLES . . . AND HIDDEN THEM THROUGHOUT CENTERVILLE. KEEP YOUR EYES OPEN FOR THESE WZZZ BOOTY BOTTLES CONTAINING VALUABLE PRIZES FOR THE FINDERS. KEEP YOUR EARS OPEN FOR CLUES ON HOW TO FIND THE WZZZ BOOTY BOTTLES. HERE'S A CLUE NOW:

* * * *

WHEN YOU'RE OUT—LOOK ABOUT—FOR THE WZZZ BOOTY BOTTLES. WHEN WITHIN—STAY TUNED IN—FOR CLUES TO THE WHEREABOUTS OF THE WZZZ BOOTY BOTTLES HIDDEN THROUGHOUT CENTERVILLE. FINDERS KEEPERS— AND THERE ARE VALUABLE PRIZES TUCKED INTO THE WZZZ BOOTY BOTTLES—SO, LOOK FOR THEM.

* * * *

DJ: HERE'S A WZZZ BOOTY BOTTLE BULLETIN.

News Voice: A WIDESPREAD SEARCH IS ON IN CENTERVILLE FOR WZZZ BOOTY BOTTLES HIDDEN THROUGHOUT THE CITY BY THE RADIO STATION. VALUABLE REWARDS FOR THE FINDERS ARE CONTAINED IN THESE WZZZ BOOTY BOTTLES. LATEST PERSON TO FIND A WZZZ BOOTY BOTTLE IS (Name) OF (Address) IN CENTERVILLE, WHO FOUND A BOOTY BOTTLE AT (Location). STAY TUNED TO WZZZ FOR FURTHER BOOTY BOTTLE BULLETINS AND CLUES AS TO THE WHEREABOUTS OF THE WZZZ BOOTY BOTTLES. HERE'S A CLUE NOW:

DJ: (Reads clue.)

THE HAPPIEST SOUND IN THE WORLD—Next to WZZZ 2.13

This is a contest promotion that you can use to tie in with the "Happy Habit," "Happy People," "Happy Sound," on-air theme material that you will find in the "On-Air Theme" section of this book.

How It Works

Your DJs announce that you know WZZZ has the happy sound. Now you want to find out what is "The Happiest Sound in the World—Next to WZZZ." Listeners are asked to write in stating what they think the sound is. A winner will be selected and you will capture on record his happiest sound and present him with whatever it is that makes the sound.

Each day, the DJs read a number of entries to stimulate interest in the promotion. Tape as many of these sounds as possible and put them on the air. Here are some of the sounds you are sure to have suggested. We list them here so you can get ready and have them taped in advance: 1. the sound of a baby laughing (you will probably have more people suggesting this one than all the rest combined); 2. the sound of a babbling brook; 3. the sound of a wind rustling through tall trees; 4. the sound of the ocean surf breaking on the shore; 5. the sound of rain on a tin roof.

Getting a Winner

One way to get a winner is to separate all entries into groups. The sound getting the most votes is announced as "The Happiest Sound in the World—Next to WZZZ" and by a drawing the winner is then selected from this group. In this case, since you will probably end up with the baby sound, you will have to borrow an infant and bring it and the winner to the station and try to get the child to laugh. Another way to get a winner is through a group of judges who have been selected for any logical qualifications.

Actually, people are not going to participate in this promotion with the idea of winning. They will participate in sizable numbers because of the pleasant connotation of the promotion. Their biggest rewards will be in having their names announced over the air with the contest in progress.

Good Tie-In

This is really a very simple promotion. But it gives you an excellent opportunity to put additional emphasis on the "Happy Sound" theme you use throughout this period.

Happiest Sound—On-Air Copy

NEXT TO WZZZ—WHAT IS THIS HAPPIEST SOUND IN THE WORLD? . . . (Recorded sound of one of the suggestions from a listener.) IN THE OPINION OF _____ OF _____ IN CENTERVILLE, THE SOUND YOU JUST HEARD IS THE HAPPIEST SOUND IN THE WORLD—NEXT TO WZZZ. WHAT DO YOU THINK IS THE HAPPIEST SOUND IN THE WORLD—NEXT TO THE HAPPY SOUND OF WZZZ? SEND YOUR SUGGESTION IN TODAY TO WZZZ—RADIO 460—THE HOME OF THE HAPPY SOUND.

* * * *

WZZZ—HOME OF THE HAPPY SOUND—IS LOOKING FOR THE SECOND HAPPI-
EST SOUND IN THE WORLD. WE'RE ASKING YOU TO NAME THE SOUND YOU
THINK THE HAPPIEST IN THE WORLD NEXT TO WZZZ. _____ OF
_____ THINKS THE HAPPIEST SOUND IN THE WORLD NEXT TO
WZZZ IS THE SOUND OF BIRDS CHIRPING EARLY ON A SPRING MORNING.
SEND US YOUR SUGGESTION TODAY. IF YOUR SOUND IS PICKED AS THE WIN-
NER WE WILL GIVE YOU WHATEVER IT IS THAT PRODUCES THE SOUND.

* * * *

IS THIS (recorded sound)—OR THIS (recorded sound)—OR THIS (recorded sound) THE
HAPPIEST SOUND IN THE WORLD NEXT TO THE HAPPY SOUND OF WZZZ?
THESE ARE SOME OF THE NOMINATIONS WE'VE RECEIVED FROM LISTENERS
IN OUR SEARCH FOR THE HAPPIEST SOUND IN THE WORLD—NEXT TO WZZZ.
WE'RE STILL LOOKING. SEND US YOUR CANDIDATE FOR THE HAPPIEST
SOUND IN THE WORLD—NEXT TO THE HAPPY SOUND OF WZZZ.

* * * *

WHAT'S THE HAPPIEST SOUND IN THE WORLD? ANSWER: WZZZ—RADIO 460,
NATURALLY. WHAT'S THE HAPPIEST SOUND IN THE WORLD—NEXT TO
WZZZ? ANSWER: YOU TELL US. WE'RE LOOKING FOR THE SOUND THAT,
NEXT TO WZZZ, IS THE HAPPIEST SOUND IN THE WORLD. SEND IN YOUR
NOMINATION TODAY. IF THE SOUND YOU SUGGEST IS JUDGED THE WINNER,
WE WILL PRODUCE FOR YOU WHATEVER IT IS THAT MAKES THE SOUND.
STAY TUNED TO THE HAPPY SOUND. WE'LL SOON KNOW WHAT IS THE HAP-
PIEST SOUND IN THE WORLD—NEXT TO WZZZ.

MONEY HOUSE
2.14

Once again, this contest, basically: 1. is a very simple promotion; 2. can be
explained easily and quickly, 3. can be entered by anyone in your listening area;
4. will not take an excessive amount of airtime to operate; 5. has a built-in element of suspense; 6. requires that people listen to your station in order to play
the game; and, 7. is fun. All of these elements contribute to make this a good,
solid, workable promotion.

How It Works

Arrange a method for the random selection of single numbers ranging from 0 through 9. You can use bingo balls, a carnival wheel, or any other simple system—preferably one that has an audible sound. Once each hour your disc jockey randomly selects three numbers. The first person to call your station who has these numbers in her street address in any order wins a prize. If she has the numbers in her street address in the exact order given, she wins a larger prize.

Following, you will find a great many details on how to handle the WZZZ Money House game. There are many variations on the theme that you may wish to use, but, basically, what we have mentioned above is all there is to the contest. Everything is simple and clean.

Probability of Winning

With this contest you will have a winner each time you put the game on the air. Here are the mathematical probabilities:

- 30% of your total listeners will be potential winners after the first number has been called.
- 6% of your total listeners will still be in the game with a chance to win after two numbers have been called.
- A little more than one-half of 1% of your total listeners will have all three numbers and are possible winners if they call in.
- One-tenth of 1% of your total listeners will have the numbers in the order given and qualify for the big prize.

This means that, if you have 10,000 listeners, 3,000 of these people will be in the running after one number is called; 600 will still have a chance after two numbers; 50 will have all three numbers right. Of this 50, 10 will have the numbers in the order given.

Now, do not let this quantity of potential winners frighten you, because only *one* of them will win. Having a fairly large number of *possible* winners simply makes the contest that much better.

The mathematical probability percentages will hold true regardless of how many listeners you have.

Suspense

This contest is loaded with suspense. As you will see in the format we give you as a suggestion at the end of this promotion, your DJ should not announce all three numbers at the same time. Instead, he should space them at least 10 minutes apart. This gives you a real listener hook because, as previously noted, 30 percent of your listeners will be potential winners after the first number has been announced. In addition, your listeners will be intrigued because there will be a winner each time you play the game.

Some Ground Rules

In playing the game, listeners will use only the last three numbers in their street address. If a street address has only two numbers in it, a zero is to be added by the listener to serve as the final digit. RFD box numbers can be used in the same manner as street numbers. Apartment dwellers simply use the street address of their apartment building. People whose address ends in a one-half use the final three whole numbers in their address to play the game.

Checking Winners

An additional advantage to this contest is that listeners do not have to be at home in order to win. You can check your winner simply by checking the telephone directory, the red book (the reverse listing which gives names and telephone numbers against street numbers), or the city directory.

A Major Promotion

If you wish to turn this into a really major event, here is a way to do it: After your winner has been determined and he has informed your DJ of his full street address and street name, the DJ pulls a sealed envelope from a container. In the container are envelopes with slips of paper inside with written names of every street in your coverage area, or in that portion of your coverage area where the game is being played. (There are many other ways of selecting the street. This is simply an easy suggestion.)

The DJ opens the envelope and, if the street named is the same as that of your previously determined winner, a much more sizable prize is the result. The prize is larger, of course, if the winner has the numbers in the order given than if he has them in mixed order.

The addition of this extra twist will not complicate the handling of the promotion as previously outlined. The resulting drawing power of the promotion will be increased tremendously.

If Your Signal Covers Several Towns

Your station may be one with a signal that covers a fairly wide area. Giving the audience in outlying areas an equal opportunity to play the game can be handled quite simply.

Set up a rotation schedule for all of the areas you wish to include, then arrange the list on the basis of size and importance. Draw up a frequency ratio like this: The smallest and least important area should be assigned a frequency of 1; a more populous area a frequency of 2; and so forth, on up to your own city.

Now set up a master list. If you have given your own city a frequency of, say, 12, put the station down 12 times. Then insert the other areas among this basic 12, putting each down the number of times indicated by your frequency ratio. This master list should be placed on the board and your DJ should check or initial each area as he uses it. (Do not let all of this confuse you. It is really very simple.) Be sure that on your rotation schedule you do not have the same area coming up at the same hour each time.

When you play the game for your city, everyone in your listening area is qualified to play. When it is for other areas, you state that "This hour the WZZZ Money House game is for listeners in Cooperville and vicinity." If the outlying towns are not of *major* importance to you, we suggest that you forget everything mentioned above and play the game without this added complication. People in these other areas can call in and try to win if they wish.

Another Variation—Take the Third Caller

Here is another way you can add interest to this promotion. Before your DJ calls the final number in the hourly sequence, he announces that the winner for that hour will be either the first or the second or the third correct phone call received. This makes a very easy addition to the game and one with an even greater suspense factor.

We suggest that, if you do decide to incorporate this extra feature, you wait until the contest has been going for several weeks. Otherwise, you will be throwing too much at your audience all at once and it will be hard for them to grasp.

Occasionally, we suggest you use this technique to determine a winner with other promotions. It is a very good added bit, since it will appeal to people who do not call in to contests because they feel their call will not get through to the station in time.

Timing

You will probably only wish to run this promotion 11 times a day—once an hour between 7:00 A.M. and 6:00 P.M. However, do not overlook the possibility of running it on into the evening hours; it can do much to build your evening audience. Situations vary, but in most cases you will probably not conduct this promotion on Sundays.

The Prize

Since you will have a winner each time this promotion is aired, you must necessarily keep your basic prize small. Giving away merchandise prizes and linking the promotion with some of your sponsors has certain advantages; however, the contest will work most effectively if your prize is cash.

The size of your prize will, naturally, be determined by the size of your market. What we suggest here should just be a guide and should not restrict you. If you go to merchandise prizes, you should offer something of value roughly equivalent to the cash prizes suggested.

Here is a possible schedule for prizes:

- *Basic Prize*—for a winner who has a street address with the three numbers called, but in mixed order: $1 or $2 in cash.

- *Larger Prize*—for winners who have the numbers in the order announced; since a winner of this type should come up on an average of one out of five times, the prize should be five times the basic prize, i.e., $5 or $10 in each.

- *Major Prize*—to be used if you include the street matching twist suggested; $100 for winners with the numbers in mixed order and the matching street; $1,000 for winners with the numbers in the order announced and the matching street. The point here, of course, is that the prize should be large enough to virtually compel listeners to stay tuned in.

Money House Game Format

TIME NOW TO PLAY WZZZ MONEY HOUSE. GET THE LAST THREE NUMBERS OF YOUR STREET ADDRESS OR RURAL BOX NUMBER IN MIND BECAUSE THOSE ARE THE NUMBERS WITH WHICH YOU PLAY THE GAME. IF YOUR ADDRESS HAS ONLY TWO NUMBERS, YOUR THIRD NUMBER IS AUTOMATICALLY A ZERO. NOW HERE WE GO. (Rattling of bingo balls as number is selected.) THE FIRST NUMBER THIS HOUR IS A (number). IF THERE IS A (number) WITHIN THE FINAL THREE NUMBERS OF YOUR STREET ADDRESS, YOU ARE IN THE RUNNING TO WIN FROM TWO DOLLARS TO ONE THOUSAND DOLLARS. IN JUST A FEW MINUTES WE WILL BE ANNOUNCING TWO MORE MONEY HOUSE NUMBERS. IF YOU HAVE ALL THREE WITHIN THE FINAL THREE NUMBERS OF YOUR STREET ADDRESS, IN ANY ORDER, YOURS CAN BE THE WZZZ MONEY HOUSE.

* * * *

A FEW MINUTES AGO WE ANNOUNCED THE FIRST NUMBER IN THE WZZZ

MONEY HOUSE GAME FOR THIS HOUR. IT WAS A (<u>number</u>). NOW, HERE WE GO FOR THE SECOND NUMBER. (Bingo ball sound). IT IS A (<u>number</u>). IF THE FINAL THREE NUMBERS OF YOUR STREET ADDRESS CONTAIN A (<u>number</u>) AND A (<u>number</u>), YOURS MAY BE THE WZZZ MONEY HOUSE. DON'T GO AWAY BECAUSE WE'LL BE ANNOUNCING THE THIRD NUMBER TO DETERMINE OUR WINNER IN JUST A FEW MINUTES.

* * * *

WE'RE READY NOW TO SELECT THE FINAL NUMBER IN THE WZZZ MONEY HOUSE GAME FOR THIS HOUR. THE FIRST NUMBER WAS A (_____), THE SECOND NUMBER WAS A (<u>number</u>). IF THE FINAL THREE NUMBERS OF YOUR STREET ADDRESS CONTAIN—IN ANY ORDER—A (<u>number</u>), A (<u>number</u>), PLUS THE NUMBER I'LL ANNOUNCE IN JUST A MOMENT, YOURS CAN BE THE WZZZ MONEY HOUSE. IF YOU HAVE ALL THREE NUMBERS, CALL WZZZ AT (<u>telephone number</u>). THE FIRST PERSON TO CALL WITH THE CORRECT NUMBERS WILL BE OUR WINNER. IF THE NUMBERS OCCUR IN MIXED ORDER IN YOUR STREET ADDRESS, YOU MAY WIN TWO DOLLARS—OR EVEN ONE HUNDRED DOLLARS IF YOU MATCH OUR MYSTERY STREET. IF YOU HAVE THE NUMBERS IN THE ORDER GIVEN, YOU MAY WIN TEN DOLLARS—OR, IF YOU MATCH OUR MYSTERY STREET, TOO—ONE THOUSAND DOLLARS. THAT NUMBER TO CALL AGAIN IS (telephone number). NOW, HERE WE GO. THE THIRD NUMBER IS (Bingo ball sound) . . . A (<u>number</u>). THAT'S IT . . . A (<u>number</u>), A (<u>number</u>), AND A (<u>number</u>). IN JUST A FEW MOMENTS WE WILL KNOW WHETHER WE GIVE AWAY TWO, TEN, ONE HUNDRED OR ONE THOUSAND DOLLARS TO THE PERSON LIVING IN THE WZZZ MONEY HOUSE.

The mystery street envelope is opened after the winner has been determined.

Money House—On-Air Promo Copy

MONEY! MONEY! MONEY!

* * * *

MONEY IN THE HOUSE NUMBER MEANS MONEY IN THE HOUSE IF *YOURS* IS THE WZZZ MONEY HOUSE. STAY TUNED FOR DETAILS.

* * * *

THE NUMBER OF YOUR HOUSE CAN MEAN DOLLARS TO YOU IF YOURS IS THE WZZZ MONEY HOUSE. STAY TUNED TO THE MIGHTY 460 FOR DETAILS.

* * * *

THROUGHOUT THE DAY—AT HOME OR AWAY—PLAY THE WZZZ MONEY HOUSE GAME. KNOW YOUR HOUSE NUMBER, KNOW THE 460 SPOT ON YOUR RADIO DIAL. THESE TWO NUMBERS MAY ADD UP TO A NUMBER OF DOLLARS FOR YOU IN THE WZZZ MONEY HOUSE GAME! STAY TUNED FOR DETAILS.

* * * *

IT PAYS TO STAY! IT PAYS TO PLAY! IT PAYS TO STAY TUNED TO WZZZ RADIO FOUR-SIXTY. IT PAYS TO PLAY THE WZZZ MONEY HOUSE GAME THROUGHOUT THE DAY ON WZZZ. STAY TUNED, IT'S COMING UP.

* * * *

Following are a group of bright and spritely air promos to be used in connection with the WZZZ Money House. Each is a simple two-voice promo and you should be able to tape all of them in a single, short session. It is a good idea to develop pre-recorded material for most of the promotions you air.

Anncr 1: THERE'LL ALWAYS BE AN ENGLAND!

Anncr 2: THERE'LL ALWAYS BE A WZZZ MONEY HOUSE. ELEVEN A DAY ON WZZZ.

* * * *

Anncr 1: A ROLLING STONE GATHERS NO MOSS!

Anncr 2: A RADIO NOT TUNED TO WZZZ GATHERS NO MONEY IN THE WZZZ MONEY HOUSE GAME.

* * * *

Anncr 1: A STITCH IN TIME SAVES NINE!

Anncr 2: A DIAL ON FOUR-SIXTY MAY WIN MONEY IN THE WZZZ MONEY HOUSE GAME!

* * * *

Anncr 1: HICKORY, DICKORY DOCK, THE MOUSE RAN UP THE CLOCK RADIO.

Anncr 2: AND SET THE DIAL AT FOUR-SIXTY TO PLAY THE WZZZ MONEY HOUSE GAME.

Anncr 1: NICE MOUSIE.

* * * *

Anncr 1: LITTLE MISS MUFFET SAT ON A TUFFET AND LISTENED TO WZZZ ON HER PORTABLE RADIO.

Anncr 2: ALONG CAME A SPIDER AND SAT DOWN BESIDE HER, AND THEY PLAYED THE WZZZ MONEY HOUSE GAME TOGETHER.

Anncr 1: THE SPIDER WON.

* * * *

Anncr 1: JACK SPRATT COULD EAT NO FAT, HIS WIFE COULD EAT NO LEAN.

Anncr 2: BUT BOTH PLAYED THE WZZZ MONEY HOUSE GAME.

Anncr 1: AH ME, HUNGRY BUT HAPPY ON WZZZ.

* * * *

Anncr 1: HI, DIDDLE DIDDLE, THE CAT AND THE FIDDLE, THE COW JUMPED OVER THE MOON.

Anncr 2: THE LITTLE DOG JUST LAUGHED AND PLAYED THE WZZZ MONEY HOUSE GAME.

Anncr 1: ARE THERE NUMBERS ON DOG HOUSES?

* * * *

Anncr 1: JACK AND JILL RAN UP THE HILL, TO LISTEN TO WZZZ.

Anncr 2: JACK FELL DOWN AND BROKE HIS CROWN, BUT JILL CLEANED UP IN THE WZZZ MONEY HOUSE GAME.

Anncr 1: SPENT IT ON ANOTHER MAN, I'LL BET.

* * * *

Anncr 1: THIS LITTLE PIGGIE WENT TO MARKET.

Anncr 2: AND THIS LITTLE PIGGIE STAYED HOME AND WON AT THE WZZZ MONEY HOUSE GAME.

Anncr 1: KEPT THE MONEY, THE HOG.

* * * *

Anncr 1: SIMPLE SIMON MET A PIE-MAN.

Anncr 2: WHILE PLAYING THE WZZZ MONEY HOUSE GAME ON THE MIGHTY FOUR-SIXTY.

Anncr 1: SAID THE PIE-MAN, "YOU'RE NOT SIMPLE, SIMON."

* * * *

Anncr 1: HUMPTY DUMPTY SAT ON A WALL, LISTENING TO WZZZ AND PLAYING THE WZZZ MONEY HOUSE GAME.

Anncr 2: HUMPTY DUMPTY HAD A GREAT FALL.

Anncr 1: BUT NOT BEFORE HE COLLECTED.

* * * *

Anncr 1: LITTLE JACK HORNER SAT IN THE CORNER AND LISTENED TO WZZZ.

Anncr 2: PLAYED THE WZZZ MONEY HOUSE GAME AND WON.

Anncr 1: IT'S BETTER THAN PLUM ON YOUR THUMB.

* * * *

Anncr 1: THERE WAS AN OLD WOMAN WHO LIVED IN A SHOE, AND HAD SO MANY CHILDREN SHE DIDN'T KNOW WHAT TO DO.

Anncr 2: HAD A LUCKY SHOE-NUMBER AND WON A POTFUL IN THE WZZZ MONEY HOUSE GAME.

Anncr 1: SHE BOUGHT A BOOT.

* * * *

Anncr 1: OLD MOTHER HUBBARD WENT TO THE CUPBOARD AND TUNED IN WZZZ ON HER KITCHEN RADIO.

Anncr 2: SHE CLEANED UP PLAYING THE WZZZ MONEY HOUSE GAME.

Anncr 1: THAT DIDN'T HELP HER POOR HUNGRY DOG, THOUGH.

* * * *

Anncr 1: THERE WAS A LITTLE GIRL, WHO HAD A LITTLE CURL, RIGHT IN THE MIDDLE OF HER FOREHEAD.

Anncr 2: WHEN SHE WAS GOOD SHE LISTENED TO WZZZ AND PLAYED THE WZZZ MONEY HOUSE GAME, AND WON.

Anncr 1: BUT WHEN SHE WAS BAD, SHE WAS STILL HORRID.

* * * *

Anncr 1: MARY HAD A LITTLE LAMB WHO LISTENED TO WZZZ.

Anncr 2: AND WON AT THE WZZZ MONEY HOUSE GAME.

Anncr 1: NOW MARY FOLLOWS THE LAMB.

* * * *

Anncr 1: THREE LITTLE KITTENS LOST THEIR MITTENS, AND DIDN'T KNOW WHAT TO DO.

Anncr 2: SO THEY TUNED WZZZ AND WON AT THE WZZZ MONEY HOUSE GAME—THEN THEY COULD AFFORD NEW MITTENS.

Anncr 1: RABBIT-LINED, NO LESS.

2.15   TRAFFIC COUNT

This giveaway is based on a prize that is ideally suited to the good weather when people are outside and active. It is flexible, so that from a few basics you can add to the prize to make it as sizable as you desire. The giveaway is also based on a contest that strongly ties in with the theme of safe driving and "on-the-go" radio.

The major prize is a complete barbecue dinner for the winner and his family or a specified number of friends, prepared and served by the WZZZ disc jockeys, with one of them acting as "chef." At the conclusion of the dinner, all of the barbecue equipment is awarded to the winner. The dinner should be held in a public place, such as a park or resort, for additional publicity.

The contest that determines the winner is the WZZZ Traffic Count. There are three natural pegs from which you may choose to hang the Traffic Count, making it more than just a promotion stunt:

1. You may bill it as part of WZZZ's continuing campaign for safe driving, putting an on-the-scene reminder out to drive safely and to illustrate graphically the vast number of cars on the road in the summer.

2. You may take the WZZZ Traffic Count to demonstrate the popularity of your town or area as a tourist mecca in the summer.

3. You may tie the Traffic Count in with your summertime theme of "on-the-go" radio, with WZZZ wishing drivers a good trip and reminding them that WZZZ is with them on their car radio.

How It Works

At a conspicuous vantage point on the main highway on the edge of your town or city, two (or more on rotating shifts) of your disc jockeys conduct the WZZZ Traffic Count. The team counts every vehicle passing the checkpoint from 6 P.M. Friday evening to midnight on Sunday. This is done for four consecutive weekends. Your listeners estimate the total number of vehicles that pass during the WZZZ Traffic Count for the entire period. In addition, you have three weekly contests, with smaller prizes, for the best estimates of the first three weekly checks.

To get the best mileage out of this promotion, we suggest you handle it this way: Arrange your promotion so that the final traffic check of the series is done for the three days of either the Fourth of July or Labor Day weekends, when thousands of cars are on the road. The traffic count is also taken on the three preceding weekends.

For the first three weekends, listeners are asked to mail in their estimates of the number of vehicles counted by the WZZZ Traffic Count. (You are, of course, plugging the major prize throughout this period.) Entries should be postmarked no later than midnight Friday before the start of each traffic count. Select the listener estimate closest to the actual count for the specific weekend—he or she will receive a smaller weekly prize. Announce this winner and his or her estimate, but *not* the actual count made by your disc jockeys. Announcing the actual count made by your disc jockeys would enable listeners to keep a running total, making it easier to estimate the number on the final weekend.

Before the final weekend of the WZZZ Traffic Count, listeners submit their estimate of the total number of vehicles counted in the four weekends of the promotion. The winner will receive your big prize. As a tiebreaker, ask entrants to include an estimate of the number of vehicles counted on the final weekend. This figure will not enter in unless there is a tie, which is unlikely. You may, however, wish to award a weekly prize to the best estimate in this tie-breaker category as an additional gimmick.

More about the Prizes

As we said before, your quarterly giveaway for the summer season is a flexible one. From a new basic item, the number of things you may add to the prize is limitless, and therefore, the prize can be as big as you care to make it.

The part of the prize you will have the most fun with is the barbecue dinner, prepared by one of your DJs and served by the rest of them. The valuable part of the prize is the outdoor barbecue equipment you are awarding the winner. The prize should consist of at least a picnic table and benches, barbecue cooking tools, barbecue spit and stand, charcoal, and a number of steaks or pounds of ground beef for barbecuing.

You may make the prize as valuable as you wish by adding such things as a carving set, beach umbrella, portable serving cart, patio furniture, apron, gloves, cocktail equipment, and so forth—plus a supply of steaks for one week, two weeks, or the entire summer.

The weekly prizes should be smaller, but in the same theme. A good prize is to provide the weekly winners with four pounds of hamburger a week for a period of a month. Or, you might give them any single item necessary for outdoor barbecuing.

The Checkpoint

For added publicity, make sure your disc jockeys are out where the public can see them while they conduct the traffic count. Set them up in style with a beach umbrella, hammock, ice-cooler—the works. Also include a large sign at the site announcing "The WZZZ Traffic Count —Drive Safely—Tune 460." Other signs might read "Do Not Feed," "Men Working?", and so on. Set up a large trash barrel for deposit of litter-bags. Arrange for cut-ins or reports from the site of the WZZZ Traffic Count.

Get Local Cooperation

Do not overlook the possibility of getting cooperation from local groups interested in promoting tourism in your area. You may even wish to turn your checkpoint into a tourist hospitality station, complete with area maps, dining, hotel and motel information, and so on.

Traffic Count—On-Air Copy

THOUSANDS OF CARS ARE ON THE ROAD IN SUMMERTIME. HOW MANY OF THEM PASS THROUGH CENTERVILLE ON HIGHWAY 171? WZZZ IS FINDING OUT WITH THE WZZZ TRAFFIC COUNT. THIS WEEKEND AND FOR THE FOLLOWING THREE, THE WZZZ DISC JOCKEYS ARE COUNTING EVERY VEHICLE PASSING THE WZZZ TRAFFIC COUNT CHECKPOINT AT THE CITY LIMITS ON HIGHWAY 171 FROM 6 P.M. FRIDAY TO MIDNIGHT SUNDAY. WHAT'S YOUR ESTIMATE OF THE NUMBER OF CARS PASSING THE WZZZ CHECKPOINT ON A SUMMER WEEKEND? FOR THE FIRST THREE WEEKS WZZZ WILL AWARD A PRIZE OF (name prize) TO ESTIMATE CLOSEST TO THE ACTUAL WZZZ TRAFFIC COUNT. HOW MANY CARS WILL PASS THE CHECKPOINT FOR THE FOUR WEEKENDS—INCLUDING THE THREE-DAY FOURTH OF JULY WEEKEND? THE CLOSEST ESTIMATE OF THIS TOTAL NUMBER OF CARS WINS THE FABULOUS WZZZ OUTDOOR LIVING SET, (details of prize). PLUS A COMPLETE BARBECUE DINNER PREPARED AND SERVED BY THE WZZZ DJs. WZZZ ASKS EVERY DRIVER TO DRIVE SAFELY—AND EVERY LISTENER TO ENTER THE WZZZ TRAFFIC COUNT.

* * * *

WIN A WONDERFUL BARBECUE DINNER PREPARED AND SERVED BY THE WZZZ DISC JOCKEYS FOR YOU AND YOUR FAMILY. AND YOU GET TO KEEP THE BARBECUE AND PATIO EQUIPMENT USED FOR THE DINNER—A DESIGN FOR OUTDOOR LIVING. ENTER THE WZZZ TRAFFIC COUNT—WEEKLY PRIZES, TOO. STAY TUNED FOR DETAILS.

* * * *

HOW MANY CARS PASS THROUGH CENTERVILLE, TOURIST OASIS OF HIGHWAY 171, ON A SUMMER WEEKEND? WZZZ IS FINDING OUT WITH THE WZZZ TRAFFIC COUNT. LOOK FOR THE WZZZ DJs COUNTING CARS AT THE CITY LIMITS ON HIGHWAY 171. ENTER THE WZZZ TRAFFIC COUNT BY ESTIMATING THE NUMBER OF CARS. WEEKLY PRIZES PLUS A FABULOUS GRAND PRIZE. DRIVE SAFELY, AND STAY TUNED TO WZZZ 460 FOR DETAILS.

* * * *

EVERYBODY IS COMING TO CENTERVILLE IN THE SUMMERTIME, AND WZZZ IS COUNTING THE CARS—WITH THE WZZZ TRAFFIC COUNT. FOR THE NEXT

FOUR WEEKENDS WZZZ DISC JOCKEYS ARE COUNTING EVERY CAR PASSING THE WZZZ TRAFFIC COUNT CHECKPOINT ON HIGHWAY 171 AT THE CITY LIMITS. YOUR ESTIMATES OF THE WZZZ TRAFFIC COUNT MAY WIN YOU VALUABLE PRIZES—STAY TUNED FOR DETAILS.

2.16 HOW DOES YOUR GARDEN GROW?

Here is another promotion that provides both fun and valuable community goodwill. Get this promotion under way so that it culminates during the peak of the flower-blossoming season in your area.

How It Works

Make arrangements with one or more institutions in your area, such as retirement homes or hospitals, that will welcome bouquets of flowers to lend cheer to the surroundings. All entries in your contest will be earmarked for these institutions. Then you ask your listeners to make up bouquets of flowers with representative blooms from the varieties of flowers blossoming in *their yards*. The person submitting a bunch of flowers with the greatest variety represented is declared the winner. All entries should be tagged with a card stating how many different flowers are represented.

Be Sure to Get Pictures

You may decide to have the entries delivered to your studios, or if they are not convenient to the public, you should arrange for a collection spot in a central area—perhaps a downtown garden supply shop or florist. In any event, be sure to get pictures for local and trade publicity as the mountains of blossoms accumulate *and* when the bouquets are placed in the institutions to bring delight to the people there.

Items

Be sure to announce regularly where the flowers are destined to wind up. Many people will bring bouquets for this purpose even though they have no intention of winning your contest. Be sure to ask that all entries be in water-filled containers so they will still be fresh when you deliver them to their destinations. A canning jar makes a good container. You will want to check the winning entries to be sure that the flowers actually came from that person's yard rather than the local park or greenhouse.

Prizes

You may have just one grand prize, or include first-, second-, and third-place prizes, as well. They may be as big or as little as you care to make them—but they should be related to gardening. The prizes are not the important thing, for many people will be, in effect, donating flowers to the institutions, and others will be taking advantage of another opportunity to show off their "green thumbs." You may run this contest for a week, two weeks, or as long as people keep bringing in entries.

How Does Your Garden Grow?—On-Air Copy

WZZZ ASKS "HOW DOES YOUR GARDEN GROW?" WE'RE LOOKING FOR THE LOCAL GREEN THUMB THAT'S RAISED THE GREATEST VARIETY OF FLOWERS IN THEIR OWN YARD. WE WANT TO REWARD THIS ABILITY. BUT WE'VE GOT A DOUBLE MOTIVE. WE'RE GOING TO CHEER UP THE SURROUNDINGS AT THE CENTERVILLE RETIREMENT VILLAGE. WE'RE ASKING GARDENERS TO BRING IN A BOUQUET WITH BLOSSOMS FROM EVERY ONE OF THEIR OWN GARDEN FLOWERS—AND EVERY ENTRY GOES TO BRIGHTEN THE LIVES OF CENTERVILLE'S SENIOR CITIZENS. BRING YOUR BOUQUETS TO SMITH'S GARDEN SHOP IN DOWNTOWN CENTERVILLE. TO THE PERSON BRINGING IN THE BOUQUET CONTAINING THE GREATEST VARIETY OF FLOWERS, WE'LL AWARD A WONDERFUL ARRAY OF GARDENING EQUIPMENT FROM SMITH'S. WZZZ IS ASKING, "HOW DOES YOUR GARDEN GROW?"

* * * *

WZZZ ASKS "HOW DOES YOUR GARDEN GROW?" GOT A GREEN THUMB? IS YOUR YARD FULL OF MANY DIFFERENT FLOWERS? BRING A BOUQUET FROM YOUR OWN YARD WITH EVERY FLOWER REPRESENTED TO SMITH'S GARDEN SHOP IN CENTERVILLE. THE BOUQUET WITH THE GREATEST VARIETY REP-RESENTED WINS A VALUABLE GARDENING PRIZE. ALL ENTRIES GO TO BRIGHTEN UP THE CENTERVILLE RETIREMENT VILLAGE.

NOTES TO YOU CONTEST   2.17

This is a good daytime contest that can be limited to one show or extended over the 9:00 A.M. to 4:00 P.M. period. We suggest that you assign it to a single DJ and confine it to that show. The contest is simple to conduct, has an excellent built-in listener hook, and can be continued over a period of time without wearing thin. In addition, the listeners who do not actively participate to the extent of trying to win the prize will have almost as much fun with this one as those who do.

How It Works

If you have a piano in your studio, you are all set. If you do not, go out and buy a toy xylophone or a toy piano and you are ready to start.

Each day you select a song to be used for the contest. These should always be songs that will be familiar to virtually everyone in your audience. The song is played one note at a time during the program. The first person to call in and identify the song wins your prize for the day. It's as simple as that.

How the Notes Are Played

The first note (you may wish to give two notes as a starter each day) should be given near the top of the show. The remaining notes are played throughout the show at indefinite times.

Your DJ should tell listeners to keep their ears to the radio because along the line, without any warning as to when, he will play the whole series of notes given up to that time. Whenever he does play such a series he should alter the tempo from that of the actual song. Each time a single note is played, the DJ should identify it as the first, fifth, seventh, or whatever note in the series. You may wish to give verbal clues to the song, too, but this is not at all necessary. The contest will work just as well without them.

The Prize

This is not a major contest and should not be treated as such. The prize could be a compact disc, theater tickets, or anything of this nature. A commercial tie-in can be incorporated easily into this contest with the resultant prize being something from a sponsor's store.

2.18 TIME CONTEST

In other sections we have talked, at length, about the necessity of keeping your contests simple if you want them to be effective. Here is a case in point. The entire basic premise of the "WZZZ Time Contest" can be stated in these eleven words: "How many hours and minutes has WZZZ been on the air?"

There is a great range of possibility concerning how to develop the promotion, so, do not limit yourself to the suggestions we set forth here. As we have also said before (so often that you are probably getting sick of hearing about it), the more of your own originality and the more local flavor you put into any of these promotions, the greater the response. The basic soundness of this promotion makes it highly adaptable.

How It Works

You simply ask listeners: "How many hours and minutes has WZZZ been on the air?" They send in estimates on a postcard. The first correct answer wins whatever prize you have set up for the contest. Someone in your office, of course, is going to have to go back over the logs and determine exactly how long you have been broadcasting.

To Make It Simpler

You may wish to simplify this and have a contest of shorter duration, using a prize of less significance. In this case, we suggest that your question be: "How many *hours* has WZZZ been on the air?" The promotion will still be an effective one if you decide to handle it this way.

Ground Rules

There are a number of ways to determine your winner:

1. Broadcasting time must be estimated correctly up to midnight of the day on which the postcard entry is postmarked.
2. Broadcasting time must be estimated correctly up to noon of the day on which the card is received at the station.
3. Your DJs can pull a number of the cards from the hopper each hour; to win, the drawn card must estimate the time correctly up to the beginning of that hour.
4. A combination of the card-pulling and method 1 or 2 can be used.

Realize that, while all of this may seem overly difficult on the surface, you are going to be providing clues that will help your listeners.

Clues

Put a fairly steady stream of clues on the air all the time this promotion is going. Start out with generalized ones and work toward specific ones. Here are just a few examples (you will have to provide dozens more):

1. WZZZ went on the air at 10 A.M., May 21, 1948.

2. During its first three and one-half years of operation, WZZZ was on the air from 7 A.M. to 8 P.M. daily.

3. Be sure to take into account the loss and gain that results from daylight saving time each year.

4. Transmitter failure put WZZZ off the air for a total of 6 hours and 18 minutes during the first half of 1950.

5. Starting at 7 A.M. on June 8, 1955, WZZZ extended its broadcasting to a 24-hour-a-day operation.

If you decide to link this promotion with one or more of your sponsors, it would be a good idea to have clues posted in the stores of these sponsors, too. This will help build traffic for them.

In addition to the type of clues indicated above, you can also include more generalized clues of this nature: "WZZZ has been on the air for more than five thousand hours" . . . "WZZZ has been on the air for more than fifteen thousand hours" . . . "WZZZ has been on the air for more than twenty-two thousand hours" . . . gradually building up to the vicinity of the actual figure.

The Prize

The range of possibility here is virtually unlimited. Here are just some of the things you might consider:

1. Any quantity or type of merchandise from sponsors.

2. A clock radio, plus a clock for every room in the house.

3. A very sizable money prize that diminishes from $10 to $100 each day you fail to get a winner. (While we're on the subject, whenever you use a prize like this, give some thought to running it this way: Get a carnival wheel with numbers from 1 to 100 on it. Refer to this as your "Money Wheel." Spin it at a specified time each day. The number on which the pointer comes to rest indicates the amount by which the prize diminishes.)

4. Offer a travel prize that starts out by offering the winner a trip to any point 12,500 miles away—that's halfway around the world. Then, each day that you fail to get a winner, the distance is reduced by a set number of miles or by the number of miles indicated by a spin of your wheel. Naturally, there is a lower limit below which the prize cannot go, say 300 or 500 miles. If you do not use this prize in connection with the contest we are discussing here, keep it in mind. It is a good one. It gives you the chance to talk up the various places a person might go if he wins the prize that particular day.

Outside Stunts

Because of the nature of this promotion, you can let your imagination roam, developing ways to call additional attention to your contest and your station.

Someplace in your town there is undoubtedly a clock standing on the street, probably in front of one of the jewelry stores. Your DJs can "lease" this from the owner and make a great ceremony out of winding, oiling, cleaning, scrubbing, adjusting, and so on. In addition, you can easily develop a pitch to advertising agencies using printed pieces keyed to the idea "Any time is good time when you're sold on WZZZ." These are but a few of the possibilities.

Time Contest—On-Air Copy

Echo Chamber: TELL US THE TIME . . .

Anncr: . . . THAT WZZZ HAS SPENT BRINGING THE TOPS IN ENTERTAINMENT AND INFORMATION TO THE CITIZENS OF CENTERVILLE SINCE WZZZ WENT ON THE AIR.

Echo Chamber: TELL US THE HOURS . . .

Anncr: . . . OF LISTENING PLEASURE OVER THE YEARS THAT WZZZ HAS PROVIDED FOR THOSE WHO DIAL THE MIGHTY 460

Echo Chamber: TELL US THE MINUTES . . .

Anncr: . . . THOUSANDS UPON THOUSANDS OF THEM SPENT SERVING YOU, THE LOYAL WZZZ LISTENERS.

Echo Chamber: TELL US THE TIME . . .

Anncr: . . . IN THE WZZZ TIME CONTEST. STAY TUNED TO FOUR-–SIX–OH FOR MORE DETAILS AND IMPORTANT CLUES.

* * * *

Sound: Clock ticking loudly to establish, then alarm rings, then out for:

Anncr: IT'S THE WZZZ TIME CONTEST (ticking resumes under). WZZZ IS ASKING YOU TO ESTIMATE THE TOTAL NUMBER OF GOOD-LISTENING HOURS AND MINUTES THAT WZZZ HAS BEEN ON THE AIR AS OF THE DAY YOU SEND IN YOUR ESTIMATE. (Alarm rings) IMPORTANT CLUES . . . (ticking under) BROADCAST THROUGHOUT

THE DAY TO HELP YOU FIGURE THE TOTAL TIME WZZZ HAS
BEEN ON THE AIR. (Alarm) WONDERFUL PRIZES (ticking resumes,
<u>describe prize</u>) FOR THE NEAREST ESTIMATE TO THE NUMBER OF
HOURS AND MINUTES WZZZ HAS BEEN ON THE AIR SINCE 7
A.M., MAY 1, 1937. (Alarm) IT'S THE WZZZ TIME CONTEST.

2.19   PIE IN THE SKY

Here's a simple outside stunt that will pique the curiosity of your listeners and
draw a large response—especially if your station is located on or near a busy
thoroughfare.

How It Works

The station obtains a sturdy balloon of moderate size, such as a weather balloon, which can often be purchased as military surplus. Some promotion ven-
dors also sell advertising balloons. The station call letters and frequency are
painted prominently on the balloon; it is filled with helium, and flies above the
studios, anchored securely at a fixed height.

Check with the local authorities or the FAA to see how high the balloon
may be so that you do not create an illegal flying hazard. Suspended in a small
package below the balloon is a "mystery object," which must be identified.

The Contest

You may have the listeners participate in several ways. If you wish, simply have
them write in their ideas as to the identity of the mystery object hanging in the
basket below the balloon. Your DJs read the entries as they come in until they
come to a right one. Or, have listeners send in postcards with just their names
and phone numbers. Every hour the DJ places a phone call to one of the
entrants. We have found the latter method to be the most effective. With both
methods you may choose to give a daily clue to the identity of the object, recap-
ping the clues every so often.

The Prize

The prize may be just about anything you choose, but it should be fairly valuable since you are only giving one prize. The idea is that the mystery object
represents "Pie In the Sky" for whoever the lucky person is who identifies it.
If you select something of value as the mystery object, it can be the prize.

A Word of Warning

Your balloon will attract attention. It may, however, attract attention of the wrong kind. Be sure to have the anchor rope fastened where it can be reached only by station personnel. It might prove somewhat embarrassing should the whole contest disappear overnight.

Pie In the Sky—On-Air Copy

THERE'S PIE IN THE SKY OVER WZZZ. IT'S PIE IN THE SKY FOR THE LUCKY LISTENER WHO GUESSES THE IDENTITY OF THE MYSTERY OBJECT SUSPENDED FROM THE BALLOON NOW FLYING OVER WZZZ. SEND IN YOUR ENTRY TODAY—THERE'S PIE IN THE SKY FOR THE RIGHT ANSWER—HERE'S A CLUE:_____.

* * * *

Echo Chamber: (Solemn) HIGH IN THE SKY OVER THE WZZZ STUDIOS, THERE'S PIE IN THE SKY FOR WZZZ RADIO LISTENERS.

Anncr: IT'S THE WZZZ GOOD-LISTENING BONUS BALLOON. GUESS THE IDENTITY OF THE MYSTERY OBJECT SUSPENDED BELOW THE WZZZ GOOD-LISTENING BONUS BALLOON! WIN A VALUABLE PRIZE! HERE'S A CLUE:_____.

* * * *

THINGS ARE LOOKING UP. IN CENTERVILLE EVERYTHING IS LOOKING UP AT THE WZZZ GOOD-LISTENING BONUS BALLOON FLYING OVER THE WZZZ STUDIOS. IT MEANS PIE IN THE SKY FOR SOME LUCKY LISTENER WHO CAN IDENTIFY THE MYSTERY OBJECT SUSPENDED BENEATH THE WZZZ GOOD-LISTENING BONUS BALLOON. SEND IN YOUR ENTRY TODAY—THINGS MAY BE LOOKING UP FOR YOU.

* * * *

DO YOU THINK YOU CAN GUESS THE IDENTITY OF THE MYSTERY OBJECT SUSPENDED BELOW THE WZZZ GOOD-LISTENING BONUS BALLOON? THE BALLOON IS UP OVER THE WZZZ STUDIOS AND IT MEANS PIE IN THE SKY FOR SOME LUCKY LISTENER. SEND IN A CARD WITH YOUR NAME AND PHONE NUMBER. EVERY HOUR WZZZ CALLS SOMEONE LOOKING FOR THE

RIGHT ANSWER. IF YOU ARE CALLED AND CAN IDENTIFY THE MYSTERY OBJECT, IT'S PIE IN THE SKY INDEED FOR YOU. CLUES ARE BROADCAST THROUGHOUT THE DAY. HERE'S ONE NOW: _____.

2.20   KEEP COOL CONTEST

In the hot summer months, WZZZ is the coolest sound around. It is a natural tie-in for the WZZZ Keep Cool Contest. This is not a major promotion, but it is one with which you can have a lot of fun—and attract a lot of attention, too.

How It Works

During one of those hot spells when the mercury in the thermometer is trying to break right out of the top of the tube, your afternoon DJ appeals to listeners for suggestions on how to keep cool. Like hiccup cures, everyone has a pet theory on how to beat the heat.

When the suggestions come in, the DJ selects the five that are the most interesting and tries them out, one a day, for a week. He should try them out between 4:30 and 5:00 P.M. when the homebound traffic is the heaviest. You will probably have to run a line outside of your studios so that the DJ can be seen.

The Result

You are sure to get a wide variety of suggestions. The poor guy may end up doing part of his show while sitting on a cake of ice. Or he may get lucky and work from a hammock while he is fanned by four lovely young ladies. Be sure to get pictures of all the methods he uses. The earlier you can stage this one the better, as far as subsequent publicity locally and nationally is concerned. If you wait until the end of August, you will be too late for any additional publicity.

Prizes

Tangible rewards are not at all necessary with this promotion. You will get plenty of cooling suggestions just by asking for them. If you do go to prizes, one may be given for the best overall suggestion submitted and used—or you can give a prize to each person whose suggestion is used each day. A good prize would be an electric fan, an air conditioner, or something similar in keeping with the promotion theme. Nothing major though.

Keep Cool Contest—On-Air Copy

HELP (<u>afternoon DJ</u>) BEAT THE HEAT. THE SHOW IS COOL BUT THE DJ ISN'T. (<u>Afternoon DJ</u>) IS ASKING FOR YOUR SUGGESTIONS ON KEEPING COOL. HE'LL TRY THEM OUT ON HIS SHOW—ONE A DAY FOR A WEEK—IN WZZZ'S KEEP COOL CONTEST. THE COOLEST SUGGESTION WINS A BREEZY AIR CONDITIONER, AND (<u>afternoon DJ</u>) GETS HELPED OUT OF A HOT SPOT.

* * * *

Music: "It's Too Darn Hot" or "We're Havin' a Heat Wave" up to establish then under for:

Anncr: THAT'S THE THEME SONG FOR (<u>afternoon DJ</u>) THESE SUMMER AFTERNOONS WITH THE MERCURY IN THE 90'S, BUT HE'S LOOKING FOR A WAY OUT WITH THE WZZZ KEEP COOL CONTEST. HE'S ASK-ING ALL OF YOU TO SEND HIM YOUR PET METHODS FOR KEEPING COOL. HE'LL TRY OUT THE BEST ONES ON HIS SHOW, ONE A DAY FOR A WEEK. THE ANSWER MAY HELP ALL OF US BEAT THE HEAT, AND THE BEST SUGGESTION WINS A BREEZY AIR CONDITIONER. ENTER THE WZZZ KEEP COOL CONTEST AND HELP (<u>afternoon DJ</u>) OUT OF THE HOT SPOT. HE'LL CHANGE HIS THEME SONG TO:

Music: Up with "Baby, It's Cold Outside" to establish and out . . .

DOLLAR SCHOLAR   2.21

The promotion under consideration here is a simple one to operate. Handled with zest and showmanship, it can give you a real lock on the school-age audi-ence in your market. You may wish to schedule this for both your early morn-ing and late afternoon shows, or simply confine it to the P.M. segment. However, do not overlook the possibility of running this promotion during the early morning hours as well. It can help your ratings a great deal during those hours when, if your ratings are up, there are a number of local accounts that you can corral.

How It Works

School kids in your area are invited to become WZZZ Dollar Scholars. To do so they simply send in a postcard with their name, address, grade in school, and name of their school. Be sure to specify that only postcards—not letters—will be eligible. These postcards will become the file you use in conducting the promotion.

Ask that the kids either print or type the information on the postcards. By doing so you will spare yourself some hectic deciphering problems. You send them in return a WZZZ Dollar Scholar card, which you have printed, with their individual number on it. The numbers are assigned on a consecutive basis as the requests are received. The same number should be put on the postcard you received. These postcards are then placed in a mixing bin you will use for the promotion.

Playing the Game

The disc jockey conducting the contest spins the mixing bin and then withdraws a card. He first announces that the winner for that hour will be from whatever school is named on the card. Fifteen or twenty minutes later, during which time he has plugged the name of the school several more times, he announces the card number and tells the audience that the card holder has two minutes in which to call the station and identify himself. Winners receive a prize of one dollar.

Be sure to announce the names of those who fail to call in when their number is announced. You can be sure that the friends of these people will tell them about it the next day at school. And you can be equally sure that such people will be ardent listeners thereafter.

Multiplying the Prize

As an additional gimmick, you might try this: After announcing the school, but before giving the card number, spin a carnival wheel to determine a specific grade in school. Then, if your winner is in that grade in school, he wins two or five dollars instead of just one dollar.

Honor Roll Students

You may wish to put additional emphasis on the "scholar" part of this promotion. If so, you can specify that honor roll students will automatically win double the regular prize, or that in addition to the regular prize such students will also win an album. Lists of honor roll students can be obtained easily from the various schools. Be sure at all times, though, that you are using a current honor roll list.

Duplicate Prize for School

Another addition that can be included in this promotion is for you to award a duplicate prize to the school your winner attends. This can be earmarked for a particular school fund, whether athletic, scholarship, or whatever. We suggest that it go to a scholarship fund.

As a matter of fact, get some extra mileage out of this promotion by letting the funds accumulate over the year and award it to the top graduating scholar in each school at the end of the school year. In this case, refer to it as "The WZZZ Scholarship Fund." By doing this you should gain the blessings—and the cooperation—of school officials.

Sign Up the Homeroom Class

Here is a way you can get the school kids actively working to sign up additional WZZZ Dollar Scholars for you, with the resulting additional listeners. Announce that when the entire homeroom class in any school has been enrolled as WZZZ Dollar Scholars, you will present each member of that class with a station T-shirt.

Sign Up the Whole Grade

Carrying the point above one step further, announce that student listeners should try to sign up every member of their grade in their school. When all the members of a particular grade have become WZZZ Dollar Scholars, a special drawing will be held to award two portable stereos (or more, or some other prize) to lucky individuals in that grade.

Sign Up the School

You can carry this idea one step further and announce that when everyone in a particular school is signed up as a WZZZ Dollar Scholar, the station will supply the DJ and records for a special dance for the school. This can be built up into a very big event. And once it starts snowballing you will have a hold over the school-age audience that will be very difficult for any other station to break.

Monthly Prize

Here is an additional twist to generate even more excitement about your promotion. Daily winners can become eligible for a monthly prize drawing. This prize should be something like a portable radio, a portable stereo system, a dozen CDs, or something else of this general nature. Logically, the prize should fall into the realm of music.

WZZZ School Reporters

If you are making a particular play for the teenage audience, you might include this. A WZZZ "Reporter" is named for each school. These reporters call in at a specified time and day each week and are interviewed by your afternoon DJ.

They can tell about events taking place at their schools, give information on the current musical likes and dislikes of fellow students, and so forth. Hold an occasional group meeting with the WZZZ Reporters at which your air personalities are present and soft drinks are served. This will tend to keep up their enthusiasm in the program.

2.22 PIN MONEY CONTEST

We have said frequently before that a contest does not have to offer a big prize in order to create excitement and audience. The Pin Money Contest is a case in point. This contest is designed primarily for the at-home audience and should most logically be scheduled during the late morning or the early afternoon show. A contest of this nature can be continued for a fairly extended period of time without wearing thin. Keep this in mind when you are making your plans.

How It Works

The idea behind this promotion is that everybody has the need for some pin money of their own—a little ready cash they can use to spend on themselves. The operation of the promotion is very simple. Get a large map of your city and have it mounted on a backing of some kind.

As the contest is run, your disc jockey blindfolds himself and sticks a pin into the map. He then announces the name of the street he has hit with the pin. The first person living on that street to call in wins the prize. If you want to add a little suspense to the promotion, have your DJ first announce the section of the city in which the pin has been stuck, play a couple of records, and then announce the actual street name.

The Prize

The value of the prize should be kept small. The prize could be the awarding of $7—a dollar a day for a week. Or the prize can be an amount that matches your frequency to give you the opportunity for additional mentions of your spot on the dial. It would be a good idea to have your DJ inform winners that they will be expected to use the money to buy something for themselves, since this is the idea of the contest.

A Prize Variation

If you want to enlarge the scope of the promotion, you might try this: Have a basic prize as suggested above. After your winner has been determined, the DJ asks for her street address. If, by chance, she lives in the exact block in which the pin has stuck, her prize is multiplied. You can offer 5 to 10 times the normal prize to such a winner.

Another Variation

Another way to broaden the base of operation for this promotion is this: Request that listeners send in postcards with their names and addresses *and* a pin. These are placed in a container and one postcard is picked at random each day at the start of the contest. The person whose postcard is picked receives a matching prize, or some other prize. Then, her pin is used to stick in the map to determine the street location of your regular winner.

Store Tie-In

If you want to make a commercial tie-in with this promotion, it can be done very easily. The basic contest does not change. You just announce that the first person from the street selected who gets to the sponsor's store with proper identification will be your winner. In this case, the prize should have the same value, but it should be in the form of credit on merchandise at the store. If you conduct this in connection with a major department store or any other large store having a number of different entrances, be sure to specify the location in the store where potential winners must report in order to qualify for the prize.

ELECTION CONTEST

2.23

This promotion will have everyone singing your praises for good work done in the public interest. It also provides an easy way to promote the extensive election coverage that station WZZZ will be doing.

How It Works

This one is really very simple. The winner of the contest is the person who comes closest to guessing what the total popular vote will be in the election. The twist is that each entry blank is a pledge to vote and to qualify for the prizes the winners must have cast their ballots in the election. This can be verified from the election rolls kept at each precinct. Do not feel that you have to wait for a national election to run this promotion. Actually, the smaller elections are the ones that need this sort of "get out and vote" campaign.

Where to Get Contest Entries

Contest entry blanks are picked up and put in ballot boxes at one of your sponsors' business locations. You may wish to conduct this promotion in cooperation with one of your gasoline accounts, or perhaps with a supermarket chain. Or it may be feasible to have all of your local sponsors participate.

Merchandising Your Election Promotion

Encourage the various business outlets that will serve as a source of contest entry blanks to offer additional prizes. Then, if a person has picked up his entry blank from, say, the ABC Supermarket and he turns out to be a winner, he also receives the additional prize offered by the supermarket. This creates traffic for your sponsors and allows them to take the greatest advantage of the promotion.

Publicizing Your Promotion

In your on-the-air publicity, emphasize that each contest entry is also a pledge to vote. Be sure that your promo spots all contain strong plugs for the election return coverage you will be carrying.

For the Younger Set

Open your contest to those under 18 years by allowing them to win if someone from their family has cast a ballot in the election.

2.24 KIDS' CAR CONTEST

With the beginning of fall comes a feverish round of high school rallies and parades as the high school football season gets under way. Here's a contest that takes WZZZ right to the heart of these intense activities on the part of the teenagers, in a manner they can hardly resist.

The WZZZ Rally Car

From one of your city's used car dealers, WZZZ obtains a sharp-looking and mechanically sound second-hand car. It can be an older model, but it should be fairly "snazzy" looking, and unless your climate is severe, a convertible will have the most appeal for this promotion. The car is then painted all over with the WZZZ call letters over the regular paint—in all angles and different sizes, just as many as you can possibly get on the car. You then make arrangements to have the car participate in all of the local high school pep rallies, parades, and at the games. A good way to arrange this is to provide it for the use of the high school cheerleaders.

How It Works

By now you've guessed the plot. The youngster with the most accurate estimate of the number of times the WZZZ call letters appear on the car is awarded the car. The appeal of an automobile—almost *any* automobile—to teenagers is immense. They simply have to estimate the number of "WZZZ's" on the car, mail their estimate to the station, and hope to win. The attention the WZZZ Rally Car receives will be well worth the money it costs you (if you can't trade it), and it should not cost you much to begin with. Remember, it should be an older car, but one that is nice looking and in good mechanical shape.

Note of Caution

To win the car, many youngsters will be willing to go to almost any length. For this reason you should take careful precautions to ensure that the car is never left someplace where anyone can spend time actually counting all the call letters. Actually, you will be painting such a quantity of call letters in such mixed up patterns that counting them would be a half-day project, so there is not too much danger, although a quick-thinking photographer might take pictures and try counting that way.

HIGH SCHOOL DRIVING CONTEST 2.25

The natural and spirited competition that exists between different high school student bodies can be capitalized on in an effective safe driving promotion aimed at these older students who comprise a large portion of the listening audience of many stations. Again, this promotion may be jointly sponsored by WZZZ and any one of the many service organizations in your area, or even a commercial organization such as the Automobile Dealers Association.

How It Works

Each high school in your area is assigned a total of 10,000 "good driving points" each month. When a student is arrested for a traffic violation or is involved in a traffic accident, points are deducted from this total. The school with the most points at the end of the month is the winner of the WZZZ Safe Driver Plaque for that particular month.

Your local safety council or members of the traffic division of your police department or both will be happy to help you work out a system of points to be deducted for various violations. The number of licensed drivers in each school will also be a factor in determining your winner and points will have to be pro-rated with this factor in mind. Naturally, the cooperation of school officials and the police department is necessary for this promotion. But these groups are vitally concerned with teenage traffic problems and will cooperate with you whenever possible.

Do Not Be Negative

You must continually emphasize the positive factors in a promotion such as this. Your object is not to malign the bad drivers, but to honor the good drivers.

WZZZ's Role

The station doing the promotion airs a running tabulation of the violations and traffic mishaps marked up by each of the participating schools. This publicizing of the competition will intensify the students' desire to contribute to their school's good record. If teenage drivers are a problem in your city, the figures you announce will increase public awareness of this fact and often result in more parental discipline of young drivers. If the teenage drivers of your city have consistently fine driving records, you will be doing them a genuine service by publicizing this fact.

Safe Driving Trophy

A traveling plaque can be awarded each month to the school with the best record for the preceding month. WZZZ should make arrangements for the plaque to be awarded to the student body by one of your on-the-air personalities at one of the all-school assemblies. At the end of the school year a permanent trophy may be the award given to the school with the best overall record. You may wish to go further than just awarding a trophy by setting up a prize of some substance that is awarded to the winning school at the end of the year. An excellent suggestion is to try and get a major automobile dealer or group of dealers to award the winning school a car for use in the institution's driver instruction classes.

2.26 WIN YOUR OWN HOLIDAY

Here's a promotion with a prize the winner could never buy for himself—one that's been reserved for the truly great people of history, now offered to one of your listeners. Just as Columbus, Washington, and Lincoln have their own "days"—the winner of your contest, let's call him Joe Glutz, gets a wonderful "Joe Glutz Day," celebrated by the entire community in his honor. What's more, the contest itself is simple and does not attempt to judge greatness, so any entrant may end up with a special day in his honor.

How It Works

From among all the entries you are going to select five *at random* as finalists for the prize. Therefore, all you need for an entry is a name, address, and phone number submitted on a regular post card.

The Selection

As we said, the five finalists are selected purely at random. Rather than merely drawing five cards from the stack of entries, however, the selection of these five finalists should be done with as much pomp and ceremony as possible. Here, for example, is one way you might do it: Have entries include also their birthdate in addition to name, address, and phone number. As the entries come in, segregate them into 366 piles (accounting for February 29 birthdays).

Make the drawing in this manner: In one hat or bin place the numbers 1 through 31, in another bin place the names of the twelve months of the year on separate slips. Each finalist is selected by:

1. Drawing a number to determine what day of the month.
2. Drawing the name of a month to pin down a specific birthday.
3. Drawing a name from the stack of entries having a birthday on the selected day of the selected month. This is repeated until you have five finalists.

A Production

Make as much of a production out of the drawing for the five finalists as possible. After all, one of the five will have a special holiday named for him. Have a civic official or a local celebrity conduct the drawing. Hold it in a public place or on the premises of a sponsor with as much ballyhoo as possible.

The Next Step

Then determine your final prize winner from among the five finalists. The essence of this contest is the novelty and desirability of the prize. The selection of the winner, since it is random, can be accomplished very simply, with just a drawing for example. But every good or goofy idea or gimmick that you incorporate into the selection of your holiday winner will increase the overall effectiveness of the entire promotion. Here, for example, is one method you might choose to select your grand prize winner.

Posterity Poker

Emphasizing that you are giving a common person a chance for his own holiday through an entirely "at random" selection, announce that your five finalists will play "Posterity Poker"—a hand of "showdown" poker played over a period of five weekdays, with the winner being named grand prize winner "for posterity." At five given times each weekday for a week, one card is "dealt" for each of your five finalists. The one having the best poker hand at the end of the week is declared your grand prize winner.

No attempt is made to rank the remaining four finalists, and they all receive similar prizes for being finalists. Again, it is a good idea to add some ceremony to the bit by having the cards "dealt" by a civic personality—perhaps in the window of a sponsor's store—with the hands on display there throughout the week the hand is played.

"Joe Glutz Day"

Well, now good old Joe Glutz is winner of his own special day entirely in his honor. Time is the only limit to the number of stunts and gimmicks you can bring into the picture to make the day truly memorable for good old Joe, and for all of your listeners who follow him in his glory. There are but a few "musts" for the day, and from there on your imagination provides the rest. Be sure that you have either the mayor, or better yet, the governor, proclaim an official "Joe Glutz Day." Try to get the local newspaper in on the deal at this stage for pictorial coverage and publicity as the "common man" celebrates a holiday in his honor.

Celebration Suggestions

- Hold a civic breakfast or luncheon in Joe's honor, with city officials praising Glutz to the skies for his real or imagined attributes.
- Stage a full parade with "the works" in the way of bands, convertibles, and so forth—and lots of ticker tape and confetti.
- Don't forget the commercial angles, with your sponsors and all stores holding special "Joe Glutz Day" sales and bargain offers.
- If the theater is included in your entertainment of your prizewinner, make sure that he's in the box seats, and that his attendance is acknowledged, perhaps announced from the stage and spotlighted in the manner of visiting royalty.
- Bury a time capsule with a special message to the future from Joe Glutz, perhaps in combination with any cornerstone laying or ground-breaking ceremonies being held that day.
- If you use this promotion at a time when the horse-racing tracks are open, arrange a "Joe Glutz Handicap" as the feature race of your holiday.
- Wherever your "dignitary for a day" travels, try to arrange a police-siren escort for his limousine—and a portable red carpet should accompany him.

2.27 CALL LETTER SLOGAN CONTEST

The best thing—and the most unique thing—about this promotion is the prize. The prize, at least for publicity purposes, can be considered a promotion by itself. The contest asks for a little ingenuity of the part of your listeners. Yet it is so simple that anyone can enter. It hinges on those so-very-important letters, *your* call letters, which you are constantly striving to keep in the ears and eyes of the public.

How It Works

Ask your listeners to send in a four- (or three-) word slogan for your station, each word starting with a letter from your call letters in proper sequence. (If you make a point of mentioning that all entries become the property of the station, you will have a great backlog of slogans for future use.)

A Variation

While you will probably want the slogan to refer to the station, you vary the bit by having the slogans relate to any campaign you may be pushing, such as the March of Dimes or a similar civic activity. This provides you with an excellent opportunity to emphasize your station's public service programming.

Doubling the Effectiveness

You can multiply the effectiveness of this promotion by including a relatively simple twist. Tell listeners that, in addition to sending their slogan to the station, they should also send it through the mails to a friend. The friend's name, as well as the sender's, should be listed on the entry. The station then places a series of calls each day to the friends so listed. If a friend can give the slogan, both parties win a special bonus prize.

The Prize

The prize for this promotion is "the prize that can't be bought." The winner will receive a set number of spot announcements on your station devoted to promoting himself. Your writers prepare the spots glorifying John Doe or Jane Doe as a citizen, businessperson, good samaritan, or whatever. Here you have definitely offered as a prize something that the winner could never have purchased for himself. The winner's "campaign" should run for two or three days on the air, with several spots each day. The nature of the prize will bring you more entries (and entries from outside the usual range of contest participants).

Promoting the Call Letter Slogan Contest

It would be a good idea to run teaser promos on the contest that place primary emphasis on the prize. Such as: "Stay tuned to find out how you can enter the WZZZ Call Letter Slogan Contest and have a chance to win the prize that can't be bought."

2.28 SNOW SEARCH

If your station has a parking lot and is located in a central area, Snow Search is a fun promotion you can try some snowy winter day. Or you may choose to stage it in an advertiser's lot. In either case, be careful it doesn't develop into a riot or the area's most memorable snowball fight.

How It Works

Spring this on a morning following a night of steady or heavy snowfall. Your morning disc jockey announces that the station manager has told him that he lost a $100 bill in a waterproof envelope in the WZZZ parking lot the night before. Rather than shovel up all the snow looking for it, the manager has agreed that whoever finds the envelope in the snow gets to keep it. The station has roped off the parking lot, and will serve coffee and doughnuts to whoever cares to join the search. Then put on your mittens and stand clear.

C-Note in the Snow

Of course, the bill has been planted in a plastic envelope the night before, and the parking lot blocked off so that the overnight snowfall completely obliterates any clues to the whereabouts of the bill. Your DJ on shift during the search should be in a position to call a "play-by-play" on the hunt, but not be vulnerable to a flung snowball. Participants should be advised that they will not be allowed to use shovels. This will increase the hilarity and duration of the stunt.

A Note of Caution

Make sure that a member of the station staff knows where the bill is in the snow and keeps a sharp eye open for the finder. If someone were to discover the bill and sneak off without mentioning it to anybody, you would have a pretty nasty-tempered crowd on your hands when no bill was found.

Sell It

This stunt has an excellent sales potential for any retail client with a good-sized parking lot. Let the store management take over the job of serving coffee and doughnuts inside the store to build traffic. In this case, it might be that a number of gift certificates were also "lost" in the snow and will go to whoever is lucky enough to discover them. It's a wild way to get a parking lot cleared of snow!

Variations

If yours is a relatively snow-free locale, this promotion as outlined here is obviously of no use. But don't just cast the idea aside. Put it in your file and save it for use as a summer promotion at a beach site. In this case, the money will be "lost" in the sand. It will work just as well.

A similar approach can also be used to build a crowd for a realtor who is selling lots in a new development. Again, the basic handling of the promotion will be the same.

With all quickie, one-shot promotions of this type, you must be particularly careful to have everything clearly arranged in advance; otherwise, there is a good chance that the promotion will go amiss and you will not have time to rectify matters before everything is lost.

THE NAME'S THE GAME—I   2.29

This is another of those adaptable promotions that we are so fond of throwing your way. Adaptable because you can make them as big or as small as you wish, because you can run them as station promotions and include them in every show or limit them to a single personality and a single show, and because of the widespread possibilities for variations that are available to you. We feel sure that such an approach is very sound.

Your overall approach to promotion should be built around a single item. This gives your listening audience the opportunity to become familiar with a fairly detailed promotion. It also gives you a running item for a reasonably long period of time that lends continuity to what you are doing. Although such promotions will appear quite simple on the surface, they are actually quite complex; just making it *seem* simple makes it complex.

How It Works

Listeners are invited to send in their names on postcards to participate in your new continuing promotion. These names are then put on tape. When "The Name's the Game" is played, the tape is run at fast forward on your tape machine. Then, the tape is punched up to regular speed and the first complete identifiable name is the winner. That person has two or three minutes to call the station and correctly identify himself in order to win the prize.

That's about as simple as a promotion can be, isn't it? Well, for the listening participants anyway. You should *strive* for apparent simplicity. While the handling of it from your end is not quite so simple, it is well worth the trouble.

Taping the Names

To begin with, ask all of your listeners to send in postcards with their names, addresses, and telephone numbers. This is the only entry they need make for your new game. You will simplify your whole operation if you specify that only postcard entries will be accepted.

In all contest-type promotions there are always a few who will try to take advantage of you—a few who will send in multiple entries. In this case, the simple method of preventing this is to take all postcard entries as they come in and file them alphabetically or enter them in a computer database. Before making up your list of names to be taped, the cards should first be checked against this file and any duplicate names eliminated. If you overlook this, you are going to have headaches later.

You should schedule the recording of names on a daily basis. When doing this, allow about a two or three second pause between each name. This will ensure that no listeners will hear their names as the tape slows down and get the feeling they should have been eligible for the prize. Remember, the tape should be run at fast forward, then punched into regular speed, with the first complete name thereafter being the winner for that time.

Frequency

Frequency, of course, is entirely up to you, after you have considered how you wish to conduct the promotion. "The Name's the Game" will work best if you conduct it throughout your daytime shows, say, from 6:30 A.M. until 10:00 or 11:00 P.M. While promotions such as this are normally run once an hour, we suggest that you give serious thought to using a much greater frequency: once every 30 minutes, or even once every 15 minutes.

We are well aware of the programming difficulties involved. However, it is perfectly possible to conduct this promotion and never take more than 30 seconds of airtime to do so. And this means that getting it on the air every 15 minutes is perfectly feasible. The advantage in this approach should be obvious: Your audience is never more than a few minutes away from another chance to win and, therefore, the tendency to turn the radio off or to switch the dial is cut down considerably.

Checking Winners

On any promotion of this type, there is always the possibility of someone trying to foul you up. A name is announced on the air for a prize, and you are going to have to have certain safeguards against a person calling in and falsely trying to identify himself as the winner. Therefore, you will do well to have a set formula for handling calls. The person taking the calls should first ask the person to identify himself by name. The next questions should be: What is your address and telephone number, so that we may call you back and verify you as a winner?

When dummy calls are received, the person will almost invariably say, "I'm not at home now. I'm calling from a different phone." In this case, you should immediately ask, "When was your entry mailed?" If you still have some doubt whether this is the correct winner, inform the person that you will call them at a specified time at the telephone number you have listed.

Prizes

Prizes, of course, depend entirely upon how large or small you care to make this promotion. Here are some possibilities, scaled into three different categories:

Small Prizes: There are many possibilities in this area. You can offer merchandise certificates tied in with a commercial sponsor. The value of these will depend on the size of your market and the size of the schedule purchased by the sponsor.

Since the title of this promotion is "The Name's the Game," a prize might be the services of a secretary for 3, 6, or 12 months. You should be able to arrange this through a secretarial school. The winner would have all of his or her personal correspondence handled for the specified period of time.

Your winner could select 10, 20, or 50 songs that he particularly likes. These would be played on the air, with special dedications made. Then, the winner would receive copies of the records.

Medium Prizes: Larger merchandise prizes arranged through commercial sponsors are a possibility here. A family weekend at a nearby resort would also make a nice prize. Do not overlook this as a means of lining up summertime resort business. Or, you can give your winners a small merchandise prize and enter their names in the final big prize drawing that comes at the end of your promotion.

Large Prizes: Most of the major record companies offer album or CD services. A subscription to one of these would be a very impressive prize. You could scale it to a 3-, a 6-, or a 12-month subscription.

The winner might receive a complete new wardrobe. In this case, you'll want to have the clothes monogrammed to tie the prize in with the name of the promotion. If you are tying in with a department store or a supermarket, you could give your winner three minutes in the store to pick out any merchandise he or she touches. Naturally, the prize winner should be blindfolded.

Cash Prizes: Of course, you can always offer a cash prize on a promotion such a this, if your budget will allow for it.

Bonus Prizes

To put a real hook into your listening audience, you may wish to consider offering bonus prizes along with the regular prizes. Within the promotion announcements, you make it known that major prizes will be offered. However, there is no telling when one of these will come up. The bonus prizes should be such things as a trip to Europe, a car, or jewelry. To handle this, 30 to 60 seconds after a name is announced on the air a special gong or other sound signal is heard. This signifies that a bonus prize is to be given away. Your DJ should break into whatever else is going on at that time to announce the bonus prize. The addition of this gimmick will give you a real continuing listener hook and will add a great deal of suspense to your promotion.

Sponsor Tie-In

A promotion such as this has very obvious commercial possibilities. Because of the frequency, you should have no difficulty at all in arranging for prizes in return for plugs. Most logically, it should be sold to a sponsor, or a group of sponsors, on a participating basis. A promotion that has such a powerful built-in listener hook will lose none of its effectiveness through a commercial tie-in.

2.30 THE NAME'S THE GAME—II

This is a giveaway promotion with a very strong commercial tie-in. It is very simple to explain and conduct, and it has a positive listener hook.

How It Works

Listeners are asked to send in postcards with their names and addresses to be eligible to enter your "The Name's the Game" contest. Large batches of these are then distributed to a group of cooperating merchants. The cards are placed in the show windows of the stores.

Potential winners' names are placed in a special frame in the windows of the participating stores. Periodically, one of these names is read over the air. A person then has 30 minutes to find the store with his name in the window in order to collect the prize being offered. That's all there is to it. See how simple it is?

What Stores to Use

This can be particularly effective during the February and March period when stores are looking for a good reason for a special sale. The sponsoring stores can include: 1. all the stores in the downtown area; 2. a selected group of downtown stores; or 3. all of the stores within a major shopping center or mall. Any of these will work. However, it is necessary to have a sizable group of stores that are within close proximity to one another. It just will not work as well if you have only two or three stores lined up.

Naturally, participation in the promotion is predicated on the purchase of a spot schedule on your station. But then the stores will be running a major sale in conjunction with this, so they will want to advertise anyway.

Handling Entries

There are two ways to handle entries in this contest: Listeners can send in postcards to the station, or you can arrange it so that they have to go into the participating stores to enter. Combining these two approaches, you might accept both postcard entries sent to the station as well as entry blanks at the stores who then pass the entries along to the station. No purchase should be necessary in order to enter.

After the entries have been received, you should divide them into equal batches and distribute them to the participating stores. Each store should then take its batch and pile it in a prominent display window. This window should contain signs explaining the whole promotion so that the public knows what is going on and can get in on the fun. There should also be a special frame on the window or right next to it. The cards of potential winners are placed in this frame. If the windows are used, you will want to have loudspeakers outside of each to let the public know the name of each possible winner as it is selected.

An Alternative

The stores may want the entries placed inside with the thought in mind of building store traffic. There are no special problems in this and the promotion will work just as well. In this case the names of winners should be announced over the stores' public address systems. Keep in mind, however, that the stores should get as much traffic with the event staged in the display windows; after checking the store windows to see if their name appears, all of these people are going to have to be doing something until the next winner is announced and that something undoubtedly will be shopping.

Timing

This promotion can be used in connection with a one-day sale, a two-day sale, or a three-day sale. Three days is probably the limit.

During the actual promotion you will want to announce a new winner every 30 minutes. A good deal of the success of the promotion depends on this frequency of winners to maintain maximum interest and response.

Pulling Winners

All of the participating stores will have a special location where the names of winners will be put on display, be it in a window or inside the store. Every 30 minutes each store should pull a new entry card and mount it on the special board. However, you will announce only the name from one store during any 30-minute period. From there it is up to your listener-winner to tour all of the stores to find the particular store where his or her name is posted. They should be allowed the 30-minute interval between games to do this. If they don't find their names in 30 minutes, they don't win the prize.

Fanfare

Some excitement should be created in each store as the new entry cards are drawn and posted. A member of the public—preferably a child—can make the drawing from the big container that holds all of the entries at a particular store.

Rotation of Stores

If you have, for instance, 12 participating stores, then you should have a winner from any one store every six hours. You will want to rotate the location of the winners throughout all the stores on an equal basis so that they will all get an equal amount of traffic. However, if you run this promotion over several days, be sure that the stores are not rotated in a predictable manner or else someone will figure out the pattern and have an unfair advantage.

The stores should know in advance from a schedule you provide when the winners will be from their stores. Then, an executive from the store where the winner's name will appear should have the responsibility of calling the station immediately after the drawing so that the name can be put on the air.

Prizes

The prizes logically should be merchandise that the participating stores provide. They will be amply repaid for these prizes through the advance and running publicity on the items that you will carry on the air.

The prizes should be of some significant value. Naturally, the prize for each half-hour drawing should be from the store where the winner's name appears. All of the prizes should be publicized in your on-air promos as a group. However, within each half-hour drawing the nature of the prize should not be announced. You should reveal the prize only after you have a winner, or have failed to get a winner. The prizes each store is putting up should be placed in their display windows and prominently marked.

You are not going to have a winner each time you play the game, so the stores will not have to put up as much merchandise as it might initially seem. If the stores agree to put up a prize for every entry card posted, even though these names are not announced on the air, these prizes should probably be in the $5 to $10 range. The prizes for your regular half-hourly winners should be in the $25 to $50 range.

You will have a promotion that is many times as effective if you get each store to put up one major prize in the $500 to $1,000 range, in addition to smaller prizes. Remember, these are not necessarily going to be given away. But they do provide you with a great talking point. And the downtown streets and stores will be jammed with people if they think they have a chance to win any one of a dozen prizes that has a $500 to $1,000 value. You can easily see how this will be the clincher in making your promotion.

Special Sale

There are, obviously, a great many benefits that the participating stores get out of this kind of promotion. Initially, they get increased store traffic as people come in advance to register for the contest. Then, there will be thousands of people in their places of business while the contest is running.

With the right prize structure, no one will be able to afford to go home while the contest is on. And, of course, the stores individually or collectively will be running special sales concurrently with the promotion. Throughout the promotion the salespeople in the stores should wear badges that state: "My name is Sally. Play the Name Game." Using the Name Game slogan, the stores have an excellent opportunity to promote and sell their nationally advertised merchandise. There are innumerable other possibilities.

If handled properly, this promotion can be a real sales blockbuster, both for the stores involved and for the station. It will take time for you to organize and sell it. But it has all the elements of an outstanding giveaway.

THE CALL OF THE WILD   2.31

On numerous occasions, we have said that while radio is a "sound" medium, relatively little use is made of sound in radio today. Here we are suggesting a major promotion that makes some use of unusual sounds as a means of catching the ears of your listeners, in order to build and maintain an audience. In this case, we are dealing with the sounds of animals.

How It Works

Set up 10 animal sounds. (A little further on, you will find some suggested animals to use.) The sound of each animal is used for a full day. The animal sound is aired once an hour. Listeners are asked to identify the "Call of the Wild." The first person to send in a correct list of the animals wins the prize.

There is little chance that you will hit a winner during the first 10 days of the promotion. The sounds, by themselves, will be quite difficult to identify. The reason for this is that we are used to hearing these sounds in connection with a word description of the animal involved or with a picture of the animal. By themselves, the sounds can be confusing. And this is an advantage.

After the first run-through of the 10 sounds, start over again. This time use two sounds each day with a clue to go with each one. Again, the sounds and clues should be used once an hour; this time on a rotation basis. If you still do not have a winner after the first set of clues, continue to give additional clues. Try increasing the number of sounds and clues to three each day.

A Variation

Another way to conduct the promotion is this: Start out each day with the animal sound. Then, on the same day, add a clue an hour until you get a winner. After 10 days you will have 10 winners. You can award each a small prize, or you can have a runoff. The runoff can be conducted over a three-, four- or five-day period with additional sounds given over the air. Each winner is permitted to get assistance in identifying the sounds from his friends or from any other source. The winner of the runoff would be the previous winner with the greatest number of correct identifications of the new sounds. For the runoff, the animal sounds by themselves, without the aid of clues, should be used.

Use the Promotion All Week Long

We urge that you use this promotion seven days a week, instead of just five days. Anything you can do to bolster weekend listening will be to your advantage. This will also help to give continuity to your listenership, since the weekend is the time when dial-switching is most frequent.

The Sounds

The animal sounds we suggest are available in most standard sound-effects libraries. If necessary, you could go to the local zoo and record the actual animal sounds, but this will be less effective in the long run.

Sponsor Tie-In

The Call of the Wild lends itself readily to a tie-in with your sponsors. One way to do this is: Prepare a list of 50 different animals. The 10 you use on the air will be included in this list. Announce on the air that these lists are available at the outlets of whatever sponsor group you are working with.

You can use a single sponsor or all of your sponsors. You can use a chain of outlets, or you can associate the promotion with a product and have the lists available at all of the local outlets that carry the product.

Prizes

You have a wide range of possibilities when you go to select the prize to be used in connection with the Call of the Wild promotion. One logical possibility would be to award a fur coat to your winner. A really *big* prize that could be used here would be to award a trip to Africa for a safari. Other possibilities include: A week at a hunting or fishing lodge, a camping trailer, camping equipment, hunting equipment, and fishing equipment.

The Animals and the Clues

1. Elephant

Clue #1
My home is far across the sea,
But in the circus you've seen me.

Clue #2
In the land of Sanskrit I am known,
Yet I also have a wilder home.

Clue #3
Teak is a product that I know.
I've also fought a buffalo.

Clue #4
Play a piano and there I'll be;
Think of Sabu and you'll know me.

2. Lion

Clue #1
My home is far away from here,
But I've got relatives very near.

Clue #2
I'm not a hippie, but I've got a pad.
When Frank Buck saw me, he was glad.

Clue #3
The bounding mane will give a clue.
You'll find me south of Timbuktu.

Clue #4
I am the king of all that I see.
A hairy neck and a roar identify me.

3. Monkey

Clue #1
I'm one of nature's handy creatures.
You've seen me in Mr. Burrough's features.

Clue #2
I'm at home on Luzon and Borneo.
Up the Amazon I sometimes go.

Clue #3
Children like me—adults, too.
'Cause I'm the hit of every zoo.

Clue #4
I like peanuts. I swing in a tree.
If you're an organ grinder, you need me.

4. Mouse

Clue #1
I've got four feet beneath my body.
If you've got me, you may be shoddy.

Clue #2
Scamper, scamper, as fast as you can,
I'm never known as a ladies' man.

Clue #3
Out in the woods are hickory trees.
I like something that rhymes with "bees."

Clue #4
I'm not stirring when Santa's around.
If you know Walt, then me you've found.

5. Parrot

Clue #1
My eye is evil. My bite is severe.
My home is very far from here.

Clue #2
I'm not saying much. I'm not trying to please.
But I'm not a young man on a flying trapeze.

Clue #3
I'm just as pretty as I can be,
But that's not why people talk to me.

Clue #4
I like saltines. I fly through the air.
I'm not jolly, but you're almost there.

6. Pig

Clue #1
I am known both far and wide,
And what's important is not all inside.

Clue #2
I'm an important actor in life's play.
You can see me almost every day.

Clue #3
Kermit and Gonzo, they know me well.
My long, lush eyelashes should ring a bell.

Clue #4
If you eat like me, you're very uncouth.
To be in a sty should be your reproof.

7. Turkey

Clue #1
Here's help in the mystery to be unraveled:
I was an American first before I traveled.

Clue #2
Under the axe you may look,
And you'll find me in a McGuffey's primer book.

Clue #3
I've trotted through straw and hay,
And even drummers know my way.

Clue #4
Captain Miles Standish, John Alden, too,
Sometimes ate me, and that's a clue.

8. Alligator

Clue #1
All my friends say I'm a pleasant fellow,
But if you saw me you'd be apt to bellow.

Clue #2
I'm a throwback biologists say,
To things that were another day.

Clue #3
When I've got a toothache, you can be sure
No dentist will want to give me a cure.

Clue #4
I swim like a fish. Women wear me well.
I've got a long tail. That's all there's to tell.

9. Moose

Clue #1
If you look for me in highland reaches,
Don't bother with kilts; you can wear breaches.

Clue #2
Mine is a real wilderness call.
Only Paul Bunyan would think me small.

Clue #3
At an important club I'm always on hand,
And when I horn in, I'm not in the band.

Clue #4
I'm a bull of a fellow. In the north I abound,
As well as in trophy rooms where I am found.

10. Bear

Clue #1
To help you find me, I'll shed some light:
Take Horace's advice and then turn right.

Clue #2
I'm known as a fighter—a dancer, too.
I'm found in almost every zoo.

Clue #3
I'm black and brown and sometimes white,
And often found 'neath the northern light.

Clue #4
I'm known as a grouch; sleep the winter through.
Some of my friends have made a rug for you.

JUNIOR HIGH I.Q.   2.32

In all probability one or more of your disc jockeys is already featuring some kind of trivia quiz that has listeners phoning in the answer with a small daily prize going to the first correct caller. If you have such an on-the-air gimmick already under way, try this innovation for a few days.

How It Works

Many folks are quick to claim kids today are not getting a proper education in the public schools. So, you set out to find out how the adults stack up against the kids on the kids' own grounds. From a local 8th or 9th grade civics or history teacher, get a list of common questions asked on the exams the teacher gives to her classes. Use these for the daily questions. The only stipulation is that the winners must be adults.

Over a period of a week or two your DJ can have a lot of fun with this variation of the daily question and can often provoke some interesting comments and observations from listeners. This also gives you a chance to point out the real educational job being done by our schools today. Be sure to talk with your local school board and get their cooperation before you start.

Working through the Schools

You may be able to work out an arrangement with the schools so that the junior high school teachers know in advance what question you will be asking on a particular day. They can then make a point of including this in their class work on that day so that the young students can go home and ask a parent if he or she had been listening to WZZZ—and if either knows the answer to the question.

SPRING CLEANING   2.33

Whether it's the nesting instinct or the fair weather, the American family annually picks the springtime for an assault on the equilibrium of the household.

This has come to be known as spring cleaning time. Here's a novelty promotion that you can apply to one or all of your DJs to entertain the people at home during the day and gain some very favorable comments from your various sponsors.

How It Works

This contest can be handled as a promotion for a single DJ or can run throughout the day. Since it is oriented to the at-home person, however, if you select a single show on which to do the promotion, it should be that of the mid-morning DJ, since he has the greatest concentration of at-home people in his audience.

In the period of a week, or at the most, two weeks, when the contest is run, you ask listeners to send in a list of all of the advertisers on WZZZ whose product or service can figure in to the entrant's spring cleaning project. With each advertiser named they also include how that product or service would be used.

The emphasis is on imagination rather than actuality to include the maximum number of WZZZ advertisers on the list in some capacity—the one who can with some degree of logic or ingenuity produce the longest list of advertisers figuring into her spring cleaning plans is declared the winner.

For Example

How the various soaps, cleansers, and products of that nature can fit into the list is obvious. But to illustrate how an entry may work in other advertisers, here is an example of what a person might say:

I took a look at my CASIO watch and said it was time for a ten-minute break . . .

during which I enjoyed a cup of FOLGER'S COFFEE . . .

and a piece of WONDER BREAD . . .

spread with CRUNCHY PEANUT BUTTER.

Then, I put on my BURLINGTON COAT . . .

got into my FORD . . .

and drove down to the THRIFTWAY MARKET . . .

to get some LIPTON'S NOODLE SOUP for lunch.

On the way I stopped at a TEXACO gas station to fill the tank . . .

and looked at some FIRESTONE TIRES while I was there . . . etc.

In effect, what you are asking for is the entrant's story of her spring cleaning project using as many of the WZZZ sponsors as she finds possible.

Selecting a Winner

The judging should be done on the basis of number of sponsors' names worked into the story. As a tie-breaker, you will want to use the most interesting plot developed.

The idea is simple enough so that you will get some very entertaining and imaginative entries. These will make delightful reading for your disc jockeys.

The Prize

There are many prizes that you can arrange for this contest in keeping with the spring-cleaning-time theme. A supply of any cleaning product is an obvious suggestion. Unless you are trying to turn this into a truly major promotion with a large prize (and this is not advisable), then this is about the most effective prize: If you are running the promotion on just the mid-morning DJ's show, the prize is his or her services as a spring-cleaning servant for an entire day. If you are running the contest throughout the day with all of your DJs participating, then the grand prize consists of having the entire corps of disc jockeys invade the winner's household on a given day to do a bang-up (figuratively speaking) job of spring cleaning. The picture possibilities and additional mileage you can gain from such a prize make it a particularly good way to reward your winner. Of course, you can, if you wish, also award a number of runner-up prizes. These would most likely be cleaning products.

"WALKING WORKER" CONTEST   2.34

This is a highly effective promotion on a major scale in which you can adjust the length of time when you run it and adjust the size of the prizes you award. The "Walking Worker" contest is obviously patterned after the old "Walking Man" promotion. Handled correctly, you will have everyone in your listening area talking about the contest—and looking each day for WZZZ's "Walking Worker."

How It Works

Each day a mystery representative is selected from the ranks of one of the jobs that requires a fairly large amount of walking during the course of a day. Listeners are told the person's profession and are given clues as to his location. The first listener to identify the mystery representative by asking, "Are you the WZZZ Walking Worker?" wins the prize being offered. Basically, that is all there is to it. But there are many ramifications.

Advantages

There are many advantages to using this approach. To begin with, you make audience participation much easier than in the old "Walking Man" promotion because you have narrowed the possibilities down to a specific category. People in this category are readily recognizable. And on the day that you select a mail carrier, for instance, you get the big plus of all the word-of-mouth promotion that will go on among the mail carriers themselves.

Types of Walking Workers to Use

There are only two basic requirements for the Walking Workers you use: walking, or being on their feet, must be a basic part of their jobs, and they must be readily available to the public. A stockroom clerk in a local department store simply would not fill the bill because he cannot be seen and queried by your listeners. Here are some suggested types you can use:

Mail carriers	Waitresses
Newspaper deliverers	Clerks in supermarkets
Clerks in department stores	Police officers who walk a beat
Gas station attendants	Bank tellers (good only on
Hotel bellboys	days banks stay open late)
Waiters	

Use a Pedometer

Get a pedometer (an instrument that can be attached to the belt that tells how far a person has walked) for use with this promotion. Be sure to check it out thoroughly before you start to make certain it is working properly. They can be a little tricky. You can use the pedometer as the basis for determining your prize, as detailed later.

Different Category Each Day

Each day your mystery walker is selected from a different profession. The contest is run only during the normal business hours when that person is working at his or her job and, thus, available to the public. If he or she has not been discovered, the mystery walker's name and where he or she could have been found are announced on the air. Also, the total distance he or she has walked is given as a sort of "hats off" to people in that job category.

The Prize

If you are giving away a cash prize, the pedometer can be used to determine how much a person wins. The amount of the cash prize can be based directly on how far the mystery walker has gone when he or she is discovered, or you can start with a set cash prize that decreases as the day progresses—how much it decreases is determined by how far the mystery walker has gone. In the first case: the more steps the mystery walker has taken, the larger the prize. In the second case: the more steps, the smaller the prize. (Naturally, the pedometer should be worn out of sight.)

By using the pedometer to determine your prize, you can pretty much control the size of the prize to keep it within the limits of your budget. This is done simply by attaching a set value for each pace, foot, yard, or mile walked by your mystery walker. For example, suppose your mystery walker is a waitress and she is discovered when the pedometer reads 6,336 paces. Since her normal pace is 30 inches, this means she has gone 15,840 feet or 8,280 yards or 3 miles.

If You Are Awarding	The Prize Is
1 cent a pace	$ 63.36
1 cent a foot	$158.40
1 cent a yard	$ 82.80
$10 a mile	$ 30.00
10 cents a pace	$633.60
$100 a mile	$300.00

and so on.

Or, inversely, your set prize can decrease by these amounts. So, you see, you can adjust the prize to your taste before setting the promotion in motion. Remember, you will not have a winner each day. However, as the promotion catches on, winners will become more frequent.

Make a Few Trial Runs

We suggest you obtain a pedometer and make a few trial runs using people who might be expected to walk as much or more than anyone you select as a mystery walker in the contest. In this way you will learn the approximate maximum reading you can expect on the pedometer. This will give you a little clearer idea as to which way you want to go in scaling your prize structure.

Selecting Walking Workers

Naturally, you will have to select your mystery walkers with a great deal of care to ensure they are honest and reliable. You should have no trouble, however, finding people who will go along with the stunt and "play it straight." A simple rule you might include in the contest is that the winner cannot be a fellow employee of the mystery walker. You may even wish to stipulate that the winner cannot be a member of the same profession.

You will want to arrange to reward your mystery walker in some way. Perhaps you can line up a local shoe store to provide a pair of shoes in return for the plugs.

Clues

You will add to the excitement of the contest and involve a great many more people if you give clues throughout the day that will help people discover your mystery walker. At the beginning of the promotion each day you will announce the type work in which your mystery walker engages.

Later you can give some of his physical characteristics. Starting in a general way and gradually getting more specific, you can start narrowing down the area in which your mystery walker can be found. When you have a mystery walker who is moving around town, you can use such clues as: "Sometime between one and two o'clock this afternoon the WZZZ Mystery Walker will be on Main Street somewhere between the sixteen hundred and thirty-five hundred blocks."

Badges for Listeners

This is an excellent extra gimmick to include since it will help get a lot of additional publicity for your promotion. Arrange to have inexpensive badges made up for listeners to wear. The badges should be available not only at your station, but at as many other sponsor outlets as possible. When a listener wearing one of your badges discovers the mystery walker, the prize is automatically doubled, or there is a bonus prize.

If you are in a position to offer a really large prize in this contest, you may want to make it mandatory that the person who wins must be wearing a WZZZ badge.

Length of the Promotion

Any contest of this type and scope must be run for a long enough period of time to become popular and do you some real good. You should not consider this just a "quickie" promotion. The contest itself is durable enough to be run for as long a period as you choose.

"PICTURE PUZZLE" CONTEST

This powerful promotion will capture the imagination of your entire region with its simplicity and suspense. It has as many "extras" going for it as anything we have seen yet, including the effective summertime plus of an outdoor attention-getter to capitalize on the automobile traffic. In addition, if you follow our suggestion, you will have a very appealing giveaway prize to add tremendous incentive to the contest.

How It Works

You're all familiar with the childhood puzzle whereby you connect the numbered dots to form a picture. That is the basis of the WZZZ Picture Puzzle Contest; you prepare a picture on this principle utilizing a large quantity of the numbered dots. The picture may be of a person, place, object, or event, and it should be quite complex, but clearly identifiable when completed. For the contest you prepare a large number of entry forms covered with the arrangement of numbered dots.

Each day (or several times a day if you wish a contest of shorter duration) you announce a pair of numbers to be connected by a line. The winner is the earliest postmarked official entry form containing the picture correctly drawn and identified. There is no limit to entries just as long as they are on the correct entry blank.

The Picture Chart

As an additional attention-getter for your contest, you arrange a large billboard in a prominent spot with the same arrangement of numbered dots. Each time you announce a pair of numbers to connect, the line is drawn on the billboard, but a day later.

The billboard serves another important function: anyone can enter the contest even after it's well under way simply by going down and copying from the board onto their official entry. The one-day delay in posting the numbers on the billboard permits you to give a fair advantage to the faithful who follow the contest on your station, and this becomes important as the contest approaches the point where the next line can be the clue to the entire puzzle.

Readily Saleable

Because this contest requires listeners to pick up the puzzle on the official entry form, it makes an appealing promotion to pitch to an advertiser with a large number of outlets, such as a drugstore or gas station chain. The outdoor billboard also adds to this appeal, since it could be readily placed at the sponsor's site, drawing attention and traffic. Your sponsor should bear the cost, or at least split the cost, of having the entry blanks printed.

Some Ground Rules

Be sure you strongly emphasize to your listeners that the dots are not connected in numerical order. Also, be sure that your mystery picture cannot be readily identified by connecting just the outside perimeter of dots. Some listeners are sure to try this gambit. Make clear that the winning entry must have all the dots correctly connected, and the picture identified. There is no bar to trying to guess the rest of the picture after it is partially complete, however.

The Prize

Of course, any prize that is sufficient in value for the scope of this promotion may be used. It's possible that if you tie in with a particular sponsor or advertiser, they may provide the appropriate prize. In the same token, the prize that we suggest for this giveaway can be used for any strong promotion contest that you come up with. It is, however, best suited to the summer months.

Complete Camping Comfort Kit

The prize we suggest consists of camping equipment. There can be unlimited flexibility to the prize to suit your budget and requirements. For example, in its simple form you might offer a pair of sleeping bags, an air mattress, and a tent. From a base as simple as this, you can expand the prize to any degree, to ultimately include just about every piece of camping equipment on the market, up to and including one of the small camper/vans popular today. The selection of attractive items in this category for your prize is very extensive, and you stop adding when you have built a prize to suit your needs.

Puzzle Plus Prize

If you do elect to use the camping equipment as the prize for your Picture Puzzle contest, you can strengthen the tie between contest and prize by having your mystery picture with an outdoor theme, such as a "Smokey the Bear" poster warning against forest fires. This is not an essential tie-in, but another plus if you choose to adapt to it.

Setting Up the Picture Puzzle

Once you have decided what finished picture you are going to use, spend considerable time carefully planning the picture puzzle itself. The puzzle should include many more numbered dots than will actually be used in the finished

picture. If possible, set up the dots in a geometric design that gives the participants no clue whatever as to what the finished picture will be.

In announcing the numbers on the air, remember that it is not necessary to
give the numbers in a sequence that produces a continuous line. You can connect two dots on one side of the puzzle, then the following day connect two
more on the opposite side of the puzzle. The idea is to try to connect as many
dots as possible without giving the answer away.

Cumulative Prize

In your prize structure, you may wish to consider a cumulative group of prizes.
This way, you would include an additional prize each day until you get a winner. In connection with the winner, be sure to state that the earliest postmark on
a correct entry will determine who wins. Or, you can start with a really huge
prize and reduce it by an item each day.

Adding a Little Flair

As few people as possible should be aware of what the completed picture is.
Once you have worked it out, it would be a good idea to put an actual copy of
the completed picture in a sealed envelope and have it deposited in the vault of
one of the banks with which you do business. This will give you the opportunity for a little extra ballyhoo—and will protect you from anyone who might
claim that you changed the design part way through the promotion.

Summer-Long Series

Since this is a very powerful promotion, you may wish to extend it throughout
the summer. Consider the possibility of making this a summer-long series in
which you move on to a new puzzle as soon as you have a winner in the current
contest.

TWO CAN WIN   2.36

This is a very simple contest promotion. The size of the prize is completely
adjustable to the circumstances. And, by its nature, this is a promotion that has
a chain effect that should help you reach an ever wider audience.

One major advantage of a promotion such as this is that it achieves a goal
toward which you should be constantly working: it encourages listeners to tell
friends and neighbors about your station and encourages them to listen.

How It Works

This promotion should be limited to a single show. It will work best if you use it on your late morning show or your early afternoon show because its primary appeal will be to people at home.

Listeners are asked to send in postcards. On these cards they should list their own address, plus the names and addresses of three friends they have called and told to listen to your station. Begin promoting the contest about a week before the actual start date so you will have sufficient cards in to do a good job.

At some time during his show your disc jockey selects a card at random. (If you wish, the card can be drawn in advance so that your receptionist will have the information, too.) From the card, the DJ reads one of the names submitted. This should never be the name of the person sending in the card. If the person whose name is announced on the air calls the station within one minute, she wins whatever prize is being given away and the person who submitted her name receives a duplicate prize.

Frequency

This contest can be run just once a show, or it can be run as often as once an hour. The frequency is entirely up to you. However, it is obvious that by running it once an hour you will have a continuing hold over your audience.

Prizes

The daily prizes for this contest should be relatively small in size. And, for contests of this type, it is probably best if you arrange to either trade-out for the prizes, or, better yet, use it as a sales tool to clinch an account. The sponsor will be amply rewarded for his contributions of merchandise by the free plugs he will receive. Any household items will serve well for daily prizes, such as soap products, dishes, foodstuffs, or even services.

A Major Weekly Prize

You may wish to tie in a major weekly prize with this contest. There are two ways to do this: The daily winners you come up with can simply be finalists who have a chance for the big prize at the end of the week, or, in addition to the daily prizes they receive, your daily winners can become finalists. It can work well either way. However, in the second case you need to award only one major prize because in this case only the name of the person actually drawn is eligible to win.

The major prize should be awarded in the same manner as the daily prizes: A name is announced and the person has one minute in which to call the station and properly identify herself.

To keep a hold over your listeners it is important that, if your major prize drawing is to be on a Friday, the winners for that day are also in the running for the big prize. This means that you will run the regular drawings earlier in the show and hold the big drawing near the end of the show.

In the case of the daily prizes, if the person whose name is announced does not call in within the allotted time, no prize is awarded. However, in the case of the weekly prize, if you do not get a winner on the first name called, a second potential winner should be announced. This should continue until you get a winner.

Checking Winners

You want to check your winners closely when they call in. Because you are announcing a name on the air, it is always possible for a false person to call in and try to identify herself as the winner. One method of checking is to simply ask for the person's telephone number and tell her that you will call her right back. Then, check the number in the telephone book to make sure that it is the right person.

A much better way of checking is to use the reverse directory if there is one for your community. This is the directory that lists the people in your town by street address. The person receiving the call at your station simply opens the book to the address of the potential winner. Then, when the call is received, ask the person to give you the names of her neighbors on each side.

Getting Additional Entries

You are looking for the largest possible number of entries in this contest because each card you receive means that four separate people or families are involved. A listener should be told that, although her name has been submitted by someone else, she has the opportunity of sending in a card of her own with the names of three other people she has told to tune in. As we said earlier, the chain reaction achieved is one of the biggest advantages of this contest.

CASH CLUB 2.37

This is another long-range continuing promotion with a built-in listener hook that will keep everyone in your coverage area tuned to your frequency. The WZZZ Cash Club is inexpensive and effective in gaining listeners.

How It Works

Your listeners are invited to send in for their WZZZ Cash Club cards. Each card is numbered. As you mail them out, keep a master list of names against numbers. You can do this most easily by specifying only postcard entries and then simply numbering the cards. You may wish to run this once in each show, or you can limit to just one show.

Your DJ reads a number on the air. If the holder of that card calls the station within one minute (the time limit will depend on your situation) and identifies himself, he wins. Winners are simply checked by name against number on your master list for verification. Do not insist that winning calls come from the actual card holder.

Encourage members to tell friends and relatives what their numbers are so that if it is called they can still win. In this way your school-age members will be sure that their mothers know their numbers and listen to your station. When you do not get a winner, your DJ should announce the name of the person who failed to call. His friends will tell him about it and you can be sure he will be listening the next time.

The Prize

The prize can be a small cash award. This promotion can work effectively if you offer only one dollar to start and increase it one dollar each game until you have a winner. Or you can use merchandise prizes and convert this into an outstanding sales promotion.

Setting Up Your Master List

In the beginning your promotion will have a better sound on the air if you start your numbers at 500 and then use only every other number. Between 500 and 750, use even numbers; between 751 and 1,000 use odd numbers, and so forth. In this way you will get up into the big impressive numbers quickly. And you can always go back later and pick up the numbers you skipped.

Outside Events for Cash Club Members

You will add interest to your promotion and increase the desirability of becoming a WZZZ Cash Club Member if you schedule some outside events for Cash Club members only. This can be a special movie showing arranged through one of your local theater chains, or it can be a special discount on CDs, records, or tapes at one of your local outlets for WZZZ Cash Club members who show their membership cards when making a purchase. These Cash Club special events can also be used as merchandising gimmicks that can be offered to potential sponsors or ones you already have on the air.

Plan for a Long Run

This promotion will be most effective if you plan to continue it over a long period of time. The interest and excitement over the promotion will actually build the longer it continues.

Timing

To gain the largest possible audience for the Cash Club, it is fairly important that you include it as a feature in your 6:00 to 9:00 A.M. show. Otherwise, you virtually eliminate the workers and the students. We suggest that you consider running it once an hour. However, be sure that you vary the time within the hour so that you maintain your audience and eliminate the people who otherwise would simply tune in to catch the Cash Club announcements.

PRICE PARADE   2.38

If certain elements of this promotion bear a marked resemblance to features of a highly successful television program, it isn't a complete coincidence. But why argue with success? The "Price Parade" is a sure-fire traffic builder for a group of participating sponsors. And the prize is exciting and substantial.

How It Works

Each day a Price Parade "item of the day" is announced frequently throughout the day, together with the name of the store where it is featured. For example, on Monday the item of the day could be a General Electric toaster at Howard's Appliance Store. On each subsequent day of the week a new item is added from a different retail outlet. By Friday you have named five different products from five different stores.

Listeners are told with each announcement to visit the stores and find out the exact retail prices of the items as featured in the stores. They then send in on a postcard, postmarked not later than midnight Saturday, the total cost of the five items. On the following Wednesday a drawing is held from all of the entries, and the first card drawn that correctly lists the total cost of the five items is declared the winner. The prize is the five items.

It's Flexible

We have suggested here a format for a weekly contest. On this basis you can repeat the contest each week for as long as you wish. You can, however, conduct this as a major one-time promotion by simply continuing the contest for a longer period of time, building both the prize and the suspense until you end the entire contest with a single drawing for the whole booty—perhaps 15 prizes instead of five, if you choose to run the promotion for three weeks.

Another area of flexibility is the size and nature of the prizes. In a major one-time promotion you could arrange prizes up to cars, refrigerators, TV sets, and so on. On a continuing series of weekly contests your prizes can fall into much less costly categories and still be sufficient to sustain a high degree of interest in the contests.

Sponsor Cooperation

Each time you introduce a new "Price Parade" item of the day you also recap those mentioned previously during the week. The object is not to get people to visit the specific store on the specific day, but rather to be sure they visit it sometime before the end of the weekly contest.

To ensure maximum benefit from the traffic-building potential of this contest you must get certain agreements from the participating stores. One requirement is that they display the contest item openly with the price clearly marked. Another is that they keep the price constant throughout the week of the contest so that people visiting the store on different days will get the same information.

Yet a third requirement to observe is that the store not give out price information on the contest item on the telephone. The station backs up this latter rule by mentioning on the air that listeners must *visit* the stores to get the prices. Since all of these requirements are in the interest of the participating sponsors, you will have no difficulties getting them to cooperate. The stores should naturally do as many concurrent in-store displays and special feature sales as possible to capitalize on the traffic created by the contest.

Look This One Over Closely

We think this is potentially one of the most rewarding contest ideas that we have ever offered, and we hope that you give it serious thought. Not only is it an intriguing and appealing feature to your listeners, but the built-in flexibility in both length and scope are prime attractions of this idea. It can be one of the biggest major contest promotions to ever hit your area. But, thinking small, this idea will work for you even if your items are such things as: 20 pounds of potatoes from Schultz's Grocery, 10 pounds of hamburger from Clancy's Market, and 500 Band-Aids from Johnson's drugs. Go to it!

DO-IT-YOURSELF CONTEST

We keep talking about simplicity in promotions. You will be hard-pressed to find one that is any simpler than this. Still it is off-beat enough to have considerable appeal for your audience.

How It Works

The best way to get into this is to simply start out with the premise that the station is tired of running contests. So you have decided to run a contest to end all contests.

The rules are just this: To enter, a listener sends in a postcard with his name and address—and his estimate of how many entries will be received in the contest. Nothing more. The listeners themselves create the contest. And it is a lot of fun.

Variation

One slight variation on the above that you might want to use is this: Entrants include their phone numbers on the postcard rather than an estimate of the number of entries. Calls are made and the person answering is asked at that time to give his estimate of the number of entries in the contest. Wrong answers should be announced on the air. This way you will have to continue until you get an answer that hits the number on the nose. When a listener guesses wrong, you should inform him whether he is high or low so that other listeners will have a better chance.

Prizes

You can offer prizes of almost any type in this kind of contest, but try to make the prizes as offbeat as the contest itself. Here are a few suggestions:

- In your area there is some nearby spot that is the butt of many local jokes. For instance, San Franciscans always make jokes about Los Angeles. The first-prize winner gets a weekend at this spot. The second-prize winner gets two weekends at this spot.

- The winner gets maid or butler service for a day. The "maid" or "butler" is the person whose estimate of the number of entries is farthest from the actual number.

- The winner gets a series of spot announcements on your air. These should be ridiculously laudatory.

2.40   MUSICAL BILLBOARD CONTEST

This is a simple contest that will involve your listeners actively, provide some good commercial tie-ins, and get your station some excellent publicity around town.

How It Works

You make arrangements with an outdoor advertising company to place WZZZ Musical Billboard signs on their regular boards. This can work well, too, if your arrangements are with a company handling neon signs. Your musical signs are small 1-foot-by-1-foot signs with musical symbols and your station call letters. These are mounted on three different billboards or electrical signs each week. The first listener to call in and correctly identify the locations wins the prize you are offering.

Size of the Signs

We suggest your signs be no larger than 1-foot by 1-foot. You want your listeners to have to work to locate them. The sign company should be able to provide you with a design and with the right colors. The company, of course, has the responsibility of putting these up.

Timing

You can change the locations every day, two or three times a week, or once a week. It all depends on how hard you want to push this. Remember that this promotion should run for a considerable period of time.

Locations

Unless yours is a fairly small city, you will want to confine the three signs being used to a specific area of town during any given week. If you get them spread out too far, it will be virtually impossible to get any winners. In your on-air promos for this you should also state the area where the signs will next appear.

Clues

Do not overlook the possibility of giving clues about the location of the signs on the air as an added listener hook.

The Prize

Probably the best prize for this type of contest is a cash award of $10, or an amount matching your frequency. This prize money should be put up by the sign company as their contribution to the promotion since they will be getting a great deal of publicity as well as some real sales advantages.

Sales Possibilities

You will want to exercise control over where the musical signs go for two reasons: first, because you do not want them appearing on the billboards of competitors of some of your good accounts; second, you will want them to go on some of your clients billboards. And your salespeople should receive lists of the locations of all musical signs so they can make sales calls on firms where such signs appear who are not current sponsors. Of course, you will have to plug the location of the signs after you hit a winner.

LIARS CONTEST   2.41

This is a promotion that can be staged at any time of year; however, this is a natural for the two or three weeks just ahead of the opening of fishing season, which takes place in late March or early April in most areas. There is something about fishing and lying that seem to go together. This is not to say that all fishermen are liars, but certainly, most of the good liars do fish.

How It Works

The details of this contest are apparent in the title. You stage a liars contest. Offer an oddball prize and then have fun. There is nothing particularly complicated about this. You will be provided with some clever on-air material for your air personalities to use.

Some Possibilities

Instead of simply asking listeners to send in a lie of any sort, set up a basic story or peg and ask them to provide the ending. This could be something like: "I had been sitting alone in the boat for hours. The water was rough and getting rougher. All of the other boats had left the lake to seek the safety of the shore. Suddenly there was a tug on my line . . .". Or even: "The big one got away because . . ." and then let your listeners take over from there.

A second possibility is to stage your contest for the biggest lie in five words or less. Another is to offer the prize to the person submitting the biggest lie about your station or your air personalities or both.

An Added Bit

Naturally as a result of this contest you are going to get a lot of good on-air material that will keep your listeners laughing. But do not overlook the possibility of compiling the best lies submitted into an inexpensive little booklet for use as a mailing piece to local and national agency people. The suggestion about lies about the station or air personalities is particularly adaptable to this.

The Prize

You may want to offer a weekly prize for two or three weeks, or a top prize to "the biggest liar in town" with a number of secondary prizes. No matter, the prize should be in keeping with the tenor of the contest. Here are a couple of possibilities: A 1990 convertible Cadillac—hubcap; or a full year's supply of hot air. There are thousands of other silly things possible, but these give you an idea.

The Judges

You'll need someone to select your winners. You will want to use a number of the entries on the air and these can just be used as examples of the type of thing you are receiving without them necessarily being winners. As a judge you might get the officer who runs a lie detector at the local police station, or a traffic judge who hears a great many lies from the people who appear before him.

As a side issue, do not overlook the possibility of trying to find out whether men or women are the better liars.

2.42 CHRISTMAS TREE BONFIRE

Here is a fine post-Christmas promotion that combines constructive public service with hard-hitting station publicity. Community members should praise you for the project and safety value of the promotion. The fire department officials will be grateful for your efforts, too.

How It Works

This promotion is about as simple as any you can run. Around the middle of Christmas week your station goes on the air with the announcement that on a specified day you will pay twenty-five cents for old Christmas trees. (See conclusion on p. 117 for variation on this payment.) You do this as your contribution to the city's fire prevention program.

Fire hazards, as you know, are extremely high during the immediate post-Christmas period. Each year thousands of fires result directly from dried out Christmas trees still around homes. Your object is to get the trees out of the homes and eliminate the danger. This important message will reach even those who do not take up your offer of paying for the trees.

The Bonfire

What do you do with the trees you collect? You burn them, of course, at the city's biggest public bonfire. This should be a spectacular event and the long nights in January mean that you can stage it early enough in the evening so the kids can attend and still have the darkness necessary for an exciting fire display.

Timing

You should kick this promotion off on the air about three or four days after Christmas. In this way, you will get it off the ground in plenty of time to ensure complete success. You will also be alerting the public to the danger of dried Christmas trees around the home at the most effective time.

Most people are in the habit of keeping their Christmas tree up through New Year's Day. You will want to schedule your bonfire for January 3, 4, or 5. You will probably want to put your bonfire on at about 7:00 or 7:30 in the evening.

Location

Obviously, you are going to require a large open area for a bonfire the size of this one. You may be able to make arrangements with the city to use a local garbage dump for the promotion. A big football field would also work well, with the added advantage of bleachers for the crowd. You will require a field that is dirt, not grass. And you will have to arrange for the removal of the ashes after the fire.

Collection of Trees

You can simply have people bring their old Christmas trees to the site of the bonfire. It will be necessary, however, to have someone on hand at the site throughout the week to receive the trees because many people will want to bring them before the night of the bonfire. In this case, you will also have to provide a way of paying the people who get there before the night of the fire.

You may be able to make arrangements with the city for the use of the city garbage trucks to help you carry out this worthwhile project. If the garbage trucks are available, you can set up collection points throughout the city where people can take their Christmas trees. The fire stations throughout the city would make daily pickups and deliver the trees to the site of the bonfire.

One thing to remember: If you do accept trees at the bonfire site before the night of the fire, you will probably have to make arrangements for a guard. Some pranksters might be tempted to fire up the trees in advance of your planned event.

Get the Schools in the Act

Encourage the schools in your area to undertake the collection of old Christmas trees as a group project. The money realized would then be turned over to the schools. In addition, you can offer a $25 bonus to the school bringing in the most trees. Also, the winning school gets to select a "Bonfire Queen" who will reign at the burning ceremony. Each school should select a queen candidate in advance and the runners-up would serve as princesses.

If you plan to get the schools into the act, it will be necessary to get information about the promotion to them in advance of Christmas vacation to provide enough time to line up committees before school lets out.

The Show

The bonfire itself is going to attract a very large audience for you. But you want to stage the bonfire with as much hoopla as possible. Set up a public address system. You might even build a small stage. Be sure that all of your air personalities are on hand to put in an appearance. Appoint one of them as emcee for the event. They can even play records before the bonfire starts to keep the crowd amused.

Civic Officials

The mayor and other civic officials should be invited to attend the bonfire, as well as the head of your local safety council. People from these categories will be included in the short program you will put on just before the fire is started.

Fire Department Participation

Naturally, it will be necessary to have fire department units at the bonfire as a safety measure. Invite the fire chief, too, and ask him to make a short speech. You can be sure that his remarks will be laudatory.

Setting the Fire

You can simply walk up and put a match to your giant pile of old Christmas trees, but why be prosaic when you can easily dramatize the setting of the fire? Here are some possibilities:

- Have on hand from the fire department one of the ladder trucks with a ladder that can be telescoped high into the air. A fireman (or, perhaps, a high school student selected with proper fanfare) mounts this ladder carrying a flaming torch which he then flings onto the pile of Christmas trees.

- Somewhere in your city there must be a good archer. Set him up a reasonable distance from the pile of trees. Wrap a cloth around the tip of an arrow and soak this in an inflammable fluid. The arrow is then set afire and the archer shoots it into the Christmas trees.

- Dig a shallow trench that spirals around your pile of trees. It should make three or four loops around the trees before running it under them. This is then filled with inflammable fluid (the fire department can tell you what to use) and set afire with proper fanfare. The crowd will gasp with excitement as the flames spurt around the trench heading for the old Christmas trees.

- You can arrange something similar to the above using a long fuse, which can then be set afire from your temporary stage. You might choose the principal of the school that wins your collection drive as the person who starts the fuse.

In Conclusion

Although you offer twenty-five cents for each old Christmas tree turned in, there will be many people who will not want to accept the money. You can consider giving such funds to your local safety council to further their fire-prevention work. One thing to remember is that this can be a tremendously successful promotion even if you offer nothing for the old Christmas trees.

CHRISTMAS CARD CONTEST   2.43

Even at Christmastime, the simple ideas are often the best. Since everybody is sending Christmas cards, why not get on their lists, and at the same time, plug a worthy charity and make a lot of other people happy?

How It Works

All of your disc jockeys appeal to their listeners to send them a Christmas card. The cards are addressed to the listener's favorite WZZZ personality. The DJ receiving the greatest number of cards addressed to him or her gets both

Christmas and New Year's off. This stipulation is simply to give your people an additional talking point within the promotion.

The Simple Contest

A drawing is made from the cards sent in and the card drawn wins for its sender an appropriate small prize. You may want to have a separate drawing and prize for the cards sent to each disc jockey. Consider having children select the winners for you.

Be sure to require that each card come in an envelope with a Christmas Seal on it. Simple? Yes sir. But it is a good mail-puller and a good chance to plug the Christmas Seal campaign in an interesting way.

A Second Benefit

There is another pleasant aspect to this promotion: your air copy for it should specify that the cards themselves contain only the name of the sender. After the drawing, your disc jockeys will add their names to the cards and these will be sent on to people who might not otherwise receive such Christmas greetings.

Getting Your Mailing List

Your mailing list for the cards should include recipients such as:

- Patients in children's hospitals
- Patients in veterans hospitals
- Children in group foster homes
- People in retirement homes

You can get the specific names from such institutions. And, since many such institutions have ladies' guilds that work in their behalf, you might even get them to help you with the addressing.

2.44 CHRISTMAS TREE CD GIVEAWAY

This is a promotion that will be a lot of fun to conduct and it can be a very effective gesture of goodwill at the Christmas season.

How It Works

About the 8th or 10th of December one of your air personalities begins complaining that there is no tree in the station lobby. He states that someone should do something about it.

In the meantime, find the location of an area where you can go out and cut down a tree. This is much better than getting a tree from a lot. One of your newsmen informs the air personality that he has located the place where a tree can be cut and suggests that the personality should bring a couple of other station employees and go out and get the tree.

When the tree is brought back to the station and set up, the personality states that it would be fun this year to decorate the Christmas tree with small toys. These toys will be given to one of the organizations that gathers toys each year and distributes them to needy children. Many fire departments conduct such campaigns, as does the Marine Corps Reserve. Contact the organization you are going to work with in advance so you can get the most publicity mileage out of the promotion.

How to Get the Toys

The air personality around whom this promotion is being built announces on the air that on a given day he will give away his entire show to listeners who will contribute a toy to be used for the decoration of the Christmas tree. He explains that on the day in question he will give away every record he plays during his show to individual listeners who call in and pledge a toy for the tree. To qualify, listeners must call in their pledges while each record is playing.

Eliminating Problems

This promotion is going to create some problems at your switchboard. To minimize this, your personality should announce that calls will be limited to three exchanges for each CD given away and only people calling on these telephone exchanges qualify for that particular CD. Set up the series of exchanges on a page in advance.

Planning the Show

Plan the entire show in advance so you are sure you have duplicates of all of the CDs to be played. Call on the distributors if you need help in this area.

Be sure that the names of the winners are placed on each CD as it is played to avoid later confusion. The listeners receive their CDs when they bring their toys to the station.

TRAVEL TICKETS   2.45

As the highways and byways of our nation become more congested every day, the idea of a Sunday drive or a short trip around the state becomes more of a threat than the pleasant outing it used to be. Additionally, considering the low rates of some commercial forms of transportation, it hardly pays to take your own car, even on short trips. So, here is an on-air contest promotion tailor-made for your statewide bus service. It is an ideal combination of sales and contest that is fun for your audience and brings home in a most forceful way the low cost of bus travel.

How It Works

The contest is conducted in conjunction with a spot schedule purchased by the transportation company advertiser. Your announcer tells listeners that it is time to play for WZZZ Travel Tickets. To heighten the drama, the announcer then spins a carnival wheel containing the names of all the sizable cities and towns in your state. When the arrow stops at a certain city or town, the disc jockey offers two round-trip tickets to that city to the first person calling within two minutes who can come within fifty cents of guessing the cost of a single round-trip. If there is no winner, the DJ gives the correct cost. Winner or not, each time the game is played, it effectively points out the low-cost message of the bus company.

Variations

In some cases, it may be more practical to offer tickets to a major city or tourist attraction some reasonable distance away, rather than give tickets to the city selected by the wheel. The contest would still be conducted on the basis of selecting a city with the wheel. Your tie-in with the bus company may develop along these lines: Instead of using cities and towns only within your state, you may wish to put the names of major cities throughout the country on your carnival wheel. This, too, will work well within the format.

Something to Think About

Obviously, a person who has secured the round-trip costs is going to have a decided advantage in this contest. Rather than being a detriment to the promotion, this is actually a big plus. As a matter of fact, it would be a good idea to encourage listeners to go to the bus station and secure such information. This will simply serve to reinforce the low-cost message that the bus company is trying to get across.

GAS STATION KEY PROMOTION

This promotion will work well with any chain of gas stations. It can also work with a single gas station, but not as well; besides, your greatest advantage as far as sales go comes from working with a chain.

In addition to being a real sales builder for the gas stations involved, this contest can be a real audience-builder for you. With a promotion of this type, you should be able to get a heavy schedule for a long period of time. The promotion is simple enough and has enough interest to give it staying power for the long haul.

As with many good promotions, the Gas Station Key promotion will take a little effort to set up; however, once it is set up properly, it can be handled with complete ease. The point is: Make sure you have all of the little wrinkles ironed out before you start.

How It Works

To begin with, when you are talking to the gas people (let's call their company Texafield here), you should talk in terms of a large weekly package. The Texafield Company offers a free key chain to any driver who stops in at one of their stations—no purchase necessary. The chains are quite inexpensive when purchased in quantity. Also, offering a gift will prove an immense traffic builder for all of the Texafield stations as they start into the promotion and should get things off to a good start.

Each key chain carries a registration number. These numbers are announced once an hour on the air and if the person with the right number gets to any Texafield station within 10 minutes after the announcement he receives a prize. It's as simple as that.

Setting It Up

If the contest is run at the same time each hour, the Texafield dealers will automatically know whether a winner arrives within the allotted 10 minutes. If the contest spots run at varied times, however, you will have to provide each dealer with a weekly or monthly listing of the scheduled contest times in advance.

When a driver comes into the gas station for his key chain, the gas dealer gets the driver's name and address and lists it opposite the number of the key chain. This information is then turned in to the Texafield main office where a continuing master list is kept. (It should be the responsibility of the gas company to prepare this master list. They should want to anyway, since it gives them an excellent mailing list for future use.) Copies of the master list and supplements to it are sent to you.

Additional Promotion

Most certainly there should be banners at all Texafield dealers calling attention to the contest. It is up to you whether you or Texafield bears the cost of these, or whether you split the cost.

Number Selection

There is no set pattern for selecting the numbers that will be announced over the air. You can pick them out of a hat, simply set them down arbitrarily, or use them on a quota basis by area or dealer—one method is about as good as another. Do *not* try to make a bit out of selecting the number on the air. It takes too long and, remember, you are dealing with commercial time here.

Alphabetical Listing

A good idea is to have a second master list set up on an alphabetical basis. This will give you a cross-check on people who are picking up a number of key chains in order to increase their chances of winning. When such duplicate entries are discovered, all but the first registration number should be removed from the listing you use on the air.

Checking Winners

The simplest way to check winners is to have the dealer call into the station with the winner's name. This way you can get the dealer's name and the name of the winner for use on the air.

The Prize

The best prize in a contest of this type is five gallons of gas; however, the Texafield people may wish to push seasonal products, other products besides gas, or services. The nature of the prize should be left up to them.

2.47   MYSTERY HOUSE

Here is a very simple station promotion that is designed to fill the listener rolls for your frequency, garner extensive goodwill for your station, and spread your call letters throughout every section of your listening area. In addition, it will cost you next to nothing.

How It Works

Announce that somewhere within your listening area there is a WZZZ Mystery House. The first person to ring the doorbell of that dwelling and ask, "Is this the WZZZ Mystery House?" will win a brand new bicycle. The value of the prize will be determined by the size of your market. If you wish to go beyond a bicycle, you can use a small moped or motor scooter as the reward.

The selection of the house will be up to your discretion. Naturally, you will want to have the permission and cooperation of the house's residents. You won't want it to be the home of anyone connected with your station.

Second Round or Alternative

You can do a second round on this promotion at a later date by offering a prize that will appeal to the 16- to 20-year-old group instead of the younger group. In this case, the prize should pertain to your music. It could be a portable stereo system, copies of all of the singles on your current list, or even a CD subscription service offered by one of your record distributors. By linking the second round or alternative promotion to your music you are provided with a logical opportunity to talk up this phase of your programming.

What Happens

The result of this promotion will be hundreds or thousands of kids knocking on virtually every door in your coverage area promoting good old WZZZ for you. Homes that have not heard of your promotion will tune in to find out what is going on. Listeners already with you will stay tuned to find out how the event turns out. And those participating in the promotion will have to stay tuned in to hear the clues that will give them the best chance of finding the WZZZ Mystery House.

Timing

If you stage this promotion during the summer months, it can be run on a continuing basis; however, if you put it on during the school months, we suggest you spare yourself criticism and headaches by limiting the promotion to weekends; you can hold interest by announcing clues as to the location of the WZZZ Mystery House all week during after-school hours. In any case, the clues are a listener hook that should be employed to get the maximum effect from this promotion.

Additional Twist

An additional gimmick that can be used is this: If the person who finally locates the WZZZ Mystery House can give your station frequency, he receives a bonus prize. This is a good way to get in extra plugs for your spot on the dial and have it register in the minds of your listeners.

Merchandising

The merchandising possibilities inherent in this promotion are obvious. Any merchant will be most anxious to provide you with a bicycle, moped, or whatever your prize may be for the plugs he will receive on the air. In addition, he should be encouraged to take a paid schedule on your station at the same time to augment his on-the-air mentions and get the maximum advantage from them.

Also, encourage the merchant providing your prize to supplement his on-the-air plugs with posters in his store telling about the promotion. At the same time, whenever you air clues as to the location of the WZZZ Mystery House, these automatically become prime listening times and adjacencies should be sold.

On-Air Copy

The following gives you some suggested on-the-air copy for use with this promotion, including teaser copy, straight copy, and promotion copy designed to create and maintain interest in your promotion. Remember that you must maintain a degree of levity in your overall approach; if your promotion is not fun for you, it is not going to be fun for your listeners. At the same time, create an aura of mystery and excitement that encourages continued listening. Develop a production intro for use with your clues to heighten the effect. And work up as many side issues as you can think of for your DJ's to talk about on the air in connection with the promotion.

FIND THE WZZZ MYSTERY HOUSE AND WIN A BICYCLE. STAY TUNED FOR DETAILS.

* * * *

THERE IS A WZZZ MYSTERY HOUSE SOMEWHERE IN (city). IF YOU FIND IT, YOU WILL WIN A TWO-HUNDRED DOLLAR (brand) BICYCLE. STAY TUNED FOR DETAILS.

* * * *

SOMEWHERE IN (city) THERE IS A WZZZ MYSTERY HOUSE. AND THE FIRST

BOY OR GIRL TO FIND IT WILL WIN A BRAND NEW TWO-HUNDRED DOLLAR (make) BICYCLE. HERE'S HOW YOU CAN WIN: JUST RING THE DOORBELLS IN YOUR NEIGHBORHOOD AND ASK, "IS THIS THE WZZZ MYSTERY HOUSE?" IF YOU ARE THE FIRST TO FIND THE WZZZ MYSTERY HOUSE, THE PERSON WHO ANSWERS THE DOOR WILL GIVE YOU A (make) BICYCLE TO RIDE HOME. THAT'S ALL THERE IS TO IT. SO, START LOOKING FOR THE WZZZ MYSTERY HOUSE. AND STAY TUNED TO WZZZ. EACH DAY WE WILL BROADCAST CLUES THAT CAN LEAD YOU TO THE MYSTERY HOUSE.

* * * *

Sound: (Spook noises)

Child: GOSH, IS IT HAUNTED?

Anncr: (filter) NO, THE WZZZ MYSTERY HOUSE IS NOT HAUNTED.

Child: IS IT A CASTLE—OR A MANSION?

Anncr: THE WZZZ MYSTERY HOUSE IS JUST AN ORDINARY HOUSE—MAYBE IN YOUR NEIGHBORHOOD.

Child: WHAT'S SO SPECIAL ABOUT IT THEN?

Anncr: THE FIRST BOY OR GIRL TO FIND IT WILL WIN A BRAND NEW (make) BICYCLE.

Child: GEE, HOW CAN I WIN?

Anncr: JUST BY RINGING DOORBELLS AND ASKING, "IS THIS THE WZZZ MYSTERY HOUSE?"

Child: AND IF IT IS THE MYSTERY HOUSE?

Anncr: THEN THE PERSON WHO ANSWERS THE DOOR WILL GIVE YOU A NEW TWO-HUNDRED DOLLAR (make) BICYCLE TO RIDE HOME.

Child: AND I JUST ASK "IS THIS THE WZZZ MYSTERY HOUSE?"

Anncr: THAT'S ALL.

Child: WELL, WHAT AM I WAITING FOR?

Anncr: REMEMBER TO STAY TUNED TO WZZZ FOR THE CLUES THAT CAN TELL YOU WHERE THE MYSTERY HOUSE IS.

Child: (off) OKAY!

SECRET OF THE DAY

This promotion stirs up fun—and listeners. If you handle it right, you will have the whole town talking—and laughing—about your Secret of the Day. There is nothing complicated about this promotion. It is easy to handle and fun.

How It Works

The Secret of the Day promotion works best if you assign it to just one of your disc jockeys. Each day he has a different Secret of the Day, which are gag phrases like the examples you will find below. This phrase is posted on the board and all of your announcers should plug it and the promotion.

The DJ who has the promotion on his show should run it about two times an hour. He simply places a telephone call at random. If the person called answers with the Secret of the Day, he wins whatever prize you have set up. That is all there is to it. You can do a twist on the promotion by having listeners send in postcards with their names, addresses, and phone numbers. These cards are then drawn at random and your calls are made on the basis of them.

You get a lot of word-of-mouth publicity on this type of promotion. Your listeners will be answering their telephones with your gag phrases while the show is on the air. Whenever it is not WZZZ calling, they will have to explain why they answered the phone in such a ridiculous manner, thus creating another potential listener for you.

To Facilitate Handling

If it is impractical to have the announcer place his own calls for this promotion, it will work just as well if you have your office receptionist place them. Then the names of any winners can be taken into the studio to be announced.

Prizes

The prizes for the Secret of the Day promotion can be almost anything. Tapes or CDs provided by the distributors in return for plugs make fine prizes. Or you can use the products of regular sponsors in a merchandising tie-in.

Warning

Stay clear of any Secrets of the Day that involve your call letters. This is an area that will run into trouble with the rating services.

Some Suggested Secrets

- "Wait until I tell you what happened last night."
- "Hurry up, the boat's leaking."
- "The coast is clear."
- "You'll never guess what happened."
- "Hurry up, the sauce is burning."
- "I don't care. I just don't care."
- "I said I was sorry. Now, what do you want?"
- "This is one of my bad days."
- "To be or not to be, that is the question."
- "I'm not here. I'm not here to anyone."

LUCKY TELEPHONE NUMBERS   2.49

This continuing, long-range promotion is designed to stimulate interest in your station, in order to gain and hold listenership. Lucky Telephone Numbers is easy to work and makes exciting radio.

How It Works

To prepare to play Lucky Telephone Numbers, produce two master carts. On the first, record the names of all of the telephone exchanges in your listening area. (If you are covering more than one city, use the exchanges proportionally, i.e., half of the exchanges should be from your primary market, two-thirds of the remainder from your major secondary markets, and the balance from your other smaller markets.) The exchanges should be arranged in a jumbled order on the cart.

How to Conduct the Game

Determine what telephone exchanges you want to include in the contest, then record onto a cart each exchange number (the three-digit prefixes) you plan to use in the contest. In fact, make sure each exchange gets onto the cart several times, but randomize the order in which the exchanges are recorded.

When it is time to play the cart back, the DJ should cycle the cart (without playing it on the air or through the cue channel) a random number of times so that no one can predict which exchange will be played on the air. By the way, a good way to determine random numbers from 1 through 12 is to glance at a sweep second on a clock or watch. Whatever number is closest to the second hand is the random number.

The Prize

We strongly urge you to give a cash prize instead of a merchandise award. The value of the prize will be determined by your market. You can start by offering $10, increasing the prize by $1 each game until you get a winner, and then start over again. Or you can start at $100 and increase it by $10 each game or each day until it is won.

Keep It Simple

It is not wise to load up a promotion such as this with additional gimmicks—say, offering a bonus prize if a winner can answer a question after he calls in. This promotion is strong enough by itself and will be more effective if it is kept as simple as possible. While the details as given here may seem rather complicated, you will find that, in operation, Lucky Telephone Numbers is quite easy to produce and understandable to the listener.

To Get More Winners

If you find that you are not getting sufficient winners using the system outlined, you can vary it by setting up the number cart with alternate three-digit and two-digit numbers, or one with only two-digit numbers. Then, when a two-digit number comes up, a listener need have only a matching exchange and final two digits in his telephone number to win. You may want to make the prize bigger and the winners less frequent. To do this, use four-digit numbers.

Scheduling

We suggest that you schedule Lucky Telephone Numbers 10 times each day, Monday through Saturday. The game should be scheduled at a different time each hour to ensure maximum listenership. Your DJ should plug it in advance:

"RIGHT AFTER THE NEXT RECORD WE WILL BE PLAYING LUCKY TELE-PHONE NUMBERS AGAIN."

You will get much more mileage from this promotion if you schedule it 10 times each day than if you try to run it only two or three times a day. Do not overlook the possibility of running it into your nighttime hours. And remember, the longer you continue Lucky Telephone Numbers on your station, the greater the interest generated among your listeners.

Publicity

In the beginning, be sure to give heavy on-the-air publicity to your winners. The sooner you have some winners to talk about, the more successful the promotion will be. But *do not* start out using two-digit numbers just to get some fast winners, because then you cannot switch to three-digit numbers without looking bad in the eyes of the public.

The Format

The format following is merely a suggested outline. Have your disc jockeys follow it for the first week or so, and then let them operate the promotion on an ad-lib basis.

Anncr: TIME NOW TO PLAY WZZZ'S LUCKY TELEPHONE NUMBER GAME WORTH THIS HOUR $_____. WE'LL SPIN THE WHEEL OF FORTUNE TO FIND THE LUCKY TELEPHONE EXCHANGE FOR THIS HOUR. HERE WE GO.

(Play a cut from the exchange cart.)

Anncr: THAT'S IT. THE LUCKY TELEPHONE EXCHANGE FOR THIS HOUR IS _____. ANYONE WITH THE _____ EXCHANGE IS A POTENTIAL WINNER. AND THIS HOUR THE LUCKY TELEPHONE NUMBER JACKPOT IS WORTH $_____. IN JUST A FEW MINUTES WE WILL SPIN THE WHEEL OF FORTUNE AGAIN TO GET THE THREE DIGITS THAT WILL DETERMINE OUR LUCKY TELEPHONE NUMBER WINNER. SO STAY TUNED. REMEMBER, ALL YOU NEED DO IS MATCH THE EXCHANGE JUST GIVEN - AND HAVE THE FINAL THREE DIGITS IN YOUR TELEPHONE NUMBER MATCH THOSE WHICH WILL BE ANNOUNCED IN JUST A FEW MINUTES. IT'S SIMPLE. IT'S FUN. IT'S PROFITABLE. IT'S WZZZ'S LUCKY TELEPHONE NUMBER GAME.

* * * *

(About 10 minutes later)

Anncr: JUST A FEW MINUTES AGO WE DETERMINED THE WZZZ LUCKY TELEPHONE EXCHANGE FOR THIS HOUR. IT IS _____. NOW WE'LL SPIN THE WHEEL OF FORTUNE AGAIN TO GET OUR LUCKY TELEPHONE NUMBER. IF YOUR EXCHANGE IS _____ AND THE FINAL THREE DIGITS OF YOUR TELEPHONE NUMBER FITS WITH THE SAME AS THOSE YOU HEAR, CALL WZZZ. THE FIRST PERSON TO CALL WILL WIN $_____. HERE WE GO.

(Play the exchange cart again.)

Anncr: THAT'S IT. THE WZZZ LUCKY TELEPHONE NUMBER FOR THIS HOUR IS _____. IF YOUR EXCHANGE IS _____ AND THE FINAL THREE NUMBERS OF YOUR TELEPHONE NUMBER ARE _____, CALL WZZZ NOW AT (your telephone number). THE FIRST PERSON TO DO SO WILL WIN $_____. AND REMEMBER, WE PLAY THE LUCKY TELEPHONE NUMBER GAME ALL DAY EVERY DAY. SO STAY TUNED TO WZZZ.

2.50   THREE AGENCY CONTESTS

When you are making a big pitch for national business, an agency contest is one of the most effective ways to bring your message home to the time-buyers. As a general rule, it is a good idea to conduct a concurrent contest for local time-buyers to solidify your efforts at all levels. Keep in mind that time-buyers are a pretty sophisticated bunch. They are not easily impressed and if you do not catch their eyes and ears with a contest promotion that has immediacy and originality, you might just as well skip it.

How It Works

Inform time-buyers that during the next three months you will be running trade ads and that stories about your station operation will be appearing in various publications. The time-buyer who cuts out and collects your call letters from the most different ads and stories wins.

Adding a New Twist

The time-buyer who develops the best slogan promoting your station wins the prize. Nothing very original here, you say. But what if you tell them to call in their slogans long-distance collect instead of using the mails. And while you've got them on the line, give them a sales pitch. Remember, you will be picking some of the best brains in the country and they will be supplying you with a large group of slogans you can use on the air and many other places.

Getting Some Help

The winner of this contest is the person who finds three errors in your printed program schedule. Tell the time-buyers that your national rep can help him find the errors. These errors should be something like showing your coverage pattern smaller than it actually is, stating that you are Number 2 in the market when you are actually Number 1, and putting one of your DJs in the wrong time slot.

You will really get entries in this one if you put in an additional prize for the secretary of the time-buyer who wins. A week after your original contest mailing, drop a line to the secretaries asking them to make sure that their boss gets his or her entry in so that they, too, can win a prize. Sneaky? You're darn right it is—but effective.

Prizes

The prizes, too, should have a certain flair that will appeal to time-buyers. How about offering a queen-sized water bed to your winner. Or dinner at the best restaurant in your town, and then fly him in for it. Maybe a $500 charge account at Brooks Brothers. Or catering service for a party he can throw for up to 50 people. Offer an African safari and you will have one of the best agency contests ever.

How to Use These

We have suggested that you do not use any of the contests outlined here as is. Rather, let these serve as a starting point, work in your own modifications, make them truly your own original plans.

THE "JOE SMITH SMELLS" CONTEST 2.51

This contest is for laughs and publicity. It is the sort of fun-type promotion your station should be running regularly, because this type of promotion will have the people in your area saying: "Have you heard WZZZ lately? Boy, there's something going on there all the time!" And if this "something going on" feeling is not what you are striving for at your station, then you have missed the whole point of radio today.

How It Works

Joe Smith is your top disc jockey. He starts wondering on the air about what the most popular smells are, and he decides to run a contest to find out. Listeners are asked to send in lists of their 10 favorite smells to the "Joe Smith Smells" contest. The person submitting the winning list (and you will have to make up your own rules for judging) will receive the things that create these odors. The tougher the items are to secure, the more fun you will have.

Continuing Publicity

You will probably wish to run this promotion over about a three-week period. Be sure your DJ reads lots of the lists over the air to keep up interest. You should also compile an overall list of the 10 favorite smells for use on the air, in local and national publicity.

Make Way for the Babies

Just so it will not come as too much of a surprise, you might as well know in the beginning that about two out of every three lists you receive will include as a favorite the smell of a freshly washed and powdered baby. This should most certainly be one of the items on the winning list.

Putting the Capper on the Promotion

After your winner has been selected, set it up so that he is presented the items on his list during an on-the-air interview. Be sure to get still photographs because you will want them for publicity purposes. And since several of the items will be in the hard-to-find category, ask your listeners to help in locating them. The winning list may contain such things as: a branch from the southern pine forests of Louisiana, café espresso like they make in Rome, sun-dried sheets, and, of course, that baby we mentioned. Anyway, the more people you can get into the act, the better your promotion will be.

2.52 LUCKY DOLLAR PROMOTION

If you are looking for listeners, this promotion will get them for you. But, remember, it is much easier to get listeners than it is to keep them. This WZZZ Lucky Dollar promotion is going to cost you money, so make sure that it is money well spent. Get your overall programming shaped up into that exciting listening pattern you have been working for. Then blast off with this one and watch those ratings skyrocket.

How It Works

The operation of the Lucky Dollar promotion is quite simple. Tell listeners to write the serial number of a dollar bill they have on a postcard and mail the postcard into the station. They must then keep the dollar bill in their possession. Ten times a day you select a card at random and read the serial number. If the holder of that dollar bill calls your station and correctly identifies himself within one, two, or five minutes (the length of time allowed will depend on your coverage area), he wins the cash prize.

The Prize

The prize offered should be cash and it should range from one hundred to one thousand dollars. Get a carnival wheel and set it up in your studio. The wheel should have about one hundred stops and these should be divided up on the following ratio:

$100—50 stops	$ 600—5 stops
$200—10 stops	$ 700—4 stops
$300—10 stops	$ 800—4 stops
$400—10 stops	$ 900—2 stops
$500— 5 stops	$1000—2 stops

Before selecting the serial number, your disc jockey should spin the wheel to determine how much the prize will be if there is a winner.

Publicity

Be prepared for thousands and thousands of entries on this promotion. Run newspaper ads showing pictures of winners receiving their checks. And be sure to get money into the ad headline:

ANOTHER $400 WINNER IN THE WZZZ LUCKY DOLLAR CONTEST!

Variation

If you are covering only a single city with your signal, you may wish to have winners come to the station with their winning dollar bills within 30 to 45 minutes in order to collect.

HOUSEHOLD HINTS   2.53

Here is a simple little contest that can be run on a continuing basis. Don't ignore this one just because it seems so obvious and easy, it can become a major bulwark on your late morning programming. There can be even greater benefits, too, as you will see.

How It Works

This contest will work best if you spot it on your late morning show (or the show that has the biggest homemaker audience on your station). You simply ask listeners to send in household hints—tips on how to make housework and homemaking easier. They need not be original. Each day you will give a small prize for the best hint of the day, plus a weekly prize for the best hint of the week. This should prove to be one of the steadiest mail-pullers on your station.

The Prizes

The prizes need not be of great value. Something like a gift package containing household cleaning products is ideal for the daily prize. Your weekly prizes should be a hair dryer, knife sharpener, starter set of stainless steel, or something of that nature. All of these prizes can be easily promoted through your sponsors in return for the plugs they will receive. It is best if the daily prize is an expendable item, such as soap products, to encourage the people to continue to send in hints even after they have won once.

Additional Publicity

After you have this promotion on the air for a short time, you will probably be getting requests from listeners for copies of the hints used. For a very modest cost you can send these out on a weekly basis. Have a form printed up with your call letters, the DJ's picture, and so on, and then copy the hints each week. It is amazing how far-reaching this added publicity can be. And, if you are smart, you will put the people at the local advertising agencies and their spouses on the list to receive the hints each week.

Getting Even More Value from the Hints

When you are arranging for the prizes for this contest, talk to your sponsor about eventually bringing out a booklet of hints. This can be an excellent merchandising gimmick for him and excellent promotion for your station. The sponsor can use the booklet as a giveaway in connection with his goods. It is the logical end product of your promotion. And it demonstrates the sort of creative merchandising that radio can do so well.

2.54 SURPRISE PACKAGE

This promotion is potent. While it is relatively simple to operate once you have it set up, the WZZZ Surprise Package will take a considerable amount of work to organize. We suggest you reserve this promotion for that time when you are making an all-out concerted effort to reach the Number 1 spot or regain the top position in your market. This promotion can do it for you.

How It Works

The Surprise Package is organized in a similar manner to the WZZZ Cash Club. Listeners write in to get their WZZZ Surprise Package numbers. Check the other promotion on p. 107 to see how details of this are handled. Once again, numbers are read over the air and the person holding the card with that number must call in and identify himself within a specified period of time. But here the similarity stops.

The Prizes

The WZZZ Surprise Package should contain 200 to 600 different prizes. The top prize should be something of real value such as a two-week vacation for two to Hawaii or Europe, a car, or a fully equipped boat of the 25- to 30-foot class. There should be a number of cash prizes in the Surprise Package such as $1000, $500, $250, $150, $100, and $50.

Other prizes can be five pounds of ground chuck from a supermarket or a $15 merchandise certificate from a cleaning establishment. Just be sure that there is a liberal sprinkling of good prizes in the Surprise Package.

Who Gets What Prize

When a WZZZ Surprise Package number is read over the air no indication is given as to whether the winner will receive the car or the hamburger meat. Only after a winner calls in and correctly identifies himself is the prize determined. There are two ways to do this: A description of each prize can be typed on a slip of paper and placed in individual sealed envelopes, or you can use a carnival wheel with the prizes indicated at the various stops.

When you have a winner, or when the allotted time has elapsed and there is no winner, an envelope is selected and opened or the wheel is spun and the prize announced. Keep the time limit as brief as possible for receiving winning calls. The possibility of winning a prize worth several thousand dollars will keep the vast majority of radio listeners in your area tuned to your station.

Securing the Prizes

Virtually all of the prizes offered should be secured from your various sponsors in exchange for the plugs they will receive. You will have to put up the cash prizes yourself. Keep talking about the big prizes in the Surprise Package when you talk about this promotion on the air. Remember, this is a promotion that will gain momentum as you continue.

2.55   WHERE IN THE WORLD

This is a great mail-pull contest that should do very well for you. As it is set up here, it is designed to run four weeks, but you can continue the contest as long as it is effective by simply writing more four-line poems.

How It Works

On the air listeners hear rhyming clues from which they are asked to guess "Where in the World?" The clues pertain to cities throughout the world and it is necessary to identify the city.

Clues to a specific city are run each weekday, Monday through Friday. All of the clues on a given day are about the same city. After listening for the entire week, listeners send in the names of as many of the cities as they can identify on a postcard.

Naturally, since the clues are relatively simple, you are going to have a large quantity of potential winners each week. That is all on the plus side. From all of the entries submitted in each weekly contest (entries must be post-marked no later than Saturday of each week), only one card is drawn to be the winner.

The Prize

The size of the prize won is determined by the number of correct answers there are on the winning card that is drawn. For instance, your prize might be cash. If the winning card has five correct answers, he wins $500. Four correct answers and he wins $400, and so on. A card must have at least one correct answer to qualify for the contest. You can award the prizes in the same manner if you use merchandise instead of money: the more correct answers there are, the bigger the prize.

Timing

You will want to run the clues at least once every two hours throughout the day. On the following pages we have given you four rhyming clues for each city. These can be rotated throughout the day.

Clues

In producing these clues—and they should be put on cart—include music very softly in the background as an additional clue to the city.

Berlin

Music: "Auf Weidersehn"—"Wunderbar"—"Lili Marlene"—"Danke Schön"

Think of a once walled city in a land
Known for Mozart, Beethoven, and Bach.
A city to the east that's west
Where at Christmas they sing "Stille Nacht" (shtilluh-nakt).

Think of a city famed for its wall
Think of Dietrich and Lili Marlene
Think of Goethe and Willy Brandt
And Gesundheit and Auf Weidersehn.

They are fond of Liebfraumilch (leeb-frow-milsh) wines
Where the Brandenberg Gate boldly stands
Where men drink beer out of big steins
And once there were goose-stepping bands.

You will like the lovely Tiergarten
Where frauleins stroll on the strasse
In a once divided city
Where they don't use water, but wasser (vahsser).

* * * *

Cairo

Music: belly dance music

Think about a dashing sheik,
And of pyramids on the Nile.
Think of a desert kingdom's capital,
And the sphinx's inscrutable smile.

Can a camel go through the eye of a needle?
Where was it that pharaohs sat?
How many grains of sand in the desert?
What was home for Farouk, the fat?

If you know of a famous belly dancer
And where beauteous Cleo was queen

Then you can find the capital city
Where pyramids and camels are seen.

There is a story about old King Tut
That will help you find this place
Where Anthony and Caesar battled
Where Ozymandias left no trace.

* * * *

San Francisco

Music: "California, Here I Come"—"I Left My Heart in San Francisco"

This town was built on a goldrush,
On many a hill and a valley.
They've got a huge park by the ocean;
And Stanfords both Leland and Sally.

Think of Coit Tower and Telegraph Hill.
Then, the Twin Peaks you must find.
When Horace Greeley said, "Go West,"
He must have had this place in mind.

It's a city surrounded by water.
On a gate of gold it looks.
Everyone remembers 1906
When the earthquake really shook.

* * * *

Vienna

Music: "Tales of the Vienna Woods"—"Vienna Waltz"

Look for the grand house of opera,
Where they sing arias a language Germanic.
They've also got woods more famous
In the music world than the botanic.

Many rulers have reigned in this country
That's the home of waltzes by Strauss.
What we need is the capital city
Of the famous Hapsburg House.

The zither is the national instrument.
The mountains are called Alpine.

The capital is on the Blue Danube
Where they're noted for drinking wine.

It's a city that's famous for song,
For the waltz and Danube so blue.
The biggest city in the country
Was conquered before World War II.

* * * *

Calcutta

Music: "Song of India"—"Calcutta"

Think of the Black Hole—what a disaster!
Think of a populous city in Asia
Home of beggars and sacred cows
And maidens in saris to amaze ya.

Think of the Hindus and think of the Sikhs
Know that killing a cow is a sin
Think of the capital of West Bengal
And a waterboy named Gunga Din.

Kipling wrote many a story here
A clue that should help you in finding
A sub-continent's largest city
Near the mouth of the Ganges so winding.

In a land where Nehru ruled
And people worshipped Gandhi
Find its largest city
Where kids spend rupees for candy.

* * * *

Chicago

Music: "Chicago"

Think first about the stockyards,
Then, Don McNeill's "Breakfast Club."
Next, think of a windy city
And a famous baseball club.

Know the scene of many gangster movies;
Know where The Untouchables call home.

Know where Al Capone played loop-the-loop;
And the name of Carl Sandburg's poem.

* * * *

Copenhagen

Music: "Wonderful, Wonderful Copenhagen"

Think of a land in northern climes
Think of Hamlet and Elsinore
Then, think of a capital city
On a Scandinavian shore.

Think of a famous pastry
From a land ruled by kings
Where Hans Christian Anderson
Wrote about childish things.

In a little country far to the north
Ophelia from Elsinore was peering
Now, name the capital city
Where the people like Cherry Heering.

Shakespeare wrote about this land
Something's rotten there, he said.
Near this capital Hamlet sought revenge
But ended up dead instead.

* * * *

Dublin

Music: "When Irish Eyes Are Smiling"

If you find the land of the Blarney Stone,
Then, hum an air of Mother Machree;
Now, shout out "Sure and begorrah,
The biggest city is for me."

If your mother comes from Ireland,
Then, you should know this town,
Where they only drink the water
To wash the whiskey down.

First, you must think about shamrocks
Then think of colleens pretty.

Know the home of the Kennedy clan
And then name the capital city.

If you believe in leprechauns
And the wearing of the green,
Then, you should name the city
Where Molly Mallone was seen.

* * * *

Hollywood

Music: "Hurray for Hollywood"

It has the brothers named Warner
Who have helped many a star
It was here that Hope and Crosby
Built the Road to Zanzibar.

Here they put people's feet in cement
Here things were once very silent
Before Al Jolson taught them to talk
And now everything's noisy and violent.

In this well-known suburb Disney started
And this is home for Lassie, the dog.
They invented snarled freeway traffic
And they even invented smog.

It's part of the West Coast's largest city
Many famous people here get their start
We don't want this southern metropolis,
Just the name of its starring part.

* * * *

Honolulu

Music: "Sweet Leilani"—"Aloha Oe"

Here you'll wear a loose-fitting muumuu
Or don a colorful aloha shirt
The native women do a traditional dance,
Wearing flowers and grass skirts.

It wears a diamond in its head
Yet, it's not Samoa-land.

We're looking for the capital city
Of a place known as "Aloha Land."

The hula is the national dance
And good exercise, they say.
They'll give you flowers to wear 'round your neck,
But here it is called a *lei*.

In a Polynesian atmosphere
Waikiki is less than frantic.
You can catch island fever here,
A disease that's most romantic.

* * * *

London

Music: "Foggy Day in London"—"England Swings"

Remember the bold King Richard
Who was so Lion-Hearted.
Remember, too, Anne Boleyn
Who from her head was parted.

On these names let your mind affix:
William Shakespeare and George, one through six.
Because, you see, they provide a clue,
As do Profumo and Winston, too.

You must know which princess has the Tony
And know where the pussycat's been
Know what happened to Dick Whittington
And the location of Christine's sin.

You see, Amber was forever
Playing about this town
Some said she was such a swinger
She made the bridge fall down.

* * * *

Madrid

Music: "Lady of Spain"—"Bolero"

You've probably built a castle here,
North of Gibraltar, south of France;
Home of castanets, Moors, and matadors,
Guitars and the Flamenco dance.

In this land of the fighting bull
You must name the major city.
It will help to think of olives
And of señoritas pretty.

Franco fought a civil war.
Hemingway tolled a bell.
Manolete fought a rugged bull
In the Latin cap-it-tell.

Think of the Pyrenees; think of cork;
Think about rain on the plain.
Think of people for whom the bell tolled
And give their capital's name.

* * * *

Mexico City

Music: "South of the Border"

In this ancient home of the Aztecs
The bells have a ring most Spanish.
The señoritas are feminine
And the mustached men are mannish.

You must go south, not west, young man,
South of the border to where
Montezuma ruled the Aztecs
A mile and a half in the air.

This capital is named for its country:
The home of the brave Pancho Villa.
You may not think much of cactus
Until you've tried their tequila.

Think of Hernando Cortes,
Of Maximilian and his Carlotta.
Think of tortillas and tacos
And cucurachas that they've gotta lotta.

* * * *

Miami

Music: "Moon Over Miami"

We admit the summers are sunny
In the large Florida town we seek,

But as a winter playground
It's really at its peak.

Seek not the capital city,
But find the most famous town
In the southern state that competes
To wear the sun king crown.

The Everglades you'll find nearby
And many keys provide a clue.
Their sun is something else again,
And that goes for their oranges, too.

By this town there's a famous beach.
It's a place of sun and sand
Where Easterners flock each year
To seek a winter tan.

* * * *

Moscow

Music: "Midnight in Moscow"—"Volga Boat Men"

You must know Napoleon burned this town
And know of a square that's red;
Know about icons and samovars,
About caviar and black bread.

Think of the hammer and sickle.
Think of novels by Tolstoy;
The capital city of Lenin and Stalin
And the famous ballet Bolshoi.

Think of Ivan, Peter, and Vladimir
And a country where Catherine was great.
Then, think of the capital city
Of this dialectical, material state.

In this land that's famed for vodka,
Where the Iron Curtain falls,
They never serve Molotov cocktails
Behind the Kremlin walls.

* * * *

New Orleans

Music: "Come to the Mardi Gras"

They still call it the Crescent City
Near the mouth of our mightiest river
And the naughty ladies on Bourbon Street
Give the town a shake and a quiver.

Think of a city with accent French
With streets Canal and Royal;
A town on the mighty Mississippi
That to the South is loyal.

Its setting is near the bayou country,
This place where jazz was born;
And in a Rampart Street establishment
Louis Armstrong first blew his horn.

Some claim they like the famed restaurants
And the wild Mardi Gras lures some.
Others say they like the stately homes,
But most seek out French Quarter fun.

* * * *

New York

Music: "East Side, West Side"—"New York, New York"

Peter Stuyvesant called this place home,
Where the Yankees won many a pennant;
And Bobby Kennedy even moved here
So he could run for the Senate.

Mayor Lindsay was once a Congressman;
And LaGuardia was a little flowery.
Go to sides both East and West,
And from Harlem to the Bowery.

Wall Street, Park Avenue, the subway,
Broadway theatre and Columbia scholars;
You'll find it all on an island
For which the Dutch paid 24 dollars.

Ziegfeld and Minsky started here.
Empire State will give you a clue.

Giants and Dodgers once played here,
And Gypsy Rose Lee did, too.

* * * *

Rio de Janeiro

Music: "Flying Down to Rio"

Think of South America's largest country.
Think of the home of the samba.
Think of the fun of Carnival.
Think of a picture of Carmen Miranda.

They invented the bossa nova
And made a Sugar Loaf out of stone
They invented a girl from Ipanema
And call Guilberto their own.

In the land of the mighty Amazon,
Near the home of the vicious piranha
Is this city whose name means river
And a beach called Copacabana.

This city is a former capital.
The people are called Brazilanos.
It has recently become the home
Of many swindling Americanos.

* * * *

Rome

Music: "Arrividerci Roma"

Horatio stood at the bridge
After Romulus got his start
Noble Caesar delighted in ruling
While Nero just fiddled about

It wasn't built in just a day;
And seven hills provide a clue.
Spaghetti is the national dish
But, for that matter, Sophia is, too.

Think of lions dining at the Coliseum.
Think of Lucretia and her poisons.

Think of Councils Ecumenical
And the home of Cleo's boyfriends.

* * * *

St. Louis

Music: "St. Louis Blues"—"Meet Me in St. Louis"

Joseph Pulitzer is a name to contend with
So is a paper called Post-Dispatch
And so is the mighty Saainen Arch
Where Budweiser brews many a batch.

In this town a world's fair was held
On the banks of the mighty Missouri
Famed for a zoo with platypus and gnu
And also for many a brewery.

There are many songs about this fair town
One says it's there we should meet
Another says I've come a long way from there
And the last one is blues with a beat.

T. S. Eliot was born in this town
Known as the Gateway to the West
Where the mighty Missouri goes rolling by
And baseball wears a Cardinal crest.

MARINE SIGNAL FLAG CONTEST   2.56

Boat sales are booming all over the country. It is one of the fastest-growing sports industries going. The spring fishing season and the prospect of summer sailing make the late spring months a big selling time for small craft. Here is a contest promotion tailored directly to the needs of a local marine or boat dealer.

How It Works

As you know, marine signal flags—the ones used for sending messages—are normally used on larger boats. This contest involves the use of such marine signal flags, each of which represent a letter of the alphabet.

Each week for a period of four weeks your advertiser displays a sequence of these flags on a pole of standard size outside his place of business. The flags spell out a specific word or phrase when decoded. Your listening audience is invited to stop by the store to pick up a sheet that identifies the entire flag alphabet. To enter the contest, they figure out the code word or phrase and submit it with their name and address. A drawing is held from among the correct entries at the end of each week and prizes are awarded.

Those entering are invited to submit a card at the end of the four-week period with all four code words or phrases on it. The correct entries are again segregated and a drawing is held for a more major prize.

This promotion is a healthy traffic builder—as advertised on your station.

Prizes

These, naturally, should be from among the marine items that your sponsor is pushing. The major prize could well be a day-long or weekend cruise, complete with crew, on one of the sponsor's larger craft.

2.57   STORMING THE BASTILLE

Here is one of the seldom-celebrated holidays (at least in this country) with which you can have a lot of fun. This one provides a marvelous opportunity to promote a sizable summer sale at a time when the stores in your area will be looking for something—in mid-July.

How It Works

Sell the idea of a Bastille Day Sale to a shopping center in your market. Back up your sales pitch with the story of the all-out effort you will be placing behind the promotion.

In the parking lot or on the mall of the shopping center you set up your "bastille": a cage or pen large enough for one of your DJs to do his show from, plus room for prizes. On the door of the "bastille" is a large combination lock. Whoever can work the combination and open the door in a given time, say, 30 seconds or one minute, has successfully "stormed the bastille" and gets his pick of the prizes within. Each time you have a winner, the lock is changed. You can use a lock with keys and give participants a chance to select a key from a large box of them; however, this will mean that you cannot use clues.

When

You may wish to make a "day" of it by shifting your operation to the "bastille" with all of your music people participating. Or you may choose to stage this promotion on one shift only during the hours of heaviest customer traffic at the shopping center.

Clues

You will want to announce clues to the winning combination on the air (and have this piped throughout the shopping center on a PA system). Additional clues can also be posted throughout the center in the various stores. A good idea is to use a scavenger hunt technique, which leads "bastille stormers" from store to store in search of clues.

Bell Timer

Get a timer of some type with a loud bell. This is to be used on location at the shopping center. The timer should be so activated that it rings loudly one minute after it is started. Use it each time a "bastille stormer" tries the combination lock.

Bastille Stormers

In order to get a chance at the combination lock on your "Bastille," each person should present a "Bastille Stormer" ticket, which he can pick up free at the sales counter of any of the participating stores. To avoid repeaters, you can state on the ticket that a person gets only one try. Or you can have different-colored tickets for each store and a person can get one try for each different ticket he presents.

The person who successfully "storms the bastille" has his choice of any prize inside. After this person has received his prize, the "bastille" is again locked with a new lock and the game continues.

Prizes

You will want to line up prizes from all of the participating stores. The more prizes the better. Working through the shopping center association, you will have to agree on a fair way to determine what value in prizes should be received from each store. Make certain there are at least two or three big prizes in the "bastille."

Annual Promotion

Bear in mind that this promotion can easily be turned into a major annual event. This should be indicated to the shopping center people when you are making your initial sales pitch.

2.58   LANDMARK SANDWICH CONTEST

Ever since the Earl of Sandwich crammed his roast duckling between two pieces of bread to take with him while he rode to the hounds, sandwiches have been big the world over. Here is a promotion that allows you to capitalize on this fact and have a lot of fun in doing it. You will probably want to stage it in the summer. The promotion has some excellent commercial possibilities, too.

How It Works

You announce that you are giving your listeners a chance to participate in your Landmark Sandwich Contest. They design a sandwich especially for one of the landmarks of your area. They may choose any landmark or point of interest in the area such as a mountain, lake, or park, and then design a sandwich made from appropriate ingredients.

Participants send the recipes and photographs of their creations to the station any time during the month up until about the last week. For example:

- A sandwich named after a mountain in your area might be mounds of "snowy mashed potatoes and white turkey between slices of foggy sourdough bread."

- A concoction that might suggest the conglomeration of human elements in a particular section of your city might include liverwurst, anchovies, caviar, and chili on French bread.

- One of your listeners might come up with a sandwich named after your farmer's market, which would contain homegrown specialties.

The possibilities are really unlimited.

Selecting Winners

You will want to choose at least 50 to 100 preliminary winners. This preliminary judging can be done on the basis of the recipes and photographs submitted. Some of the people on your staff can probably handle this.

Final Judging

Final judging should take place on a Saturday or a Sunday at a public park to which the public is invited to attend and watch the fun. All of the finalists bring their sandwiches here for the judging. You will have to make arrangements to have tables set aside. You may even want to invite a group of underprivileged children to attend and help eat the entries.

The final judging should be done by a combination panel of experts from the fields of food and fine arts. The basis for the judging should be for the most original, skillfully designed, artistically presented, and edible sandwich.

Prizes

Top prize should be a deluxe sandwich-making kit that includes a brand new stove, a refrigerator-freezer, an electric blender, a hibachi, and other kitchen utensils—plus a year's supply of bread, pickles, and peanut butter. Runner-up prizes can include dinners for two at a number of the fine restaurants in your area.

Sales

There are obvious sales opportunities in this to any of the companies handling normal sandwich ingredients.

SECTION

3

Outside Stunts

HANDLED PROPERLY, THESE OUTSIDE STUNTS CAN BE ONE OF YOUR BEST means of publicizing your station. Through them you can reach hundreds of thousands of people who do not normally listen to your station. Through such stunts you can convert these people into listeners.

Keep all of your stunts simple and colorful. Work for ones that can be staged in major public places. The type of outside stunts we suggest here serve a different purpose than your normal on-air promotions. For one thing, these provide your best opportunities for local, regional, and national publicity. Most of them by their very nature are visual. They lend themselves to the type of pictures for which newspapers are always hungry. Let's face it—you will always have a certain amount of difficulty getting local newspaper coverage on your regular contests. Most newspapers have contests of their own and they are not willing to give too much space to your activities unless it is very unusual. But these outside stunts do have a legitimate news and humor value that many city editors will go for.

Rather than do one such stunt a week and quickly wear out the effectiveness of the technique, stage one a month and devote the extra time working out all of the details that will ensure you achieve the greatest impact. Always remember that the audience you are primarily interested in with these stunts is that portion of the public who are *not* regular WZZZ listeners. You are trying to create the impression that there is a lot of fun and excitement going on at WZZZ and that, if they do not tune in, they are going to be missing something.

3.1   WZZZ LIKES TEACHERS

Work through your local school board or school administration office on this one. It's a nice way to build a good relationship between your station and the local schools.

How It Works

Each day you air material about a different local school. Also, you record short messages from the students at the school. Through a local florist or your local florists' association, arrange to get flowers—red roses or some appropriate flower that is in season.

Have your personalities appear at the school and present one of these flowers to each teacher. Using stock forms your printer has, you can quite inexpensively have attractive certificates printed as a "Salute to the Teachers of Grant Junior High School." This certificate should be presented to the principal for distribution to the teachers, perhaps as a part of a school assembly.

Since most schools have a PA system feeding each room from the office, you may wish to devote two to five minutes of airtime during the late morning to the school and arrange to have this piped into all of the rooms. This is a fairly simple yet effective stunt. And it should create lasting goodwill for your station.

DISK JOCKEY CHALLENGE BET   3.2

Here is another stunt that can stir up a lot of talk in your market. It runs along the lines of the ever-popular "gentlemen's bet."

How It Works

Two of your air personalities make a bet on some event like the ones suggested below. You will get more mileage out of this stunt if the bet concerns some event not connected with the station. The interesting twist is that no money will change hands; the audience draw comes from the creative payoffs. More about that appears below.

Some Possible Bets

- The bet could be about the outcome of a local baseball game or track meet.
- It could be about the number of women wearing jogging shoes who will pass a downtown intersection within a given time.
- The bet could even be about when the thermometer passes 70 degrees in the morning or when it will next rain.
- Tie the bet into a weight-loss challenge.

Paying Off the Bet

The payoff should be something utterly ridiculous. Here are some suggestions for what the loser should do:

- Push the winner through town in a wheelbarrow.
- Pull the winner through town in a rickshaw.
- Lead a burrow or donkey carrying the winner through town.
- Do his/her show astride a donkey or in a bathtub in front of the studio.
- Lead a chimpanzee around town with the chimp wearing a sign identifying it as the loser. The losing DJ must wear a sign reading "(Winner's name) IS THE WORLD'S GREATEST RADIO PERSONALITY."

- Spend a day and a night in a small tent on top of the studios with a sign similar to the one mentioned above.

If the bet has been about which local team will win a game or meet, one of the pay-offs could be staged at the next game or meet. Be sure to get the local paper to take a picture of the payoff.

3.3   PUBLIC SERVICE UNDER GLASS

While this promotion itself will run for only a few days, it still must be considered a continuing promotion because you will spend a couple of months in advance preparation and publicity.

The promotion we are suggesting here is a big one. It is going to take a considerable amount of time to organize and set up. It will also take a lot of effort to operate. But the rewards are sizable and tangible. Once you have tried the WZZZ "Public Service Under Glass" promotion, you'll want to make it an annual event. This is the sort of promotion that we like to call "creative public service."

What Is Involved

Operating in behalf of some charity, you move your entire broadcast operation into a show window of a major department store downtown or at the mall. From this location you broadcast for a period of two to five days. We believe two or three days is the most effective. Throughout this period you will go "under glass" to conduct a major campaign for the charity you have selected.

Which Charity?

Because of the scope of this promotion, you must tie-in with one of the largest charity campaigns. An ideal one is the March of Dimes campaign, which takes place each year. The United Way is another very good possibility. Perhaps your area has a local children's hospital that has an annual fund drive.

The problem arising from using this promotion with one of the smaller charities is that a small organization probably won't be in a position to give you the full-scale cooperation you will require. A small charity probably won't be able to take advantage of all the benefits this promotion offers, either.

Where to Set Up

One of the main show windows of a large department store is an ideal location for your complete remote broadcast. Depending on the commercial traffic patterns in your community, the remote will be downtown or at the mall. You must have an area large enough to hold your entire remote broadcast operation plus room to stage the many stunts you'll be conducting.

The store in which you put this remote is going to receive a tremendous amount of publicity. A huge amount of traffic should also be in the store as a result of your operation. Therefore, it is only natural that you should have the store pay for the transportation charges involved in setting up the remote, as well as the line charges to pipe the audio back to the studio.

Newspaper Advertising

In cooperation with the participating store, consider putting in a full-page newspaper ad for "WZZZ Under Glass." The ad artwork should probably include photos of all your air personalities that will actually work at the remote site. You can even set up a shot that simulates the remote.

The ad copy should point out that your station and the store are devoting all this time and effort to help ensure the success of the charity campaign. The broadcast times of your various DJs should also be included, along with information on any special highlights that will take place. You may be able to get the store to cover the cost of the ad, or you may have to split the cost. Either way, it's a good investment for everyone concerned.

Handling the Broadcast

Your remote broadcast should be timed to coincide with the major push of the charity's campaign. Try to arrange to handle your whole broadcast day from the remote. Otherwise, you'll be shifting program materials back and forth every day with mass confusion as the result.

If you must limit your remote operations to less than the full broadcast day, the early evening shift is ideal because of the heavy sales traffic in the store during the evening hours. Broadcasting the early morning drive-time show from the store is also good because that's probably when your ratings are highest, and you can generate interest for store traffic later in the day.

Remote Newscasts

Plan to have your news operation work from the remote site as well. You'll want to give the impression of having the entire broadcast setup being bodily transferred from your regular studios to the department store. Your news coverage is a vital part of the broadcast service you provide, and your audience will be interested in seeing that too.

Yes, you'll incur extra costs in setting up news wire service, network audio, and police/fire monitors at the remote site, but the convenience and audience response will make up for the costs. The store should be willing to cover these costs as well, since they add value to the promotion.

Setting Up the Window

The display department of the store should have the responsibility of dressing the window, but you should work with their staff, making suggestions for layout and decorative touches. Here are some things to consider:

- Be sure to set up a sound system outside the window so that the audience can hear what is going on. Make sure sound quality is top-notch and sufficient volume is available to get above the noise level.

- The backdrop in the window area may be easily made from a copy of the charity's outdoor billboards. This will tie things together visually for the charity's overall campaign.

- Have your station call sign, frequency, and station logo or slogan prominently displayed. Photos, names, and shift schedules for the air personalities should be displayed as well.

- The news area will probably be set up somewhat separate from the on-air combo operator's position. The combo area can include posters from record distributors, while the news area should have local and area maps, clipboards for sorted-out wire copy, and so forth.

- If you use computerized program logs and scripts, provide a spare monitor by the window where the audience can see it.

- Just for visual interest, perhaps you can borrow someone's cat to hang around in the window remote site. Be sure to provide a kitty litter box in some shielded spot.

Kicking Off the Remote

On the initial day of your remote broadcast, kick off the show with as much hoopla as possible. Try to arrange for a parade from your studios to the store for starters. Sometime between noon and 1 P.M. is a good time for this.

All of your on-air personalities should be available for the parade. Get as many representatives as possible from the charity as well. If you can get representatives from the store, from local government, and from beneficiaries of the charity, so much the better.

The final phase of the campaign for most charities is a city-wide door-to-door solicitation. In the case of the March of Dimes it culminates in a mother's march. Arrange your remote broadcast to coincide with this. The parade to the store and the kick-off ceremonies can serve to get your broadcast off to a strong start, and will spotlight the final phase of the charity's fund-raising campaign.

Adding Some Flash

Have as many activities as possible going on simultaneously. The idea is to have a great many things beside the broadcast to attract and hold a live audience. This is going to take work and planning. Remember, you will be staging a round-the-clock show for three to five days. The live audience will be vast and fluctuating, so keep them amused.

Besides staying busy with handling program materials and running the board, your air personalities can stay busy doing the following things:

1. Get haircuts, shaves or manicures.
2. Take dancing or karate lessons.
3. Use an exercise bike, rowing machine or treadmill, with competing tallies kept by all of your remote staff using the equipment.
4. Converse via intercom with live audience.
5. Invite audience members into the booth for a close-up look.
6. Play darts, cards, or board games, or shoot baskets with paper wads.

Get Your Distributors Involved

As another stunt you can arrange with your record distributors to cooperate with the charity drive. This will mean working out in advance all of the music you will play throughout the remote. (Or you can confine this bit to just certain segments of your remote.) The distributors should supply copies of everything you will be playing. Then, after you have played a given record or CD, it can be auctioned off to the highest bidder with the money going to the charity.

In addition, you may want to pick up a fairly large number of singles, albums, and CDs, and auction these off too. You could also use this system to cull a lot of deadwood out of your own record library. The auction itself should be handled by some representative of the charity. You can auction the records off to people in the live audience at the remote broadcast site, or you can offer them to the first person to call in and make a pledge for the charity. Obviously, such calls should be handled on a special phone line set up in the remote booth for that purpose.

The Charity's Part

You are doing a massive job for the charity involved. Therefore, so that they may receive the greatest benefits from your efforts, you have every right to expect them to do a real job of promoting and merchandising your operation. Plugs for your station and its remote broadcast should appear on all the printed materials put out by the charity. To make this work smoothly, however, you must work as far in advance as possible. All of the workers for the charity, on all levels from the top to the bottom, should be completely briefed on what you are planning.

Your remote site should serve as the secondary headquarters for the charity during the final phase of the campaign. And this site should be the activity center where the charity will stage virtually all outside bits.

Complete Cooperation Is Essential

You will need complete cooperation from the charity if this promotion is to succeed. It will be absolutely necessary for the charity to have some of its people on hand at the broadcast site at all times, ready to answer questions, hand out literature, and most importantly, receive contributions. *No one on your staff should be directly involved in the collecting or handling of money.* Everything in this area is the responsibility of the charity.

Some Guest Disk Jockeys

You can create some additional excitement for your remote programming by lining up a group of "guest DJs." These can include persons like the governor, the mayor, the president of the chamber of commerce, the head of the department store in which you are operating, the local winner of the Junior Miss Pageant, student government leaders from the local high schools, selected students from the local college radio stations and broadcasting departments, the local police/fire/emergency dispatchers, the charity's president, and other people of local prominence. In advance of the remote broadcast, you might even run a little contest that you invite listeners to enter. The winners will then be given the opportunity to become guest DJs. Naturally, all entries in such a contest should be accompanied by a contribution to the charity.

Each of your guest DJs should be limited to 15 minutes on the air. They should work directly with your regular air personalities. Be sure you plan things in advance, though, so that chatter is kept to a minimum. Throughout your broadcasts you will be talking extensively about the charity, so there is no need for these guest DJs to belabor the point unnecessarily.

Other On-Air Visitors

Arrange with some restaurant (or group of restaurants) to cater the show for the whole remote crew. (If the department store sponsoring the event has food facilities, make the food arrangements there, of course.) The food for your working air personalities should be served with as much flair as possible by regular waiters from the restaurant. This is all part of the overall plan of continuity to tie your remote broadcast together as both an on-air show and something worthwhile for the live audience.

Guest Appearances from Notables

Arrange for special guest appearances of all the available personalities in the area. Be sure to set up an advance roster of these people and schedule them with the idea of having some feature attraction on at almost all times. Such guest appearances should be primarily for the benefit of the live audience. Otherwise, you will end up with a lot more talk on the air than you want. Be sure your sound system setup allows for use as a local PA system as well as serving as an air monitor.

Your guests should be reasonably legitimate entertainment personalities, not just a group of nondescript characters.

An All-Star Show

To put a real capper on your operation, plan an all-star show to be staged on the final night of your remote broadcast. This show should include any entertainment personalities you can put your hands on, local or otherwise. Your air personalities should act as hosts for the show and should be featured prominently in it.

If the remote originates from a downtown department store, work through your city hall to arrange to have the street out front blocked off for the evening to accommodate the crowds. Depending on the performers' union requirements and other complications, you may or may not wish to air this all-star show. It will work effectively either way, however.

Include a block dance as a part of the show. You can rope off the dancing area and make the admission charge a contribution to the charity.

Working Schedule

With the possible exception of the period from 10:30 P.M. to 7:30 A.M., you should plan to have at least one of your other personalities on hand in the remote booth to help out the person on the air. This will take some advance scheduling, but remember that you are doing this to get public exposure for your personalities to the greatest degree possible.

The second air personality can help with public interaction, covering phones and such. Remember, you still have a radio station to run, and the on-air personality needs to be able to devote enough attention to that task to keep your air quality high.

Printed Promotional Materials

If you do not already have them, prepare publicity photo handouts of your air personalities. There will be a heavy demand for autographed copies of these from the live audience. Don't have the autographs printed on in advance—that should be done live and handed out as requested for maximum impact.

Don't just have the photos duplicated at a local photo lab; it's more economical to have large quantities of the picture printed on an offset press. The photo should be captioned with the DJ's name, airshift hours, and the station's call, frequency, and logo.

In Conclusion

As you can see, this is a fairly complicated promotion to take on. However, if it is handled properly, it should be one of the most rewarding activities of the year. And the resulting publicity and goodwill will be well worth the effort.

The list of details is fairly long, however, so you must start early and keep on top of things for preparations to be complete. Here's a checklist:

☑ Set up a conference with the charity to make certain that they understand the full scope of what you are undertaking in their behalf. Work out a general plan of operation.

☑ With one or more key people from the charity, set up a meeting with the manager of the store in which you wish to stage your remote broadcast. Work out a fair understanding about what cooperation is needed on the part of the store manager, including location and space requirements, electrical, lighting and telephone needs, furnishing and decorating the remote booth, and transportation and setup costs.

☑ Have your DJ publicity photos taken professionally, and the captions typeset at a quality print shop. Don't shortchange this or permit yourself the false economy of shoddy publicity photos.

☑ If you do not already have one, you should have a remote portable broadcast console constructed. This should be well made and attractive, with the thought that you will use it again in the future.

☑ Work out a schedule of who will be on the air when, and who will be on standby at the remote site. This permits your air personalities to make their plans accordingly. Remember, if you do not employ board engineers separate from the announcers, you'll need someone to ride the board back in the control room at the station.

☞ Make certain that the charity is planning to include the station in all of the printed materials it will be preparing. Make arrangements to supply them with logotypes, pictures of your staff, and any other materials they will need for such printing.

☞ Make arrangements with the distributors for tapes or CDs if you plan to make a record auction part of your show. This will mean working out well in advance as much of the music as possible so that the distributors can start lining up duplicate copies of the recordings for you.

☞ Start working out a list and schedule for the guest DJs from the civic area that you serve.

☞ Arrange for the food catering, on-air haircuts, and other stunts and activities that will be going on during the remote.

☞ Start lining up entertainment personalities who will be making guest appearances.

☞ Go to work on your plans for the all-star show; these details are much too involved to leave to the last minute.

☞ Above all, put your program director to work early on the actual handling of the various phases of this remote broadcast. If such details are not worked out, you will end up with almost endless talk on the air. And it should not be necessary to point out that such vast quantities of talk are not going to do you or the charity any good.

THE JOKE PANEL 3.4

This promotion provides the basis for a highly successful outside stunt that can be repeated again and again. In addition, it will give excellent exposure to your air talent.

How It Works

Set up your air personalities as a Joke Panel, a group prepared to be challenged by any outside group to a joke-telling competition before a live audience.

The Competition

The joke-telling competition should be based on telling a joke in a given category. Once the category is selected, each team has one of its members tell a joke on that subject. There are several ways that the categories can be selected.

The simplest method is to have the categories listed on slips of paper and then drawn at random from a box. Or you can set up a carnival wheel on which the categories are listed. This is then spun each time a new category is needed.

Judging the Competition

There are several methods to judge who wins such an event. Here are a couple of possibilities:

1. You can have a panel of judges who determine which team tells the funniest jokes. They should probably give each joke a point score.
2. You can have the audience vote to determine a winner. The best method for this is to have your chief engineer set up a large laugh meter. This would then be used to judge the laughter that each joke received to arrive at a total score and the winner.

Jokes and Categories

On the following pages you will find several dozen jokes broken down into categories. These should only serve as the broad general starting point for your joke file. Each member of your Joke Panel undoubtedly will have jokes of his own in most of these categories to add.

Accidents

I once fell off a six-story building, but I wasn't hurt. I was wearing my light fall suit.

I once swallowed a penny and I laughed for a week. Lincoln's whiskers kept tickling my stomach.

A friend of mine was in a freeway accident recently, and he needed so many stitches that the doctor used a sewing machine.

I swallowed a roll of film the other day. I called the doctor right away and he said to wait awhile and see if anything develops.

Animals

I bought a monkey yesterday. I paid $50 for him, but he won't cost me anything for food. There was a big sign on the cage that said: "Do Not Feed The Monkey."

Elephants are found in Africa, although they are so big that hardly anyone ever loses one.

While I was camping in Africa I had a terrifying experience. I woke up one morning and had to shoot an elephant in my pajamas. How he got into my pajamas I'll never know.

Babies

I know a woman who had triplets one day and twins the next. One of the triplets got lost.

Whenever our baby's birthday comes around, we open his piggy bank and buy him a present. Last year it was a microwave oven. The year before it was a VCR.

Our neighbors think our baby is spoiled. But they're wrong—*all* babies smell that way.

Banks

I get the feeling that the bank I use is on rather shaky legs. Last week I wrote out a check for $20 and they sent it back marked "No Funds."

Barbers

I won't tell you what kind of barber (name of DJ) goes to, but last week he went in for a haircut and they were all out of them.

My barber—what a guy! When he shaves you, you don't even know he's got a razor on your face . . . it feels more like a file.

Baseball

Baseball—great game. The WZZZ team played against a team last summer and the score was 83 to 72. It was a pitcher's duel.

The gang here at WZZZ organized a baseball team last spring. We played lots of games and had a perfect record going up till mid-August. Then we won one.

I played baseball in high school. I was the most accurate pitcher in the league, too. Every time I threw the ball, I hit the bat.

Bravery

I'm a brave guy. Just this morning I saved the lives of three men. I didn't let my wife have the car.

Remember that big fire in (town) last week? I was there. I dashed right in and saved 18 lives—well, two cats.

Business

I have an uncle who is in business. He's a southern planter. That mean's he's an undertaker in Georgia.

Butchers

My butcher is a real joker. Last Saturday I went in and asked for a dollar's worth of steak. He let me smell the knife.

I'm not saying that our butcher is a crook, but I put our newborn baby on his scales and the kid weighed 15 pounds.

Cars

The engine in my car stopped running yesterday and I had to call a garage for help. You know, they charged me $40 just to tow me *one* mile. But I got my money's worth—I kept my brakes on.

(Name of another DJ) is really the big wheel around here at WZZZ. And I mean that literally. I'm not going to name-drop and tell you how big his car is, but one of the accessories is a tugboat with a pilot.

Childhood

When I was a kid my parents wouldn't let me smoke. So I used to buy breakfast food, sit around and puff rice.

My parents moved a lot when I was a kid. But I always caught up with them.

I come from a musical family. My father sang first bass, my brother sang second bass, and I sang shortstop.

My family used to do some singing. Papa sang bass, Mama sang tuna. We weren't a professional group—we just sang for the halibut.

When I was born everyone was so happy. The doctor rushed up to my father and said, "Congratulations! I think it's a baby."

My parents really treasured us kids. When I was born my Mother said, "Isn't he a treasure?" and Dad said, "Yeah, let's bury him."

When I was a kid, our family was patterned after the U.S. government. Mom and Dad handled the legislation, and my older sister was the Supreme Court— and she was a conservative.

Christmas

I'm all for Christmas, but I really think that gift-giving has gotten out of hand. Take last year, for instance. I finally found out why folks are always singing about a White Christmas —when you get the bills you turn pale.

This last Christmas the toy makers came out with something really educational. It was the one that's supposed to help a child adjust to today's world. No matter how you put it together, it's wrong.

Remember, only _____ shopping days until Christmas—plus another five weeks to the February you don't have to pay 'til.

Clothes

I got a new shirt a couple of weeks ago and the clerk who sold it to me said it was color-fast. He was right—the color certainly came out of the cloth in a hurry.

You've heard about the clothes they're making out of paper—but have you heard about the new ones made out of milk? Just great for moths with ulcers.

College

Going to a school like Oxford has its advantages. You can write home for money in Latin.

I didn't go to college—I slept at home.

I wanted to go to a coed college but my family wouldn't hear of it. They said I could go to any college in the country providing it wasn't coed, so I went to Vassar.

Courtship

I remember Loretta. She said her heart belonged to me, but the rest of her kept going out with other guys.

A girl I was once courting had a strange father. He thought I was a fish. At least he always said, "Holy mackerel, are you here again?"

I guess I'm too old for Santa Claus. I sent him a note saying I wanted something with an hour-glass figure for Christmas. I got a cello.

Crime

I knew a real clever crook over in (town). He opens combination safes with his feet. It may sound silly, but it drives the folks in the fingerprint lab crazy.

I've got a friend who was arrested for stealing an apple from one of those open-air fruit stands. They booked him for impersonating a police officer.

Dancing

When I graduated from the Arthur Murray dance school, I was voted the student most likely to return.

The ads for these dance schools are something! One school claimed they could teach me how to dance if I knew how to walk. That's my trouble—I don't know how to walk.

Dentists

For years I thought I had long white teeth—until my dentist pointed out to me that I just had short gums.

Boy, have I got a great dentist. The last time I went to him, he pulled one tooth and I screamed, "Hey, that wasn't the one." And he said, "I know, I'm coming to it."

My new dentist found a way around using Novocain. First you get in the chair, and the receptionist comes in and hands you the bill. After you pass out, they start drilling.

Doctors

I've got a crazy doctor. I was getting a checkup recently and he told me to walk over to the window and stick out my tongue. I said, "Why?" And he said, "I don't like the guy next door."

My doctor told me to stay off my feet. So I took up ice-skating.

Dogs

(Name of DJ) has a poodle named Fang. A very smart dog! (Name of DJ) says to him, "Fang, are you coming or aren't you?" And Fang either does or he doesn't.

When I was a little kid I had a dog named Spot. I'll never forget the day he disappeared. He drank some Mr. Clean—and GOODBYE SPOT!

Drinking

(Name of DJ) is a great guy. I always go to his birthday parties and help him drink up his presents.

I know a fellow who got plastered and he doesn't even drink. A ceiling fell in on him.

Driving

I used to be a safe driver, but I gave it up. Who wants to drive a safe?

I'm not saying that my son is a bad driver, but if the road turns when he does, it's a coincidence.

My wife said she wanted to learn to drive, so I got her a hammer and some nails.

I know some people who just moved to the area from Florida. They don't know how to handle driving in snow down there, but they knew a trick I'd never thought of. When they hear snow forecasted on the radio they go ahead and drive the car into a ditch—that way they beat the rush and get a tow truck right away.

Education

When I was a kid, my father helped me with my homework. Why, without him I would have never been in the fourth grade—I would have been in high school.

I finally left school because the principal said something I didn't like. He said, "You're expelled."

I don't know how many of you have experienced this same thing, but there is one thing I learned in college. I learned I should have stayed in high school.

Etiquette

Here's a point of etiquette to remember: Never chew tobacco, except when you're wearing a brown suit.

Never add cream and sugar to your coffee after it is in the saucer.

Family

Everyone in my family is called Bruno—except Mom, of course. Naturally we wouldn't call her Bruno. Bruno is her sister.

When I was working in Boston, I went with a girl who came from a family that was sooooooo old, it was condemned.

In our family, we run the house on a 50/50 basis. I wash the dishes, and my wife sweeps them up.

The secret to marital bliss is a house with two bathrooms.

Farming

I was brought up on a farm in Kansas. I'll never forget it. In the summer there it got so hot that the cows gave evaporated milk.

I have a friend in (town) who bought a truck farm—but it failed. He planted nine trucks and not one of them came up.

I used to work on a ranch some years ago. They bought four new horses and were looking for a groom. That's when I left—I wasn't ready to get married.

I don't think dairy farming is such a good business to get into. Everything you have you owe to udders.

Fighting

I remember a fight I had when I was in college. My opponent only came up to my chin. Trouble is, he came up once too often.

After my first amateur boxing match the referee gave me a can of varnish. It went with the shellacking I got.

I'll never forget a fight I once had. It was in a high school smoker. My opponent kept hitting and hitting me. Finally I brought one up from the floor . . . which is where I happened to be at the time.

Fishing

You know, one thing that's bothered me for years is: Are *all* fishermen liars, or do only liars fish?

I'll never forget fishing one day off the coast of California. I hooked a 900-pound tuna. He pulled on the line and I pulled on the line. He pulled on the line and I pulled on the line. Then, the line broke—and I got away.

Flying

The WZZZ air traffic reporter is really good. He can fly on instruments. Of course, he prefers an airplane.

You've got to have steady nerves to be a pilot. Why, if I was in a plane and the motor stopped, I'd just jump out and come down by parachute. And if the parachute didn't open, I'd just come on down anyway.

I went flying with the WZZZ air traffic reporter the other day. We flew so high there was nothing else up there but the stars and taxes.

I went flying with the WZZZ air traffic reporter again last week. Boy, that guy flies low! We were sooooooo low, he had me reach out and push the crosswalk button so we could get across a busy street.

Food

You know those home economics courses that the kids take in school? I had a girlfriend who once made me a rhubarb pie two feet long. She said she couldn't find a smaller rhubarb.

I understand that the Bicarbonate Soda Makers of America are putting out a new cookbook. It features dishes like fried sausages smothered in chocolate fudge gravy.

Just before coming here tonight I spent two hours picking splinters out of my teeth. But that's what I get for eating a club sandwich.

Football

When I was playing football someone once offered me a thousand dollars to throw a game. It would have been against my principles to take the thousand dollars—and a thousand dollars against my principles looked pretty good, so I took it.

I remember one football game I was in back in high school. One guy grabbed me by one leg and another guy grabbed the other leg. Then they said, "Make a wish."

Gambling

I'm against gambling myself—and what's more, I'll bet anyone two to one they don't legalize it.

I was in a card game not long ago. I could tell right away that the game was crooked. Nobody was playing the cards I dealt them.

I'm not saying that, as a card player (name of DJ) is a shifty dealer, but when he plays he shuffles his sleeve.

Golf

I'm a real golf nut. I even play in the winter in the snow. Instead of a regular golf ball, I use a lump of coal.

(Name of DJ) would be a great golfer except for one thing. He stands too close to the ball after he hits it.

I'm not too bad at golf, I guess. I broke 80 once—on a nine-hole course.

Health

Yesterday my doctor called me. Boy, was he sore! He said my check came back. Well, that makes us even—so did my cold.

Someone once told me that I've got more than three million organisms living on me. And that's not even counting my in-laws.

A couple of weeks ago I was bothered with shooting pains. First they came, then they disappeared, then they came back again. I guess they went out to reload.

Hobbies

My brother's got an unusual hobby. He likes to double-park . . . one car on top of another.

My wife has two hobbies. She swims and knits. It makes the wool a little soggy, but that's life.

Honeymoons

My wife and I have been married for some time now and the honeymoon is over. These days the only time we hold hands is when we play cards.

Horses

When you think of horses, you think of racehorses. And I remember last year out at (racetrack) a fellow was touting me on a horse to bet on. He said it was a sure winner because the jockey had halitosis so bad that the horse would win just trying to get away from him.

They say a horse is like a dog—man's best friend. But who wants to come home and have a horse jump up in your lap?

Hospitals

Out at the hospital, during every operation they wear masks. That's so if something goes wrong, nobody can identify them.

I got sick up in (town) not long ago and had to be taken to the hospital. And it was small. Didn't have private accommodations, just semiprivate . . . two to a bed.

Hotels

When I first got to (town), I stayed in a hotel downtown that advertised it was air-conditioned. And they were right. I've never seen air in such condition.

I remember a hotel I stayed in once. The bed was so hard I had to get up two times during the night to get some rest.

Housing

I'd like to buy one of those houses made of glass. And just for kicks I'd put in brick windows.

They say the newest homes feature things hidden in the walls. Nothing new about that. I once lived in a house that had things hidden in the walls. Every night we'd set traps for them.

You should see our house. It's the kind of place you can do a lot with if you're handy with money.

Hunting

In Africa once I came face to face with a ferocious lion. He crouched, then he sprang at me. But I was too smart for him—I ducked and he sailed right over my head. A week later I saw that same lion—do you know what he was doing? Practicing shorter jumps.

The last time I went duck hunting, even the decoys got away.

Ignorance

I'm not going to say that (football coach) has any ignorant players on the (school) team . . . but one tackle he had last year—that guy was sooooo dumb that when he won his varsity letter, someone had to read it to him.

There have been a few ignorant people here in (town). I remember one guy—they gave him the key to the city, and he locked himself out.

Insurance

One insurance company I heard of has paid over $2,000 for broken legs alone. I wonder what they do with all of them?

Invention

(Name of opponent) is a big man around campus in this town. He's the guy who invented the coed car pool.

My brother once invented an alarm clock that doesn't ring. It's for people who don't have a job.

I'm the guy who invented the *turkaroo*. I crossed a turkey with a kangaroo—and you can stuff it from the outside.

Jobs

A friend of mine in Hollywood has one of the oddest jobs I know of. He sells calamine lotion to cowboys with itchy trigger fingers.

I know a guy—he doesn't have an unusual job, but it's unusual for him. He's a one-armed sculptor. He puts a chisel in his mouth and hits the back of his head with the hammer.

My brother used to be a baseball player. Then his eyes went bad, so he became an umpire.

Lawyers

Lawyers have a new career opportunity these days, working in laboratories. It seems that the labs were having some trouble with the mice they use, so they started using lawyers—the lab technicians get attached to the mice, and there are some things that the mice just wouldn't do.

Laziness

Lazy—that describes my brother. He joined five unions so he would always be sure to be on strike.

(Name of DJ)—now *there's* a lazy guy. He was born with a silver spoon in his mouth and he hasn't stirred since.

Letters

Someone just handed me this letter. I think it's from (town). Look at the stamp—George Washington is holding his nose.

Manners

Here's something my mother taught me. Always put your hand over your mouth when you sneeze. It keeps your teeth from falling out.

Marriage

I met this wonderful girl and I finally asked her to marry me. But she said "No" and we've lived happily ever after.

(Name of DJ) is the bachelor on the WZZZ staff—and he says that he's not going to get married until he finds a girl who likes what he likes . . . *him!*

Men

I guess (name of DJ) qualifies as a man . . . and I'm not going to say that he's cheap—he just has ingrown pockets.

I understand that (name of man on opposing team) is a three-letter man here in college . . . I.O.U.

(Name of DJ) used to be a heavy drinker, but not anymore. He went on a diet.

Military Life

I want you to know that when I was in the Army, I was in the *shooting* Army— one night I won fifty bucks.

When I was in the service I was on KP so much I got a medical discharge for having dishpan hands.

I was an officer when I was in the Army. They made me a second lieutenant. They had to—I was too young to be a private.

Money

(Name of DJ) does very well in the broadcasting business. So well, in fact, that recently he has been buying St. Bernard dogs just for the brandy.

You probably read in the papers recently that the (music group) was offered a quarter-million dollars to play a one-night stand here. But I'm not interested in that kind of deal—it's not a steady paycheck.

As you may know, WZZZ Radio is owned by (some major local business leaders). And far be it from me to tell you they are getting rich off of this place, but last week our manager sold his Lincoln because the ashtrays were full. And the week before that he got rid of his Rolls Royce because it was facing the wrong direction.

Mothers-in-Law

My boss's mother-in-law never shows up at their house during the winter. She goes to California with them.

I just got back from a pleasure trip. Took my mother-in-law home.

What's a mother-in-law? I think she's a retired longshoreman.

Movies

When I was working down in California, I had a chance to appear in a motion picture. It was one of those big war epics. There were 100,000 soldiers on one side and 150,000 on the other. It would have been a big-budget movie except for one thing—we used real bullets.

I really think movies have gone downhill in recent years, but there are a few exceptions. I saw a great one the other night—in fact, it was so good that they are talking about making a book out of it.

There was a movie playing in town here recently—one of those super spy flicks, you know, and it was really bad. The story was taken from the files of the FBI—and they never missed it.

Navy

I was in the Navy during the war. I had the honor of being the first sailor in history to get seasick in the recruiting office.

When I was in the Navy we had one sailor on my ship who got washed overboard so often they couldn't get him dry behind the ears—so they made him an ensign.

Newspapers

I saw a great ad in the paper last Sunday; it gives you an idea of how bad the housing situation is getting. It said, "For sale: small furnished house, $69,000. If interested, will kill present occupants—20 chickens."

There was a help-wanted ad in the paper a couple of weeks ago. "Wanted: young man with fast car. Opportunity to make $5,000 for one hour's work. Apply at North Side Dry Cleaner's. If cop is watching, apply at *South* Side Dry Cleaner's."

Night Clubs

There's this place downtown—they have three waiters for every table. One gives you the check, and the other two revive you.

Parents

Some say we're all descended from monkeys. That's not true. My folks came from Wales.

Philosophy

I'll give you a bit of modern-day philosophy: What this country needs is a man who can be right *and* be president, too.

Living in the past has only one advantage—it's cheaper.

Picnics

Last summer we went out on a picnic one Saturday. What a picnic! The food was so bad I felt sorry for the ants.

Police

(Town) has one of the great police departments in the country. Not long ago a burglar, wearing calfskin gloves, robbed a safe. And a (town) detective took the fingerprints—five days later he arrested a cow.

Politics

In the campaigns last fall, things were so dull that I'm sure the candidates were writing their own speeches.

During the last elections I made so much money betting on the Democrats that I became a Republican.

Private Eyes

I was a private eye for a short time. I remember one time I was face-to-face with a killer. I aimed my gun at him and told him if he took one more step, I'd let him have it. So he took one more step and I let him have it. Who wants a lousy old gun anyway?

Private eyes have all sorts of troubles—like the one who got back to his office and found it turned upside down. He knew it was upside down because he tripped over the chandelier.

Psychiatry

(Name of DJ) is really cheap. He goes to a psychiatrist who is sooooo poor he can't afford a couch—he uses a lawn chair.

Radio

Our radio station is like any other radio station. We carry quite a few commercials for soap. You've heard them—they tell you how soothing their brand is. Well, now that they've made the soap less irritating, I wish they'd start working on the commercials.

Recreation

For recreation I like to fish. I have found the greatest place in the world for fishing. No, I'm not going to tell you where it is. But let me tell you this—those fish are so anxious to bite that you have to hide behind a tree to bait your hook.

I went fishing once—and I caught a huge head cold.

Some people go for outdoor recreation and some people go for indoor recreation—like playing bridge. And let me tell you, bridge is really a wonderful game. Especially for some folks. It gives them something to think about while they're talking.

Restaurants

I used to go to a seafood restaurant over in (name of town). But there was one thing wrong with their fish. Long time no sea.

(Popular restaurant) is probably this area's fanciest eating place. But not all of us can afford to go there. That place is so expensive, I can't even afford the tip.

Secretaries

What a secretary we've got here at WZZZ. One day I asked her to take dictation and she said, "Where to?"

Show Business

When I first got into this business, I had stage fright so bad that they called me Old Man Quiver.

There is an example of show business right here. There's a guy down there who thinks we're so bad he keeps saying "*Up* in front."

Sports

I play quite a bit of golf. Yesterday, I broke 80—and that's a lot of clubs for one day.

When I got out of high school, I thought I was a pretty tough kid. And I was a good fighter so a friend of mine talked me into taking a fling at boxing. After my first fight, the referee came over and picked up my hand. Then he picked up my legs, and my teeth, my jaw . . . .

Television

Personally, I think it's television that is bringing radio back.

This was not one of the great seasons for TV shows. You remember (show name)—it was so bad that even the camera operators didn't watch it.

Travel

When you travel to France there are four words you should learn. "You forgot my change."

Travel, it's great. It's wonderful in Southern California this time of year. You can open your window and hear the birds coughing.

Las Vegas is a wonderful place to travel to. But there are poor people in Las Vegas, too. Of course, they weren't poor when they got there.

Troubles

Last year I got in a lot of trouble with the Internal Revenue Service. You know that little box at the top of your tax form that says: DO NOT WRITE IN THIS SPACE? Well, I wrote in it.

If you think you've got troubles, just consider the nearsighted hen who sat on a snowball.

Vacations

Last year I spent a lot more on my vacation than I planned to. I forgot that post-card postage had gone up again.

I took my family on a vacation last month and it really was a change for me, a change for my wife—and a few thousand changes for the baby.

Wealth

Some people say that (name of DJ) is wealthy. I don't know about that. I do know he weighs 200 pounds—and only 152 without his money belt.

I once knew a kid who was sooooooo rich . . . that he mixed alphabet soup with buckwheat flour and served monogrammed pancakes.

Weather

It rains a lot here, but not where I come from. It's dry. I remember one day a farmer got hit by a raindrop and he fainted. They had to throw buckets of sand in his face to revive him.

Palm Springs—now there's a place for weather—all of it hot. The last time I was there, one day I stepped into a pool of water and my feet didn't even get wet. I looked down and saw the water just disappearing. It was so hot, the tongues of my shoes were lapping it up.

Weddings

We went to a wedding recently. It was one of those high-class California-style weddings. The bride wore a veil so long it almost covered her jeans.

You know in the wedding ceremony when the bride promises to love, honor, and obey. Sometimes I think that's the world's oldest joke.

Wives

My wife has been missing for three days now. I'd go down to the police station and give them her description—but they'd never believe it.

My wife is not one of the great cooks in the world. All she knows how to do is fry things. And lately I have become a little suspicious of her. She keeps putting ground glass in my food—claims it cuts the grease.

I had a terrible dream last night. I dreamed my wife and Kim Basinger were fighting over me—and my wife won.

My wife has changed a lot since I married her. She's changed my friends, my habits, my food . . . .

Wolves

(Name of DJ) is a sort of a wolf. At least he's the only guy I know who buys a dozen of those cards that say: *"To the only girl I ever loved."*

(Name of DJ) says he's not a wolf—but if I was Little Red Riding Hood, I wouldn't even trust him with my grandmother.

THE WZZZ SIGN PAINTERS   3.5

Get a billboard from an outdoor advertising company for each of your disc jockeys. Lease the boards for a period of 30 days. Have the outdoor company cover each board with white paper and you are ready to start.

How It Works

Assign a billboard to each DJ. It then becomes his or her responsibility to decorate it in any way that seems fit. The station provides the paint, a ladder or scaffold, and coveralls with your call sign and the DJ's name on the back.

The DJ then works on the billboard for an hour a day, giving the teaser effect from the boards as they gradually take shape. There are certain components that should go on each board: your call sign, frequency, station logo/slogan, the DJ's name, and the hours of the DJ's airshift. Aside from that, the DJ is allowed a free hand in determining the content (within the limits of good taste). Your air personalities will be working on their signs for about two weeks.

After the sign boards have been completed, invite the art directors (and possibly presidents, too) of local ad agencies to lunch. Take them around to view each board. They are the judges who select the best (or worst!) billboard. This will give you a chance for additional publicity on the stunt.

Billboards today often feature very slick and sophisticated artwork and photography. The simplicity or crudeness of your DJ's creations will assure their noticeability.

On-Air Copy

Most of the on-air plugs for this promotion will come naturally in the DJ chatter as they try to explain, excuse, or justify their own billboards, or to level "artistic criticism" at the efforts of the coworkers. However, here are some on-air spots that may suggest a theme or may be used as teasers.

HAVE YOU NOTICED ANYTHING UNUSUAL IN THE WAY OF BILLBOARD ART AROUND CENTERVILLE LATELY? IT'S THE WZZZ DISC JOCKEYS AT WORK WITH OUR DO-IT-YOURSELF BILLBOARD KITS. WE EACH HAVE BEEN GIVEN OUR OWN BILLBOARD, BRUSH, AND PAINT. THEY TOLD US TO CREATE BILLBOARDS PUBLICIZING OUR OWN SHOWS. SO, WE'RE DOING IT. AND WE'RE TAKING IT PRETTY SERIOUSLY, TOO—ALTHOUGH IT MAY NOT LOOK IT. THE BILLBOARDS WILL BE JUDGED ON THEIR ARTISTIC MERIT (IF ANY). YOU CAN SEE THE WZZZ AIR ACES AT WORK ON OUR DO-IT-YOURSELF BILLBOARDS EVERY DAY. I'LL BE WORKING ON MINE AT (location) FROM NOON TILL 1 P.M. TODAY. DROP BY AND SAY HELLO.

* * * *

THE WZZZ DISC JOCKEYS HAVE EACH BEEN GIVEN THEIR OWN BILLBOARD TO DECORATE AS THEY SEE FIT. IF YOU'RE DRIVING BY AND SEE ONE OF THEM AT WORK, STOP BY AND OFFER YOUR SUGGESTIONS. AT LAST REPORT, THEY COULD USE SOME HELP.

* * * *

WE WZZZ DISC JOCKEYS HAVE FINALLY GOTTEN WHAT WE WANTED. WE'VE EACH GOT A WHOLE BILLBOARD TO ADVERTISE OUR OWN SHOWS. BUT THE CATCH IS—WE HAVE TO DECORATE THE BILLBOARDS OURSELVES. AFTER ALL OUR HOLLERING, WE'VE GOT TO COME UP WITH SOMETHING GOOD, SO IF YOU FOLKS AT HOME HAVE ANY IDEAS ON HOW WE SHOULD DO IT, DROP US A POSTCARD. BETTER YET, STOP BY OUR SIGNS AND BE SIDEWALK SUPERVISORS. I'LL BE UP THERE, WORKING ON MY BILLBOARD AT (location) EVERY WEEKDAY FROM NOON TILL ONE. COME ON OUT—AND BRING A PAINTBRUSH.

* * * *

Voice #1: (Echo) THEY SAID IT COULDN'T BE DONE!

Voice #2: TAKE SEVERAL DISC JOCKEYS FROM RADIO Z-46—WITH NO TRAINING IN ART OR PAINTING. GIVE THESE PEOPLE BRUSHES, PAINT, A BILLBOARD—AND LET THEM CREATE THEIR OWN LIVING TESTIMONIALS TO THEIR SHOWS.

Voice #1: THEY SAID IT COULDN'T BE DONE!

Voice #2: HAVE THESE WZZZ DISC JOCKEYS CREATE OUTSTANDING EXAMPLES OF BILLBOARD ART—DRAWING THE ADMIRING GLANCES OF THOUSANDS OF RESIDENTS OF CENTERVILLE.

Voice #1: THEY SAID IT COULDN'T BE DONE!

Voice #3: (female) WELL, I'VE SEEN THOSE WZZZ BOARDS, AND I SAY IT HASN'T BEEN DONE!

NEEDLE IN A HAYSTACK   3.6

Here is an outside event that is a party for some of the young people in your area and a lot of fun for the station. It will attract the younger set, including the participants and their parents who will come to cheer the kids on.

How It Works

WZZZ invites a number of Boy and Girl Scout Troops or similar groups to compete in the "WZZZ Needle in a Haystack Hunt." The station provides refreshments for the entire group. A needle or moderately small nail (make sure it's blunt) is tossed into a haystack that has been piled up in the WZZZ parking lot. The different groups draw straws to determine who goes first. Then each group in order gets 10 minutes to try finding the needle. Your sportscaster or one of your DJs calls the play-by-play on the frantic search that takes place.

The "Needle in a Haystack" hunt is intended to be a simple fun-type outside promotion, but in some areas it will be received with tremendous enthusiasm. In this case, you may wish to award a trophy to the winning troop, with their troop name and number inscribed on it. They can keep the trophy, or a more-elaborate "traveling trophy" can be defended and passed to the winning troop each year.

The Prizes

Whichever group is successful finding the needle receives a prize for the entire gang. Prizes can include something for the group as a whole, such as a cruise, a movie, a pizza party, or an afternoon at the pool, or each individual in the winning group may receive a prize, such as an item of camping equipment.

Follow-Up Gimmicks

As an additional prize, the WZZZ air personalities become honorary members of the scout troop on the following Saturday. On that day, your air staff works with the winning troop doing good deeds with the real scouts supervising. The DJ/scouts fan out through the downtown area or mall to help folks carry packages, walk dogs, change flat tires, and so forth. Be sure to inform the local papers and TV stations of your activities so they can cover the good deeds and get some pictures.

On-Air Copy

HOW LONG DOES IT TAKE TWENTY YOUNG BOY SCOUTS TO FIND A NEEDLE IN A HAYSTACK? WZZZ FINDS OUT THIS SATURDAY WHEN SCOUTS FROM TROOPS _____, _____, AND _____ IN CENTERVILLE SEARCH FOR A NEEDLE IN A HAYSTACK IN THE WZZZ PARKING LOT. THEY WON'T WIN MERIT BADGES IF THEY FIND IT BUT THE WINNING TROOP WILL GO FOR A WEEKEND CRUISE AS THE HAYSTACK-HUNTING CHAMPIONS OF CENTERVILLE. COME DOWN AND JOIN THE FUN THIS SATURDAY IN THE WZZZ PARKING LOT. THERE ARE REFRESHMENTS AND FUN FOR ALL IN THE "WZZZ NEEDLE IN A HAYSTACK HUNT."

* * * *

CENTERVILLE BOY SCOUTS HUNT FOR A NEEDLE IN A HAYSTACK THIS SATURDAY IN THE WZZZ PARKING LOT. COME DOWN AND WATCH THE STRAW FLY AS TROOPS _____, _____, AND _____ COMPETE FOR THE HAYSTACK CHAMPIONSHIP. THERE'S A WONDERFUL PRIZE FOR THE WINNING TROOP. THIS SATURDAY IN THE WZZZ PARKING LOT—THE "WZZZ NEEDLE IN A HAYSTACK HUNT."

3.7 SUMMER OLYMPICS

Setting up a local "Summer Olympics" for the young people of your area is an ambitious yet tremendously effective outside promotion for the summertime. This takes some effort to set up, but you can be assured of help and cooperation from civic groups and officials. It can be done on a small scale, but it is expandable to the point where hundreds can participate. It'll become the focal point of local attention when it is held.

How It Works

The promotion is this: WZZZ sponsors a Summer Olympics event for local youth. It can be done by your station alone, or in cooperation with other entities like the local newspaper. The event should be held on a Saturday, or it can span the entire weekend. The variations on this idea are so many that we won't even try to map them all out. Let your imagination be your guide.

You May Need Help

As mentioned above, getting the best effect from this promotion will require considerable effort. For this reason we strongly suggest you consider inviting cosponsorship, either with a civic organization, a commercial outlet, or both.

This promotion will undoubtedly appeal to civic organization, such as the JAYCEEs and Kiwanis clubs. Their cosponsorship is of value because they represent enthusiasm, influence, and available labor.

In addition, many local firms participate wholeheartedly in community activities such as this, and they represent all of the above qualities—plus money for underwriting expenses. Types of firms you might approach with the offer of cosponsorship of the Summer Olympics include car dealers, sporting goods outlets, and department stores. You will also need the help and cooperation of the local park board or school district if you use their facilities, equipment, officials, and advice.

Do not be scared off by the frequent reference to "you"—perhaps you envision more work than the busy schedule of your station and staff permits. But keep in mind that many people will be anxious to assist. When you propose a major sports event focused on your local kids during the summer, plenty of people will agree that this is a good idea and will work hard to make it successful. Your contributions of strong on-the-air support for them and the project will be the major direction of your effort, and the key to the success of the "WZZZ Summer Olympics."

The Scope of the Event

The "WZZZ Summer Olympics" will be effective on about any size scale. You may confine it to a four-hour period on a Saturday afternoon with a limited schedule of track and field events confined to a certain age group. Or you may make this an interschool or even intercity event involving a wide range of outdoor sports. You're not competing with regular school athletics at this time of year, so this can be a major event for the kids.

Perks and Precautions

- Have participants register upon arrival on the day of the Olympics. Include on the registration form a standard release statement protecting the sponsors of the event from liability in case of injury or property damage. (Ask your station's lawyer to help you on this one.)
- Check with soft drink distributors in your area. Many of them have portable concession stands that you can rent (or borrow at no charge!).
- Arrange for adequate portable restroom facilities to be donated.
- Arrange for the donated use of one or more tents to shelter staff and officials from sun, wind, or rain.

Work with Organized Groups

In any case, you will have to work with existing groups of youngsters. Depending on what age group you decide to direct the meet toward, teams may represent some of these groups: Boy Scout or Girl Scout troops, neighborhood YMCAs, community centers, church athletic teams, or teams organized from athletic programs at city parks and playgrounds.

If you intend to make this a major sports event, contact the high school track coaches in your listening area. Teams could be entered representing different schools, providing you with youths trained in track events and possibly aided by the coaches themselves. You will have to get to work in the spring, well before the start of summer vacation, if you decide to go in this direction.

3.8   HOT DAY PROMOTION

When the thermometer has reached the summer peak point for your area, and after the heat wave has continued for a few days, try these "cool" gimmicks:

- Have your air personalities fan out through parks, malls, the downtown area, and so on and hand out hand-held fans with the station's call, frequency, and logo imprinted on them.
- Hand out WZZZ ice cubes—inside each cube is frozen a nonsoluble capsule (available through drug wholesalers) in which you place a piece of paper. Most of the papers carry station plugs, but some may contain gift coupons for prizes that can be claimed at the stores of your sponsors.

CONVERTIBLE CAR 3.9

Buy one of your air personalities a cheap old car, which he or she is going to convert into a convertible to take advantage of summer weather. Your DJ starts by cutting a small hole in the top with a saber saw or pneumatic cutting chisel. This hole is expanded each day or new ones started elsewhere on the car. As the summer wears on, the whole car takes on a "swiss cheese" look, until little is left but the frame and motor.

The car can be put on display at stores and malls, used in parades, or just driven around town. Be sure to hang signs (on whatever is left!) indicating that this car is the "WZZZ Special Summer Convertible."

Caution:

- Be sure your DJ uses protective clothing and safety glasses while cutting down the car.

- Consult with a mechanic about what portions of the car should not be cut away for safety reasons.

ELECTION BET PAYOFFS 3.10

Following every general election a rash of people do zany things to pay off election bets that proved to be ill-advised. Your DJs can have some good fun on the air and get some exposure to the public by challenging each other to back up their political beliefs with a bet.

How It Works

To pay off on the bet, the losing air personality must endure some attention-getting stunt. With this in mind, here are some suggestions that can pay off both in on-air topics and publicity for the station. Each situation offers photo opportunities that should interest your local papers.

Egghead Golf

Loser's penalty is to play one hole of golf at a local course. The "ball" is an egg—*not* hardboiled. Every time the raw-egg golfball breaks, your DJ must tee up and start toward the hole again.

Poster Picking

The loser is put in charge of WZZZ's poster-picking parade. With a large truck, tractor, or horse-drawn wagon (or a caravan led by an elephant and a donkey) and a troop of scouts, the loser tours your city, collecting every political campaign poster in sight. The scouts fan out, pick up the posters, and load them in the truck. For every poster collected in the effort, WZZZ pays the troop a nickel to go either into the troop treasury or toward the troop's selected charity.

The vehicle, of course, has prominent signs and an attention-getter such as a bell or electronic horn that plays tunes. From time to time your mobile unit can check in with the little caravan to see how they're doing. (This is a variation on the "Pennies for Political Posters" promotion and can be effectively developed into a strong annual event to help clean up the city after election day passes.)

Political Fence

Since the loser "was on the wrong side of the political fence," he or she must find a way to get to the other side. In a large department store or shopping center, the losing DJ sits "on the wrong side of the fence"—an actual section of fence with a gate in it.

The gate is secured by a combination lock. The person who can work the combination and get the DJ "on the right side of the fence" wins a merchandise prize from the store or group of stores. Clues are broadcast on WZZZ and the loser stays there, even missing a shift or more if necessary, until someone wins with the right combination. Since this is a promotion of a sales nature, it can be given good air support. You may want to develop it into a major contest by including additional requirements and tying the clues into the store or shopping center.

3.11 ATHLETE OF THE MONTH

This promotion will work particularly well if your station places any emphasis on sports coverage. It can be continued throughout the school year without wearing thin. In fact, it should gain momentum as it continues and can easily develop into something repeatable.

How It Works

Nominations for the WZZZ Athlete of the Month are received by the station. Depending on how the nominations are handled, judging can be done by your sports director or news staff, a group of high school coaches, or some outside group of judges. The monthly winners become eligible to run for the title of WZZZ Athlete of the Year come June.

Nominations

Getting nominations for the "Athlete of the Month" promotion can be handled in several ways. The nominations can be made by the high school coaches for the sports being played in the various times of year. In this case, there should be two nominated from each high school. Your own sports/news staff can make the nominations. Or nominations can be thrown open to the public. If so, without any fanfare, a preliminary judging of the nominees from each school might be done by the individual coaches involved to get the list from each school down to two or three. We suggest that you make nominations open to the public, since this involves more people in the promotion.

Judging

The best manner to handle the judging is to have it done by a group of local sports luminaries. They will be glad to do it. This will keep the coaches and you off the hot seat. If the former sports stars you select for judges have any local high school background, be sure to maintain a proper balance of representations among all the schools.

The Award

Get a suitable plaque or cup through a company that specializes in trophies or through a jeweler who handles this type of thing. In addition to "WZZZ Athlete of the Month," the name and school of each winner should be engraved on the plaque or cup. This should be given to the school of your next winner the following month. The winners should receive for themselves printed certificates proclaiming them as "WZZZ Athlete of the Month." Any printer either stocks or can get fancy certificate forms, which are then imprinted with the information you specify. The cost is nominal and such certificates are very handsome.

By all means try to have one of your air personalities present the award at a school assembly. The added impetus that this will give to the whole promotion is immeasurable.

Year-End Award

From the nine monthly winners will be selected the young person to be named "WZZZ Athlete of the Year." The individual winning this important title should receive a personal plaque or cup to keep. A matching trophy should go to the school for permanent display.

3.12 DISC JOCKEY RACES

Numerous sporting events take place in your area during the year. Here are some suggestions on how to get your DJs on the scene promoting your station. The people in charge of such events will be anxious to cooperate with you since the appearance of your air personalities will assure them a large quantity of publicity for the event. Your station's participation will also help bring in the crowd.

Horserace Track

If there is a horserace track in your area, either a commercial one or one at the county fairgrounds, set up a special Saturday event in which your disc jockeys participate. Perhaps this race can be part of a charity fund-raiser or just a promotional stunt for the county fair.

You might try a burrow or donkey race if the animals are available. Everyone will have a lot more fun if the animals are balky. You can add a crazy twist if each racer uses a different animal, such as a donkey, a cow, an elephant, or a llama.

Dress your DJs in the most outlandish manner possible for the race. The WZZZ call letters should be clearly featured on the costumes, of course.

Stock Car Races

If there is a stock car track in your area, here is a way for your station to participate. Get a feud going between two of your DJs on the air—they can argue about who is the better driver. The result of the grudge match between your air personalities is a demolition derby for just the two of them. If the track does not have cars available for this, you can get them through a used car dealer who will gladly provide them in exchange for the promotional value of sponsoring the event.

Paint the cars brightly with the station's call, frequency, logo, and the name of the disc jockey. Humorous slogans are fine, too, as are "racy" names for your two drivers: "Hurricane Hank" or "Fearless Frank." Start the event out as a legitimate stock car race. Then, after a couple of laps one DJ might bump the other. Or, if one is getting way behind, he can stop and wait for the other to come around. Then the demolition derby part begins, continuing until one car can't go anymore.

Consult with professional racers familiar with demolition derby racing. They'll help you prepare both the cars and drivers for this kind of race. Keep it safe and fun for everyone.

Ping-Pong Ball Derby

Lay out a course, and have a contest between your DJs. Whoever pushes the Ping-Pong ball across the finish line first is the winner. The only snag is that the ball must be pushed by noses only.

Stilt Race

Your air personalities can all "get up in the world" by competing on stilts. Each time a participant falls off, he or she must go back to the starting line and begin again.

Ostrich Race

Several groups of these animals tour the country and are used in various promotional events. Such a race among your disc jockeys should pull a good-sized crowd. The DJ's ride in sulkies similar to those used on horse-trotting races. An ostrich is a real runner and the race should be exciting. Adding to the fun, you can steer an ostrich with a long-handled broom by holding it out on either side of the bird's head. To turn right, just hold it by the animal's left eye—and hope for the best!

You'll need a large group of "handlers" to keep things under control; once you get an ostrich running, the only way to stop it is to have three or four husky guys there to grab him and stop him.

ANIMAL SAFETY SYMBOL   3.13

If yours is a station that is really promoting traffic safety and accident prevention, you'll go to considerable lengths to build community awareness of your station's emphasis on it. Here is a means of reaching youngsters with your traffic safety message. It capitalizes on the idea that animals always fascinate the very young.

Not a Promotion—A Theme

This isn't a specific promotion, but rather a peg to hang your traffic safety pitch on, and to increase its effectiveness. In every locale you'll have varying situations where this theme will gain you mileage.

A living safety symbol of this sort is a natural attention-getter at any public gathering and will get frequent exposure in the newspapers. It offers something visual plus helps accomplish something of positive community interest. *And*, your call letters get exposure.

How It Works

The idea is this: WZZZ obtains a bird or animal as the station's traffic safety symbol, which is used solely to associate safety and WZZZ. "Elmer, the WZZZ Safety Elephant" (or whatever) gives advice, safety tips, and makes public appearances with WZZZ air personalities. The appeal here is to get the safety message to the kids—they'll pass it on to the grownups. Your living safety symbol should be used on posters and mailers, and take part in traffic safety campaigns conducted by other organizations.

Renting or Borrowing an Animal

Unless your station's facilities are pretty unique, we don't suggest you set up a branch zoo out back by the west tower! You can rent or borrow the animal you choose to use as a safety symbol from a farm, a zoo, or circus, or from some other source in your area. You may end up with a Safety Elephant, a Cautious Cow or Camel, a Traffic-Wise Owl, a Prudent Pig, a Beware Bear—who knows?

Using the Animal

Here are some specific ways to use the safety animal:

1. On the opening week of school, WZZZ's Safety Elephant escorts young-sters across the school crossings at elementary schools in your area. He wears a sign or poster warning motorists to use extra caution now that school is back in session.

2. Schools visited by WZZZ's Safety Elephant are awarded a special pennant to fly above the school as long as none of the youngsters are involved in a traffic mishap going to or from school.

3. Run a contest asking youngsters to draw a poster of WZZZ's Safety Ele-phant with a safety slogan caption. Reproduce exactly the winning poster or posters for use on school bulletin boards, or use them as ads in community newspapers.

3.14 HUNTER'S SAFETY VISION CHECK

With the advent of the fall hunting season, here's a simple yet extremely timely and effective promotion that again emphasizes your station's constant concern over serving the citizens of your area. As the vast army of hunters increases every year in most parts of the country, this promotion makes a good annual event that will not lose its impact no matter how often it is repeated through the years.

How It Works

This is a joint promotion with your local optometric association or with a large local optometrist's firm. It simply consists of setting up facilities whereby WZZZ offers free eye examinations to hunters prior to the start of the hunting season. The purpose, obviously, is to increase hunting safety.

The facilities may be located in the WZZZ parking lot or lobby if the station is located in a good spot for this. If not, make arrangements to set up an eye check downtown, or in a shopping center or mall. Or you can make arrangements with a mobile home dealer to provide a trailer where you can set up a temporary eye-check station.

Duration

This is a quickie promotion designed to create a service impression on your listeners. You will probably not want to conduct the safety vision check for more than one or two days at the most. However, you will want to give it a heavy volume of on-air promotion a few days prior to and all through conducting the check.

Vast crowds aren't as important in this promotion as the fact that your station and the local optometrists are thoughtful enough of the public welfare to provide the service. Naturally, you'll share the credit with the optometrists.

TOYS FOR TOTS DANCE   3.15

In every area a number of organizations gather used toys for repair and redistribution to needy children at Christmas. In the United States one of the best examples of this is the annual Toys for Tots campaign staged by the Marine Corps Reserve. However, the promotion can be easily modified and adapted to suit the needs of any other group that regularly conducts such a campaign for used toys. For instance, it is a common practice in many areas for the local fire departments to do such work.

The Toys for Tots Dance is another promotion that is a creative public service—a public service program that does a fundamental and imaginative job, and that goes beyond the mechanism of mere spot announcements.

How It Works

Working directly with an organization that collects used toys for poor children at Christmas, your station organizes and stages a big public dance. The price of admission is a toy to be turned over to the charity group. Essentially that is all there is to it. You gather a large number of needed toys, do a major publicity job for the overall toy collection campaign, and everyone involved has a wonderful time in the process.

Cooperation from the Charity Group

Obviously, because of the scope of this promotion, you are going to need considerable outside assistance. The sponsoring organization of the toy collection campaign should be in a position to provide such assistance. Since you expect to attract hundreds of couples to your dance, you are going to need this group's cooperation supervising the dance. They can probably do a more effective job than your station staff anyway. Perhaps they can also handle the advance preparations, such as arranging for the dance hall, decorations, refreshments, and chaperons (and bouncers).

The charity's active participation in the event will generate an overall enthusiasm that will help assure the success of your dance, so enlisting their participation in the setup (and cleanup) details will pay off for everyone concerned.

Targeting an Age Group

There are many types of dances you can stage: rock, 50s, swing-era, square, bluegrass—it all depends on your format and local interests. Your station's music format will probably be the determining factor. If there is any doubt about the public's acceptance of the style of dance you're putting on, be sure your promos are specific about the music, dancing style, and age groups expected. You won't be able to please everyone's tastes in a single event, so you should head off anything that would lead to resentment and an unsuccessful event. Making your promos specific about the dance's target audience will help.

Getting the Hall

One thing to remember in lining up a hall is to be sure to get one that is large enough. If you promote your dance properly, you should have a huge turnout. The best bet is a hall that is regularly used for dances and that has plenty of floor space and seating.

The hall should be donated for the purposes of this charity dance. The owners will receive an ample return in publicity since every time you mention the dance on the air you will be talking about their facility. Also, they will get a monetary return through the operation of the concessions on the night of the dance. And, except under the most unusual circumstances, you will be much better off to leave the operation of such concessions to the owners of the hall.

Music

You have your choice of recorded or live music. Try to line up a live group if at all possible—a dance with live music is about 75 percent better than one using canned music, even if a good dance-style DJ is present.

Do not automatically assume that the local musicians unions will not cooperate. Such unions have a special fund set up to cover free appearances. Also, it may be possible to get approval from the union's board for its members to appear at your dance. Remember, this can be an opportunity for the union to get some well-deserved publicity. Most of the public thinks that musicians are always taking, without realizing the many contributions they make to worthy causes. It is reasonable to talk to the union and suggest that the station share billing with them, something like " . . . the big Toys for Tots dance is being staged by WZZZ and the Centerville Musicians Union."

Even if you cannot arrange for live music, you can still have a highly successful affair with recorded music. However, in this case you will have to doubly emphasize the other parts of the program you will be putting on at the dance.

An Entertaining Program

A dance such as this provides you with an excellent opportunity to get personal exposure for your air staff members. So plan to have them all on hand. If any of them are performers in their own right, be sure to include their acts in the show. And all of them should rotate as emcees throughout the dance.

To bolster the promotion, you will want to line up any "name" talent that is available for appearances at your dance. Be sure to give them plenty of on-air publicity because the use of their names will help increase the turnout.

Do not—repeat, *do not*—inflict any lengthy speeches of gratitude by members of the charity group on the people who come to the dance. Keep the show moving. Remember, they came to dance and have a good time. If you wish to have the head of the charity say a very few words of welcome and thanks at the end of the intermission, that's all right. But limit it to that.

Dollar Dance

As stated, the admission price to the event is a toy. But you can raise some extra operating cash for the charity by staging a special dollar dance during the evening. At some point when the dance floor has been completely cleared, have a special dollar dance—the only dancers will be those couples who drop a dollar in the bin up front. Don't have more than one of these during the evening. You can either collect at the beginning of the dollar-dance segment of the program or instruct everyone to dance by the dollar bin during the number and make their contribution.

Types of Toys

In your on-air promos for the dance you will want to specify that the price of admission is a toy—Either new toys or ones that are in reasonably good condition are acceptable. Also specify that admission price is one toy per person, not one per couple.

Many people will go out and buy a new toy in order to be able to attend your dance. For an occasion like this you should not be bothered with individuals showing up with toys so old and worn that they are useless. However, be sure to emphasize that used toys are perfectly acceptable. In so doing, you will help promote all of the other phases of the charity's campaign to collect toys.

You may want to consider storing the toys for a day or two after the dance. Perhaps some dancer's younger sister or brother will come wailing to you about a toy given up involuntarily, and if you still have the toys on hand there's a chance that it can be located and returned. The returned toy will be more than made up through the goodwill generated for the charity and your station.

Additional Toys

Undoubtedly, there will be many people anxious to contribute a toy to the campaign after hearing about your dance, yet they won't be able to attend the dance. You should inform these people that the toys can be dropped off at your station. You can also place collection bins in a shopping mall near a children's toy store.

Perhaps the charity group has volunteers who can go out and pick up toys. If so, your station can be the clearing house for phone calls from donors, and you can then turn this information over to the charity, or have your lobby be the dispatching point for the volunteers.

In all probability, the charity will arrange for several pickup points around the city as a part of its overall campaign. You can promote these through a tag announcement on your regular spots for the dance. At any rate, you should certainly make an effort to get additional toys besides those that will be brought to the dance.

Final Report

After the dance is over, you will want to inform the public about the results of your effort. This is often overlooked in this type of promotion. The report should state how many toys were received, how much money was contributed at the dollar dance, and how many needy children will have a happier Christmas because of the generosity of your listeners.

Annual Affair

If your Toys for Tots Dance goes as well as we think it should, you will want to plan it as an annual affair. Promotions like this have a habit of gathering momentum over a period of years. Besides, after the first year you will have ironed out most of the problems and will have a comparatively simple time of it on future occasions.

CHRISTMAS AT THE ZOO   3.16

While everyone is bustling about buying presents and bubbling with the spirit of Christmas, few give thought to the animal friends who give them so much enjoyment throughout the summer months. But a compassionate WZZZ disc jockey is dedicated to making sure that there is Christmas at the zoo!

How It Works

About two weeks before Christmas one of your DJs announces that the animals at the zoo will not be forgotten this holiday season. To ensure their having a Merry Christmas, your air personality will take them all presents two days before Christmas.

For the next few days the DJ compiles a list of appropriate gifts for all of the animals, enlisting the help of listeners to make up the list and donate the gifts. Then, two days before Christmas, the WZZZ Zoo Santa delivers all the gifts to the animals, inviting everyone to join in the fun. The deliveries can be taped or covered live—a good photo opportunity for the local papers and TV stations.

Coordinating with the Zoo

If you decide to set up a Christmas at the zoo, be sure to enlist the cooperation of the zoo officials in your plan from the start. Especially if the gifts consist of food for the beasts, the animal experts will want to have a hand in it from the beginning. In fact, a good part of the stunt on the air is to call the zoo daily and confer with them on the air about what the appropriate gifts should be. Zoo officials will be happy to cooperate for the publicity they will receive—a reminder to the public that the zoo is a year-round attraction and enjoyment.

Publicity

Be sure you get pictures of your "Christmas at the Zoo." And don't forget to invite the local papers and TV stations; there is a good chance they'll want to cover the event.

One publicity shot you might consider working out is a twist on the old image of Santa and his sleigh pulled by reindeer. Instead, have your DJ dressed as Santa, and have him pull a sleigh in which a reindeer is seated—a *real* reindeer, if the zoo has one available.

Include the Public

Get everyone in on the act as much as possible. In addition to asking for their help in selecting the gifts, ask them to donate gifts. Of course, on the day of the event, you'll want to invite the public to be on hand to serve as "Santa's helpers."

3.17   TOY BOAT RACE

This is an outstanding summertime promotion that's wild and amusing. If you have any doubts about its appeal to the general public, just consider the times you have put a small boat, stick, or even a leaf into a stream and watched in fascination as it drifted off.

How It Works

You announce that you are staging your "First-Annual Toy Boat Race." Anyone can enter a craft. The requirements are minimal:

- The craft can be anything that floats.
- It cannot have a source of power.
- The name and address of the entrant must be attached to the craft.

• It must be less than three feet long and at least six inches long.

This means that almost anything can qualify as an entry—a regular toy boat, a tree branch, an old jogging shoe, or anything that will float through the entire race.

Running the Race

The entrants will not race their craft themselves. This will be handled by your air personalities and other designated officials of the race. Each craft has a number attached to it as a means of identification. The race can be staged on a major river or a small stream. It can even be staged on an ocean shore.

The craft are started in groups of about 10 and sent off from the starting line about two minutes apart. Those that make it to the finish line are timed in. The total elapsed time is used to determine the winners. You can also stage the race by categories, either according to size or type of craft.

Bringing Out the Crowd

Be sure to pick a racecourse setting where a good-sized crowd can come out and witness the race. Have your air personalities out on the water in regular boats acting as officials. And try to have some local celebrities enter a craft in the race and encourage them to come out and participate. You may even wish to have a separate "celebrity" race.

Prizes

To add to this promotion, have a large number of prizes to award to the winners. There should be a couple of prizes of real value, a large number of relatively small value, and a few goofy ones. The ideal top prize would be a real boat, complete with motor and trailer.

Judges

You will need a fairly large number of judges. Most of them should be at the finish line. They will all have to have synchronized watches. Their main job will be to time the boats in at the end of the course. These times will then have to be balanced against the starting times to determine the elapsed time for each craft that finishes.

Sell It

This promotion is a natural to sell to a boat marina that has a location on or near your racecourse. If you do sell it to such a sponsor, ask the account to provide boats for your air personalities to use. This should give excellent exposure to the boating outlet's product.

You can use the marina's place of business as a spot where the entering craft can be brought and displayed in the days ahead of the race. The promotion can also be sold to other types of sponsors, and their places of business can still be used as a location for displaying the craft.

Name That Boat

To add some fun and personality to this promotion, encourage the entrants to name their craft, perhaps prodding them toward unusual names. This will provide you with some good material to use on the air.

Make It an Annual Event

We are sure that once you see how much fun and excitement this promotion generates, you will want to make it an annual affair. Each year you can add some new twists to keep it alive.

3.18 SURVIVAL TEST

Here is a happy sort of promotion to capitalize on the interest that survival tests and obstacle courses have gained. It contains built-in publicity angles that almost assure you of good coverage in the print media. In addition, it will give your station and one of your DJs excellent outside exposure.

How It Works

Basically, what you conduct is a survival test in reverse. Instead of trying to find out how much hardship a man can endure, you try to determine how long your DJ can stand absolute luxury and service. The reason you do this, of course, is in the interest of research. With new labor-saving gadgets entering our lives daily, it is important to know if we can survive the luxuries that progress has made possible.

The WZZZ Survival Test involves putting one of your DJs into the finest hotel in town, with the entire place at his disposal during the stay. He should also do his regular show from the hotel suite and do telephone bits with the other DJs on their shows. His every wish (within limits, described later) is met until he breaks under the strain of living in the lap of luxury. The stunt should run one to two weeks.

A Word of Caution

This may be a holdover from the old days, but in the public mind radio people have a general reputation for fast and loose living. Add to this the fact that you are placing one of your DJs in a hotel, and you can see the possible danger of things getting out of hand—at least in the minds of some.

Therefore, you must make absolutely sure that no accusations can be made against your station staff or the hotel. Avoid any wild parties in the suite or any excessive drinking on the part of your staff or their guests. Be sure that your DJ conducts himself with complete dignity throughout this survival test. Don't allow unescorted guests (unless it's your morning man's wife!) to be in the hotel suite. No matter how careful you are, there will be certain people who will want to assume the worst, so make sure you don't provide them with any ammunition.

Hotel Arrangements

You should have no difficulty making arrangements with a quality hotel or motel to host your survival test. The publicity both on and off the air will make it well worth their participation. Most hotel people have been well-schooled in the need for and the benefits of publicity and promotion, so there should be no problem convincing them.

Your disc jockey should be given the finest suite in the place, plus whatever he calls for in the way of service. This may include hair styling, shoe shines, and special food. The quality of the service, along with his overall marvelous treatment, will be described on the air to the listeners. If the special services are provided by businesses outside of the hotel, they should also receive on-air plugs in return for rendering the service as a trade-out.

The Details

About a week prior to the survival test, your disc jockey announces that he has been asked to undergo a test in the interest of research, but he is not sure whether he wants to go through the ordeal. Since advancing the common good of humanity is paramount, however, he feels duty-bound to go through with it. He states that he will undertake the test as soon as he can find an appropriate place. He asks listeners to suggest various types of tests he might undergo, as well as places in which the test should be conducted.

On Wednesday of the week prior to the test, he should start reading various suggestions on the air. On Thursday, he mentions that among the survival test suggestions he has received is an invitation from the manager of the Biltmore Arms Hotel suggesting that his survival test be designed to see just how much absolute luxury a man can endure. After speculating about this, he decides that this is indeed the best test, particularly since it deals with an area of human endurance that has undergone little direct research.

The test is therefore scheduled to begin the following Monday morning. Your disc jockey takes the weekend to rest and prepare himself for the ordeal. Then you are ready to start.

Don't Spare the Fanfare

Your man should arrive at the hotel in a chauffeur-driven limousine, with a van behind carrying all of his luggage. He should be met at the door by the manager and as many members of the staff as possible. Naturally, there should be a red carpet across which he makes his entrance. There should be banners in the lobby announcing: "The Biltmore Arms Welcomes WZZZ Jimmy Parsons for His Survival Test." Members of the hotel staff should wear badges proclaiming: "I'm at the service of WZZZ's Jimmy Parsons."

Be sure to have the local press on hand to witness the start and various phases of the test. Make sure that the press knows they are welcome to visit the suite throughout the survival test to interview the "guinea pig" and to share in the refreshments that are constantly available.

Ground Rules

The conditions and requirements of the test should be announced in advance and repeated many times each day during the survival test. These include:

1. Throughout the test, your DJ must remain within the hotel grounds. If he leaves, the test is over.

2. Throughout the test, except for the most basic necessities, your disc jockey must do nothing for himself. Everything possible must be done for him. When he sips a soft drink, someone else should open it and pour it into a glass filled with ice. When he gets dressed, a valet should be present to help. When he says, "Gee, I'd like a steak" someone should get it for him immediately. When he rises to leave a room, someone should open the door for him.

3. While the ultimate in luxury seems appealing, it can also get a little overpowering. If your disc jockey complains at any point in the survival test about too much luxurious living, the test is automatically ended.

4. As a part of the survival test, your disc jockey will undergo a daily "happiness checkup" to measure his state of mental well-being. This should be administered by a psychologist and the results should be aired.

Additional Bits

Have a nurse on call at all times to assist your DJ in the event that he should succumb to too much luxurious living. A doctor should also give him a complete physical examination before the test starts. The doctor should drop by for daily checkups to see how your DJ is standing up under the pressures of such a lifestyle.

During his stay, your DJ should pay courtesy calls on each department of the hotel. He should go prepared with a tape recorder (carried by someone else, of course) and interview various hotel employees about their duties and anecdotes of life in the hotel.

You will probably wish to schedule a special luncheon or dinner for some of your sponsors. If it is not practical to invite all of them, select the lucky few by having a drawing. This will also be an excellent opportunity for the hotel to demonstrate its facilities and services to this select group. A good way to sell this to the hotel is to point out that members of your sponsor group are in a prime position to recommend the hotel to out-of-town visitors.

Consider publishing a daily report on the various "ordeals" that your DJ will be undertaking each day. This can be released to the press, used for distribution within the hotel, given out at the station, and used as the basis for ad-lib comments by your other air personalities expressing their envy or sympathy.

An entourage of hotel employees should accompany the man who is making the survival test everywhere he goes. They will act as his own personal staff and serve all of his needs. One employee should be designated to carry a radio tuned to your station and to ensure that your DJ has the best of everything at all times. You may wish to have your man moved about the hotel in a special wheeled chair similar to the ones found on the boardwalk at Atlantic City.

There are numerous things that you and the hotel people can arrange to contribute to a life of ease for your disc jockey—the more the better. Just make sure that as many of them as possible take place in the public areas of the hotel so that you will get the benefit of maximum exposure. If your man still covers his own air shift during the survival test, the remote booth should be as sumptuous as possible, in keeping with the tone of the whole promotion.

Finally, He Can Stand It No Longer

Of the first day of the survival test, your DJ will be nothing but enthusiastic about this glorious situation. This feeling will continue through subsequent days, and he'll make frequent references that he can "go on like this forever." Finally, his eagerness will begin to wane and he will begin to doubt that having everything at his beck and call is all it is cracked up to be.

At the conclusion of the test he breaks down and announces that he just can't take it anymore. The service at the hotel has been just too wonderful. He is overcome. The life of luxury and idleness has done him in at last. An ambulance should be summoned and he should be carried to it on a stretcher. On his way out, your DJ should be carried around to each department so that he can thank everyone for their overwhelming attentions to him during his stay. Arrange for him to be taken to a hospital for a complete checkup.

A Variation

Why not set up a challenge between two of your air personalities? Have one take the "lap of luxury" route at the hotel, while the other is outfitted for a relatively austere survival test camping in the wilderness. The idea, of course, is to see which can endure the longest. Odds are that the winner will be the wilderness man.

A Final Note

This is the sort of simple, sure promotion from which you can get a lot of good publicity. It is relatively foolproof, since it is virtually impossible for it to fail. So put it on your schedule of things to do and get going.

3.19 ON A BICYCLE BUILT FOR TWO

We have suggested before that you will get a lot of promotional mileage out of pitting two of your disc jockeys against each other. The logical ones, of course, are your early morning man and your late afternoon man, particularly since these are probably your two strongest personalities. The running feud between them will provide an effective method of working in cross-plus on the air. It also provides you with the ideal starting point for numerous outside stunts.

The stunt suggested here is just one of many you can use. In other promotions we suggest numerous other ways through which you can take advantage of the conflict situation between your two DJs.

How It Works

Once the rivalry is established, one of your DJs should issue a challenge to the other. In fact, to get a little extra fun out of it, he might ask listeners to call or write in suggestions as to what sort of a test he can enter into with the other DJ. In the end, he resolves to challenge his opponent to a bicycle endurance test to see who can travel the farthest in a day. Be sure you make it an endurance test and not just a race, because this way you have a logical reason for the two to stick together as they ride.

The other DJ accepts the challenge, of course, but says he will spell out the ground rules for the endurance test. The second man states that he wants medical help close by and so specifies that they will ride on tandem bicycles. The second person on the bike will be a nurse—obviously someone with first aid skills. Each DJ then proceeds to ask for volunteers from the listenership to ride along. Set up interviews for the "medics" at the station. Ability in first aid and fitness for an endurance bike ride should both be factors—this is not something for a frail person!

Some Things to Check

When arranging for the tandem bicycles, make sure that you get ones that are in good condition. If possible, try to get bikes that have multispeed gearing, particularly if your race will be held in hilly country.

Double-check your station's medical and liability insurance policies to make sure that your staff and the guest-riders are all covered should anything happen to anyone during the endurance test. Dress all four people in white sweat suits and white biking shoes. Your DJs' sweatshirts should have the station call letters imprinted on, plus the name of the DJ. The other team members should have similar sweat suits with the station call sign plus "Joe Smith's Medic" imprinted on the back.

Have the bikes equipped with a few essentials. Some of these are available from your local bicycle shop or other outlets. Each rider should be provided drinking bottles and a small frame-mounted bag for snacks, lip balm, and so on. Check with Radio Shack™ or another electronic store for AM/FM portable radios designed for mounting on bicycles. Fit both of your bike-riding air personalities with two-way wireless communicators, permitting them to converse with the chase car. They can also be interviewed while going down the road.

Arrange for one of your news cars to escort the two biking teams throughout the endurance test. If you cannot spare a regular news car, have banners or signs made that you can attach to a chase car that will follow the riders.

Starting the Endurance Test

Conduct the endurance test on a Tuesday, Wednesday, or Thursday to avoid traffic problems. Saturday and Sunday are not suitable days for this kind of event either.

The starting point should be about 35 miles away from your town. The ideal spot is on the far side of town about this distance from your station. In that way, the riders will move through at least two different towns.

The starting time should be about 6:45 A.M. so that you can take advantage of the morning drive time exposure on the roads and on the air. When setting up your schedule, try to arrange things so that the teams reach your town about 3:30 or 4 P.M. in the afternoon.

You should be able to arrange a free breakfast at the starting point and a nice lunch along the way at restaurants on the route. If the finish line is near a health club, the teams can work toward the goal of a relaxing soak in a hot whirlpool once the race is done.

Perhaps you can incorporate stops at bicycle shops or service stations along the route as well. These can be used as "pit stops" where the riders take needed breaks and the bicycles get checked over. Much hoopla is built on this to make it resemble the pits at a large stock car race, complete with pit support personnel for each team. Give particular attention to tire inflation and wear, as well as lubrication and adjustment of the pedals, chains, gears, and brakes. Naturally, the pit crews have T-shirts imprinted to resemble the clothing worn by the bikers.

The start, finish, and pit stops all provide the best photo opportunities. Take the angle of the sun into account in setting this up for the best lighting—don't let the camera face into the sun.

Publicity Coverage of the Event

Be sure to have a good professional photographer along to get plenty of pictures. Consumer-quality cameras handled by amateurs will rarely get what you want; call the local paper and see if a member of their staff is available to handle the shooting.

Contact the local TV stations in advance and tell the assignment editor of your planned route. Give plenty of suggestions for coverage, keeping in mind that the visual interest is very important to good TV news reports.

They're Off!

Arrange for frequent updates about the current location of the riders. Speculate about how each team member is doing and on each team's chances of completing the course. Using the wireless microphones mentioned above, conduct brief interviews with the two air personalities several times during the race, getting first-hand impressions of how things are going, remarks about the terrain, how the bikes are handling, and expressions of appreciation for the medic/biker member of the team.

Be prepared for many people to drive out to the race route just to see your tandem testers. Make the DJs easy to find. Perhaps you can put up conspicuous posters along the route and set up checkpoints every 5 or 10 miles where the riders are required to stop and have cards punched to verify that they have completed each leg of the trip.

Be sure that your people ride on the far right side of the road so that they do not create a traffic hazard. The chase car should carry a sign on the roof saying "bicycle race ahead" or something similar. Be particularly careful during peak traffic times or in congested areas.

The Winner

The termination point of the endurance test should be somewhere on the other side of town away from the starting point. Let's hope that there is one definite winner, rather than a draw. With a winner, you will have more to talk about on the air. Also, having a winner provides the logical basis for the loser to come back with a challenge of another type of test to get even—and you are on your way to another outside promotion.

WALKING ENDURANCE TEST 3.20

You have already seen how a running rivalry between two of your air personalities can be used as the basis for both on-air and outside promotion stunts. The "On a Bicycle Built for Two" promotion was a part of this pattern. Here is another to help you carry the feud along.

How It Works

One of your DJs challenges the other to a walking endurance test. After the prior publicity, and with much fanfare, they set out to see who can walk the farthest. Essentially, that's all there is to it. Following are suggestions on how to make this promotion really go.

Where to Walk

One way to handle this is to have your personalities start their walk about 10 miles out of town. If there is a neighboring town some distance off, they can start from there. If yours is a major city that spreads over a wide area, pick your starting point about 10 miles from the center of town. The idea is to arrange things so that your disc jockeys walk the widely traveled sections of your city so that they achieve maximum exposure.

Another way to set up the Walking Endurance Test is to lay out a specific course. Arrange it to be around an area measuring a mile on each side. In this case you probably stand a better chance of getting a large group to walk along with your air personalities. Also, the course can be plainly marked with signs that call attention to the event. A quarter-mile track at the high school or university is another location for this promotion, although walking 40 laps on a quarter-mile track will be fairly tedious for the walkers.

Get Your Listeners into the Act

As always, set things up so that your listeners can participate. Have your DJs ask on the air for suggestions about how they should protect their feet or prevent sunburn. Ask for suggestions about how to train for the event, proper diets, walking methods, race strategies, and so on.

Ask the Experts

Check around—there may be hiking clubs in your area. The local camping supply outlets should know. Try to get two hiking groups to adopt your disc jockeys. The club members can help train the DJs and may even want to walk along on the day of the event. Through tying this promotion in with the hiking clubs, you have the opportunity for a great deal more advance publicity on the Walking Endurance test as your dueling DJs prepare.

Training for the Walk

To provide contrast and talk points, have one of your DJs train on an austere "health nut" diet—a strictly Spartan approach. The other DJ should use the "lifestyles of the rich and famous" approach with relatively little regard to diet and physical training. A note of caution, though—both of your DJs should be given a complete physical to make sure this promotion is within safe medical limits for them. Don't mess with someone's health!

Dressing for the Walk

Be sure to have your DJs dressed in special custom-imprinted sweat suits for the walk. Pick wild colors and have the station's call and logo plus the DJ's name imprinted on the suit, back and front. In like manner, have the "chase car" decorated with signs advertising the event. The car can also carry special foods, ointments, first aid kits, and gag paraphernalia to add some laughs.

The Schedule

When arranging details for the endurance walk, remember that your DJs will probably cover about three miles per hour for the first few miles. Considering the fact that DJs are notorious for not being in the best shape, this pace will undoubtedly slack off once they get to about the 10-mile mark.

Try to set things up so that your people go through the center of town or through a local mall around noon. Have the whole entourage take a lunch break (with reserved tables) in a public place.

The lunch break will be provided by the restaurant as a trade-out for the promotional value you will give them. Naturally, there should be a sign in the restaurant's window and over the reserved tables calling attention to the fact that the "WZZZ Walking DJs Will Eat Here at Noon."

Wrap-Up

The WZZZ Walking Endurance Test ends when one of your air personalities decides that enough is enough and can go no farther. The limit is probably 20 to 25 miles, since you're not interested in having them kill themselves. Whichever DJ wins, the other should naturally claim that he won by foul means. Be sure that you do not end up with a draw. By having a winner, you are in a natural position to have the loser issue yet another challenge, and you're on the way to another promotion.

THE SPRING CAMPOUT   3.21

This promotion should be a lot of fun for everyone involved and should achieve maximum exposure for your station. The month of May is the ideal time for your Spring Campout. And this event should work well annually.

How It Works

Move the entire broadcast operation to a local mall or shopping center for its entire business day. Set yourself up in tents and surround yourself with as many elements of outdoor life as possible. Use tents for studios, picnic tables to hold the equipment, folding chairs, camp lanterns—the works. The gimmick is that the station is camping out, even if the tents are actually indoors along the central concourse of a mall.

The Spring Campout can run on Thursday through Saturday, or you can go for six to eight days. At any rate, it should be more than a one-day affair. Depending of your capability of running a full remote, you'll need to decide whether or not to originate the newscasts from the "camp site." You should, however, be prepared to hand out photocopies of today's local, area and national headlines each day.

Sell It to Camping Outlets

Obviously, the expenses of this kind of remote can be traded out with the mall and several sponsoring stores. The camping and sportswear stores can equip the "radio campsite" and clothe your air personalities in return for promotional signs at the remote and mentions on the air.

On-Air Competition

Have at least one live-action contest or stunt each day. Here are some suggestions:

- Have your air personalities play broom ball hockey on roller skates against a team made up of local kids;
- Have a tree cutting or log sawing contest;
- Set up a campfire building contest, judged by how fast someone can build a fire that can burn through a piece of string strung across the fire three feet above the ground;
- Have a tent-pitching race.
- Stage a mountain climbing contest.

The local Scouting council office may have other ideas for outdoorsy competitive events similar to the ones used by Scout camps.

Handouts

Have lots of printed material and trinkets ready to give away to visitors to the remote site—plenty of folks are going to come and see you. Custom imprinted pens, balloons, key chains, fans, kites, bookmarks, cost very little and are real crowd-pleasers. Somewhat more tangible giveaways (coffee mugs and T-shirts) can be given away to " . . . the third person who walks into the WZZZ Campout tent and hoots like an owl."

Take this one step further and have special "Honorary WZZZ Camper" badges made up, each with a unique serial number. The numbers can be used as the basis for drawings for major prizes of camping equipment or vacation travel packages.

Displays

Have a group of displays near your Spring Campout tent. These should include a good cross section of new camping equipment. Try to have a display of luxury camping gear and recreational vehicles as well.

Arrange with the local Boy and Girl Scouts to have some of them present during your campout remote, demonstrating various outdoors-oriented skills. Get in touch with the local state fish and game commission and invite its participation, including handouts on local recreational areas, conservation methods, displays of stuffed (or live) animals, and so on.

CHARITY RIDE OR CHARITY EXPRESS   3.22

Here is a flexible and outstanding outside stunt promotion that you can use to benefit a local or national charity drive. It is effective and attention-getting, with excellent picture possibilities. About all you need to make it work is some salve for the treatment of saddle sores.

How It Works

Your equestrian DJs, riding in relays, stage a marathon horseback ride to reach a goal of so many dollars for the selected charity. Whoa, now—not a *real* horse! They'll be riding one of those mechanical ponies found out front of supermarkets, drugstores, and so on. If you are a parent, surely you are familiar with these machines because your children are probably constantly begging for money to ride them.

Arrange for the horse either through the local amusement company that handles them or with a store that has one on its premises. Make sure you get one that is in good condition! The event itself may be staged inside or out in the most public and well-trafficked spot you can obtain. Uniqueness and flair will make this stunt pay off.

The Marathon

You may choose to announce that your disc jockeys will stage a marathon ride on this noble steed until a certain amount in contributions is reached. In this case, your people simply ride the pony in the public place, exhorting everyone to contribute to the charity by putting money in a pair of saddlebags mounted on the pony.

You can make an additional appeal to would-be contributors by inviting youngsters to join the DJ on the pony for a short ride in return for a small contribution. In this instance, the ride continues throughout the business hours each day until the goal is reached for the charity.

Goal Gallop

With some charity efforts, you can set up a more visual method of conducting the promotion. If the charity you are aiding has an out-of-town headquarters or center of operations, you can set as your goal an amount in dollars equal to the distance in miles from your town to the charity's headquarters. In this case, announce that it will take a dollar a mile to get the WZZZ disc jockeys to the goal and that they will keep riding until they get there.

If you are working with the March of Dimes, for example, this could be the distance to the Georgia Warm Springs Foundation, supported by the March, in Warm Springs, Georgia. Arrange for a large map to be mounted near your horse. Then as the miles are ticked off, a red line on the map will show the progress toward the goal.

Changing Riders

Unless you use this promotion primarily to publicize one individual as a continual canterer, it is a good idea to change riders two to four times an hour. This will add to the pace of the stunt with a dramatic sequence recalling the pony express days. It will also make things easier for the riders who are prone to motion sickness.

Have one rider leap off while the other mounts the horse at full gallop. If the money donations are being placed in saddlebags, the fresh rider should bring along a new set of saddlebags, and the dismounting rider can be escorted by "armed guards" carrying water pistols to where the money is tallied and locked up.

Name the Horse

Naturally, you'll give the electric equine a name. You can ask listeners to call or write in suggestions. You can name him after a local mountain, hill, or other geographical site. Or you can have his name relate to the station's logo or slogan. Anyway, be sure to come up with a name of some sort. This will add considerably to the flair and personality of the promotion.

Signs

Large signs calling attention to the event should be used at the riding site. You can probably promote these free through a local sign painter or typesetting shop. Also, be sure that the store at which the event is staged mentions the promotion in its advertising. Naturally, you will give the store promotional mentions on the air.

Support Staff

The charity group with which you are working should be called upon to supply people to be on hand during the ride. These people should be the ones to actually handle the contributions—not your station staff.

Representatives of the charity may also take turns in the saddle, alternating with your announcers. Off-duty riders from the station and charity should still be nearby to hand out promotional literature and answer questions.

Publicity

Be sure to capitalize fully on the picture possibilities this stunt will provide. Since the entire effort is for a charitable purpose, you will probably have fairly good luck getting the local newspapers to cover your "ride." You should also have a phone available for the rider to talk to the studio to report his progress. If you are conducting a long-term ride over a period of several days, you might even consider the possibility of a remote line, but local circumstances will determine if this is advisable.

On the Air

A running series of reports on the progress of the WZZZ charity riders should be carried on the air. Listeners should be urged constantly to get out and see the event and make contributions. You may wish to use short taped bits by officials of the charitable organization as part of the on-air promotion.

BARBERSHOP QUARTET SINGERS 3.23

One of the very active and promotion-minded organizations all across the country is the "Society for the Preservation and Encouragement of Barber Shop Quartet Singing in America," the SPEBSQA. A similar all-female group of national standing is the "Sweet Adelines."

On your staff there are certainly at least four people capable of singing with a greater or lesser degree of proficiency. Only the totally tone-deaf are incapable of fairly passable barbershop quartct singing.

How It Works

Get in touch with one of the barbershop groups in your area. Tell the members that you are anxious to develop a group of your people into a barbershop quartet. With a little practice and within just a few weeks, your quartet will have developed into a fairly competent foursome and will be in a position to entertain publicly.

Now your DJs will be able to appear on a regular basis at the many public events staged by other barbershop groups, giving both parties excellent exposure. You have also put the wheels in motion for a fairly large organization to be busy on the outside promoting your station because of the promotion job the station is doing for the organizations.

In addition, your singing disc jockeys can now go out and put on a real show at schools and local clubs. And you will promote your station's image through the DJs' group appearances. You may even bundle a whole station promotion spot campaign for use on the air, featuring your singing DJs.

3.24   THE ULTIMATE SCARECROW

Tying your station in with the local, county, or state fair is a good idea. Use this promotion as a delightful attention-getter for WZZZ by honoring one of the most significant contributions to the history and development of agriculture: the scarecrow!

How It Works

WZZZ announces that this year the station will sponsor a new competition at the fair—"The Ultimate Scarecrow." In honor of the farmer's silent partner, listeners are invited to construct the best scarecrows they can and enter them in the "WZZZ County Fair Ultimate Scarecrow Contest."

Scarecrows entered may be any size, shape, or gender, and dressed in any way as long as they are decent. The one fast rule is that each scarecrow must bear the station's call letters, either on a sign or somehow incorporated into the dress of the scarecrow.

Work with Fair Officials

You will obviously need a fair amount of space to accommodate your corps of scarecrows. At even the smallest of fairs, space is at a premium. Therefore, contact the fair authorities well in advance. Your approach should be that they donate the space for your scarecrow contest; of course, this is a trade-out for the extensive publicity WZZZ will give to the fair.

Ask the fair authorities to put the scarecrow judging on the regular schedule of events, along with the agriculture, livestock, and other awards ceremonies. Have ribbons awarded to the winning entries. Your requests are quite reasonable, for the fair will get valuable free publicity and advertising by cooperating with you.

Judging Categories

There are many categories from which you may choose to award ribbons: most elaborate, scariest, best-dressed, worst-dressed, and so on. You will need to have your own special ribbons made up for these categories, as the fair officials usually have only the standard first-, second-, and third-place varieties. A large group judging categories will add considerable variety to the personalities of the scarecrows being entered.

A good additional gimmick is to establish a special category for the scarecrow that most resembles one of your DJs—the morning man, for instance. For this category to work best, much advance ballyhoo is needed on the air and in newspaper ads that include photos of your DJ. The judging for this category should be handled by the other air personalities from your station. Naturally, you'll want to get pictures of the morning man standing alongside his "clone."

Prizes

Awarding ribbons is probably sufficient to generate interest in the "Ultimate Scarecrow" contest at the county fair, but tangible prizes are an incentive, even if they are fairly modest in value.

An Angle to Consider

To add some community service and goodwill lustre to this promotion, consider confining your entries to members of a specific group, such as 4-H clubs or Future Farmers of America. In this case you would then present prizes of savings bonds, cash, or scholarships to those who win. This approach is an excellent goodwill-builder, and in no way detracts from the appeal of the overall promotion.

3.25 BALLOON RALLY

Here's an outside stunt that can prove to be the wildest publicity-grabbing event ever held in your area. Its possibility depends on two things: first, that you have in your area a sports car club, and second, that you can locate a hot-air balloon and a qualified pilot.

How It Works

Set up a "hare and hounds" rally with the balloon as the hare and the sports cars as the hounds. The balloon will carry the pilot and one of your air person-alities with the intent of landing about three hours later. As soon as the balloon is launched, the cars begin the chase, following as best they can. The first driver to reach the balloon after it lands is declared the winner. As with any car rally, the drivers must obey all traffic rules implicitly.

The Play-by-Play

Arrange for the flying DJ to make reports and announce the location of the bal-loon. Frequent on-air progress reports will be of interest to your listeners, especially if the balloon is heading near their part of town.

Certainly you will have the station's call letters displayed on a huge banner hanging on the sides of the balloon. This will further promote listenership as people notice the balloon floating overhead.

Note: VHF and UHF hand-held radios are ideal for communicating between the balloon and your station. Perhaps your news department already uses these. Cellular telephones, however, may not be used in any type of air-craft. An airborne cellular telephone would interfere with distant cells and really mess up the system.

The Safety Factor

Do not try to stage this rally unless it is sponsored by an established car rally organization. The members of sports car clubs are conscious of the importance of safe driving and will not want to risk adverse public opinion through unsafe driving. As an additional safeguard, however, each car can have an observer/passenger assigned by the rally officials. The observer helps the driver keep track of the drifting balloon and also makes sure that no traffic laws are vio-lated. Breaking any traffic law should automatically disqualify a competitor.

Use a Real Pilot

Balloon flying is a science. Don't dare set a DJ adrift on a borrowed balloon. Even if you're trying to get Joe Stokes out of your afternoon lineup permanently, don't put the rest of the town at risk. Use a qualified balloonist and rely on the pilot's judgement about weather conditions needed for a safe flight and a proper landing area.

The Prize

The best prize for this event is a suitably inscribed trophy. These people will be competing for the sport of it, and they'll treasure a trophy or plaque much more than a prize of money or goods.

Pictures

Be sure that the local papers and TV stations are notified in advance. Talk to the assignment editors personally to make sure they understand the schedule. Have photographers on hand to record the whole event from the ground, and try to have your DJ or the balloon pilot shoot some pictures from the air.

Emphasize the need for safety for all involved. Remind your balloonists to tie any cameras and two-way radios securely to the balloon so that nothing gets dropped. Likewise, assure the public that the rally drivers are instructed to observe traffic rules strictly.

SPEAKERS BUREAU 3.26

Although this promotion cannot really be classified as a "stunt," it does fall within the outside activities category and is therefore included in this section. The WZZZ Speakers Bureau can do a real job for you in the area of community relations. As you continue to use it and expand its range over the months ahead, you will realize that it is one of the most effective long-range publicity tools you have.

How It Works

The idea itself is quite simple. Your air personalities, and any other member of your staff who seems suited to the task, are organized into a speakers bureau. Community organizations and other groups are notified that your people are available for public appearances at meetings.

The entertainment chairperson of any organization is always hard-pressed to line up good programs for meetings month after month. Therefore, these people will love to make use of your services as soon as they know your people are available.

Handling Bookings

To avoid confusion, one person at the station should handle all bookings. A regular calendar should be maintained so that you do not get one individual committed to appearances at several different places at the same time. Naturally, the station's most popular personalities are going to be requested most often. So you will have a problem maintaining a fairly even balance in appearances among all of your people.

Put very strict limits on the number of appearances any single individual can make in a week. When a request comes in, the tentative speaker should be asked if he or she can make it, and then the event should be scheduled on the master calendar to avoid conflicts.

How to Alert the Public

Develop a regular series of public service announcements on the WZZZ Speakers Bureau for on-air use. These should state very simply that WZZZ personalities are available for certain appearances at civic clubs, community organizations, and other groups. Program chairpersons should contact the station for further information.

A letter explaining the service should be sent to all of the various organizations that might make use of the bureau. It will probably be best if you direct this letter to the president of the organization. In addition, after the WZZZ Speakers Bureau has been in operation for several months, send out a follow-up bulletin to keep the organizations aware of the fact that you are still in business.

If yours is a large community, or if your signal coverage includes a large area, there will probably be a number of chapters of main organizations, such as Elks, Jaycees, and Scouts. In addition to contacting each chapter individually, be sure to get in touch with their regional or state headquarters so that information about your Speakers Bureau can be included in the organizations' newsletters.

Thank You Note

It is a good public relations gesture for the personality involved to send a short note of thanks after the speaking engagement.

The Purpose

Explain to your people that they are not being booked as an entertainment package. Stand-up comedy is not the intent. This is a serious public relations job that is important to your overall operations. Your people should also be reminded that the programs on which they appear are on strict time schedules, so they should stay within their allotted time period and wind up promptly. Better to have the audience wanting more than wishing for less.

Speaker's Guide

Simplify the whole setup by preparing a speaker's guide to assist your people in handling this outside work. This will not only make their jobs easier, it will also assure a relatively high quality of performance. Some suggestions are given here, and a copy should be given to each of your staff involved in the Speakers Bureau.

Suggested Format for Speeches

Here is a general outline of how the speeches should probably shape up:

- General Introduction
- Purposes of the WZZZ Speakers Bureau
- The Impact of Radio Broadcasting on Today's World
- WZZZ's Policies on Selecting Music and Programming
- News Coverage
- Sports Coverage
- WZZZ's Community Service Efforts
- What's My Job?
- Conclusion
- Questions and Answers

The Speech Format—Expanded

The following is a reiteration of the format with suggestions for how to flesh it out.

General Introduction

- Toss in a quick story or joke, usually relating to life in a radio station. Use this to relax the audience.
- Tell the audience that you are going to be brief and won't load them down with a lot of facts and figures.

- Try to give the impression that you are relaxed and are not there to "sell" anything, even your station.
- Express thanks for the opportunity to meet the group and for their invitation to have you say a few words about radio broadcasting.

If the person who has introduced you has not done as complete a job as you think is necessary, add on a few more items about yourself. (A prepared biography with pictures of you should have been supplied to the organization in advance of your appearance.)

The Purpose of the WZZZ Speakers Bureau

Tell the audience why you are here, for instance:

- The station has established the Speakers Bureau solely as a public service to friends and listeners.
- The station feels that public relations is a very important commodity in a highly competitive world.
- This is a chance you and your associates have wanted for a long time, to get out on the other side of the microphone and meet your listeners personally.
- Radio broadcasting has a very important story to tell, a story that cannot be told on the air but which can be outlined at a meeting such as this.
- Because so many people have a high degree of interest in radio today without any real knowledge of its workings, that you welcome the opportunity to fill them in on a few of the details.

The Impact of Radio Broadcasting on Today's World

- Explain briefly how listening and programming patterns have changed over the years.
- Point out how many of these changes were motivated by the advent of stereo FM, broadcast television, cable TV and satellite networks.
- Explain how, contrary to the belief of many, there are more radios today than ever before, with more people spending more time listening to radio than ever.
- Give some examples of the effective sales jobs radio is doing for its sponsors.
- Explain in completely nontechnical terms about some of the new equipment that adds to the overall quality of production.
- Give them a rough idea of what a modern radio station looks like and what goes on in the studio when you are working.

Station Policies on Music

- Point out how the music format provides for a balance and sets the mood of your particular station.
- Explain how your music library is set up, how new records are auditioned and rated, and how your air personalities learn of new releases for airplay.
- Tell the audience how a good radio show is planned in advance with great attention given to the details. "Ad-libs" are carefully worked out in many cases, and records are not just fished randomly out of a box and put on the air.
- Point out how a music show has frequent (though informal) breaks for information, such as time and temperature checks, weather updates, and traffic reports.
- Describe other feature programs, where they come from, how they are produced, when they are scheduled, and so on.
- Explain your station's policy about breaking into regular programming with important news bulletins.
- Tell briefly about the Emergency Broadcast System, and how it is used for more than "air raid" warnings.
- Tell how the entire programming activity of your station is under the guidance of the program director, whose long background in the business is so important to the creation of your particular format.

News Coverage

- Explain that your news department is the most aggressive in the area.
- Outline how your station's regular newscasts are formatted, such as:
    - ~ five-minute "news in brief" coverage hourly
    - ~ fifteen-minute wrap-up at 7 A.M., noon, and 6 P.M.
    - ~ headlines on the half-hour
    - ~ weather updates at 20 after and 20 till the hour
    - ~ locally-produced features, interview shows, editorials
- Introduce and tell about each member of the news staff.
- Describe the news-gathering equipment and techniques, including wire services, police/fire/emergency radio monitors, two-way and ENG equipment, and traffic spotters in helicopters, airplanes, and cars.
- If you use a news tip system that involves listeners calling in about news stories, explain how it works, what safeguards you have to ensure reliability, and what special fast-breaking stories were covered sooner than they would have been otherwise.

Community Service

- Point out that the station is more than just a business, that it constantly strives to be an effective part of your growing community and is determined to make serious and valuable contributions to the life of your area.
- If you editorialize on the air, explain your policies governing this and give some information about recent editorial campaigns.
- Detail the amount of public service time your station airs each day, week, or month. Tell about the various PSAs you schedule.
- Tell your audience how weather and traffic information are an important part of the public service you perform.
- Explain the importance of the job you do when there is a disaster, serious weather conditions, or school closures.

What's My Job?

- Explain briefly exactly what you do for the station, including your air-shift schedule and off-air duties.
- Bring in some humorous anecdotes about offbeat things that have happened at the station, especially during your show.
- Sketch out what some of the other staff members do.
- Point out how, by its very nature, radio is a cooperative effort requiring coordination among people.
- If you use any special production techniques or other resources in preparing for your show, explain these.

Conclusion

- Go back and briefly hit the key points again.
- Work in a strong pitch for the radio business itself.
- Thank the group for inviting you.
- Tell them that you'll be glad to answer questions they might have.

Possible Questions

Here are some questions that might get tossed to you, so have some answers ready.

- How far away can your station normally be heard?
- Who selects the music played on your station?
- What time does your morning man get up in order to do his show?
- What about payola?

- How does your station handle religious programming?
- Does your station use a satellite network?
- Has television hurt radio?
- How much music do you play in a typical hour?
- How much news do you have on the air in a day?
- Do you always have someone on duty in the news room?
- Do you have to buy all of the records you play?
- How much does a spot announcement cost?
- Who produces the commercials?
- Why do some station call signs start with a K, others with a W, and others with a C?
- How many commercials do you run in an hour?
- Is there a limit to the number of commercials you can run?
- Why do some of the local AM stations go off the air or get so weak at night?
- What happens when I call in a request for a certain record to be played?
- What happens to your old records?

"Free Money" Campaign   3.27

Two of the most compelling words in the English language are "free" and "money." Here is a happy promotion that combines both. The result: more listeners.

Getting Listeners Ready

Produce some teaser spots to be aired frequently. These spots should be very brief. Have the words "FREE MONEY" with reverb or echo, followed by another announcer stating, "Stay tuned to WZZZ."

If you prepare a display ad for the local papers, have them use GIANT-sized type normally reserved for the start of a war or the end of all taxation. The ad should contain only your station call and logo, and the words "FREE MONEY" in the giant type.

The on-air teasers and newspaper ads should break three days before the actual start of your "Free Money" promotion.

How It Works

On the day your promotion starts, go on the air with the announcement that WZZZ disc jockeys are on the streets of your city giving away free money. All a person needs to do to get some of the free money is to walk up to the DJ and say "I listen to WZZZ."

The DJs should be spotted in various sections of the city on a rotation basis. Each should be given $15 to $25 or more to give away each time he or she is out. Each WZZZ air personality should be wearing distinctive WZZZ T-shirts or warm-up suits to help people find them on the streets.

The money given out should be crisp, new $1 and $5 bills. Have small promotional flyers printed and attach them to the bills with paper clips. The flyers can say: "It pays to listen to WZZZ." They should be signed by the DJ that hands them out.

A Precaution

You don't want your air personality mugged for the money. Always have your people work in pairs—preferably with both wearing the distinctive T-shirts or warm-up suits. Have them carry relatively little money at a time, keeping additional cash securely locked in the car or van they're using. If one of your air people is female, team her up with the burliest male member of the staff.

Tell the Ad Agencies

To be sure that the people who place ads on your station are fully aware of the promotional job you are doing, have your air personalities and sales staff tour the agencies while the Free Money campaign is going on. The theme should be: "It Pays to Advertize on WZZZ."

Any ads placed on WZZZ during the three-day campaign automatically enters the time-buyer in a prize drawing to be held after the campaign is over. The prize here will depend on your station. This is an excellent time for your air personalities to get to know the agency people personally and bring home the job that WZZZ is doing.

The Listener Hook

This promotion should be run only about three days. During this time, give periodic announcements about general locations of the air personalities handing out free money. This activity should be promoted heavily on the air.

CLUNKER CARAVAN

Handle your public service announcements so that they become a publicity and promotion tool for your station. In that way the PSAs will also do a better job for the agency being promoted. This promotion is an example.

How It Works

Have your personalities buy old cars, fix them up so that they are in safe driving condition and drive them over a prescribed course. The winning driver will be the one with the best safety record. Everyone involved will have lots of fun on this one and you will demonstrate graphically that any car can be a safe car to drive.

Cooperating Organizations

The Safety Council in your area is a good starting point. It can help you in your overall planning, coordinating your promotion with its own program, providing some general supervision, and furnishing you with a checklist for rating the DJs who drive the clunkers around town.

Check with your local police department, sheriff's office and state highway patrol. These agencies can provide a motorcycle escort, and may be able to assign troopers to ride in the clunkers and rate the drivers on safe driving.

Involve local auto rally clubs. They can provide the labor and expertise to help put the clunkers in safe driving condition.

How to Set Up Your Clunker Caravan

Have your disc jockey drivers each line up an old car from a local auto dealer. If your frequency is 1050, they should pay no more than $10.50. You can ham this up by having the DJ pay for the car with a pocket full of loose change. The dealers will be adequately compensated through on-air plugs.

Your caravan should cover a course from your station to a town about 50 miles away and back. The drivers will be rated on safe driving performance. You will want to arrange with one of your gasoline accounts for "pit stops" along the way and with a restaurant in the town for a lunch break.

Have a tow truck firm send one of its vehicles to accompany the Clunker Caravan. In your on-air publicity you should state that the clunkers will be auctioned off to the public at the end of the promotion. The proceeds will be donated to the Safety Council.

There are other obvious safety gimmicks you can work into this promotion. To spice up the event, have your DJ-drivers dress up in outlandish costumes. Have the clunkers painted garishly—including, of course, the station's call sign. Get an official starter to send them off like the beginning of the Indy 500 or a Le Mans race.

Perhaps a parallel promotion would be to set up a "WZZZ Safety Inspection" and your listeners can drive their cars in for a basic checkup on tires, lights, horn, wipers, and so forth. This also gives you a chance to expose your air personalities to the public. Be sure to have a variety of WZZZ trinkets and flyers to hand out.

3.29 BAIL OUT YOUR DISC JOCKEY

Your station receives requests continually to help various organizations in their fund-raising drives. Here is a way you can really help one of these groups and harvest a bumper crop of community goodwill at the same time.

How It Works

Suppose the March of Dimes asks you to assist in its annual fund drive. Your station agrees to raise, for instance, $10,000. Contact the mayor, the police department, and one of your local judges for their assistance.

The mayor issues a decree that four of your DJs should be arrested as "public nuisances." They are arrested, brought into court, convicted, and put into jail because they fail to pay $2500 each. The public is asked to pay the fines—of course the money is turned over to the March of Dimes.

Setting Up the "Case" against Your DJs

Start off your morning show on the specified day by having your DJs play only one song over and over. They state that they will continue playing this song until the March of Dimes reaches its fund-raising goal.

After this has continued long enough that the whole town is talking about it, the mayor issues an order for the arrest of your DJs on a "public nuisance" charge. It may be fun to have the police enter the control room and arrest your on-air person with the mike still on.

From here on, you will probably want to cover the whole thing as a remote. The mock trial should be covered by your news department. Once the DJs have been placed in cells, they should broadcast pleas for people to pay their fines so that they can be released.

Paying the "Fines"

The public can help pay the disc jockeys' fines by bringing money to your station or to the jail, or by phoning in pledges to the station.

3.30 COMMUNITY BILLBOARDS

This is not really a separate promotion, but fits in with pivotal events in your station's lifetime. Reserve this idea for a time when you are making a major change in programming, are bringing on new air personalities, or wish to place maximum emphasis on a particular phase of your programming.

How It Works

Throughout your city there are undoubtedly hundreds of community billboards available in supermarkets, coin-op laundries, hairstyling salons, and so on. Many businesses also have bulletin boards near the cash register where business cards can be posted.

Offer to trade out plugs for these various businesses in return for space on their public bulletin boards. Prepare WZZZ posters in several sizes ranging from business card dimension to poster size. When approaching a business about posting your ads on their bulletin boards, suggest that you will offer a free one-minute spot in exchange for each day the poster is on display. You may offer a free 30-second spot if only the business card ad is used.

If the cost of the airtime being given away seems overly generous, remember that many of these firms are not now on your roll of sponsors. You will get them on the air via this "free advertising" basis, giving you a good foothold to sell them on the job radio can do for their products or firms. Your salespeople will have an opening that may be possible no other way.

Go for the Maximum

Do not approach this promotion timidly on the basis that you will arrange for two or three billboards "to see how it works out." You won't get the desired results. Try for every community billboard in town for a week or two. This goes for the "portable" self-lit signs often parked in front of businesses. Instead of plugging their special of the day, have WZZZ's message posted during your campaign. Everywhere a person goes in town, he or she should see your message. If seen often enough, this type of saturation advertising makes people tune in just to find out what's going on.

If you're worried about trying to squeeze in all of those extra trade-out spots, remember to offer the firms the option of saving the spot for use at a later date. You can issue a "gift certificate" for the free spots any time during the following 12 months, for example.

3.31   BEACH BIT

Since you are going to be promoting listening to portable radios anyway, try this: Announce that the WZZZ disc jockeys and other people representing WZZZ will be touring the various swimming beaches in your area at various times. When they find someone listening to WZZZ on a portable radio, the listener immediately receives an album, cassette, or CD.

3.32   OUTBOARD MOTOR MARATHON

If your region is a boating area, here's an opportunity to stage the noisiest promotion yet. It's an outside stunt suitable for remote pickups. It might be just the event that a local boat distributor will jump at sponsoring.

How It Works

The Outboard Motor Marathon is just what the name implies: a competition to see who can keep his outboard motor running continuously for the longest time. The winner should receive a substantial prize such as an outboard cruiser or a runabout with an outboard motor attached. The prize must be of some consequence for this promotion, because the entrants will, to some degree, be jeopardizing the motors they own by running them for extended periods.

The motors are run in barrels of water, at a site such as a boathouse or pier where you can be sure that the monumental racket of the outboard motors will not draw the wrath of local citizens.

The Running

Your winner in this promotion will be the person whose outboard motor is still running after everyone else's has conked out. The odds are that your entrants will enter older motors. There is comparatively little chance of causing any real damage to the motors—the most likely reason for them to stop is a fouled spark plug.

Entrants will be willing to put their motors to the test because of the sizable prize being offered. A second motivation is personal pride; many people think of themselves as being more gifted mechanics than the rest of the populace.

Each participant should be allowed up to a five-man team to run his or her motor. Since the event may continue for some time, this will be necessary to allow for rest, eating, and so forth.

A Weekend Event—or Longer

Your outboard marathon should be scheduled during a weekend, beginning late Friday afternoon. It will, of course, run continuously from start to the last cough . . . and that could be sometime well into the following week. It will be up to the contestants to determine if they wish to compete on into the week if they are still in the running.

Since the competition is between the motors, actually the teams formed will keep a vigil on the machines. Thus, the operators will probably have to work in shifts. Your competition area should have sufficient lights, toilet facilities, food concessions, and perhaps even cots.

And the Tension Mounts

Throughout this event, especially by the second day, a tremendous amount of interest will be generated in the community by your remote broadcasts from the site of the outboard marathon. Spectators will drop by and the sponsor of the event should be sure to capitalize on this by having wares on display. Demonstration rides, having factory representatives on hand, and special sales promotions are all appropriate to this promotion.

The Prize

The winner should receive something fairly substantial. We suggest that it be an outboard-powered boat. The large volume of exposure the prize will receive can justify this major prize. Naturally, it should be contributed by the sponsor in conjunction with the manufacturer.

A very good additional incentive to entries is the award for a nominal gift to every entrant. A fuel can for the boat is an ideal possibility.

Free Fuel

Gasoline and oil for the outboards should be available at the contest site. You can try to arrange to have this provided free through one of the major gasoline distributors.

Be Careful

Pay attention to safety, especially during refueling operations. Outboard motors used in this marathon should have provision for external fuel tanks. Don't risk the potential problems that come with pouring gasoline into a small fuel tank mounted directly on the engine.

3.33 OUTDOOR COOKING COLLEGE

Within the ever-expanding borders of suburbia, the air grows heavier each summer with the aromas of outdoor cooking. Unfortunately for many, the challenges of successful outdoor cooking are hard to overcome—and some find the task impossible to master.

Here is a savory promotion stunt that you can pitch to a major supermarket. They'll turn into a big-volume client for you, and you should help them move a considerable portion of the area's barbecue and picnic items.

How It Works

On a Saturday morning or afternoon in early summer the supermarket stages an Outdoor Cooking College: a short course on the arts of barbecuing and outdoor cookery. The event, of course, is heavily promoted on your station and your disc jockeys either attend or help conduct the course, depending on their own talents in this area. The supermarket provides everything, including instructors, grills, utensils, meat, and condiments. Faculty and students enjoy the fruits of their labors in a feast following the event.

Every place you stage your Outdoor Cooking College, get the store to put up special decorations for the event. They will want to have all of their clerks wear the sort of barbecue aprons that have sayings printed all over them. The clerks should also wear chef's hats to add a little more spark to the occasion.

Benefits

Not only will the store gain traffic, goodwill, and publicity from the Outdoor Cooking College, but the store's meat counter and picnic supply aisle will show a profit throughout the summer from this promotion.

Instructors

You may already have a nutrition/cooking editor on your staff who is the ideal person to conduct the outdoor cooking class. Or yours may be a co-owned radio/television operation that has a person who does cooking features on a locally produced TV show. If the right person is not available from your immediate staff, there are many cooking experts in every town who can do the job. Maybe some of the prominent business leaders who are your sponsors are outdoor cooking experts, and they could fill the bill.

How to Sell It

This should be pitched to a supermarket as a major Saturday promotion. The station will naturally get behind it on the air. Be sure to arrange for as many of your personalities as possible to be on hand. The event should be promoted through a very heavy spot schedule on your station, as well as through the store's regular newspaper advertising.

Point out to the store buying this idea that they will get the maximum benefits by tying in a spectacular sale of outdoor cooking items to run on the same Saturday as the cooking college. Such a sale should include not only meals, but also salad ingredients, potato chips, sauces and seasonings of all kinds, plus napkins, paper plates, and many other food items relating to outdoor cooking.

Consider selling this promotion to a chain of supermarkets. In this way you conduct the Outdoor Cooking College at all of their outlets on subsequent Saturdays. You can even stage it at one store in the morning and again at another store in the afternoon.

If a local shopping center includes a supermarket, you can broaden the sponsorship of the promotion to include all stores that sell relevant items. The cooking college will then be put on in the middle of the shopping center before a huge crowd of people.

Tie in Regional and National Sponsors

When you plan this promotion, be sure to include spot schedules for regional and national sponsors who have items that are related to outdoor cooking. The cooking college gives you a natural "in" with them for the entire summer season.

Printed Materials

Either your station or the sponsoring store should prepare some handouts for the Outdoor Cooking College. You may want to split the cost on this, but try to get the store to pay the whole bill. The printed piece should carry a good strong plug for the station and for the store. It should also include cooking tips, recipes, and whatever other information your Outdoor Cooking College instructor thinks is proper.

Fun Promotions

THESE PROMOTIONS ARE FUN. IN MANY CASES, THERE IS A PRIZE CONNECTED, but this is incidental to the fun of getting through the promotion itself. Keep this in mind: In order for promotions to be effective with the audience, they should generate enthusiasm among your personnel. If your staff isn't having fun promoting your station, then your listeners won't be having a good time either.

Most "fun" promotions are of short duration. They are usually built around the simplest of ideas and are designed to create talk. This is another highly effective means of establishing the feeling of excitement that attracts listeners and holds their attention.

Fun promotions should get all of your air personalities into the act. The idea behind the promotion is to project a certain vital image of the entire station, rather than developing any single personality at the expense of the others. In the long run, word-of-mouth promotion is the best, so you are striving to get people in your listening area to tell someone else "You should hear what they're doing on WZZZ!"

A fun promotion has "spread" (the built-in ability to cause a chain reaction). In affecting one person, it spreads itself automatically to that person's circle of friends and acquaintances. The promotions in this section have the elements of "fun" and "spread" in abundance.

4.1 MYSTERY NAME

This one is easy. It is based on a whispering campaign, and you know that rumor mills work fast—and well!

How It Works

Each day, select the name of a local person. Then announce it on the air once each hour for the whole day.

THE WZZZ MYSTERY NAME FOR TODAY IS JOHN JONES.

If you wish, pick a new name for each hour, and announce it two or three times during that hour. Just announce it without further comment. That's it. No elaboration. No additional ad-libbing. Just that short announcement.

Does this sound too simple to even be usable? Just put it on the air and try it. You'll find out differently.

The Spread Goes to Work

Dozens of friends of John Jones will hear his name mentioned on the air, and they'll call him to find out what it's all about. They'll also call other people, saying, "Hey, I heard John Jones' name on the radio. Do you know what's going on?"

Sooner or later, John Jones himself will call you to find out what is happening. If he does, simply tell him, "We thought you would like to hear your name on the air. We like people and we just wanted you to know that you don't have to get elected president or rob a bank to get your name on WZZZ."

It's simple. It's easy. It doesn't cost much or involve a lot of air time. Yet you'll be amazed at the amount of "spread" you will get from this simple fun promotion.

"PRINCE CHARMING" AT THE FAIR   4.2

Everybody goes to the fair, and WZZZ is there too, represented by the "WZZZ Prince Charming" looking for—who else?—Cinderella. This promotion is ideally suited to the fun-filled atmosphere of the fair in your area.

How It Works

WZZZ's "Prince Charming" is abroad among the crowds at the fair with a glass slipper. Any woman or girl who stops him by asking "Are you the WZZZ Prince Charming?" gets to try on the slipper. If it fits, she is named "WZZZ's Cinderella" and wins the prize or prizes you have arranged. If the slipper does not fit, the person receives a consolation prize, say, a pass to some of the rides at the fair, and after a wait of 15 or 30 minutes, "Prince Charming" again begins his search.

Each day of the fair a WZZZ "Cinderella" is sought, and if a day passes without a winner, the prize is doubled for the next day, and so on, although it is doubtful that a day will pass without a winner. You can assure yourself of this if you wish by inserting clues describing the appearance of "Prince Charming" into your broadcasts.

Since a good number of people pay more than one visit to the fair, you will have to use a different person in the role of "Prince Charming" each day. You may have to substitute "Prince Charmings" during the day after there have been unsuccessful attempts to put on the glass slipper, since people then will have identified your man.

"Prince Charming" Calls

From time to time have "Prince Charming" phone the station with news of his activities at the fair: who has stopped him, what his plans are for the next hour, or any colorful items of information or fun that he has picked up while he, and WZZZ, are at the fair.

Posters at the Fairgrounds

Be sure to put up posters, or "reward" bulletins at the fairgrounds as a reminder for your listeners to be looking for the WZZZ "Prince Charming." Even people who have not heard you promoting the contest on the air will join the search when they get there and see your posters. If you are doing a remote from the fair, be sure your booth announces that the WZZZ "Prince Charming" is around the fairgrounds somewhere.

Prizes

For this contest we suggest a group of prizes rather than one major one, and since you will be awarding them each day of the fair, they should not be too large.

Arrange for the "Prince Charming" prizes through firms having booths at the fair, and get them to put up signs asking people to look for the WZZZ "Prince Charming." In return, of course, you mention the sources of the prize and perhaps plug where the booth is located at the fair.

A couple of good prizes in keeping with the "Cinderella" theme might be a dinner for two and a night on the town, and a beauty treatment or permanent at a local salon.

"Prince Charming" At The Fair—On-Air Copy

GO TO THE FAIR, PRINCE CHARMING'S THERE. WZZZ'S PRINCE CHARMING, THAT IS, LOOKING FOR CINDERELLA TO GIVE HER A HOST OF WONDERFUL PRIZES. EACH DAY NEXT WEEK AT THE _____ COUNTY FAIR,

* * * *

WZZZ'S MYSTERY PRINCE CHARMING WILL BE SEARCHING FOR THE CINDERELLA WHOSE DAINTY FOOT FITS THE GLASS SLIPPER HE CARRIES. HE'LL BE GLAD TO LET ANY OF YOU LADIES TRY IT ON, JUST ASK HIM: (woman's voice): "ARE YOU THE WZZZ PRINCE CHARMING?"GO TO THE FAIR, PRINCE CHARMING'S THERE.

* * * *

IF THE SLIPPER FITS, WEAR IT—YOU MAY BE WZZZ'S CINDERELLA-AT-THE-FAIR! EVERY DAY OF THE COUNTY _____ FAIR, WZZZ'S MYSTERY PRINCE CHARMING WILL BE AROUND THE FAIRGROUNDS WAITING TO BE ASKED: (woman's voice) "ARE YOU WZZZ'S PRINCE CHARMING?"IF YOU ARE

THE LUCKY LADY ASKING THAT QUESTION OF WZZZ'S PRINCE CHARMING, AND IF THE SLIPPER FITS, WEAR IT! YOU ARE WZZZ'S CINDERELLA-AT-THE-FAIR.

* * * *

(music, circus theme up then under)

WZZZ IS AT THE FAIR—PRINCE CHARMING IS THERE! STAY TUNED TO WZZZ-460 FOR DETAILS.

(music up to end, fade)

PROMOTE TRAFFIC SAFETY   4.3

With summer comes vacation time and hundreds of thousands of Americans take to the roads. Each year thousands of them die in traffic accidents—and many more are injured. One of the greatest services you can provide your listeners is to conduct a safe-driving campaign with special emphasis on the three-day weekends that come with summer holidays.

How It Works

Here is a humorous approach to traffic safety. This is an effective way to approach the problem. Following you will find a large group of suggested slogans to use. Ask listeners to send in slogans in the same light vein. Do not try to make a contest out of it; simply give name credit when you use a listener's slogan. Work closely with your local Safety Council in setting up your campaign. These groups are almost universally cooperative.

Possible Slogans

PULL OFF THE ROAD WHEN YOU STOP TO LOOK—IT MAY KEEP YOUR STAY FROM BEING A PERMANENT ONE.

NEVER PASS ON A BLIND CURVE—YOU MAY GET A FATAL SURPRISE.

FOLLOWING TOO CLOSE IS A HABIT YOU CAN STOP—BEFORE YOU FIND YOURSELF IN A SITUATION WHERE YOU CAN'T STOP.

SUMMERTIME IS WHEN THE LIVIN' IS EASY—BUT SO IS THE DYING IF YOU'RE RECKLESS ON THE HIGHWAY.

THE REWARD FOR COURTEOUS DRIVING MAY NOT BE OBVIOUS. BUT REMEMBER YOU'RE ALIVE TO LOOK FOR IT.

DIMMING YOUR LIGHTS AT NIGHT IS THE BRIGHT THING TO DO.

IF PEOPLE REALLY AREN'T IN A HURRY TO DIE, WHY DO SO MANY OF THEM EXCEED THE SPEED LIMIT TO DO IT?

A CURVE TOO FAST CAN BE YOUR LAST.

YOU'RE LISTENING TO WZZZ RADIO—MUSIC TO DRIVE SAFELY BY.

THE GREATEST SINGLE CAUSE OF ACCIDENTS IS THE LOOSE NUT HOLDING THE STEERING WHEEL.

WELCOME TOURISTS—PLEASE DRIVE SAFELY SO WE CAN GREET YOU AGAIN NEXT YEAR.

DON'T LOSE YOUR TEMPER WHILE DRIVING—YOU MAY NOT LIVE LONG ENOUGH TO FIND IT AGAIN.

DON'T RACE A TRAIN TO A CROSSING—THE LOSS WILL KILL YOU.

DON'T GO IN FOR ONE-ARM DRIVING UNLESS YOU'RE WILLING TO LOSE THE OTHER ARM.

DRIVE SAFELY—AND DON'T TRADE THAT SUNTAN FOR A FUNERAL PARLOR PALLOR.

DRIVE SAFELY—DON'T TRADE YOUR VACATION FOR A PERMANENT REST.

DRIVE SAFELY—REMEMBER, YOU'RE ENTITLED TO ONLY ONE FATAL MIS-TAKE.

DRIVING TOO FAST IN THE SUMMER MAY LEAD YOU TO AN EARLY FALL.

WZZZ ASKS YOU TO DRIVE SAFELY—EVERY LISTENER COUNTS.

DRIVING TOO FAST WON'T MAKE YOUR VACATION LAST LONGER—IT'LL JUST SEEM THAT WAY IN THE HOSPITAL.

DON'T LET YOUR ANXIETY TO COVER GROUND PUT YOU UNDER IT.

IF YOU WANT A COMPACT CAR, BUY ONE—DON'T COMPRESS THE ONE YOU'VE GOT IN AN ACCIDENT.

DON'T LET A FAST TRIP BE YOUR LAST TRIP.

DRIVE SAFELY—DON'T DIE IN AN AUTO ACCIDENT. IT CAN SPOIL YOUR WHOLE SUMMER.

BELT SOMEONE YOU LOVE—USE SEATBELTS.

AMIDST OUR AREA'S SCENIC SPLENDOR, TRY WATCHING THE ROAD.

SPEED DICTATION 4.4

Here is an evening-hours promotion. Set up on tape 30 seconds of dictation material. Have a typed manuscript of it handy. Play the tape; the first person to call in an exact reading of the material is your winner. Each evening, new dictation material is used and the speed is increased by 5 to 10 words per 30-second period.

The contest continues until the evening on which you can get no winner because the dictation speed is too fast. Then the winner from the previous evening is declared your grand champion. Check with a secretarial school to work out word patterns that are sufficiently difficult to provide a proper test.

"I WORK FOR A DICTATOR" 4.5

Invite the secretaries among your listeners to join your "I Work for a Dictator" club. You can have a lot of fun with this on your midday shift.

How It Works

The secretaries enter by writing to one of the WZZZ disc jockeys and requesting a membership card. You will, of course, have the cards printed up in advance, permitting fast turnaround. Your printer can handle the typesetting and work with you on a design. The advantage of the membership cards is, of course, that this will be shown around to many people who are not now your listeners. It will convey the impression that a lot of fun things are happening on the air.

The membership card should be headed: "I Work for a Dictator." The body copy on the card can state: "This is to certify that the undersigned is a member in good standing in the WZZZ I Work for a Dictator Club. Said member is hereby designated as a Dictatee and may be dictated to interminably by persons in proper authority." A line for a signature should be at the bottom of the card.

4.6 MARCH HAIR HUNT

This simple promotion is based on a very familiar pair of words that have been twisted to direct it right at the females in your audience. It includes a prize that is bound to please your female listeners.

How It Works

Announce that WZZZ is taking a page from "Alice in Wonderland" and is searching for Centerville's "March Hare"—only here it becomes "March H-A-I-R." Confine this promotion to the late-morning show.

Female listeners are asked to tape a strand or lock of their hair to a piece of paper and mail it to WZZZ's March Hair Hunt. Naturally, the postcard should also include the entrant's name, address, and daytime phone number.

At the end of the week, one of the cards is drawn from among the entries and this winner receives a complete hairstyling from a local hairdresser. That's all there is to it.

4.7 FRIDAY THE THIRTEENTH

No matter how sophisticated we may be, each of us has some superstition that we heed. Certainly we ridicule the belief in superstition while in public, but not one of us is completely free from its influence. This being the case, you have the perfect basis for a fun promotion.

Friday the Thirteenth turns up a few times each year. During these days superstitions are foremost in our minds. Your object is to test once and for all the validity of commonly held superstitions.

How It Works

Try to get at least two of your air personalities into the act. Establish one of them as the believer in superstitions and the other as the nonbeliever. About 10 days before the event, one DJ warns listeners that a Friday the Thirteenth is coming up, so they should be particularly careful. The second DJ ridicules this and states that he or she would not be afraid to test any superstition. Then the DJ who is the believer challenges the other to take the test.

Get Listeners into the Act

Ask listeners to send in lists of all the common superstitions they can think of. In a public place on Friday the Thirteenth your brave DJ will violate as many of these superstitions as possible in a test to determine if bad luck will really come.

As the lists of suggestions come in, use them on the air to spark additional interest. You can even have a drawing for minor prizes to be awarded to each entry that is read on the air.

As the promotion develops, encourage active listener participation. Ask people to assist the experiment by providing some of the various props you will need to use in breaking the superstitions. Just be careful in the wording of this request, though. You don't want to end up with every stray black cat in town.

Insured to the Hilt

As an additional feature, have your DJ insured by Lloyd's of London. Arrange for a special "superstition-breaking" policy for as large a sum as possible.

Medical Coverage

Have a doctor and nurse on hand throughout the superstition test. They should check the "condition" of your guinea pig between each experiment. Try to have an ambulance standing by, too, just in case the DJ is stricken with bad luck on the spot.

Publicity

Give as much publicity as possible to the time and place of the superstition test. Set things up so that your challenger follows a systematic program of testing the superstitions. You should be able to do a very effective remote from the site, with a play-by-play of each experiment and a "tote board" showing progress through each one.

The public will be invited, of course, to attend the event. You may want to set up a PA system with one of your other DJs. Probably the superstitious one should be the emcee for this event. You can get a good crowd and do a sponsor a good turn by holding the superstition experiment in a mall, a large store, a theatre, a supermarket, or some similar place.

4.8 LISTENER'S HOLIDAY

A limitation with many promotions staged by radio stations is that they are confined to a station's own airwaves. This is not always bad, though. One of the things promotion does is to maintain the audience you already have; the other thing is to build a larger audience for you. To enlarge your audience, you need more than word-of-mouth exposure. You must get the message across to those people who are not your present listeners. A promotion such as this is one that can get the job done.

How It Works

In your morning drive time slot, the DJ announces the name of a worker sometime during the show. If that worker is listening to the station, he or she will be told of having the day off work via the announcement on the air. However, if the selected worker is not listening, he or she will end up at work being razzed all day by fellow employees who heard the announcement.

Making Arrangements with the Employers

First, contact all of the major employers in your area. Particularly important will be the industrial groups. Inform these employers of your plans. They will be anxious to work with you because of the plugs their business will receive, not to mention the boost in employee morale it should create among their staff. It will also provide the company a novel way of rewarding faithful employees.

You should set up a contact within each firm. This will normally be the president, general manager, or some other key executive. These are actual decision-makers who select the employee to be honored with a day off. This also allows the company to choose a convenient time and to arrange for temporary help if needed.

Publicity within the Companies

This promotion must receive maximum publicity within the participating companies themselves. Arrange for stories to appear in the company in-house newsletter. Have material prepared for posting on the company bulletin boards that explains the promotion. If the company holds meetings with the workers, the promotion should be outlined by an executive at such meetings.

Handling on the Air

Prepare a standard format to be used within this promotion on the air. Listeners who are friends of the employee names should be cautioned not to call him or her. If the selected employee is not listening, let him or her go on to work—

only to find out (too late) that today could have been a holiday. Within this format, you have an excellent opportunity to give praise to the activities of local businesses and point up their importance to the community.

For the Losers

When a worker has not been listening and fails to win the holiday, the contact person should call the station to this effect so that a message of condolence can be carried on a later show. This amounts to additional plugs for the company, as well as the promotion.

When you have a loser, your morning air personality can go to the company to take this employee to lunch as a consolation prize. This provides an excellent opportunity for good exposure for the DJ and the station, gives a nice boost to the promotion, and helps the honored employee feel that not all was lost.

THE LISTENER CLUB   4.9

The WZZZ Listener Club is as inexpensive to operate as it is effective in gaining listeners.

How It Works

Your listeners are invited to send in for their Listener Club cards. Each card has a unique serial number. As you mail them out, keep a master list of names against the numbers issued. After a sufficient number of cards have been sent out, the Listener Club promotion starts on the air.

Seven to ten times each day, one of the numbers is read on the air. The holder of the card who calls the station within two minutes and positively identifies himself or herself wins. When you do not get a winner, your DJ should announce the name of the person who failed to call in. The loser's friends will make sure that he or she listens in the future.

The Prize

The prize should be a small cash reward. This promotion can work effectively if you offer only one dollar to start and increase it one dollar each game until you have a winner. In this way the promotion can cost you no more than $7 to $10 dollars a day.

Alternate Prize

Besides a cash prize, another approach is to give away some kind of merchandise. These prizes should be relatively small in value, but you are not going to be successful giving away movie tickets or anything else of that nature. You will be better off with a variety of prizes so you can continue to pile them up when you have no winner.

Setting Up the Master List

In the beginning, your promotion will have a better sound on the air if you start the card numbers above 500 and use only every other number, such as the even numbers. Once you get above 750 use only the odd numbers. This will help get the card numbers high enough to be impressive in a hurry. And you can always go back and pick up the skipped numbers later if you want to.

To prevent any one person from sending in for multiple Listener Club cards, set up a second alphabetical master list. Specify that you will accept only postcard entries. Then, after the names have been put on your master list and the cards have been sent out, file the postcards alphabetically. There is no need to double-check every membership request that comes in. Just have one person handle the mail on this promotion, and they will quickly recognize multiple entries.

Outside Events for Members

You will add interest to your promotion and increase the desirability of becoming a Listener Club member if you schedule some special outside events for Listener Club members only. This can be a special movie showing arranged through one of your local theaters, or it can be a special discount on tapes or CDs at a local record store. Listener Club members who show their cards are the only ones to get the special treatment.

These Listener Club special events can also be used as merchandising gimmicks that can be part of a special sales package offered to sponsors. The merchants can offer special sale prices to members who show their cards at the point of purchase.

4.10   DICTIONARY DROP-INS

This is another of those simple little on-air bits. It is uncomplicated and easy to do. It takes very little air time, yet gives your listeners one more reason to perk up their ears, chuckle, and talk about your station.

How It Works

Get a group of unusual words from any standard dictionary, along with the definitions. The Dictionary Drop-Ins should be confined to just one of your disc jockeys. The material provides your DJs with some interesting filler items that should be dropped into the show cold for the greatest effect. Use no introduction—just dump in the word and its definition, then move right into the music.

Some Examples

albertite—a bituminous mineral resembling asphaltum, found in the county of Albert, New Brunswick.

bubaline—of or belonging to the group of antelopes typified by the *hartebeest* and the *topi*.

chaldron—a nearly obsolete English dry measure for coal, lime, etc., commonly equal to 32 bushels.

diachylon—an adhesive plaster made of litharge and olive oil or olive oil and lard.

eudaemonia—well-being; happiness; especially in Aristotle's use, felicity resulting from life of activity in accordance with reason.

fetiparous—designating mammals, as marsupials, whose young are born very incompletely developed.

graywacke—a coarse sandstone or fine-grained conglomerate, usually dark grey, composed of firmly cemented, somewhat rounded fragments of quartz, feldspars, and so on.

ignescent—emitting sparks when struck with steel, hence, becoming inflamed; inflammatory.

jalap—the purgative tuberous root of a Mexican plant of the morning-glory family, or a powdered drug from it.

kestrel—small European falcon noted for its habit of hovering in the air against the wind.

liripipe—a pendant part of the old clerical or academic tippet; afterwards: *tippet*; *scarf*; *hood*.

monody—an ode sung by one voice, as in a tragedy; a funeral song; a dirge.

THE TIME CAPSULE   4.11

This promotion is probably several hundred years old, if not older, but it still works amazingly well. By putting in a couple of twists and a little imagination, you can make it into a winner.

How It Works

Gather together a group of items, place them in a sealed container, bury it, and leave instructions that it is to be opened at some time in the future. That's all there is to it. The secret of success in the Time Capsule promotion lies in what items you include, how you gather them, and where you place them.

When to Do It

You need some logical reason to do the Time Capsule promotion. You can stage it under the following circumstances:

1. The start of a new year,
2. In conjunction with a major civic celebration;
3. As a part of your station's anniversary promotion;
4. To capitalize on a major national or international occurrence or anniversary.

The main idea is to tie it in with something else that is going on. This will give it added meaning, especially if the other event will also provide a likely circumstance for reopening the time capsule years down the road.

How to Lead into the Time Capsule Promotion

On the air you first establish the significance of the tie-in event. Then, announce that you are going to bury a time capsule in conjunction with this event. Invite the public to send in suggestions about what should be included in the WZZZ Time Capsule. Remember that everything is possible because you do not have to include the actual item, but can substitute a photograph instead. Also, many things can be reduced onto microfilm.

What to Include

Here are some suggested things that you should include either as real samples or in photographic form:

- pictures of your air personalities
- pictures of your station, inside and out
- contemporary furniture
- current telephones
- modern bathrooms
- a list of current sayings and what they mean
- cars

- restaurant menu
- credit card
- list of top musical hits
- list of current best-selling books
- a copy of a magazine's year-end roundup of significant news events
- a copy of your publicity release explaining the Time Capsule

Hype the Event

Naturally, you want to involve the public as much as possible, so ask them to help you in locating or providing some of the items to be included. Include taped messages from the mayor, governor, and others.

Have a group of key people give you predictions about life in the future when the capsule is supposed to be reopened. Invite the general public to sign a scroll, which will be placed in the Time Capsule—this is a kind of "Hello to the Future" greeting card, and can be reduced to microfilm. Try to have a complete newspaper included, especially if the local paper does a feature story on the Time Capsule.

Build the whole day's programming around this event. Recordings of the ceremonies, related promos, and news stories can be added to the capsule's contents at the last-possible moment.

TRAVEL LOG 4.12

Summertime is vacation and travel time; each year millions of Americans are traveling throughout the United States and abroad. Of course, many of your listeners will spend their vacations well beyond your reception area. Here is a simple promotion that will keep your station on their minds. It will also permit your listeners at home to share in some of the experiences of their traveling neighbors.

How It Works

Ask your listeners to write a card or letter to the WZZZ Travel Log while they are on their vacations. Each week a portable radio or similar prize is awarded to the most interesting letter received from a traveling listener.

As a tie-in with the travel log idea, a major-prize AM/FM/shortwave portable radio is awarded to the writer of the letter from the vacation site that is most distant from your community.

A Summer-Long Promotion

The simplicity of this promotion lets you easily run it throughout the summer vacation period, from early in June through August or even into September. The entries and messages you will receive will make highly interesting items for your DJs to read on the air daily. Your air personalities can talk up the promotion, building anticipation toward the announcement of the weekly winners.

Home Addresses

In all publicity and promotion, make sure you emphasize that entries have the *home address* of the sender included. If the only address a winner gives is a hotel in Paris, you might have more than a little trouble delivering the prize.

4.13 "SPORT SHIRT DAYS" PROCLAMATION

We don't know how you feel about it, but on the really hot days of summer we much prefer the comfort of an open collar sport shirt to the confines of a white shirt and tie. However, custom and conformity dictate that "white collar" jobs are just that—white collars are worn no matter what the temperature.

Campaign for Comfort

As soon as the first genuine hot spell of the summer gets under way, your disc jockeys start a concerted campaign to get a day proclaimed "Sport Shirt Day" throughout Centerville. The proclamation should come from the mayor or the president of the Chamber of Commerce.

Promote this idea on the air and encourage listeners to send in letters to the mayor (or Chamber president) supporting the concept. After two or three days of this, have the Mayor's office issue a short, clever (and prearranged) proclamation.

This promotion needs to be arranged with civic officials and local business in advance. By arrangement, the proclamation will be issued after a few days of 90-plus degree days when the forecast calls for more of the same tomorrow.

Firms Tie-In

Invite any and all firms and businesses to issue short statements in favor of the proclamation, which you read on the air. For example, a department store might joyfully support the campaign with a statement such as:

THE BON TON REALIZES THAT CUSTOMERS CAN'T SPEND ALL OF THEIR TIME SHOPPING IN OUR AIR-CONDITIONED COMFORT, AND WE THEREFORE SUPPORT SPORT SHIRT DAYS.

Sample Proclamation

Here is a sample of the proclamation you can have issued by the mayor:

> I, John J. Jones, Mayor of Centerville, do hereby proclaim that WHEREAS the male population of the City of Centerville is a hard-working and conscientious group;
> and
> WHEREAS said male population is generally neat and well-groomed;
> and
> WHEREAS said male population has suffered without undue complaint from the days of early manhood within the confines of starched white shirt and tie, regardless of weather;
> and
> WHEREAS it is a well-recognized fact that certain meteorological phenomena make such attire impractical;
> THEREFORE I do hereby proclaim that the next day on which the weather prediction as announced on radio station WZZZ calls for a temperature higher than 90 degrees Fahrenheit will henceforth be known as "Sport Shirt Day" in Centerville; and the adult male population of the City of Centerville may on that day appear at work and on the city streets wearing a sport shirt without a tie in the full knowledge and assurance of being adequately, properly, and decently dressed.

DEPARTMENT STORE SCHOOL DAY   4.14

This is a promotion that can create a tremendous amount of goodwill for your best department store account. It is hard to imagine a promotion that would be received as enthusiastically by the community as a whole. In fact, it can be turned easily into an annual event for the department store that buys your idea.

How It Works

On a given day that has been well publicized in advance over your station, the department store declares "School Day." For that day only the store will donate 10 percent of the day's receipts to the schools of your city. Customers are alerted in advance to write the name of the school of their choice on the back of the sales slips.

Naturally, signs are posted all over the store explaining the promotion and directing customers to the deposit boxes conveniently placed near the checkout lanes and other places.

Area Promotion

Rather than having a single department store participating in the "School Day" promotion, sell the idea to all the stores in the downtown area or every outlet in a shopping center or mall.

Invite All Schools

Four weeks in advance of School Day, a letter announcing the event should go to the principal of each school in your area. The schools themselves may bring this to the attention of the students and parents. Be sure that every individual school is contacted.

To make things easy for the principal, enclose a self-addressed and stamped reply postcard with the original announcement. The principals will use the reply cards to indicate the willingness of each school to participate in the promotion and to receive moneys that will result from the purchases made.

Your on-air promotions should mention the names of participating schools. The signs on the collection boxes should also list which schools are involved.

Help by the Schools

Request that a member of each school be present at the various deposit boxes to assist people in depositing their slips correctly.

4.15 MERIT BADGE PROMOTION

This promotion gives your DJs a chance to do a first-class job of publicity for one of the nations most deserving organization: The Boy Scouts of America. The official Boy Scout Week falls in February, but this promotion is better used at another time of year.

This is one of the best and most worthwhile pegs for a promotion that we have seen in a long time. It provides a good basis for feeding the rivalry you have set up between two air personalities.

How It Works

Through on-air challenges, your two feuding DJs can set up a competitive situation to see who can honestly acquire the greatest number of Boy Scout merit badges. They should be limited to working on their merit badges for a given length of time, such as three or four months.

Your air personalities may not use any shortcuts or be excluded from any normal merit badge requirements; they must play it "by the book." Judging should be handled by Scouting representatives who normally judge the merit badge achievements of regular Scouts.

Get Some Outside Help

So that you can do a better job of publicity for the Boy Scouts, and to add an extra spin to the promotion, arrange for each of your DJs involved to be "adopted" by a Boy Scout Troop. If there is only one troop in the immediate area, have individual patrols adopt each DJ.

The scouts should be permitted to coach and counsel the DJs in their efforts. But the DJs should still have to fulfill all of the qualifications for each merit badge. In addition to the Boy Scouts, your air personalities should also call for some other outside advice from professionals within the various categories of competition.

No Limits to the Scope

Only your imagination limits the fun and stunts your DJs can devise as they compete. Remember, however, to avoid belittling the merit badge requirements or the Boy Scouts. The source of hilarity will be in seeing grown-ups sweating through the requirements that must be met by young people.

Don't be surprised if your DJs don't succeed on each attempted merit badge. At the same time, the thoroughness of the requirements will give you many honest opportunities to plug the benefits of Scouting.

Get the Book

Get a copy of the official publication "Boy Scout Requirements." This booklet, available from your nearest Scouting office, lists the detailed requirements for the many dozens of possible merit badges.

Get Official Help

Before you start this promotion, consult with the local council of the Boy Scouts. Inform the leaders of your plans and enlist their cooperation. Scouting officials are a group of real live-wires and their assistance will be invaluable. Point out to them how this promotion is designed to publicize Scouting and how it will help their recruitment and fund-raising efforts.

The Scouting officials will be able to provide the necessary judges as your disc jockeys attempt to qualify for the various merit badges. They should also be able to provide any special facilities required.

Picking the Merit Badges

When selecting the merit badges to be used, try to arrange them in various categories. Several should be the type that the DJ will do mostly on his own, but which will make for interesting talk on the air. A number should actively involve some members of the listening audience. And a couple should involve all of the Boy Scouts in your area, probably at one of their camping events.

Here are some suggested merit badges appropriate for this promotion:

Home Repairs

This merit badge outlines 26 separate repair jobs, and 14 must be completed satisfactorily to qualify for the merit badge. This gives you a chance to go on the air and ask listeners to volunteer as guinea pigs, inviting the DJ into their homes to make one or more of these repairs. The required repairs include:

- waterproof a basement wall
- repair broken furniture
- repair sagging door or gate
- repair broken picture frame
- clean out clogged sink trap
- replace faucet washer
- replace broken pane of glass
- replace all cords in a Venetian blind
- recondition a garden tool

Bugling

This one gives your DJs a chance to do some practice on the air—with the resultant horrendous sounds. The official requirements include the proper sounding of these calls:

- First Call
- Reveille
- Mess
- To The Colors
- Officers
- Drill
- Assembly
- Recall
- Fatigue
- Church
- Fire
- Swimming
- Retreat
- Call to Quarters
- Taps

Cooking

The requirements for this merit badge gives you the opportunity to stage a good outside stunt, since it is necessary to cook for a number of people. The public can be invited to attend and sample the culinary skills of your disc jockeys.

Hiking

This one will put your DJs outside in a big way. It's a good idea to invite plenty of Boy Scouts along on the hikes. They can all work toward the merit badge together with your air personalities. Certain written requirements exist, in addition to the following hiking activities:

- Take five hikes of 10 continuous miles each on five separate days.
- Take one hike of 20 continuous miles in one day.

Basketry

The Basketry merit badge, as well as the Sculpture and Woodcarving merit badges, gives your DJs a chance to produce materials that can be put on public display as a means of gaining additional publicity for this promotion. The official requirements for Basketry include:

- Plan and weave a large basket or tray using reed, raffia, or splints.
- Weave a seat for a stool or chair, using cane or rush.

Sculpture

This merit badge provides the opportunity to enlist advice from one of the many art groups in your area. Again, this is part of the plan to get your disc jockeys wide public exposure in a great variety of different areas. The requirements here include:

- Model in clay or carve in wood, soft stone, soap, or other soft material:
    - ~ a full-size human head of a type or nationality;
    - ~ a small scale model of a group of animals or people in action.
- Also, make a plaster cast mold of an apple, pear, or any other fruit or vegetable. In this mold cast a replica of the fruit or vegetable.

Woodcarving

Here is a good one for enlisting outside help. The requirements include:

- Make three handy camp articles, such a pothooks, a fork, a spoon or tent pegs, using only a knife.
- Plan and carve a design in low relief, or plan and carve in the round a simple object such as a totem animal figure or model.

Some Other Possibilities

This promotion seems to work well with these other merit badges as well:

• Archery	• Marksmanship
• Art	• Plumbing
• Athletics	• Pottery
• Camping	• Public Speaking

- Canoeing   • Radio
- Cycling   • Rowing
- Fishing   • Swimming

Timing

If you plan to use this promotion, use it during the late spring or early summer so that you will have some good weather for the outside activities. You can continue this promotion for as long as you wish. It will certainly run between one to two months at least.

Don't Be Scared Off

As you look at the total scope of this promotion, you might be a little frightened by its obvious complexities. Remember, however, that all of these activities will not be going on at the same time. You will be doing them one or two at a time.

Be sure to work out with the Scouting officials in your area the sort of publicity campaign you are going to be doing for them in advance. Some may require particular emphasis on getting new boys into the local troops. Others may need help in getting adult leaders and supervisors. Get this worked out in detail and plan it as carefully as you do the other parts of the promotion.

4.16 HAPPY BIRTHDAY

This idea is not actually a contest promotion, even though it has all of the usual elements. It provides the basis for a fine project that can be carried out over a very extended period of time. It involves your listeners in a very pleasant way—and all of their friends, too. It is simple to handle and will create no problems for you.

How It Works

Invite all of your listeners to send in postcards to register in the WZZZ Happy Birthday promotion. The card should include the entrant's name, address and date of birth.

The cards are arranged in chronological order by month and day. Each day one person having a birthday on that day is saluted by the station. They receive on-air recognition and some special gifts and surprises. That's all there is to it.

Added Features

By random selection, or whatever method you choose, one person is picked each day for the major happy birthday salute. Considerable fanfare is given to this person. You may ask people to give some additional information about themselves when registering; this can then be used on the air.

Salute all entrants for a given day with a mention on the air. Each of these should be sent a special birthday greeting card from the station. In order to set up your birthday file properly, you are going to have a large number of cards on hand when you start this promotion on the air. So give yourself about two weeks of advance birthday salutes. Let your listeners know what you have planned and encourage them to get their cards of registration in early.

Gift Ideas

You should have no problem arranging for special gifts for your birthday winners. You may wish to conduct a short telephone interview with the winner each day. It should be no problem to line up one of your bakery accounts that has delivery service to take a birthday cake to your daily winner. Flowers or plants are another possibility.

While a person normally has something already planned for his or her birthday celebration, you can present your winners with a gift certificate for dinner for two at a local restaurant. The gift certificate can be valid any time during the next month. Or one of your regular commercial accounts may wish to provide a gift certificate for a special surprise present.

Plan to use your birthday salute a number of times each day, rather than airing it at a single preset time.

Conclusion

As an additional bit to include, dig out the names of all the famous people born on each day and use these as a supplement to the local people you are saluting. The public library has this data, but you may also receive it via your wire service or find it in the various almanacs and trivia books available.

SPRING CLEANUP   4.17

Here is a public service promotion that has a great deal going for it. By using it you will attract the attention of the entire community. The response can be overwhelming!

How It Works

As an inspiration for a community or area-wide spring cleanup campaign, your station offers "a penny a pair" for all the matchbook covers turned in to the station during the "WZZZ Spring Cleanup Week."

Promote this stunt for a week or so in advance. Sell the fund-raising emphasis for civic organizations like the Scouts or church groups. Your response may be improved if you also send a direct-mail release to these groups informing them of your plans. Be sure to set aside a special area at the station for the matchbook covers turned in. Have space for a display of the collection and be sure to take some pictures.

A Natural Tie-In

Some civic agency, such as the Chamber of Commerce, may already sponsor an annual spring cleanup in your area. This is a natural tie-in for a joint promotion with plenty of publicity for everyone. Try to match your dates with an existing program. Don't buck 'em—join 'em.

The Cost

The only cost for this promotion is the amount of money you pay out for the matchbook covers turned in. The "penny a pair" figure is just a suggestion. For instance, if the promotion is an outstanding success and you collect 100,000 matchbook covers, your out-of-pocket expense is $500. We think it is a reasonable sum for a promotion of this magnitude. You can adjust the bounty on matchbooks to suit your budget, however.

Using the Matchbooks

Rather than just throwing the matchbook covers away after you have collected them, check around with veterans hospitals or similar places to see if they would like to receive the covers. Collecting matchbooks is a popular hobby.

A Related Contest

As an added attention-getter to this promotion, you may choose to run a simple contest in conjunction with your Spring Cleanup Week. A prize is offered to the listener who sends in a postcard bearing the closest guess to the actual number of matchbooks received.

The covers can be placed in a large container constructed of chicken wire. Listeners are then invited down to the station or to some other public place where your collection is on display. They can look over the pile before making a guess. Don't worry about having to go through the bin to count all of those matchbooks. Just keep an accurate account of the cash paid out and use this figure to establish the number of matchbooks collected. Make sure you have adequate storage area for all of this stuff that will come in. Perhaps a local trucking company will lease or loan you a semitrailer to serve as a temporary storage shed.

Alternative Collection Items

Instead of using just matchbook covers as your collection item, collect empty aluminum drink cans or old newspapers. Any of these can be recycled. You can run a large combined Spring Cleanup, or have separate events for each type of recyclable material.

Handling the Collection

Be sure to specify certain hours for the collection items to be turned in at the station. And be sure, too, that there is always someone besides the on-air personality present to greet, collect, and pay off. If you leave the DJ alone to handle this task (plus spin records, read the news, answer the phone, clear the news wire, and read the meters), your on-air product will quickly suffer.

If your station covers a large listening area, arrange for additional collection spots at shopping centers scattered around town. As a trade-out, perhaps you can get several garbage trucks to haul in the recycled material to a central processing point in your parking lot or antenna field. The growing piles will become an impressive reminder of everyone's duty to keep your community clean.

The World's Largest Trash Can

Construct a collection bin that at least vaguely resembles a large garbage can. If you are collecting several different items for recycling, subdivide the "garbage can" into sections internally, but preserve the "World's Largest Garbage Can" appearance on the outside. On-air patter about the overall promotion may include comments about how the "World's Largest Garbage Can" is filling up. Perhaps you can even have someone do a live remote as they stand knee-deep in the collected refuse.

Honorary Street Cleaners

Get some additional spread out of this promotion by having some wallet-sized cards printed up informing the world that the bearer is an official "WZZZ Honorary Street Cleaner." A card is then presented to each person bringing in any of the collection items. In addition to (or instead of) the membership cards, present each collector with a bumper sticker that says "I Cleaned Up with WZZZ."

What to Do with the Money

Any money you receive from the sale of matchbooks, cans, or newspapers should be used for civic betterment. A good project is to purchase some new public litter barrels to be placed along city streets. Or use the money to make "Official WZZZ Litter Bags" and give them away for use in cars.

Cleanup Announcements

Concurrent with your Spring Cleanup Week promotion, you should air an extensive series of spots urging listeners to cooperate in the general city-wide cleanup campaign. Remember that your promotion is designed to turn the spotlight of public attention on such a general campaign.

Be sure that you create an aura of fun around this promotion so that everyone will participate. Unless you do, a great many people are not going to bother to bring items down to the station. You might start things off by dressing your DJs up in street cleaner uniforms and have them go sweep out the gutters of the downtown area.

4.18   STARGAZERS

This is more of a programming idea than a promotion. Granted, it may not work in some areas as well as others, but if you do a little digging, you are bound to find some local astronomy enthusiasts.

How It Works

The WZZZ Stargazer promotion is usable during the late spring and early summer months when the nights are typically clear and warm. Set up a regularly scheduled series of programs dealing with the stars and other celestial bodies visible from your location. Invite listeners to take their radios out into the backyard and follow for themselves while an authority discusses the stars in the heavens. You will be surprised at the enthusiastic response you'll get to this program.

Scheduling

Because of the combination of long days, compounded in most areas by daylight saving time, you will probably have to schedule this for sometime after 9:30 in the evening. Naturally, to gain the largest possible audience you will want to air it as early as possible after local sunset.

Depending on your own circumstances, you will have to determine the frequency of the program. You may wish to run this every night of the week, but it can also be effective if run only once or twice a week. Regardless of the schedule, the program should be done live. Remember, this is a changing world; unforecasted changes in the local weather conditions can make a prerecorded program impractical. The program could run as long as 15 minutes, but it will work just fine as a one- to three-minute feature.

Lining Up the Instructor

When we mentioned using an authority on astronomy, we meant just that. Don't settle for using one of your DJs referring to the "morning star, evening star" almanac information provided by the news wire.

Ideally, a live remote from a nearby college observatory or planetarium is the setting for using a qualified astronomy professor or at least a well-versed amateur astronomer. You'll probably find a local astronomy club that can also help out.

Selling the Stars

Gain the sponsorship of a store that handles telescopes. If such a store doesn't want to be sole sponsor, ask if it will consider buying participation spots and adjacencies. Since the program may run in the evenings, you'll be able to offer attractive off-peak ad rates.

Do It Outside

Try to originate the program from a park or some similar outside location. Invite your listeners to bring their own telescopes and join in the fun. The "atmosphere" will help bring the broadcast alive for listeners as well.

At least once in a while, the sponsoring store should have sales representatives and some products there. This can involve an extended stargazer's night with only a portion being broadcast. The local astronomy club will also want to be there, to recruit new members.

4.19 RIDICULOUS SONG TITLES

This isn't really a promotion as such. It's a continuing bit to be used by just one of your air personalities. Decide which air shift is best suited to this kind of craziness, and keep it there.

How It Works

This is simply a collection of goofy song titles that will work best when used to introduce or back-announce music your audience already knows well. In this way, the nonuse of the true song title won't be of any consequence.

Song Titles and Intros

NOW, A MIDDLE-EASTERN CLASSIC THAT TELLS THE VITAL STORY OF WHAT THE SULTAN TELLS THE TURKISH DIGNITARY. IT'S CALLED "I DON'T RECALL YOUR NAME, BUT THE FEZ IS FAMILIAR."

NEXT, A SONG THAT DEALS WITH THE PROBLEMS AND FRUSTRATIONS OF LIFE AS IT IS LIVED TODAY . . . A SONG ENTITLED, "I'M DANCING WITH TEARS IN MY EYES—BECAUSE SOMEONE STARCHED MY UNDERWEAR."

HERE IS THE TITLE SONG FROM ONE OF HOLLYWOOD'S LATEST BIG MUSI-CALS CALLED: "HE CLIMBED THROUGH THE ROLLERS IN THE PLAYER PIANO AND TINKLED HIMSELF TO DEATH."

THIS IS A HAUNTING AND BEAUTIFUL SONG CALLED "MY EYES ARE BLOOD-SHOT BECAUSE OF MY TEETH—I WAS UP ALL NIGHT LOOKING FOR THEM."

NEXT, A BRIGHT AND BOUNCY VERSION OF THAT NEW BOY-GIRL HIT CALLED "I THOUGHT YOU WERE SPOILED, BUT IT WAS JUST THE PERFUME YOU WERE WEARING."

NOW, RELAX AS YOU LISTEN TO THAT TENDER NEW BALLAD CALLED: "A BEAUTIFUL BABY FROM HEAD TO FOOT—AND A MISERABLE MESS IN BETWEEN."

HERE'S A TEXAS-SIZED HIT FROM ONE OF THE LATEST WIDE-SCREEN EPICS—A SONG CALLED: "SOME DIRTY HORSE THIEF STOLE MY GAL."

NEXT, A SONG ABOUT MODERN MARRIAGE CALLED: "MOTHER HAD TO LET THE MAID GO BECAUSE FATHER WOULDN'T."

HERE'S A BEAUTIFUL NEW BALLAD WITH A HAUNTING LYRIC—A SONG TITLED: "IF THE BEES FIND OUT WHAT I FOUND OUT, THE FLOWERS ARE THROUGH."

THIS IS A CUTE AND CATCHY ONE—A CUT FROM THE NEW CHILDREN'S ALBUM: "MUSIC FOR FIGHTING DIRTY."

HERE'S AN OFFBEAT SONG WITH AN OFFBEAT LYRIC THAT TELLS A RATHER UNUSUAL STORY. IT'S CALLED: "THEY MADE ME JUDGE THE FLOWER SHOW BECAUSE I SMELLED SO GOOD."

LISTEN NOW TO A SONG ABOUT THE GAMES PEOPLE PLAY WITH THE INTRIGUING TITLE: "I CALLED HER CHECKERS BECAUSE SHE JUMPS EVERY TIME I MAKE A MOVE."

HERE'S A SONG THAT IS DESTINED TO BECOME A STANDARD: "LET ME CALL YOU FLOUR, 'CAUSE, BABY, YOU'VE BEEN THROUGH THE MILL."

NOW, HERE'S MUSIC FROM THE TELEVISION SHOW ABOUT TARZAN CALLED: "TARZAN GETS POISON IVY."

NEXT A LITTLE NOVELTY TUNE SET IN THE MAINE WOODS AND CALLED: "I USED TO HAVE A MAPLE CHAIR, BUT I DIDN'T LIKE IT—THE SYRUP STUCK TO MY PANTS."

NOT ALL MUSIC DEALS WITH YOUNG LOVE. HERE'S ONE THAT TELLS THE STORY OF MARRIED LOVE . . . A SONG CALLED: "AFTER THE DIVORCE I MARRIED HER SISTER—SO I WOULDN'T HAVE TO BREAK IN A NEW MOTHER-IN-LAW."

NOW, ONE OF THOSE SONGS IN THE OUTDOOR VEIN TITLED: "WE'VE BEEN SKATING FOR HOURS ON END, DARLING. MAYBE WE OUGHT TO TAKE LESSONS."

HERE'S A SONG THAT TELLS HOW A MAN FEELS ABOUT A WOMAN. IT'S CALLED "DARLING, YOU MADE ME WHAT I AM TODAY—A BUM."

NOW WE HAVE A SONG THAT IS AS UP-TO-DATE AS A POWERFUL ENGINE CALLED: "HE WAS A HIGH-GEARED DADDY UNTIL HIS SWEET MAMA THREW HIM INTO LOW."

HERE'S THE THEME MUSIC FROM ONE OF THIS SEASON'S TELEVISION FAMILY COMEDIES — A TUNE TITLED: "IF WE'RE GOING TO HAVE YOUR MOTHER FOR DINNER, MY DEAR, MAKE SURE SHE'S WELL DONE."

THIS NEXT ONE IS A BLUES SONG THAT TELLS THE STORY OF MARRIAGE WITH GREAT TRUTHFULNESS. IT'S CALLED: "ON THE SEA OF MATRIMONY, WE HAVE A LEAKY BOAT."

NEXT, TO BRIGHTEN UP THE DAY A LITTLE—THE THEME SONG OF THE FUTURE FARMERS OF AMERICA. IT'S CALLED: "EARLY TO BED, EARLY TO RISE, MAKES A MAN A ROOSTER IN DISGUISE."

HERE'S A BRAND NEW BALLAD ABOUT MATURE YOUNG LOVE CALLED: "THERE'S NO PLACE LIKE HOME—ESPECIALLY AFTER ALL THE OTHER PLACES ARE CLOSED."

NEXT, THE THEME MUSIC FROM THE MOVIE BIOGRAPHY OF JOHN DILLINGER—THE SONG THE WHOLE NATION IS HUMMING AND WHISTLING CALLED: "LADIES AND GENTLEMEN, ALL THOSE IN FAVOR OF LEAVING THIS BANK ALIVE, KINDLY HOLD UP YOUR HANDS."

YOU ALL REMEMBER THE "ANNIVERSARY SONG." HERE'S A NEW ONE IN THE SAME VEIN THAT IS TITLED: "SEEMS LIKE YESTERDAY WE GOT MARRIED AND YOU KNOW WHAT A LOUSY DAY YESTERDAY WAS."

NOW A NEW HIT ON COLLEGE CAMPUSES ALL ACROSS THE COUNTRY CALLED: "YOU MUST HAVE BEEN BORN IN THE DARK AGES 'CAUSE YOU SURE LOOK AWFUL IN THE LIGHT."

HERE'S A SONG THAT CARRIES A LOT OF FREIGHT. IT'S CALLED: "IF YOU KNEW SUEZ LIKE I KNEW SUEZ—OH, OH WHAT A CANAL."

NEXT, THE LATEST MUSICAL IMPORT FROM ENGLAND—A LILTING BLUES BALLAD TITLED: "PUT A WREATH ON THE FUSEBOX, MOTHER. DADDY GOT THE ELECTRIC CHAIR."

NOW, A SONG OUT OF NASHVILLE BY SNUFFY LINSEED, THE HILLBILLY TENOR. IT'S CALLED: "I'M IN LOVE WITH A WONDERFUL STILL."

THIS NEXT ONE IS A SONG ABOUT THE WEATHER: "HIGH WINDS, FOLLOWED BY HIGH SKIRTS, FOLLOWED BY ME."

HERE'S ANOTHER BIG HIT FROM BROADWAY—THE TITLE SONG FROM THE NEW MUSICAL CALLED: "THERE'S A CABIN IN THE SKY—SO BE CAREFUL WHEN YOU STEP OUT THE DOOR."

NEXT, A PLAINTIVE BALLAD ABOUT SPACE TRAVEL CALLED: "I WONDER WHO'S TRACKING HER SATELLITE NOW."

NOW, A TENDER LOVE SONG ABOUT HIGH SCHOOL ROMANCE TITLED: "I'LL BE LOVING YOU WHEN ALL YOUR GREEN STAMPS TURN TO GOLD."

HERE'S THE BACKGROUND MUSIC FROM THE MOVIE THAT TELLS THE SAGA OF THE NEW WEST. IT'S CALLED: "TAKE YOUR COTTON-PICKIN' HANDS OFF MY LEATHER JACKET. IT'S THE CLOSEST THING TO SKIN I'VE GOT."

NOW, MY FAVORITE SELECTION FROM AMONG THE MANY FINE SONGS IN THE NEW ALBUM: "PETER JENNINGS PLAYS DAVID BOWIE."

NOW, THE LOVELY BALLAD THAT ALL OF TEENAGE AMERICA IS SINGING— ONE OF THE BIG HITS OF THE DAY CALLED: "I'VE GOT HEARTBURN FOR YOU."

NEXT, WE HAVE AN OLD STANDARD . . . ONE OF THE ALL-TIME BIG ONES ON MY PERSONAL HIT PARADE. SO LET'S STROLL DOWN MEMORY LANE TOGETHER AS WE LISTEN TO: "EVERYTHING I HAVE BELONGS TO THE INTERNAL REVENUE SERVICE EXCEPT MY MOTHER-IN-LAW—THEY MADE ME KEEP HER."

THIS NEXT SONG WAS ORIGINALLY FRENCH. THE LYRICS HAVE BEEN TRANS-LATED INTO ENGLISH, AND THEY COME OUT AS: "I'VE GOT WHAT NO MIL-LIONAIRE'S GOT—NO MONEY."

THIS IS A NEW ONE THAT JUST SHOWED UP IN OUR RECORD LIBRARY, AND I THINK IT'S GOING TO BE A HIT. THE ALBUM IS CALLED: "FIDEL CASTRO SINGS PAUL McCARTNEY."

NOW, A SONG ABOUT A YOUNG MAN WHO GOES INTO A RESTAURANT AND MEETS A LOVELY YOUNG WAITRESS. THE SONG IS TITLED: "TAKE BACK YOUR HEART—I ORDERED LIVER."

NEXT, A SONG THAT DEALS WITH THE SORT OF PETTY BICKERING THAT TAKES PLACE AMONG NEIGHBORS LIVING IN SUBURBIA. IT'S CALLED: "YOU THINK YOU'RE SO SNOOTY JUST BECAUSE YOU SENT YOUR GARBAGE OUT TO BE GIFT-WRAPPED."

HERE'S ONE OF THOSE SONGS WITH A MESSAGE—EVEN, IF YOU WILL, WITH A MORAL. IT HAS JUST SHOWED UP ON THE CHARTS AND SHOULD GO FAR. IT'S CALLED: "BOYS WHO SWEAR WHILE PLAYING MARBLES USUALLY GROW UP TO BE GOLFERS."

THIS IS A NEW ONE NOW AND WE'LL HEAR IT FOR THE FIRST TIME TOGETHER. LET ME KNOW IF YOU LIKE IT. IT'S TITLED: "DON'T FALL INTO THE LENS GRINDING MACHINE, MOTHER, OR YOU'LL MAKE A SPECTACLE OF YOURSELF."

NOW, HERE'S A SONG THAT REVEALS SOMETHING ABOUT THE MOOD OF AMERICAN YOUTH CALLED: " 'YOU'RE THE FIRST GIRL I'VE EVER KISSED,' " HE SAID, SHIFTING GEARS WITH HIS KNEES."

HERE, NOW, A SONG ABOUT THE PROBLEMS AND MISERIES EXPERIENCED BY THE YOUNG. IT'S APPROPRIATELY TITLED: "TOO OLD FOR CASTOR OIL AND TOO YOUNG FOR GERITOL."

NOW, ONE OF THOSE SONGS WITH A SOUTH SEAS FLAVOR: "IT WAS A LOVELY NIGHT IN HAWAII AS I WATCHED THE NATIVES ROTATE THEIR CROPS."

HERE'S AN OLDIE THAT I THINK MOST OF YOU WILL REMEMBER, SO WHY NOT SING ALONG AS WE PLAY: "DON'T WORRY ABOUT THE WOODPILE, MOTHER. FATHER WILL COME HOME WITH A LOAD ON."

THIS IS A NEW SONG—DESTINED TO MOVE RIGHT ON UP THE CHARTS. IT'S CALLED: "SHE HAD ALL THE ANSWERS, BUT WAS NEVER ASKED THE QUESTIONS."

NEXT, HERE IS THE THEME MUSIC FROM THE NEW MEDICAL MOVIE: "LADY CHATTERLY'S LIVER."

ANOTHER BIG HIT FROM THAT EXCITING NEW MUSICAL GROUP, THE FOUR CLODS. IT'S TITLED: "THE RASH IS ENDED, BUT THE MALADY LINGERS ON."

HERE'S ANOTHER ONE OF THOSE GOLDEN HITS THAT MAINTAIN THEIR POPULARITY OVER THE YEARS. YOU ALL REMEMBER: "I'LL BE SEIZING YOU IN ALL THE OLD FAMILIAR PLACES."

THIS SONG COULD BE THE PSYCHIATRISTS' NATIONAL ANTHEM. IT'S CALLED: "YOU'RE FINE. HOW AM I?"

EVERYONE IS MAKING RECORDS THESE DAYS: SENATORS, BASEBALL PLAYERS: THIS ONE IS BY A DOCTOR AND IT'S CALLED: "THE OBJECT OF MY INJECTION."

NOW, HERE IS THE THEME MUSIC FROM THE NEW MOVIE: "SWISS CHEESE—SON OF COSHISE."

NOW, LET'S HEAR THE TENDER BALLAD: "MY NIGHTINGALE OF ROMANCE HAS GRAVEL IN HER THROAT."

INSULTS FOR ALL OCCASIONS 4.20

These are all quick gags—insulting remarks with which one of your DJs can flail the other. There are enough ideas here so that new ones can be used daily. We're sure you'll be inspired to create others.

Set up one of your DJs as the continuing winner, and the other as the full-time loser. These insults should be used by the winner. This gives your loser a chance to threaten a lawsuit unless his assailant stops his slanderous remarks.

Air Copy

(Name's) MONTHLY SALARY RUNS INTO THREE FIGURES. HE HAS A WIFE AND TWO TEENAGE DAUGHTERS.

(Name) ONLY HAS TWO REAL TEETH—AND ONE OF THOSE HE GOT WHEN HE JOINED THE ELKS.

(Name) WHEN HE FIRST CAME TO WORK HERE, CLAIMED TO BE A SOUTHERN PLANTER. LATER ON WE DISCOVERED THAT HE HAD BEEN A NEW ORLEANS UNDERTAKER.

(Name) WON A PRIZE FOR LAZINESS WHEN HE TRIED TO CLIMB A BARBED-WIRE FENCE WITHOUT TAKING HIS HANDS OUT OF HIS POCKETS.

YOU RECALL I MENTIONED THAT (name) WON A PRIZE FOR BEING LAZY. KNOW WHAT? AT THE AWARDS BANQUET, HE ASKED IF THE WAITER COULD BRING THE TROPHY TO HIS TABLE.

(Name) HAS ALWAYS BEEN SELF-RELIANT. WHEN HE WAS A BABY, HE WALKED THE FLOOR ALONE.

(Name) COMES FROM A COMMUNITY THAT IS SO HEALTHY THEY HAD TO SHOOT A TRAVELING SALESMAN TO START THE CEMETERY.

(Name) AND HIS DOG WERE ARRESTED WHILE STROLLING THROUGH THE PARK YESTERDAY. THE DOG SAW A SIGN ON A BENCH THAT SAID "WET PAINT"—SO HE DID.

(Name) SPENT HIS YOUTH PLAYING WITH RABBITS IN HIS BACKYARD. THEN AT THE AGE OF 10, HE GOT HIS TWO FRONT TEETH FIXED.

(Name) WENT TO ONE OF THOSE VERY STIFF, FORMAL PARTIES LAST WEEK. HIS WIFE CAME FORMAL, AND HE CAME STIFF.

(Name) DOES THE HARDEST WORK OF HIS WHOLE DAY BEFORE BREAKFAST— GETTING OUT OF BED.

(Name) LIVES IN A BEAUTIFUL LITTLE APARTMENT OVERLOOKING THE RENT.

(Name) LEFT HIS LAST JOB BECAUSE OF ILLNESS. HIS BOSS GOT SICK OF HIM.

(Name) HAS ACTUALLY LEFT HIS LAST SEVERAL JOBS BECAUSE OF ILLNESS. HE'S SICK OF WORKING.

(Name) HAS THE SAME ATTITUDE TOWARD LIFE AS THE GOVERNMENT. HE NEVER LETS HIS BEING IN DEBT KEEP HIM FROM SPENDING MORE.

A LITTLE PRAISE MADE (name's) HEAD SWELL SO MUCH THAT WHEN HE WENT THROUGH THE GRAND CANYON, THEY HAD TO PIN HIS EARS BACK.

(Name) ORIGINALLY COMES FROM A POOR PART OF THE COUNTRY. THE DOGS THERE WERE SO SKINNY THAT THEY HAD TO LEAN UP AGAINST A TREE TO BARK.

A TECHNICALITY RECENTLY PREVENTED (name) FROM GETTING A DIVORCE.

HIS ATTORNEY DISCOVERED THAT HIS MARRIAGE WASN'T LEGAL BECAUSE THE GIRL'S FATHER DIDN'T HAVE A LICENSE TO CARRY A GUN.

WORK REALLY FASCINATES (name). HE CAN SIT AND WATCH IT ALL DAY.

SOME PEOPLE CAUSE HAPPINESS WHEREVER THEY GO—BUT (name) CAUSES HAPPINESS WHENEVER HE GOES.

(Name) REALLY KNOWS THE ROPES. HE SHOULD—HE'S BEEN ON THEM FOR YEARS.

(Name) IS THE SORT OF GUY WHO GOES THROUGH LIFE PUSHING DOORS MARKED "PULL."

WHEN (name's) SHIP COMES IN, HE'LL BE AT THE TRAIN STATION.

EVEN (name) IS NOT ENTIRELY USELESS. AT LEAST HE CAN SERVE AS A HORRIBLE EXAMPLE.

MOST OF (name's) TROUBLES COME FROM HIS MOUTH. HE EATS TOO MUCH, HE DRINKS TOO MUCH, AND HE TALKS TOO MUCH.

SOME MEN ARE KNOWN BY THEIR DEEDS, BUT (name) IS KNOWN BY HIS DEBTS.

(Name) CAN ALWAYS RISE TO THE OCCASION—BUT I WISH HE WOULD LEARN WHEN TO SIT DOWN.

(Name) DISCOVERED THAT IT'S DANGEROUS TO DRIVE A CAR WITH ONE HAND. HE RAN INTO A CHURCH THAT WAY.

THE ONLY LAW THAT (name) OBSERVES IS THE LAW OF GRAVITY.

(Name) DOESN'T BELIEVE EVERYTHING HE HEARS, BUT HE USUALLY REPEATS IT.

(Name) HAS FALLEN IN LOVE WITH HIMSELF, AND HE HAS NO RIVALS.

(Name) IS THE ONLY GUY AROUND HERE WHO BLUSHES, OR NEEDS TO.

(Name) IS ALWAYS READY TO GIVE OTHER PEOPLE THE BENEFIT OF HIS INEXPERIENCE.

(Name) SAYS HE IS LOOKING FOR GIRLS WHO ARE GOOD, CLEVER, AND BEAUTIFUL. HE DOESN'T REALLY WANT ONE—HE WANTS ALL THREE.

(Name) DOESN'T HAVE AN ENEMY IN THE WORLD. ALL HIS FRIENDS HATE HIM.

(Name) IS ALWAYS CACKLING IN HIS SLEEP. I GUESS IT'S BECAUSE HE'S HEN-PECKED.

(Name) IS ALWAYS GOING AROUND BOASTING. WITH HIM IT IS NO SOONER DONE THAN SAID.

(Name) IS CONSTANTLY STRUGGLING TO KEEP THE MONEY COMING IN AND HIS HAIR FROM COMING OUT.

WHEN (name) WAS COURTING THE GIRL HE LATER MARRIED, HE ASKED HER TO SHARE HIS LOT—AND THEN HE GOT MAD WHEN SHE ASKED IF IT HAD A HOUSE ON IT.

(Name) HAS SOWED HIS WILD OATS. NOW HE'S PRAYING FOR A CROP FAIL-URE.

(Name) IS ALWAYS BRAGGING ABOUT BEING A WIT. AND I HAVE TO ADMIT THAT HE'S HALF RIGHT.

ONE THING ABOUT (name): HE REALLY HAS AN AMAZING BRAIN. IT STARTS WORKING THE MOMENT HE GETS UP IN THE MORNING—AND IT DOESN'T STOP UNTIL HE GETS DOWN HERE TO THE RADIO STATION.

(Name) IS REALLY PUTTING ON WEIGHT THESE DAYS. BUT, THEN, I GUESS I SHOULDN'T HAVE FUN AT HIS EXPANSE.

(Name's) WIFE IS A WOMAN OF FEW WORDS—BUT OFTEN.

(Name) WAS ARRESTED FOR TAKING HIS WIFE BREAKFAST IN BED YESTER-DAY. SHE WAS STAYING AT THE Y.W.C.A. AT THE TIME.

(Name's) WIFE IS SO FRUGAL THAT SHE WENT WITHOUT A HONEYMOON SO HE COULD SAVE HIS MONEY FOR HER ALIMONY.

(Name) IS SO CONCEITED THAT, ON HIS BIRTHDAY, HE SENT HIS MOTHER A LETTER OF CONGRATULATIONS.

DAFFYNITIONS

The idea of goofy definitions is probably as old as language itself. Actually, this is a form of the pun. Make these a regular feature on one DJ's show. They can be spotlighted as "The Word of the Day" or "Webster's Misabridged Dictionary."

Give some thought to asking your listeners to send in their own daffynitions. It provides just one more way of involving your listeners actively. In any case, use a production library fanfare with these to make them a standout feature on a particular show. (*Note*: For more "Daffynitions," see section 10.14.)

Air Copy for Daffynitions

INDIGESTION: WHAT YOU GET WHEN YOU HAVE TO EAT YOUR OWN WORDS.

DRESSMAKER: SOMEONE WHO KNOWS THE SEAMY SIDE OF LIFE.

WATER: A CLEAR, COLORLESS LIQUID THAT TURNS DARK BROWN WHEN LITTLE BOYS WASH IN IT.

DUST: MUD WITH THE JUICE SQUEEZED OUT.

LITTLE BOYS: NOISE WITH DIRT ON IT.

BACHELOR: A MAN WHO BELIEVES THAT ONE CAN LIVE AS CHEAPLY AS TWO.

LAW SUIT: THE CLOTHING WORN BY A POLICEMAN.

WASHINGTON D.C.: A TERRITORY HOUNDED ON ALL SIDES BY THE UNITED STATES.

RACKETEER: A MAN WITH THE COURAGE OF HIS NON-CONVICTION.

RADICAL: A PERSON WHO INSISTS ON CONVINCING US INSTEAD OF LETTING US CONVINCE HIM.

RHEUMATISM: NATURE'S FIRST PRIMITIVE EFFORT TO ESTABLISH A WEATHER BUREAU.

BANJO PLAYER: A MUSICIAN WHO HAS EASY PICKINGS.

TAILOR: A MAN WHO FOLLOWS SUIT UNTIL PAID.

TRAFFIC LIGHT: A LITTLE GREEN SIGNAL THAT CHANGES TO RED AS YOUR CAR APPROACHES.

4.22   LAUGH-OFF

This is an outstanding one-day fun promotion. When properly promoted in advance, it can gain a huge audience for your station.

How It Works

On a given Saturday or Sunday (Saturday is best) you schedule a solid 12 hours of comedy material to run from 8 A.M. to 8 P.M. Combine this with the idea that yours is "the station that put fun back into radio."

Comedy albums, featuring monologues, skits, and songs, should constitute about 75 percent of each hour, with the remainder gleaned from material produced by the station staff itself. That latter part should include as much of the good stuff you can find that has been aired over the years, such as humorous promos or even old commercials that have been saved. You probably will want to create some special new material for the Laugh-Off. This should be kept as local as possible.

Suggestions for Material

The Laugh-Off should be total humor, fully produced, with the only breaks coming for your regular newscasts. Some of the comedy albums, which you should already have in your record library, may include transcriptions of old comedy radio programs. Individual artists with comedy albums released across the years will include the following:

Abbot & Costello	Shelly Berman
Don Adams	Mel Blanc
Don Ameche & Francis Langford (The Bickersons)	Victor Borge
	Bob & Ray
P.D.Q. Bach	Art Buchwald
Orson Bean	George Carlin

Godfrey Cambridge	Tom Lehrer
Tim Conway	Jack E. Leonard
Bill Cosby	Guy Marks
Billy Crystal	Bob Newhart
Bill Dana	Mike Nichols & Elaine May
Phyllis Diller	Pat O'Brien
Fibber McGee & Molly	Richard Pryor
W.C. Fields	Carl Reiner & Mel Brooks
Fannie Flagg	Don Rickles
Stan Freberg	Joan Rivers
Andy Griffith	Rowan & Martin
Buddy Hackett	Smothers Brothers
Pat Harrington Jr.	Jackie Vernon
Spike Jones	Robin Williams
Homer & Jethro	Jonathan Winters
Bob Hope	Weird Al Yankovic
Don Knots	Yogi Yorgesson

Selling It

The Laugh-Off offers some great sales possibilities. Each hour of the 12-hour show can carry six one-minute commercials. Also, each hour can be introduced with a sponsor billboard. This format obviously means that you will have to preempt all of the regular commercials for the day. This should not be too difficult to accomplish on a Saturday.

Whatever you do, to make the Laugh-Off most effective, hold the commercial load to a minimum. It won't be a money-loser because you can charge premium rates.

Advance Promotion

Start plugging the Laugh-Off about two weeks ahead of the show date to make your audience aware of this unique departure from your regular programming. Newspaper ads are a good idea. If you can afford to run ads that feature the names of the stars who will be featured, go for it!

DROUGHT BREAKERS

Are you looking for summertime fun that can focus listening attention on your station? Here is a promotion that will do it. Simple, good listening—and if you time it right, you will have the people in your listening area at least half-believing that you have more on the ball than the cloud seeders.

This little stunt depends a lot on timing. If yours is an area that is subject to long summertime droughts, it can work well. You must wait until your area has suffered a dry spell of at least four or five weeks—long enough so that everyone is wondering out loud if it will ever rain again. Then, working in close contact with accurate weather forecasts, you put the WZZZ Drought Breakers into operation on a day when there is at least a reasonable possibility of rain to follow soon.

How It Works

When the weather reports indicate that the time is about right, go on the air in the middle of a hot, sultry afternoon and announce that WZZZ will stop talking about the weather and do something about it.

Tell your listeners that, in an effort to break the drought, WZZZ will play nothing but rain music the following day. In your record library you will find hundreds of suitable songs. Then go on the air the next day and play nothing but music that has rain in the title or someplace in the lyrics. And, if rain does come, take full credit for producing it.

Additional Twists

Whenever you give a weather report throughout the hot, sunny days of the drought, be sure to follow it with this statement: "BUT WZZZ PREDICTS RAIN!" Your teasers the day before your promotion should state: "WZZZ PREDICTS RAIN TOMORROW." This can refer either to actual precipitation or simply to the rain music you will be playing.

Selling It

Before your Drought Breaker promotion starts, have your salesmen contact the department stores to run spot announcements offering 20, 30, or 40 percent off rain gear during the day of the promotion.

4.24 *CARE* GARDEN

CARE, the international self-help organization, is recognized as one of the finest public service groups around. Your station undoubtedly has run public service announcements for this organization that has done so much to help less-fortunate people around the world. This promotion, designed to spotlight the work of CARE and demonstrate the benefits of its program, will also focus much favorable attention on your station.

How It Works

Contact your local CARE office. The people there will give you their full cooperation. Get a CARE package of farm tools, such as the hand tool kits regularly sent to underdeveloped countries. Using your CARE tools, your DJs will plan the WZZZ CARE Garden outside your station, or in some other location if that is more practical. (Check with the chief engineer before digging around between the station and the towers—you don't want to knock the place off the air!)

The DJs will cultivate the garden through the summer growing season to demonstrate graphically how the CARE program helps people help themselves. If a regular plot of ground suitable for growing vegetables is not readily available, have a large box constructed from heavy wood about 3 feet high, 6 feet wide, and 2 feet long. With a gravel bottom layer to provide drainage and a rich layer of topsoil, this garden-in-a-box will work well.

Get Professional Help

To ensure the success of your promotion, enlist the aid of a local horticultural authority. He or she will supervise the entire project and will probably wish to do much of the actual work. Plant the widest possible selection of vegetables. You need variety rather than any considerable quantity of a single type of vegetable.

Publicizing the WZZZ CARE Garden

Arrange for the most important dignitaries possible to be on hand with your DJs for the ground-breaking ceremonies. Be sure that all of your DJs do regular reports on the progress of the garden. Get plenty of pictures of every phase of the promotion for local and national release. You can, if you wish, stir up some additional interest by running a little contest as to when the first plant will break through the ground, when the first tomato will turn red, or something of that sort.

Bringing Your Promotion to Its Conclusion

About the last week of August in most areas the produce from your garden will be ready for harvest. To bring the promotion to its logical conclusion, have one of your disc jockeys and family live off the garden product, supplemented by a regular CARE food package.

4.25 RUMOR OF THE DAY

This is another easy sort of little promotion that will put a lot of laughs on the airwaves. Keep in mind that all promotions of this type must stay simple to be effective.

How It Works

Your air personality initiates a feature to be called the "WZZZ Rumor of the Day." These are ridiculous statements passed along on the air and billboarded as being strictly rumors. If you are already running some other promotion involving phone-in entries, tack on the WZZZ Rumor of the Day. If the contestant can repeat the rumor correctly, an additional prize is awarded.

Sales Idea

Tie this one in with a supermarket sponsor. Then, any person coming into the sponsoring store and repeating the rumor to the checkout cashier will get a dollar off of any purchase of $10 or more.

Format

Here's a way to package this rumor gimmick. It should help alert listeners that something is coming, and also bail you out of accusations of peddling untruths.

OPEN: "LISTEN CAREFULLY—HERE'S THE WZZZ RUMOR OF THE DAY . . ."

(insert rumor)

CLOSE: "REMEMBER, YOU HEARD IT FIRST HERE ON WZZZ—BUT IT'S ONLY A RUMOR."

Sample Rumors

BRUCE SPRINGSTEEN HAS MARRIED A 14 YEAR-OLD LATVIAN BALALAIKA PLAYER.

THE PRESIDENT ANNOUNCES A 10 PERCENT ACROSS-THE-BOARD CUT IN INCOME TAXES.

THERE WILL BE A 50 PERCENT DISCOUNT ON ALL PARKING METER FINES PAID BEFORE NOON.

BECAUSE OF GOOD WEATHER, ALL BUSINESSES WILL CLOSE AT NOON TODAY.

BECAUSE OF STAFF SHORTAGES AT THE NATIONAL WEATHER SERVICE, ALL WEATHER HAS BEEN POSTPONED UNTIL NEXT WEEK.

DISC JOCKEY SWITCH 4.26

Like most cities in the country, yours probably has some special summer events designed to give the home folks a good time. Odds are that the event also attracts some tourists. This is a promotion you will probably want to run during such special events, although it need not be limited to that.

How It Works

Make arrangements with a radio station in some other part of the country to switch disc jockeys with you for a period of one week. Your DJ will go to the distant city to spread the good word about the summer events in your area. Likewise, the visiting DJ will perform the same service for his city while on your station. It makes for good listening and will give you a change of pace that can spark your whole programming effort.

The Goodwill Ambassador

Before your DJ leaves for the temporary out-of-town assignment, have your mayor appoint him or her as your town's goodwill ambassador. Your DJ should take along some gift representative of your area to be presented to the mayor of the other city. Likewise, a variety of WZZZ station premiums should be taken as gifts for the manager and staff of the host station in the distant town. Suggest that the other station do the same.

Publicizing the Event

Have your disc jockey record a series of promos about his or her upcoming visit. Send it to the other station working with you for use on the air. Likewise, your sister station should provide promotional material for you to use on the air.

Invite your listeners to send in suggestions about what the WZZZ DJ should tell his new audience about your city. Be sure to get picture coverage of the entire event from start to finish.

4.27   BEAUTY CONTEST ON A BOAT

No matter where you are, during the summer months there will be dozens of beauty and talent contests going on. Your station will be asked to run some public-service announcements for most of these. Why not get some real sales and promotion advantage by tying in closely with one of these events?

How It Works

Contact the leaders of an organization staging the beauty contest and tell them that you wish to take an active part in the promotion of their beauty contest this year. They will be overjoyed at your offer of cooperation. It will be best if you select one of the major contests for this. A good event to get involved in is a pageant that feeds into the state competition for the "Miss America" or "Miss Universe" pageant. In many areas the Junior Chamber of Commerce sponsors these events.

Arrange to have one or more of your personalities host the contest. Also, run a heavy schedule of announcements promoting the event. Seek the involvement of Scouts or the Coast Guard to help with logistical support.

Selling It

You can get sales out of this promotion. Arrange to give the whole event a nautical flavor, which fits right in, by staging the finals of the contest at a boat marina or at a marine sales outlet. But, wherever it is staged, the contestants should arrive in boats. As well as providing good theatrical staging for the contest, it should also give the sponsor a chance to show off the wares.

As each contestant arrives at the dock, she is escorted ashore. Then she mounts the stage which has been constructed in the stern area of a cruiser up on a trailer on shore. The judges can be seated in a pontoon boat with a canopy overhead.

SECTION
5

Community
Boosters

HERE ARE SOME PROMOTIONAL IDEAS THAT FOCUS ON COMMUNITY LIFE AND personal interests of your listeners. In some cases, your radio station will be the originator and focal point of the activity. In others, however, your station covers something that is already going on, but will get an added boost from your involvement.

5.1 "MY SECRETARY DESERVES A DAY OFF"

In your listening audience there is undoubtedly a large group of secretaries. Listeners in this category will generally be among the most loyal you have. Not only that, but they are also very vocal about their likes and can do a great deal to spread the good word about WZZZ to friends and fellow workers. Here is an idea for a special promotion that you can conduct specifically for secretaries to let these people know that you are aware of them and thinking about them.

How It Works

Request that letters be written to the station telling why a particular secretary deserves to have a day off. The twist is that the letter must be written by the secretary's boss. This gives you the opportunity to involve two separate groups of people in your promotion. On the face of it, this is a rather pedestrian promotion. By following some of the additions to it suggested below, however, you will quickly take it out of this class.

Judging

To begin with, the contest letters should be judged by the secretarial assistants in your office, who are obviously the experts and the natural ones for the job. You will also get more fun from the contest by handling it in this manner. You will have to decide whether it is feasible, but you might consider having one or more of the station's secretarial staff cut promo spots for the contest.

The Prize

The prize, of course, is a day off work. You will have to provide a replacement for the winner. This can be arranged easily through one of the companies in your area that supplies temporary office help, such as Manpower, Inc. or Kelly Girls. They should be glad to do it for the plugs they will receive.

A day off should be something special. Here are some of the things your winner might receive:

• Maid service for the day

- A corsage or plant from a local florist
- A chauffeured limousine for the day
- A special luncheon at a fancy restaurant with several of your disc jockeys and the winner's boss
- A "Best Boss" certificate to be presented to the winner's employer
- Plus anything you care to plan.

INDUSTRIAL REPORTS 5.2

This is somewhat of an image-building promotion for your large industrial sponsors, but properly handled, the results can be sizable. Also, this is a long-range promotion that will create a great deal of community goodwill for your station, as well as forcefully bringing the station operation to the attention of the prominent business leaders in your area.

How It Works

Prepare a special letter to the key managers in the major businesses and industries throughout your listening area. This letter informs these key people that your station is inaugurating a special service for them and their employees. When, for any reason, an employer must notify employees about whether to go to work that day, a call to the station will get this information on the air immediately.

Advantages to You

Naturally, for this project to work successfully for everyone involved, it will be necessary for management to inform all of their workers that they should stay tuned to your station to receive these special business and industry bulletins. Information pertaining to the service should appear in the company house newsletter. Also, cards should be printed for company bulletin boards calling attention to the service.

To Avoid Misfires

There is always the possibility of a joker calling the station to state that the MNO Company will be closed for the day. To prevent such false information from getting on the air, set up a firm policy for handling all calls pertaining to the service. A list of contacts at the various participating companies should be kept at your switchboard and in the control room at all times. This should list the persons authorized to give out such information, along with their business and home phone numbers. When a bulletin is called in, never put it on the air until your contact at the company has been called back for a confirmation.

Addendum

By coupling this promotion with the "Day Off for Workers" promotion, you should end up with an earlock on a very large block of listeners. If you plan to use both promotions, we suggest that you initiate this one first, then follow it up later with the other.

5.3   "WHAT'S THE GOOD WORD?"

Here is a simple and effective community service program feature that will gain you goodwill and respect throughout your broadcast area, as well as establish or strengthen your bonds with the top business leaders of the region.

How It Works

Carefully select a group of the best-known and respected business leaders of your community: the presidents of the local department stores, major industries, banks, and so on. You contact these people and ask them to give a one-minute answer to the question "What's the Good Word?" explaining why they and their specific enterprises have optimism for the present and the future. You are not inviting them to give a commercial for their business, but to relate their specific reasons why they feel the future promises continued growth and prosperity for their interests and, hence, for the entire local economy.

Example: The manager of a local plastics plant might cite increased volume of business leading to plant expansion and more job openings, plus a larger volume of dollars poured into the local economy. Almost all of those you contact will have a bright, honest message, and will be delighted to have their say in contradiction to the more vocal and oft-quoted prophets of doom.

How to Handle It

Do not try to get involved with lengthy explanations or introductions to these brief program features. None is necessary. Simply have your news director announce it as follows:

THIS IS BOB JOHNSON WITH MR. JAMES JORDON, PRESIDENT OF THE BON TON DEPARTMENT STORE. MR. JORDAN, WHAT'S THE GOOD WORD?

The candidates you select to present their "good words" will not only be flattered at being asked, but more importantly, will respect your station for its community interest in originating such a campaign.

Frequency in Airing

This will work best if you use the message of a single individual on a given day. Play it several times during the day to give it proper exposure. Air it at least once during your morning show, then again in the late morning, early afternoon, late afternoon, and evening.

Outside Publicity

Make these messages available to your listeners in printed form. They can be obtained by writing to the station. Also, post other public spots.

A feature of this type gives you the opportunity to make an excellent tie-in with one of your local newspapers. Approach them on the basis of running your "good word" message as a regular daily feature. It will make sense for both the newspaper and the station.

"TELL US, TOURISTS" 5.4

Summertime is travel time. In all likelihood, your area enjoys a large number of visitors throughout the summer and early fall, either for several days if you happen to be a resort area, or perhaps merely overnight on their travels. In any case, here is a unique method of calling your station to the attention of these visitors. It's a gimmick that provokes comments both at home and wherever the tourists continue their journeys. It also provides you with entertaining program fare and spreads goodwill for the entire community.

How It Works

In all of the motels and hotels, travel information centers, and other logical spots, WZZZ makes available a quantity of attractive "self-mailer" folders for the tourists. The folders invite your visitors to write a brief "commercial" for their home city or state and mail it to WZZZ. WZZZ will give visitors to Centerville free spots on the air, reading the folders extolling the virtues of the regions the tourists come from. Then the station uses these cards on the air, as many as possible, selecting the best and trying to get as many areas of the nation represented as possible.

Local Interest

Whether or not the tourist actually hears his announcement on the air while he is in town is of little importance (although you can bet that the transient traffic exposed to this idea will tune to WZZZ during their stay in Centerville). Aside from the goodwill this "different" approach will win for both your station and your community, you will reap more material benefits within the community.

These "commercials" written by visitors will prove interesting listening for your regular audience, not only for what they say, but as an insight into just "who from where" is stopping in your community. Be sure, too, that you announce the project to the local Chamber of Commerce and other agencies to gain the full measure of credit for this effort of goodwill that will be a definite boon to the area's tourism.

The hotel and motel operators will gladly cooperate, recognizing this as a good thing for their business. Try to get them to place these items in each room or to hand them to guests registering at their establishments.

On the Folder

The copy on your "Tell Us, Tourist" folder should read something like this:

> Welcome to Centerville. The people of Centerville, the operators of this establishment, and Radio Station WZZZ hope you enjoy your visit with us. We're proud of our region. We know, too, that you are proud of the part of the country that you are from—and we'd like to hear about it! Radio Station WZZZ is offering our visitors a free "commercial" for the purpose of telling us, the citizens of Centerville, about your home area—maybe someday we can return the visit.

> Just write us a "Commercial" announcement about your home area on the attached card and drop it in the mail. Radio WZZZ will help you spread the word about your part of the country—as another service to you during your visit to Centerville.

Be sure to include a place for name and address on the mailer. You might wish to send a card telling the tourist that their announcement was used and that you hope they enjoyed their visit in Centerville. It's entirely possible, also, that the tourist bureau of the Chamber of Commerce may wish to send a follow-up form note or card to the guest inviting them to stop again.

5.5 LOCAL SPORTS AT ALL LEVELS

In every part of the country, summertime brings with it the opportunity for people to get out and participate in sports, rather than be just spectators. In your area each day there are local sports ranging from good semipro baseball to lawn bowling in the park . . . from American Legion baseball, Little League games, and industrial softball, to checker tourneys, marble matches, boat races, picnic contests, duffer golf matches—and many more.

The Audience Is Big

These sports do not attract the attention that the major leagues and the local pros do, but for every person participating in any of these events mentioned above, there are dozens of friends interested in the outcome. You can develop a genuine bond with the community, and a good name for your station, by reporting the results of these relatively minor sports activities. It's easy to do—especially once you get the program underway. Very possibly, WZZZ will be the only medium reporting these results. In almost every instance, you will be the first to air them—not the boxes or details, just the scores and winners.

How It Works

A reliable and free method of setting up your coverage is close at hand. Keep an eye on the local papers—not just the dailies, but the neighborhood weeklies also. Look for the purely local sports events in the offering. Get on the mailing lists of the organizations, such as the park board and service clubs, which sponsor athletic programs.

Contact the people in charge of community sports, and those in charge of the places where sports events are held. Ask them to have someone call in the results—nothing more, just the scores and the names of winners. The publicity your announcements will give the activities will make them more than happy to cooperate. Interject these items as you receive them, or perhaps at specific times in conjunction with other programming features.

All of the above may seem like a lot of trouble; however, everything you do on the air requires effort and preparation, and must be judged in light of the response. In this case, you are doing a real community service, while identifying yourself with the core of community activities.

If sports are a major service of your programming, you are making your service truly complete. If another station in your market has sports coverage tied up, you are going them one better in covering these purely local events.

Continuing Is Easy

In setting up the system to provide yourself with the scores of these activities, your only cost is the effort in contacting people. Once you start, and the station becomes known for its interest in community sports at all levels, you can easily continue this information throughout the year. Your contacts will keep in touch.

Once you set up a working system, you should make a serious effort to get these announcements sponsored, using something like: "And here are the results of some local sports contest brought to you by (sponsor) . . . ". In major markets you will not be able to cover everything at the lower levels, but you can easily cover more than your competitors are doing, and your listeners will soon know it. In small markets and in large, you can keep the hand of your station on the pulse of events that are of major importance to your listeners because they are participating in the events you are reporting.

5.6   LET'S GO FISHING WEEK

This is another promotion that will accomplish a number of things simultaneously: provide a lot of fun for everyone, focus much favorable attention to your station, and do an excellent job for some charity.

How It Works

There is a national "Let's Go Fishing Week" promotion that you can use as the basis for your event. With this to go on, set up a large tank in a well-trafficked public place. The tank is stocked with fish—probably trout. The public is invited to fish for them. They pay 50 cents to $10 for the privilege. All of the profits go to the designated charity. You are sure to attract large crowds with such a promotion because there is a great fascination in seeing and catching fish.

Involve the Charity

The charity you select to be the beneficiary of your promotion should be large enough to provide the people necessary to staff the fish tank. An additional benefit will be the resulting publicity.

Where to Get the Fish

In your area there are probably a number of trout farms that stock fish. Chances are they also will have all of the other equipment necessary to run this promotion: the tank, the pumps, and the fishing gear. In most states you will find that, since this is a privately run operation, it is not necessary for your fishermen to have fishing licenses. Be sure to check it out. The trout farm will be able to rent you the required equipment and provide the fish at a relatively low cost. These costs can be covered out of the income, with the net profit going to the charity involved.

Other Possibilities

Be sure to get as many "names" into the act as possible: the mayor and members of the city council, perhaps the governor, and any "name" attractions who are appearing in your town.

Consider doing phone reports from the tank site to keep the promotion going on the air. Also, think about tagging some of the fish with prizes going to the people who are lucky enough to catch them. Naturally, the fish should be cleaned on the spot, wrapped and given to the fishermen to take home with them.

FISH FINDER   5.7

In parts of the country where there is good fishing throughout the year, this can be a year-round promotion. In most areas, however, summertime is fishin' time—and time for the WZZZ Fish Finder.

How It Works

Calls are placed to the fishing resorts throughout your area for a report on the recent catches, water conditions, and fishing prospects. Make the calls each day, taping several different ones each day. At regular scheduled intervals throughout the day and evening, one of the taped reports is played while the board man gives some of the other reports from different areas.

They'll Cooperate

Resort managers will be most willing to cooperate with you and provide you with accurate information. False reports can be discouraged by dropping a resort from your calling list at the first hint that it is not being honest with you and your listeners.

Commercial Possibilities

Do not overlook the possibility of selling this program feature to a local sporting goods store or similar sponsor. An important selling point when you approach a potential sponsor is this: While your local ball team may feel lucky to get a crowd of 5,000 out on a Saturday or Sunday, 50,000 to 100,000 fishermen in your area will probably be out on those same days. And, once you have established the validity of your fishing reports, these fishermen will be listening to WZZZ for the up-to-the-minute information they need.

5.8   WZZZ GOES EVERYWHERE

A happy little promotion to tie-in with the On-Air Theme that you will find in another section of this book. Since your DJs will be talking up the fact that "WZZZ Goes Where You Go," try this: Use a no-prize promotion in which you ask listeners to tell you where they think WZZZ cannot go (i.e., where it would be impossible to take a portable radio and tune in WZZZ). You take it from there. It should be a lot of fun.

5.9   SCHOOL DAYS SAFE DRIVING CAMPAIGN

With the start of school in the early fall, your station's year-round public service safe-driving campaign is pegged on reminding drivers that they must use extra caution in school zones and be on the lookout when school's out. Here are some ideas that you can use to carry your "back-to-school" safe-driving campaign beyond the announcement level, and earn extra goodwill and a community service reputation in your city.

Safety Gear for Traffic Patrol

If the youngsters of the school Safety Patrol in your city are not already so equipped, as a community service, your station can provide or sponsor a drive to collect funds for white safety helmets for the youngsters throughout the city to wear on patrol duty. We don't suggest that these helmets be emblazoned with your call letters or anything of that sort, just providing the gear will encourage goodwill and publicity throughout the schools and the entire community. Another item of safety gear that can be provided by the station is a set of bright yellow rain slickers for the young patrols—again this is suggested as a public service gesture, not to serve as a walking billboard for the station's call letters.

Traffic Safety Tips

An effective traffic safety promotion can be developed by a takeoff on the "Homemaker's Hints" or "Idea of the Week" contests run by many stations. Listeners are asked to send in their suggestion for traffic safety: "Traffic Safety Tips." The ideas may apply to pedestrians, drivers, and bicyclists. The suggestions may be general points that could apply anywhere at anytime, or they may be specific to common problems of a certain community or neighborhood.

This promotion is best run by one of your disc jockeys, say, the mid-morning air personality who is talking to daytime listeners, but it can be carried throughout the day so that drive times are hit with the safety tips. At the end of the week the traffic department of your local police department, sheriff's office, or safety council (best to have the judging done by an outside authority such as this) selects the best "Traffic Safety Tip" of the week. A cash or merchandise prize is awarded the winner.

SPORTSMAN'S ALERT 5.10

This is another public-service promotion with a built-in listener hook that will help you stay on top in your market. Although we suggest that you kick this off during the fall hunting season, it can be adapted to fit every season and run as a continuing year-round promotion.

How the Sportsman's Alert Works

The Sportsman's Alert is a service you provide for contacting hunters who are out in the field in case of an emergency. Sportsmen are told to tune in your station at a specified time each day when you will be broadcasting emergency messages.

It will probably work best if you schedule the Sportsman's Alert for sometime around 6:00 P.M. Coupled with these emergency messages, give weather reports and other information specifically designed for hunters to round out the feature as a sports package. If you already have a regular sports show on the air, you can include this as part of it.

To Set Up the Sportsman's Alert

Get in contact with the state police in your area and ask for their cooperation. They will be glad to give it. Then, in publicizing your promotion, tell listeners that, if they have an emergency message for a sportsman, they should call the state police, not the station. One of your staff can check with the state police just prior to airing the feature to get any reports. No emergency messages should be aired until they have been cleared by the state police, or some such official agency.

To facilitate contacting sportsmen in the field, tell them to be sure to leave their license number and description of their car at home before starting out. They should also leave information as to approximately where they plan to be while out in the field.

Merchandising the Sportsman's Alert

This promotion makes a nice saleable package for the many sporting goods stores in your area. Since not too many of these stores have large advertising budgets, you might sell the package to five or six of them on a participating basis. Of course, the feature is a natural for any national manufacturer of sporting goods.

Keeping the Promotion Seasonal

The Sportsman's Alert can be kept on the air throughout the year by keeping it abreast of the season. The fall is the big hunting season. In the winter, skiers will have need of this special service. In the spring and summer, the fishermen are out. And in the summer, swimmers and boaters also fall within the scope of the service.

5.11   TIPS FOR TRAVELERS

In many parts of the country the winter weather fouls up all forms of transportation. Your station probably already carries traffic tips and road condition announcements as part of your regular public service programming. Here is an extension of the service that will be effective and popular with your listeners.

How It Works

Announce the effects that the weather is having on the regularly scheduled methods of transportation such as air, rail, and bus. In an area with a large volume of commuter traffic, the value of this service is obvious. But even if the majority of your listeners are not so directly concerned with travel schedules, they all like to know how the weather is affecting travel activities other than their own. The reports should be packaged within a special format to call additional attention to them.

Information Readily Available

All the information you need is readily available simply by calling the depots or terminals in the area. Compile the information and announce it, or put a phone interview directly on the air using whatever authority is available.

Sales Opportunity

A service such as this is a natural for sales to a travel agency. However, not too many travel agencies have budgets for any large amount of radio advertising. Therefore, it is a good idea to line up a group of them for sponsorship on a rotating basis. The local members of the American Society of Travel Agents (ASTA) would provide a good basis for such a group.

Additional Bit

When you initiate your reports on the air, rail, and bus transportation, make sure the officials of these public carriers know about it. Either get them to print, or have printed yourself, 3-×-5-inch slips announcing the service on your station. These should be handed out to each ticket purchaser, urging them to stay tuned to WZZZ for the latest reports in the event of bad weather. In this way you will get the widest possible spread.

WINTER-LONG SKI PROMOTIONS   5.12

Skiing has become one of the major participation sports in North America. (If your station is located in one of the sections of the country where there are no ski facilities even remotely close, you can stop reading now. What we have to say here demands snow, and, if there is none anywhere close, you will be wasting your time going further.) In most areas where snow is available, you will find hundreds of thousands of skiers. And they are all avid enthusiasts for the sport. What we are outlining here is an overall approach that includes a whole series of promotions, all designed to create the image in the public mind that yours is the skiers' station. While this means that you will be doing a considerable amount of talking about skiing during the season, it is the sort of sport that nonparticipants do not mind hearing about. Many of them will be journeying to the slopes to watch, even though they never put on a pair of skis.

How It Works

No doubt, there is a certain amount of ski information available on your station and other stations in the market. Therefore, you must attempt to do the complete job. If you do, you are going to lock in a huge, diversified segment of the listening public because no other station is going to be giving the quantity of information that you will. You will also open the way for a great deal of practical publicity. Obviously, there are sales possibilities within this approach. Heavy spot schedules from all of the sporting goods stores should be a natural result. But there are many more, and we will touch upon a number of them as we go along.

Tie-In with Ski School

You will get the most mileage out of this winter-long series of ski promotions if you arrange to link the whole thing with one of the ski schools in your area. The schools will get a vast amount of great publicity out of such a tie-in and you will have the assistance and cooperation of an organization that can help carry out your overall program. You will certainly want to try to have your call letters included within the official title of the school, such as: "The WZZZ-Central Ski School." Many of the promotions you will be doing within this format will require the active services of the ski school; in addition, you will want their aid in effecting many other parts of this approach.

Snow Reports

One of the natural things you will want to do is to set up a regular series of snow condition reports to be carried throughout the ski season. These should contain accurate, up-to-the-minute information spots from all of the major ski areas in your vicinity. Your news department can set up the call list for this purpose. It will be best if the WZZZ Snow Reports are scheduled at regular times during the day. Around 6:00 P.M. is a natural time for one such report. Also, have more frequent reports on Friday and Saturday than on the other days of the week. The reason for putting this information into a regularly scheduled package is that then you have a highly salesworthy little program feature.

Your snow reports are probably the only information feature within your ski promotion that should be sold. The other informational features should be kept as public service. But, of course, intensive efforts should be made to sell all of the spot packages possible to businesses related in any way to skiing.

Road Reports

During the winter ski season, reports on road conditions in the ski areas are highly important. You will want your news department to have sources all lined up to secure such information because you should be carrying frequent reports on the roads. You will not want to hit this too heavily during the week, but on Friday, Saturday, and Sunday such information is vital to your skiing listeners.

Ski Club Reports

If there is skiing in your area, there are undoubtedly numerous ski clubs. Make direct contact with all of the clubs in your vicinity to make certain they carry in their club bulletins a story about all of the ski information your station will be airing through the season. In addition, tell them you will be doing regular reports on ski club activities, so they should get all such information to you. This phase is particularly important because the members of the ski clubs can do much good for you.

Outside of the clubs, as well as within, they will publicize by word-of-mouth that WZZZ is the skiers' station. Also, in some of the later phases of your winter-long promotion you will want their active help and participation.

Ski Race Information

Another important part of the service you are going to perform for skiers is reports on the various ski races that will be held throughout the winter. You will want to give advance publicity to such races throughout the week (most races are weekend events). Also, you will want to have fast results on the races to carry on the air. It should be no problem to arrange to have someone phone in the results of each race to you.

Of increasing popularity are the professional ski races. Some rather sizable purses are being put up to attract the top skiers in the country. You should be able to sell spot schedules to the promoters easily because you have already established yourself as the skiers' station.

Entertainment Information

You have an excellent sales possibility in spots for the eating and entertainment places that lie along the routes that skiers take back from the mountains. You can do a real job for such businesses because you will be reaching their potential customers at times when they are most likely to hear and heed the message. Also, most of these spots will undoubtedly be running on Saturday or Sunday when you can use some extra commercials on the log.

Disc Jockey Skiers

An active promotion idea for the winter months includes having all of your disc jockeys learn to ski. Instructors from the ski school with whom you are connected can handle this easily. It will give your air personalities some good things to talk about on the air and serve to spotlight all of the other ski things you are doing.

In some places there are indoor ski arenas where beginners can get started on the fundamentals of the sport. If there is such a facility in your city, it is a good idea to get your disc jockeys to take their early instruction there. Such a ski arena will be open before there is skiing on the regular slopes, so you have the opportunity to get a strong lead-in ahead of the season.

You may also want to include some simple contest where each DJ selects two listeners to come along as his or her guests to take lessons, too. You will want your disc jockeys to continue their ski lessons out in the open once the season starts. Some of these lessons should be on weekends when you can get them out in a group and promote their appearance on the air.

Ladies' Day

You will certainly want to promote a special ladies' day when the ladies can go to the ski slope and take free lessons. This should be done on a weekday. The ski school probably already has arrangements set up for busses to take skiers to the mountain. The station may want to pick up the tab for the busses, but it is not unreasonable to ask your listeners to pay for their own transportation, since you are providing free lessons for them. Be sure to have ladies who wish to attend your free ski school register with the station in advance so that enough busses can be provided and enough instructors can be on hand. You may wish to run more than one such ladies' event during the season.

Students' Day

A similar day of free ski instruction can be offered to the students in your listening audience. The best time to stage such an event is during Christmas week when the high school and college students are out of class. It is just not practical to try to run such an event on a weekend.

Workpeople's Night

A third free ski-lesson promotion can be directed to the working people in your audience. Undoubtedly, in your area there is at least one slope that is lit for night skiing. Make arrangements for the use of this on a weeknight and invite all of the working people to participate. The response to this should be big. Also, a good deal of the transportation problem should be solved because most of these people will be making the trip in their own car.

Ski Carnival

The final event in your series of ski promotions should be a giant ski carnival staged by the station. You will want the cooperation of all the ski clubs and organizations in the area. Because of the scope of the event, you may want to plan on taking two days for this.

Your ski carnival should include all of the various ski races, each run separately according to age and ability. If the facilities are available, ski jumping is an event that will attract a huge crowd. On the first evening of the ski carnival, consider having a large group of skiers with flashlights, flares, or flaming torches come down the slope just after dark. There should be a special race of some sort for your skiing disc jockeys. You can also have a wild race in which the public uses the plastic saucer sleds to compete. The expert skiers in your area will be able to help you line up the events most suited to your slopes.

In Conclusion

You have here the basis for a long-range promotion that can produce sizable amounts of revenue for the station. Also, once initiated, your ski promotions can be repeated year after year. And, in setting your sights on the skiing public, you are going to garner a great many new listeners. It is a sensible programming approach.

NEWS TIP OF THE WEEK AWARD   5.13

The battle for news is a continuing one in today's radio. Here is a simple promotion that will let you get the jump on your competitors on many of the fast-breaking stories in your area.

How It Works

Announce that you will give a cash award for the best news tip phoned in to your news department each week. The award doesn't need to be more than $10 to work. If your frequency is, say, 990, make the award $9.90 and take advantage of this additional opportunity to plug your spot on the dial.

A clipboard with news tip forms should be kept in the newsroom to list all such tips as they come in. Make it mandatory that all such tips be listed, along with the date and time of the tip. On Monday of each week your news director and other individuals involved should meet to select the winner of the award. This simple device will bring you many news stories that you would otherwise miss, or not have on the air until much later.

Publicizing the News Tip Award

You will be running regular promotion spots on this award. In addition, tag your newscasts with a plug like this:

REMEMBER, WZZZ PAYS $9.90 FOR THE BEST NEWS TIP PHONED IN TO OUR NEWS DEPARTMENT EACH WEEK. LAST WEEK'S WINNER, JOHN ANDERSON OF (town).

A Warning

Always—repeat, *always*—check every news tip out before you use it on the air. Your regular newsroom team should follow up on tips. Sometimes news breaks when you have no news person on duty. There is always the chance of an excitable DJ thinking he has a hot scoop and putting it on the air without double-checking it. And, without a doubt, *that* will be the time you will get caught broadcasting an erroneous story on the basis of a bad tip. Check all tips out with the police department, the fire department, or some other official agency. If the tip cannot be checked, don't use it. It is better to be late than wrong.

Here is some suggested on-air copy you can use:

SEE SOMETHING THAT LOOKS LIKE NEWS IN THE MAKING? CALL THE WZZZ NEWSROOM AT (phone number). YOU MAY WIN NINE DOLLARS, NINETY CENTS. WZZZ GIVES THAT AMOUNT AWAY EACH WEEK FOR THE BEST NEWS TIP PHONED TO OUR NEWSROOM. THAT'S THE WZZZ NEWSROOM—(phone). WZZZ—REPORTING ON-THE-SPOT NEWS ALL DAY LONG.

* * * *

AUTO COLLISION? SHOOTING? ROBBERY? IF YOU SEE ANY TOP NEWS EVENT, CALL WZZZ AT (phone number). YOU MAY WIN NINE DOLLARS, NINETY CENTS FOR THE BEST NEWS TIP OF THE WEEK. AND STAY TUNED TO 990, FOR WZZZ ON-THE-SPOT COVERAGE OF ALL THE BIG LOCAL NEWS STORIES.

* * * *

DO YOU HAVE A NOSE FOR NEWS? EYES FOR NEWS? REMEMBER, WZZZ, PAYS NINE DOLLARS, NINETY CENTS FOR THE BEST NEWS TIP OF THE WEEK. SEE AN ACCIDENT, A FIRE, A SHOOTING—ANYTHING THAT LOOKS LIKE TOP NEWS—THEN CALL THE WZZZ NEWSROOM AT (phone number). YOUR NEWS TIP MAY BE WORTH NINE DOLLARS, NINETY CENTS.

* * * *

WHEN YOU SEE SOMETHING THAT LOOKS LIKE NEWS—THE TYPE OF IMPORTANT LOCAL NEWS YOU HEAR EVERY HOUR HERE AT THE 990 SPOT ON YOUR DIAL—THEN CALL THE WZZZ NEWSROOM AT (phone number). WZZZ WILL PAY NINE DOLLARS, NINETY CENTS FOR THE BEST NEWS TIP OF THE WEEK. THIS IS YOUR CHANCE TO JOIN THE WZZZ STAFF OF REPORTERS—AND MAKE MONEY WHILE DOING IT. SEE A NEWS STORY? CALL THE WZZZ NEWSROOM AT (phone number). YOUR NEWS TIP MAY BE WORTH NINE DOLLARS, NINETY

CENTS.

BETTER BUSINESS BUREAU REPORTS 5.14

This promotion can be effective anytime of the year, but particularly so during the pre-Christmas season when many cities are flooded with shady operators conducting phoney telephone or door-to-door solicitations. You will be performing a real public service with this one, and it makes good listening, too.

How It Works

There are many phoney operations. Typical of these are the magazine "salespeople" who hit a town, collect all of the advance money they can, and then disappear. The crooked pitchmen who come through with deals on photographs are common, too. Operators such as these milk the public of millions of dollars every year. The legitimate businesspeople in your area are more anxious to catch these characters than anyone because they give all business a bad name.

The Better Business Bureau in your city is set up to protect citizens from being fleeced by these shysters. You can perform a great public service by working with the Better Business Bureau in your area to develop a regular series of reports on the rackets currently being conducted. You then air these reports a number of times each day. If handled properly, the result is not only an informative programming segment, but a highly dramatic one.

Who Should Make the Reports

The head of your local Better Business Bureau is the natural person to make these reports for you. The added credibility gained by having the reports presented by him or her is obvious. Under normal circumstances, a whole week's series can be taped at one time. Set up a regular format for the manager of the BBB so that the reports are kept within a one and one-half- to three-minute block.

Some of you are going to find that your BBB manager simply does not have the right vocal equipment to do these reports. In other cases, you might find the manager reluctant to tape them for you. If this is the case, you should probably have a member of your news staff handle the job.

A Variation

Instead of having just a straight report, you might consider this: Working with information that the Better Business Bureau has in its files, develop a script that has a man giving an actual pitch like the ones being used by these shysters in your town. This will heighten the dramatic effect and should result in getting the message across in the most forceful way possible.

Concluding Your Reports

The conclusion of your reports should contain information on what a citizen should do if contacted by a salesperson who appears to be a shady operator. Any legitimate salesperson will be pleased to have a person call the BBB to check on him.

An Added Bit

You may want to make copies of these reports available to your local newspaper on an "as heard on station WZZZ" basis. Make these copies available to listeners who write in for them.

Timing

There are generally certain times of the year when these fly-by-night operators are most active in a given locale. As suggested above, in many cities this is during the pre-Christmas season. In other areas you will find large groups of these shysters around when the local track is open. Still other areas are infested with them at the height of the tourist season.

Find out what the pattern is in your town. This is not the sort of promotion you will want to run on a year-round basis. Use it when the need is greatest, then put it in mothballs and save it for use again the following year.

Publicity

It is the merchants of your city who provide the funds for the Better Business Bureau. They have a vital interest in its success. So, approach them to put posters in their stores calling attention to the "Better Business Bureau reports" you are carrying on your station. Alert the firms concerned when you are doing a report on a racket within their lines of business, for instance, send a bulletin to photographers in advance of your report on shady door-to-door photograph pitchmen.

Handling

Be sure to keep your reports short and concise. Get the basic information across quickly without becoming involved in a lengthy talk session.

When you start these reports you will undoubtedly get many calls from people who have been hit by shady operators. All such calls should be directed to the Better Business Bureau. It is not your place to be gathering such information, nor is it your place to be giving out information on operations that are allegedly shady. You will be heading for trouble if you get involved in this side of the matter.

RADAR REPORTS 5.15

Here is another on-the-air promotion in the public-service vein. Handled properly, this one will keep the drive-time listeners tuned to your station.

How It Works

Virtually every city of any size now uses police radar units to help control speeds. Contact your local police department and ask them to cooperate with WZZZ in this safety campaign. Each day, or on a weekly basis, you call the police department and get the location of one of the radar units for both morning and evening peak traffic hours. WZZZ then puts this information on the air in the form of a Radar Report.

The information you give out should not pinpoint the unit, but give a general location. Drivers will quickly get into the habit of tuning to your station to hear this. The broadcasting of these Radar Reports will caution drivers in all parts of the city to drive carefully. Your report should emphasize that you are giving the location of just one unit and that there are several operating on the city streets. This continuing publicity will be of great benefit to the police department in its safety campaign.

Production

You will increase the effectiveness of your Radar Reports if you produce a special intro for use with the spots. An electronic sound is better than a police siren. Over this, an announcer's voice says something to the effect:

THE WZZZ RADAR REPORT—BROUGHT TO YOU IN COOPERATION WITH YOUR LOCAL POLICE DEPARTMENT.

The board announcer follows this with the location of the unit. These Radar Reports should be scheduled twice an hour during peak traffic times.

Other Traffic Reports

Your Radar Reports should be augmented by other traffic reports. Drivers will come to know that by staying tuned to WZZZ they will always get the full traffic picture. These additional reports can be obtained through the Traffic Eye System, a promotion described elsewhere in this book.

5.16 TEACHER OF THE DAY AWARD

This promotion will get your station as many compliments as anything you undertake. It is simple to handle, and it makes an excellent continuing feature.

How It Works

Announce that each day you will honor a school teacher. Listeners are invited to write in, nominating the teacher they think should be so honored. Anyone can write in: schoolchildren, parents, or anyone else. Then the teacher selected is honored on the air with a salute. The disc jockey handling the feature will probably want to read a portion of the nominating letter. (It is better if you do not state who sent the letter.) And the teacher is sent a small gift. That is all there is to it.

A Word of Caution

Be sure to emphasize that you are in no way trying to single out the best teacher or anything of the sort. You are simply honoring a member of the teaching profession, and therefore, the gift honoring the teacher should be a modest one. You can no doubt make arrangements with the florists' association in your area to have a corsage or potted plant delivered to the teacher, or with a candy firm for a box of candy to be sent. Be sure you do not make the Teacher of the Day award seem too important. You will defeat your purpose if you do. It should be thought of by your listeners, and by you, as simply another one of the nice little things that your station does.

Scheduling the Teacher of the Day Award

This feature will naturally work best if it is confined to one disc jockey's show. It is suggested that you use it on your morning show, since this will give the schoolchildren a chance to hear it. If practical time-wise, have your disc jockey take the flowers or candy to the school personally. This will allow your air personality to be seen by the kids and will do a lot to boost his or her ratings.

Tell the School System

Be sure to let the school system know what you are doing, but do not let them get into the act. They may want to do the selecting of the teachers for you, but do not permit this. You can provide them with the names of the teachers honored for use in the news bulletins that they get out.

How Long to Run It

Think in terms of using the promotion throughout the school year. It takes little time or effort and the rewards you will receive from the promotion are cumulative. You are not affecting a multitude on any given day, but, rather, over the period of a month or so.

OPERATION PUSH-BUTTON   5.17

Here is a simple little promotion that will help boost your drive-time listenership—an increasingly important segment of your audience, both in quantity and in the ratings. The promotion does not involve a great deal of effort on your part, but if you continue it over a period of two or even three months, the results will be sizable.

How It Works

Contact the garages, auto dealers, repair shops, and parking lots in your area and ask their participation in the plan. The participating firms will then have employees set the left-hand push button on car radios to your spot on the dial. On this push button they will hang a tag you have had printed which states something to the effect: "To keep you driving down the happy side of the street, this button has been set for WZZZ, the happy sound in (your city)."

Rewarding the Participating Firms

At the end of each week, the firms participating in Operation Push-Button send your station a list of the cars serviced. Each firm receives a regular minute commercial spot announcement on your station for every 20, 30, or 50 car radio dials set. (The number of cars serviced for each minute spot announcement will naturally depend on what your rate is. However, in making your pitch to the participating companies, talk to them in terms of dollars, e.g., "for every 25 car radio dials you set, you will receive $30 free advertising"). You may want to run an occasional spot check to make sure that the cars listed by the participating firms have actually been serviced.

To Get the Most Cooperation from Participating Firms

The garage, etc., working with you on Operation Push-Button will make sure that the job is done right if you offer a bonus award to the shop that turns in the most jobs. This can be a merchandise award or a vacation trip, but it will be more effective if you offer a weekend-spot package each week for a month.

Making the Dial Tags Do Double-Duty for You

You will get double-duty—and a lot more listeners—from the tags you have hung on the car radio push buttons if you have each one numbered. Encourage drivers to hold onto these because at the end of the Operation Push-Button there will be a drawing based on the tag numbers for prizes. This will eliminate any possible complaint from car owners whose radio dials have been set. Naturally, you will want to conduct this drawing on the air during peak driving times. The winners must contact the station within a specified time in order to collect their prizes. This way you can spread the drawing out over a week or more.

5.18 TRAFFIC EYE

This is a promotion designed to secure for your station up-to-the-minute, on-the-spot traffic reports to bring to your in-car listeners. Work with your convenience store and gas station sponsors to set up the WZZZ Traffic Eye system. First, contact your local police department to determine where the major traffic bottlenecks are in your city. Give a copy of the list of bottlenecks to the gas station employees. Prepare an information sheet giving the details.

How It Works

Whenever there is an accident or traffic tie-up in the vicinity of one of your Traffic Eye stations, the operator is instructed to call the station. His call should be put through directly to the board man. The information is aired and credit is given to the specific station.

Merchandising

Provide your Traffic Eye stations with banners for display to inform the public that they are part of your network of traffic information sources.

5.19 STRAW VOTE

This promotion does not pertain to a regularly recognized day or week of the year, but is pertinent to the season during a national election year.

How It Works

This promotion provides you with the basis for taking the pulse, political and otherwise, of the public within your community or listening area. It is really very simple to conduct, and properly handled, you will find that you will get a lot of press and wire service coverage out of it.

Your "Straw Vote" is simply a telephone survey in which the public has the opportunity to call in and register a vote on a particular question of the day.

Wording the Question

You should be careful to word your question so that it is concise, clear, and can be answered "yes" or "no." You will be receiving a large number of phone calls and you will want to word the question so that it discourages elaboration or detailed discussion as much as possible.

Scheduling

Probably the best time to pose your "Straw Vote" question is as the final item on your news at the top of the hour. This will tend to concentrate the public calls during the ensuing few minutes and will keep your lines clear for business during the remainder of the hour. Naturally, if you have special contest phone lines, you will want to use these for the "Straw Vote." You can schedule the question to run all day long, but it will work just as effectively if you start it on the noon news and continue it through the five o'clock news, then give the results as part of your six o'clock and later newscasts.

Giving Results

You will want to give as much importance to your "Straw Vote" as possible and play it up big. Unless you can generate and are set to handle a really large number of calls, it will be best if you announce your results in terms of percentages, e.g., "72 percent of the people said yes, and 28 percent voted no."

Types of Straw Votes

The possibilities for your "Straw Vote" are almost unlimited. Any hot local issue with sharply divided public opinion is always good. Try to avoid issues upon which there is almost complete agreement one way or the other. Avoid complex issues that are not easy to explain or understand. Political questions are almost always good ones—and you can do a whole series of these matching one candidate against another. You may even wish to go into the realm of fancy and ask a question such as this: "If they were the two candidates running for the presidency, for whom would you vote: Washington or Lincoln?"

It is always a good idea to have an occasional light question.

AGENCY PROMOTION   5.20

As we have said before, agency time-buyers, particularly on the national level, are not easily impressed. You must do something on the spectacular side if you are going to catch their attention; this can do it.

How It Works

Mail from your hometown stands a good chance of getting lost in the stack that arrives on the time-buyers' desks each morning. But there is a certain fascination about mail from abroad that demands reading. Set up a campaign to bombard the time-buyers with your message, but fire it at them from all around the world. Like this:

- *From London*: "Really, old chap, all England is talking about WZZZ. Suggest you try it and buy it."
- *From Paris*: "Home was never like this. And radio was never like WZZZ. Try it."
- *From Athens*: The Greeks have a word for it—WZZZ, the station that gets the job done. "Try it and see."
- *From Bombay*: (a tiger hunt postcard) "Ever try hunting a Bengal tiger from a moving elephant? It's like trying to sell the _____ market without WZZZ."
- *From Madrid*: A note written in Spanish.

Plus similar notes from half a dozen other places around the world.

Not Too Complicated to Set Up

Does the complicated organization of setting up all of these distant mailings make you apprehensive? The simple solution to the problem is as close as your nearest travel agent or American Express office. They should be able to work out all of the details for you and the payment of one bill will take care of all of your expenses.

5.21   PROMOTING YOUR NEW DJ

When you hire a new disc jockey, you want to make as big a publicity splash about it as possible. Here is a promotion that shows you how to do it, with a listener hook that will have them tuned in before, during, and after.

How It Works

First contact one of your local automobile dealers and make a trade deal with him for a new car. The automobile dealer will make arrangements through normal business channels for your new disc jockey to pick up a car at his point of origin to drive to your city.

The Contest

Tell your listeners to send in postcards with their estimates of how many miles will be registered on the new car when it arrives in front of your station. That's all, except to remind them to include their name, address, and phone number on the entry.

Listener Hook

Once, twice, or more times each day your new DJ will call in reports of his progress. In addition, scattered throughout your broadcast day will be information about the route being followed, any detours or side trips taken, and so forth. Be sure to specify when you set up the contest that estimates must be made to the tenth of a mile. Also, be sure that the odometer on the car is taped over so no one can see it until the DJ gets to your station.

PUBLIC SERVICE: LISTENER LOSER? 5.22

Let's start out by making a flat statement just to stir things up a little: As a general rule, "public service" is the dullest thing you put on the air. Now, while you are mulling that over, let's toss a few more brickbats your way. Public service material probably occupies a greater part of your broadcast day than any other single spoken type of material, and yet it is easy to be completely lazy and unimaginative in the manner in which you handle it. You pay lip service to the idea of making full application of the "in the public interest, convenience, and necessity" clause. You tally up the vast amount of time devoted to what you mistakenly call "public service" and congratulate yourself on fulfilling your obligation. Actually, what you are doing, in most cases, is simply producing a quantity of dullness while rendering no public service at all.

The problem is this: Each of you has a basic philosophy of what your broadcast pattern should be. You strive constantly to produce the best-possible product within the format established by your basic precepts. But this great block of public service time bears no relationship whatsoever to the pattern you have set. Public service has become a thing you do automatically—and dully.

Little creative thought is ever given to it. You air the stock handout announcements given to you (and to every other station) and let it go at that. The point is, you are defeating your own broadcast pattern and failing your public service obligation.

Here are our suggestions on what you should do with this important public service time to convert it from a listener loser into an audience builder—to change it from a forerunner in the dullness derby into an integral part of your broadcast pattern and to make it do the job originally intended. There's no way you can lose

How It Works

We suggest that you set up a basic format for handling public service within which all public service time during a given week is devoted to a single organization. Of course, there will be some organizations to which you will wish to devote more time, others less. But the full-week pattern should be your basic approach. This accomplishes many things: It gives tremendous added importance to what you do for each organization, it provides you with the amount of time needed to do a real job, and it puts the burden on the organization to pull out all stops and go to work developing usable material for you.

When you talk to an organization on the basis of giving them a full week of airtime, you are not going to be satisfied with the stock handouts that come down to them from their national headquarters. Each organization must develop the local aspects of its work, which is what you are primarily interested in anyway.

When you devote a full week of airtime to an organization, the people within that organization are naturally going to go out and promote what you are doing. This will help build your audience. In order to get the optimum benefits, you are probably going to have to work a full year in advance to set up the type of public service program we are suggesting. But, once it is set up, your work will be much easier.

Because of the great variance in your broadcast patterns, we cannot give specific suggestions on how to handle public service material within the full-week format. But the material should be handled in a manner compatible with the rest of your air product. You will find that, once you make the switch to the full-week format, many of your existing problems in the area of public service will be resolved. Essentially, you will not be devoting any more time to a given organization during a year than you do now. But you will be packaging what you do in a practical manner through which both you and the organization will realize the greatest possible benefit.

SPONSOR DAY PROMOTION   5.23

If you are looking for a way to create real goodwill among past, present, and potential sponsors, try this promotion. It will give you an opportunity to show these businesspeople the sort of job you are really doing for them. This "soft sell" approach can be more effective than hours spent trying to reach each of these people with your story in another way.

How It Works

Set up a certain day as "Sponsor Day" at your station. Invite all of your past, present, and potential sponsors to a luncheon at the station. You should also invite all of the local advertising agency people, too.

Before the luncheon, take them on a tour of the station and show them all phases of your operation. Remember, these are businesspeople and many of the things that would not appeal to the general public will be of interest to this group. Explain to them such things as ratings and rates.

If possible, take one spot announcement and show them what happens to it from the time the order comes in until it gets on the air: how the copy is written, produced on tape, logged, and aired. The luncheon itself should emphasize that your guests are "guests of honor," since they are the people who make your operation possible.

Put Them on the Air

There is something flattering and ego-boosting about hearing your own voice on the air, and these businesspersons are as subject to this feeling as anyone else. So, while you have them at the station, have each of them record some station breaks for you, identifying themselves and their companies. Then, the first time you schedule these spots, have someone from your office call each sponsor to say exactly when the spot will be on the air. You might want to give each sponsor a cassette with his spot on it.

The Follow-Up

Don't forget to drop each person a little personal note of thanks for attending your luncheon.

WEATHER WATCHERS   5.24

Here is another feature to ensure your continued hold on an expanding listening audience. By developing a series of such features to fill the specific local needs of your audience, you will make sure that they stay tuned to your spot on the dial. Such public service features make it possible for you to say: "You don't miss a thing if you stay tuned to WZZZ."

How It Works

Weather and time are two of the most important informational services you provide your listeners. Time is time and there is not much you can do about it except note it; however, weather is constantly changing, even within a small area. The WZZZ Weather Watchers is a group somewhat similar to the WZZZ Traffic Eye Organization mentioned in an earlier promotion.

Set up citizens in all of the towns in your coverage area to phone in reports on weather and road conditions as a supplement to your regular weather reports. While this information can be of special importance during the winter months, the feature is also of value at all times of the year.

You can get your weather watchers by enlisting individuals you know personally in the various communities in your listening area, or you can ask for volunteers on the air. In most cases, homemakers and retirees work out the best because their schedules tend to be more flexible. Each will call you collect at a specified time to give a report.

Airing This Special Weather Information

To save time, most of the weather information should be aired by the person on the board. But about twice a day—once in the morning and once in the late afternoon—you should tape a report and use it. This will mean that each of your weather watchers will be on the air about once a week and the notoriety resulting from this will be their reward.

Little Extras

You may wish to have some cards printed up for these individuals proclaiming them WZZZ Weather Watchers. And it would be a nice gesture to bring them in for a luncheon and tour of your station. Remember, you will be affecting all of these people's friends as well and many of those in their communities.

In Conclusion

As mentioned in connection with some similar promotions, develop a production intro to introduce your WZZZ Weather Watcher reports. Give it a little flash and class. It is all part of building that "something happening" feeling into your overall programming effort.

MUSIC AWARDS

The basic element of today's radio programming in most cases is music. Here is a promotion to let you give this program element the publicity it needs. There is nothing complicated about setting up the WZZZ Music Awards promotion or in the handling of it. And if you can't turn it into some national publicity, you're not worth your salt.

How It Works

This is a general station promotion that all of your air personnel will be plugging. Announce that, in order to give recognition to the musicians who produce the records you play throughout the day, station WZZZ will be giving out Music Awards. Listeners are asked to write in to vote for their favorites. (You may wish to have printed ballots available at some of your sponsor's stores.)

Categories

Here are some of the categories for awards: Male and female vocalists (newcomers); Male and female vocalists (well established); Male vocal group; Female vocal group; Orchestra; Combo; Solo stars on various instruments; Best songs of the year—vocal, instrumental, and novelty; plus any other categories you want to include.

Balloting Reports

To keep up interest in the WZZZ Music Awards, you should have daily recaps of the balloting. These should be spotted regularly throughout your broadcast day.

The Awards

If you have one, the awards should be in the form of your station symbol, engraved with the winner's name and what it is for. If any of the winners are available, be sure to make the presentations on the air. Cover all of the musical and radio trade publications with releases, and don't forget to have the record distributors give you some assistance in getting as much national publicity as possible. After all, it is *their* artists that you are publicizing.

Don't sell this promotion short just because it looks so simple. Properly publicized, the ballots should roll in by the thousands.

5.26 SOUNDING BOARD

If you are looking for a public service feature that will net you listeners as well as plaudits, this is it.

How It Works

The WZZZ Sounding Board provides people with the chance to speak out, both pro and con, about the happenings in your city and state. You simply invite listeners to send in their cheers or jeers in 30 words or less. Select the 10 best each week and air them on a rotation basis. If the writer so specifies, you use only his initials on the air.

The items used can range from a complaint about the lack of a stop sign at a certain intersection to a boost or a blast about something happening in city or state government. Naturally, you will get some crackpot mail, but that's expected.

Bringing Items to the Attention of Officials

When there are specific complaints in the items you use on your Sounding Board, you will perform an additional public service by bringing them to the attention of officials who can act on them. You may also wish to allow officials to answer such complaints.

Let Your Listeners Take Strong Stands

Do not lessen the effectiveness of this promotion by trying to steer clear of letters that comment on controversial matters. A little controversy can do more good than harm.

5.27 PROMOTION SALES FORM

A major portion of the promotions contained in this book are salesworthy; you would be foolish if you did not approach them with sales in mind. However, as we know from experience, there is often a lack of coordination between the sales aspects and the programming aspects of a particular promotion. Sometimes no one knows exactly who is telling what to whom. Also, on the sales side, your sales manager needs to know which salesperson is pitching what promotion to which client and what the conditions of the sale are.

To help solve this problem, we have devised the Promotion Sales Form that you will find on the following page. A copy of this form should be attached to the written outline of each promotion you are planning. Copies should be in the hands of the sales department, the programming department, and the promotion department. In this way you will avoid many of the headaches involved in trying to track down who has promised what.

Promotion Sales Form
WZZZ 460

Promotion: _____

Running Dates: Start _____ Stop _____

Price: _____

Conditions of Sale: _____

Salesperson	*Client*	*Date Assigned*	*Date Presented*	*Reaction*

Additional Promotion and Merchandising Promised

On-Air Promos: _____

Newspaper Ads: _____

Signs: _____

Printed Materials: _____

Personality Appearances: _____

In-Store Displays: _____

Merchandising Letters: _____

Other: _____

SECTION

6

Promotions for Every Month

T HE CALENDAR IS LITTERED WITH ALL KINDS OF CELEBRATIONS AND SPECIAL days. Some have national recognition, others should but don't, and still others don't receive much attention. But any occasion can be made special, given a little sales work on your part. Here are some ideas for calendar-motivated promotions.

6.1   SHERLOCK HOLMES' BIRTHDAY—January 13

As they say, "Be they ever so humble, there's no police like Holmes." You might try to organize a local chapter of the Baker Street Irregulars. This and similar organizations exist throughout the world, many of the members asserting that Holmes is still alive and beekeeping in rural England.

As a simple gimmick for the one day only, have one of your disc jockeys invite listeners to call in with the names of the famous sleuths of the world of fiction in an effort to see how long a list can be compiled.

6.2   NATIONAL YMCA WEEK—January

Most YMCAs around the country are currently conducting physical fitness tests and classes in physical conditioning tailored to the needs and capabilities of those enrolled. You have a chance to help promote this worthwhile project and spotlight all the work done by the YMCA.

Fitness Tests.

Have all of the air personalities at your station go through the tests that the "Y" gives. Then enroll them in the YMCA classes for a week, two weeks, or even a month. At the end of the course they take the tests again and compete on the basis of who makes the most improvement. This stunt can provide some good items for on-air talk—and it might even create some healthy disc jockeys.

6.3   GROUNDHOG DAY—February 2

February 2nd is Groundhog Day, when traditionally the worthy rodent known as the Groundhog proves his worth as a weather prognosticator. If Mr. Groundhog emerges from his burrow and sees his shadow, superstition has it that he returns to hibernate some more, and spring is still six weeks away. How about having one of your disc jockeys—perhaps the afternoon man or woman—report Groundhog Day from the Groundhog's point of view?

How It Works

Arrange a remote broadcast from a point that is underground, be it an old mine shaft, a cellar, an air raid shelter, or better yet, a foxhole or "den" ostensibly dug by the disc jockey himself. The more publicly accessible this den is, the better. Your afternoon DJ is designated "acting Groundhog, pro tem." He stations himself in the den on the morning of February 2nd, to emerge at a fixed time to see if he has a shadow.

Broadcasts from the Burrow

Periodically throughout the morning and forenoon your DJs cut to the man in the hole in the ground for a report from the official groundhog. He can comment on how things look from the groundhog's point of view—or perhaps all you get when you cut to the den are stentorian snores from the still hibernating hog. Attempts should be made to achieve an echo chamber effect on all broadcasts from the den, as if from the bowels of the earth.

The Emergence

Make a ceremony of the moment when the "groundhog" emerges to forecast the coming of spring. Arrange to have the newspapers, the Mayor, and other civic officials on hand to pronounce judgment on whether the groundhog casts a shadow. To legitimize the whole thing, it might be a good additional gimmick to have a real live groundhog in a wire cage accompany the DJ, then the forecast becomes unassailable in the eyes of all.

You may choose to get more mileage out of this promotion by putting your "groundhog" in his burrow two or three days prior to February 2nd—*but don't choose someone with claustrophobia!*

NATIONAL CRIME PREVENTION WEEK—February   6.4

With the crime rate constantly increasing nationally and in many locales throughout the nation, this week provides you an opportunity to study the problem as it applies to your area. With a tape recorder, some effort, and imagination, you can produce an outstanding public service program effort for the duration of this week, in a manner as fascinating to your listeners as only radio can be.

How It Works

Announce beforehand that in recognition of National Crime Prevention Week your station is going to present a continuing detailed study of the crime problems in your area for the duration of the week. The study will be presented as brief reports throughout the broadcast day, with the ultimate goal being to answer these four questions:

- Is there a crime problem in your area?
- What is being done to control crime?
- What more can be done?
- What can the average citizen do?

It's Not a Crusade

Don't start off with the premise that you are crusading against crime or inadequate law enforcement or anything of that nature. The subjects you will present are vitally interesting in their own right, and don't try to create an exposé where no problem exists. If a problem does exist, then it most probably can be traced back to citizens' apathy, which is the very thing your efforts will do much to eliminate.

6.5 BOY SCOUT WEEK—February

Here is a simple little promotion that you can get a lot of mileage from over the years.

How It Works

Working with local scouting officials, your station sets up a trophy to be awarded annually to the Scout Troop in the area that recruits the greatest number of new members during Boy Scout Week. The troop gets to keep the trophy and a new one is awarded to the winner the following year. The station helps in the effort by devoting major effort to publicizing the character-building and downright "fun" aspects of scouting. As each troop gains new members they call in and the names of the recruits are given.

6.6 NATIONAL SALON WEEK—February

This promotion can get a lot of radios tuned in to your station and should result in some new business for you, too.

How It Works

Conduct a "Salute the Salon" promotion during this week. Be sure to publicize the fact to the salons first. Each day as a salute, the names and addresses of several local hair, tanning, or fitness salons are announced individually at different times. If the shop calls in within two minutes, the station awards a small prize to each of the customers in the shop at the time.

A logical and simple prize for a promotion of this nature might be a pair of passes to a local movie theater for each patron present in the salon when it won. This works well as a joint promotion for the salons—they should run specials on their services during this promotion. Of course, the possibility of their customers winning in *your* "Salute the Salon" event should be mentioned as well.

WEIGHT-WATCHERS' WEEK—February   6.7

Here is another fun promotion tied to a special week with a built-in sales hook.

How It Works

The variety of low calorie or "special" foods designed for fitness or dieting is weird and wonderful. Have one of your disc jockeys select his meals for the week from this assortment, announcing his menus each day on the air. Since there will be such items as spinach cutlets, be sure he does not poke too much fun at the foods. This provides a logical sales hook to pitch at a health food store or a drugstore specializing in dietary foods. You may be able to line up a manufacturer sponsor, too.

ST. VALENTINE'S DAY—February 14   6.8

This is the day for expressing pleasant feelings. One way is through poetry.

How It Works

Have one—or all—of your disc jockeys conduct a Valentine's Day poem-writing contest. As a prize for the best poem, have the poem dedicated to whichever DJ the author chooses. Naturally, you will want your air personalities to read quite a few of these on the air. As a judge, why not get the person who runs the greeting card counter in a local store?

Limitation

We suggest that you set an arbitrary limit of 10 to 14 lines for the length of the poems. This is to keep them readable on the air.

WASHINGTON'S BIRTHDAY—February 22   6.9

This promotion will take a little advance work, but it should provide lively programming.

How It Works

About a week before the holiday have one of your disc jockeys (you might include all of them in the act) announce that he or she, like George Washington, cannot tell a lie. The DJ invites listeners to send in any questions on postcards, and the DJ will give honest answers to as many as possible. Then, as the questions come in, your DJ selects those most entertaining and not too embarrassing and answers them truthfully on the air. You might vary this by having listeners call in their questions. Better have someone screen them before the DJ gets them.

6.10 FUTURE FARMERS OF AMERICA WEEK—February

If agriculture is at all a significant industry in your area, offer recognition to this fine organization during this week.

How It Works

If you carry early-morning farm reports, be sure to make mention of this special week there. Also, talk to successful "alumni" of the FFA in your region—men and women who are now successful in agribusiness and who attribute a portion of their success to the training they received from FFA. Get taped interviews with these people and play them during this week. Be sure to tell each person interviewed when his or her tape will be used on the air because you certainly want them to tell their friends so they can listen, too.

6.11 GREEN MUSIC/ ST. PATRICK'S DAY—March 17

As a tribute to the holiday beloved by the Irish, WZZZ devotes the entire broadcast day to the playing of "Green Music." Announce beforehand that all of the music you will play on St. Patrick's Day will be "Green Music" in a salute to the Irish. Then on the day, introduce every song by inserting the word "green" in the title and even incorporate titles that already have "green" in them.

There is nothing more to this, but it's still fun and amusing. Some of the titles you come up with will be quite entertaining. Here are some examples:

- Green Green (by the New Christies)
- The Green, Green Grass of Home (Tom Jones)
- Green Tambourine (The Lemon Pipers)

- Green Heartbreak Hotel
- Any song by "The Moody Greens" like "Nights in Green Satin"

ST. PATRICK'S DAY SALE—March 17   6.12

St. Patrick's Day is March 17. Here is an idea that can turn that to the best advantage for your station and a local advertiser. The best sales possibilities for a promotion such as this are department stores or similar retail establishments.

How It Works

As advertised on your station, and in honor of St. Patrick's Day, the advertiser stages a gigantic "Green Sale" on March 17. The attraction: a five percent discount on any item purchased if the buyer is wearing green.

Get a Bigger Crowd

As an additional crowd creator, the store can stage a contest at a specific time during the day to judge the "greenest" person, considering color of clothes, hair, skin, eyes, and so on. A prize, such as a complete spring outfit, is awarded to the winner. Your judges for such a contest, naturally, will be prominent local Irishmen.

Salute to the Irish

Your station, of course, can devote the day to a salute to the Irish. You may want to consider doing a remote from the store sponsoring the sale. You can have a disc jockey dressed as an Irishman passing out shamrocks, playing Irish music—the works.

Variation

In addition to, or instead of, giving discounts to people dressed in green, the store may want to base the sale on green items.

GIRL SCOUT WEEK—March   6.13

The thousands of girls involved in Scouting make a logical basis for promotion.

Some Suggestions

- Set up a trophy to be given away on a similar basis to that suggested for the Boy Scouts in another promotion in this section.
- Play a tape recording of a group of Girl Scouts reciting their pledge on the air.
- Have each of your disc jockeys attend a separate Girl Scout meeting and then report on the activities to his listeners.

6.14   HOEDOWN SALE—March

Spring signals the start of the gardening season and sales of seed, shrubs, mowers, hoes, rakes, hose, clippers, snippers, bulbs, fertilizer, wheelbarrows, nozzles, sprays, spades, forks, edgers, and on and on. It also brings forth some sizable expenditures in advertising by garden stores. So, here is an idea one of your garden supply stores is looking for: the Hoedown Sale.

How It Works

The Hoedown Sale is a spring super sale at your garden supply advertiser's store, featuring Hoedown No Down Payment on purchases. The whole thing takes on the flavor of an old-fashioned country jamboree as you originate remote broadcasts from the site with every possible gimmick added. You may want to make this a Saturday and Sunday event, with the garden store buying large blocks of airtime.

The Hoedown

Here are just a few of the attractions that will help draw crowds to the spring sale of lawn and garden items:

- On-the-spot broadcasts
- Live music
- Square dance exhibitions
- Station and store personnel dressed in old-fashioned country garb
- Hoedown No Down Payments featured
- Free cheese and crackers
- Door prizes
- One cent a foot trade-in allowances on old garden hose when purchasing new hose

- Free wheelbarrows of fertilizer to the first ten people pushing in their own wheelbarrows
- Prize to the first person driving a tractor to the sale
- A disc jockey wheelbarrow race

APRIL FOOL'S DAY—April 1   6.15

This is the day when your listeners will expect something out of the ordinary. Strive for humor, but keep what you do broad enough so that no one is actually fooled. If you go on the air and announce a $50,000 giveaway and later point out that it was all a joke, you are just going to end up with disgruntled listeners. Here are some things that will add brightness to your programming.

Gag Record Intros

Have one of your DJs use ridiculous introductions to the music he plays on April Fool's Day. A couple of suggestions are included for your use. This is harmless; everyone is in on the gag immediately, and it will produce a lot of laughs.

Examples:

- Mayor _____ singing his hit version of "One-way Street to Nowhere"
- Governor _____ singing "A Ticket, A Tax It."

Time and Temperature

Have your late morning and early afternoon DJs announce the time as midnight and the temperature as 212 degrees. Do not fool around with these during your 6:00 to 9:00 A.M. show. These services are too basic during that period.

Gag Bulletins

Record a special bulletin intro for April Fool's Day. It should be distinct from your regular bulletin intro, and it should have a "clinker" sound in it that lets the audience know this is a gag. Be very careful about this because you want to do nothing that will reflect on your regular news coverage.

Follow the intro with the most outlandish stories you can come up with. We are including a group of suggestions, but you will get much more fun out of ones that are keyed to local events and personalities.

THE U.S. INTERNAL REVENUE SERVICE HAS ANNOUNCED THE ABOLISH-MENT OF INCOME TAXES. STAY TUNED FOR COMPLETE DETAILS.

* * * *

THE WEATHER BUREAU HAS JUST ISSUED THIS WARNING. A SUB-ZERO BLIZ-ZARD IS EXPECTED TO HIT CENTERVILLE BEFORE SIX THIS EVENING—FOL-LOWED BY TEMPERATURES IN THE EIGHTIES BEFORE MIDNIGHT. STAY TUNED FOR DETAILS.

* * * *

IF YOU OWN A RED CAR, DO NOT DRIVE TODAY. REPEAT, DO NOT DRIVE TODAY. AS PART OF ITS CAMPAIGN FOR MORE CONSERVATIVE COLORS, THE POLICE DEPARTMENT HAS ANNOUNCED THAT IT WILL ISSUE TICKETS TO THE DRIVERS OF ANY RED-COLORED CARS CAUGHT ON THE STREETS OF CENTERVILLE AFTER NOON TODAY.

* * * *

AN EPIDEMIC OF SNEEZING HAS BROKEN OUT IN NORTHERN UTAH. AUTHORITIES ARE NOW SEARCHING FOR THE PERSON OR PERSONS WHO PUT PEPPER IN THE GREAT SALT LAKE. MORE DETAILS AS SOON AS THEY ARE RECEIVED IN THE WZZZ NEWSROOM. (Announcer sneezes.)

* * * *

THE DANGER OF FLOODS THREATENS THE ENTIRE MIDWESTERN SECTION OF THE UNITED STATES TODAY. THE MIGHTY MISSISSIPPI RIVER, WHICH DRAINS THE ENTIRE AREA WEST OF THE ALLEGHENIES AND EAST OF THE ROCKIES, HAS REVERSED ITS COURSE. WATER IS FLOWING OUT OF THE GULF OF MEXICO AND HEADING NORTH TOWARD THE CANADIAN BORDER. (If your station is anywhere in this area, top this one off by having your announcer say:) FLOOD WATERS ARE NOT EXPECTED TO REACH CENTERVILLE UNTIL . . . (fol-lowed by a bubbling sound made with a straw in a glass of water.)

Sam Hoagy

Record a single phrase, such as "What ever happened to Sam Hoagy?" Have a number of different people, both male and female, voice this. Put the cart in the studio and throughout the day have your DJs play it. The DJs should make no reference whatsoever to this intruding voice. They should make no mention even that they are aware that it is going out over the air. The mysterious voice simply asks the question in the middle of a record, while the DJ is talking, or at any other time except in the middle of a commercial.

When you get phone calls about the voices, as you most certainly will, simply state that you are trying to trace down the difficulty.

"Stop the Rumor" Bulletin

Periodically throughout the day you come up with brief, news-style "April Fool's Day Bulletins." These should state categorically that such and such a preposterous tale fostered for April 1 is *not* true. Do not use your regular bulletin sound to cue these in, but develop as ridiculous a bulletin-type sound as you can to use. Each should lead off with: AND NOW FOR AN APRIL FOOL'S DAY BULLETIN FROM THE WZZZ NEWSROOM. And close with: REMEMBER, YOU HEARD IT FIRST ON WZZZ. BUT, EVEN SO, STOP THAT RUMOR!

Listeners Join In

Ask your listeners to report any false April Fool's Day rumors that need debunking on the WZZZ bulletins. Be sure to have a number of your own made up in advance though. Then the listeners will start taking part in the stunt and phoning in some of the funny stories and tales they have heard, in the spirit of the day.

On-Air Copy—Examples

AND NOW FOR AN APRIL FOOL'S DAY BULLETIN FROM THE WZZZ NEWSROOM . . . UNDERGROUND GOVERNMENT SOURCES REPORT THAT IT IS NOT TRUE THAT CENTERVILLE IS FLOATING ON A SUBTERRANEAN POOL OF ILLEGAL BOURBON LEFT OVER FROM PROHIBITION DAYS. USUALLY RELIABLE SOURCES STATE THAT THEY HAVE 100 PROOF THAT THIS IS MERELY AN APRIL FOOL'S DAY RUMOR. REMEMBER, YOU HEARD IT FIRST ON WZZZ. BUT EVEN SO, STOP THAT RUMOR!

* * * *

AND NOW FOR AN APRIL FOOL'S DAY BULLETIN FROM THE WZZZ NEWSROOM . . . RELIABLE SOURCES CLOSE TO THE CENTERVILLE POSTMASTER REPORT THAT IT IS NOT TRUE THAT THE LOCAL POST OFFICE IS HOLDING A

BARGAIN DAY SALE ON STAMPS TODAY. NO MATTER WHO TOLD IT TO YOU, STAMPS ARE NOT GOING FOR A PENNY APIECE. REMEMBER, YOU HEARD IT FIRST ON WZZZ. BUT, EVEN SO, STOP THAT RUMOR!

* * * *

AND NOW FOR AN APRIL FOOL'S DAY BULLETIN FROM THE WZZZ NEWS-ROOM . . . THE STATE HIGHWAY DEPARTMENT—IN AN EXCLUSIVE REPORT TO WZZZ—HAS STATED THAT IT IS NOT TRUE THAT ALL CARS WILL START DRIVING ON THE LEFT-HAND SIDE OF THE STREET AT NOON TODAY. IF YOU ARE NOW DRIVING ON THE LEFT AND HAVE NOT YET HAD AN ACCIDENT, GET BACK WHERE YOU BELONG. IT IS JUST AN APRIL FOOL'S DAY RUMOR. REMEMBER, YOU HEARD IT FIRST ON WZZZ. BUT, EVEN SO, STOP THAT RUMOR!

* * * *

AND NOW FOR AN APRIL FOOL'S DAY BULLETIN FROM THE WZZZ NEWS-ROOM . . . A RELIABLE SOURCE IN THE U.S. AIR FORCE HAS REPORTED TO WZZZ THAT IT IS NOT TRUE THAT JET FIGHTERS WILL BE PRACTICING LANDINGS AND TAKEOFFS AT THE INTERSECTION OF FIRST AND MAIN IN DOWNTOWN CENTERVILLE TODAY. AIR FORCE SECURITY OFFICERS ARE NOW LOOKING FOR THE PERSON WHO STARTED THIS RUMOR AND PLAN TO INDUCT HIM INTO THE SERVICE UPON CAPTURE. REMEMBER, YOU HEARD IT FIRST ON WZZZ. BUT EVEN SO, STOP THAT RUMOR!

* * * *

AND NOW FOR AN APRIL FOOL'S DAY BULLETIN FROM THE WZZZ NEWS-ROOM . . . A HIGH OFFICIAL IN THE CITY WATER DEPARTMENT HAS JUST CALLED TO REPORT THAT THERE IS NO TRUTH IN THE RUMOR THAT A DEAD ELEPHANT HAS BEEN FOUND IN THE RESERVOIR. NO MATTER WHAT YOU HAVE HEARD TO THE CONTRARY, CENTERVILLE'S WATER SUPPLY IS PURE AND DRINKABLE. THIS WILL PROBABLY BRING TO AN END THE UNUSUALLY HEAVY CONSUMPTION OF CANNED AND BOTTLED SOFT DRINKS NOTED EARLIER IN THE DAY. REMEMBER, YOU HEARD IT FIRST ON WZZZ. BUT, EVEN SO, STOP THAT RUMOR!

* * * *

AND NOW FOR AN APRIL FOOL'S DAY BULLETIN FROM THE WZZZ NEWS-ROOM . . . A SOURCE CLOSE TO THE MAYOR'S OFFICE HAS REPORTED TO

WZZZ THAT IT IS NOT TRUE THAT A STATUE OF FIDEL CASTRO WILL BE ERECTED IN THE CENTER OF THE FIRST AND MAIN INTERSECTION IN DOWNTOWN CENTERVILLE. IT IS JUST AN APRIL FOOL'S DAY RUMOR—AS IS THE REPORT THAT SCHOOL CHILDREN WILL BE ISSUED CASTRO-TYPE ARMY FATIGUE OUTFITS WHEN THEY ARRIVE FOR CLASSES ON MONDAY. REMEMBER, YOU HEARD IT FIRST ON WZZZ. BUT, EVEN SO, STOP THAT RUMOR!

COFFEE DAY—April 6.16

This special day offers a natural opportunity for an easy and effective promotion. Here is a promotion you can use as a merchandising aid to help you with a coffee account.

Set up a free coffee booth outside your station. The coffee served will, naturally, be that of a sponsor. The booth is staffed by your air personalities. Invite the public down to have a free cup of coffee. It may be possible for you to set the booth up at curbside so coffee can be served to motorists who drive by. But check this out with the police department before you do it.

COUNT THE BEANS CONTEST—April 6.17

Another Coffee Day promotion you can stage is a "Count the Beans" contest. Start out by getting a large bag of coffee beans. Coffee beans are usually shipped in one hundred pound gunny sacks—this is the kind of bag you need.

Get a big metal washtub and record the sound of the bag of beans being poured into the tub. Use this on the air when you are asking listeners to guess the number of beans. The actual bag should also be put on display at your studios, or at some central location.

At this point, you are probably saying, "That is fine, but who is going to spend all those hours counting the beans?" Simply weigh out one, two, or five pounds of coffee beans, count them and multiply by the number of pounds in the sack. (Don't forget to weigh the empty tub first!)

The prize in a contest of this type should be a six-month or a year's supply of coffee.

SIGNIFICANT EASTER PROMOTION—April 6.18

A simple Easter promotion you can conduct that will reflect a great deal of credit on your station is this: In advance of Easter, invite a minister or priest from each denomination to come to your studios and record a one-minute Easter message which you will broadcast on the holy Sunday. Be sure to make the request three to four weeks in advance because most ministers and priests are extremely busy during the week just prior to Easter Sunday.

You can then schedule the tape recorded messages once an hour throughout the day. Most churches put out a bulletin that is handed to members each Sunday. Give each minister or priest the exact time or times when this message will be broadcast so that he can inform parishioners about this through his bulletin.

6.19   EASTER PARADE—April

Very few cities outside of New York City have a real Easter Parade. You can organize one quite easily for your town and reap a lot of benefits. This can provide you with an excellent way to sell time to clothing stores who are featuring Easter finery. If you do organize an Easter Parade, it will be almost mandatory that you cover some portion of it with remotes. Your Chamber of Commerce should be anxious to work with you on this one.

Set up a specific area for the parade. If possible, have it pass in front of your studios. You can have your air personalities out on the street with large Easter baskets of colored Easter eggs bearing your call letters to hand out to the children.

This is a simple promotion that you can easily develop into an annual affair. Be sure that it is known as the "WZZZ Easter Parade."

6.20   EASTER BONNET CONTEST—April

Take this idea to one of your local millinery shops, or to one of the local department stores. In return for a fairly sizable Easter spot schedule, you will promote a contest in which women are asked to create the most imaginative Easter hat they can from items commonly found around the kitchen.

How It Works

During the two weeks prior to Easter you can stage an Easter bonnet contest. Listeners are asked to send or bring in homemade Easter bonnets. The only requirement for entering the contest is that each hat must have your call letters on it someplace. You can arrange for local fashion experts to do the judging. Naturally, the prize should be an Easter wardrobe or a clothing prize of some type. If your studios are centrally located, all of the bonnets entered in the contest should be displayed there. If not, the bonnets should be displayed in the windows of the store donating the prize.

Building Traffic

Entries should be taken to the advertiser's shop. There, they can be put on display—or at least the best ones can. In this way a double flow of store traffic is created: the hatmakers bringing in their entries and the people who come to see the unique millinery styles. Remember, every woman who enters a hat is going to have a number of friends who will also be showing up to see that entry.

Picking a Winner

You may wish to arrange to have the WZZZ disc jockeys act as judges to select the most imaginative hat created by a local woman. Better yet, arrange for judging by a cooking expert and a millinery expert working together. Or you could have one of the society page editors from one of the newspapers act as a judge, with the resultant print publicity for your promotion.

Make arrangements to have every person bringing an entry to the store receive an inexpensive Easter corsage (providing, of course, the possibility of an additional tie-in with a local florist).

NATIONAL LAUGH WEEK—April   6.21

Here's a good-fun way of taking recognition of National Laugh Week that may or may not contribute to one of the goals of this special observance: "to encourage the development of comedy talents." This is simply a takeoff on an old party game.

With the human penchant for garbling any set of facts passed by word of mouth, it sometimes seems a wonder that even a story as flexible as a joke can survive unless written. This simple stunt shows the changes that might be made in a funny story when several people place their successive interpretations upon it.

How It Works

Each morning during National Laugh Week your morning DJ reads a short uncomplicated joke with a good punch line and records it. At the end of the shift, just as he's about to turn it over to the next DJ, he repeats the story, this time in his own words, to his relief. At the end of that DJ's shift he repeats the joke to his relief—and so on. None except the originator of the story has access to the original version. The last person in line records his version of the story as he recalls it from his predecessor. In the morning, the first teller of the tale compares the first and final versions.

6.22 LET'S ALL PLAY BALL WEEK—April

By more than coincidence, this special week falls just as the national attention is turning toward the great American game of baseball. Teams from grammar school to major leagues are training and preparing for the new season. Here are a couple of ways for your station and personalities to share in the spotlight turned on baseball.

How It Works

Set up each of your disc jockeys as the "mascot" of a different local high school baseball team. Each DJ makes it his concern to meet the coaches and players of "his" or "her" team. Be sure that your personalities turn out with the teams on certain occasions. They should also attend pep rallies held for the team. All of these activities should be talked about on the air. Also, the individual DJs engage in good-natured banter about their respective teams and create a feeling of friendly rivalry. Of course, the mascots will be expected to appear at the games to help with the cheer leading and generally to spark the team on to victory.

Future Promotions

Keep in mind that once you have established this sort of rapport between the station and the schools on the basis of baseball, you are in a logical position to continue a similar program during the football and basketball seasons as well. In certain areas, stations will want to align themselves with colleges instead of high schools. The idea will work just as well.

Station Team

Here is another idea to take advantage of the interest in baseball. Organize a station team—either baseball or softball—with your disc jockeys as the core of the team. Softball is probably the best bet since there are more teams engaging in this kind of ball. Also, there are many more facilities for playing softball than baseball. After you have lined up your disc jockeys, other station personnel should make up the remainder of the team. If possible, avoid bringing in outsiders for the team. Those who want to support the team but don't want to play can form the nucleus of a cheering section.

You can get an immense amount of community exposure, and have a lot of fun, too, by challenging and competing against other teams in the area. Because chances are your team will not be of professional caliber (or even of competent amateur standing for that matter), avoid games with regularly organized teams. Challenge teams organized by civic groups: everything from the Boy Scouts to the Ladies Auxiliary of the VFW. Other teams you can challenge might include groups from city hall, fire department, the police department, a team of college coeds, a group from the local newspaper, a representative team from local advertising agencies, and any other group that will provide fun and talk.

Challenge School Teachers

One good way to take advantage of your station team is to have them engage in games with teachers from the local high schools. Although high school baseball itself does not usually pull a big crowd, a game such as this will. If possible, arrange things so that the admission charge is turned over to the school for some suitable use.

BIKE SAFETY WEEK—April   6.23

The coming of the space age has not altered the popularity of bicycles with young people. The first bike is still one of the most wanted items in a child's world. And, unless we are getting old and jaded, they seem to start riding them at a much earlier age these days.

How It Works

On the Saturday of Bike Safety Week, following a week-long promotion on the air, your station conducts the WZZZ Bike-O-Rama. This is a bike rodeo open to all of the youngsters in your region. You stage a full-day competition, judging the entrants on how safe their bikes are, and how safely and skillfully they operate them. Prizes are awarded to the winners in whatever categories you decide to set up.

The Events

Without attempting to blueprint the entire competition for you, we'll suggest some elements on which the entrants can be judged: First, the bikes themselves should be graded for proper brakes, lights, license, fenders, chain guard, and so on—all elements contribute to the operating safety of the bicycle. Next, the entrants can be judged by a simple written exam, testing their knowledge of the rules of the road. Then you will want to test their bike-handling skill, with individual events such as a slalom course, riding a straight line, stopping in the shortest distance after a signal, and so on. There should be an area in which problems normally encountered on city streets are laid out and the participants judged on the manner in which they meet them.

Categories of Judging

We suggest you award prizes in two age brackets: one set of prizes for the 8 to 11 group, and another set for the 12 to 16 group. There should be boy and girl winners in each bracket. Within these categories you will want to award prizes for events such as those outlined above, as well as for such things as the best kept bike, the fanciest bike, and the best decorated bike.

Race

You may also wish to stage a series of races for your young bicycle riders. You will need considerable space in which to do this, so it will not be practical in all cases. Also, for the purposes of the races your categories should span no more than two years.

Get a Sponsor

You have probably figured out by now that this is a natural for any variety of advertisers to cosponsor. Obviously, you will want to pick the sort of sponsor who is in a position to come up with some prizes that will appeal to kids. A good place to look is a suburban shopping center. The entire event can be held in the parking lot of such a center.

The Bike-O-Rama is a natural goodwill and traffic builder for anyone from a supermarket to a garden center, preferably one with a large parking area adjacent. You may find that the best area will be your local park.

License Incentive

The cost of bicycle licenses and the degree of enforcement of their use varies from community to community. It has been our experience, however, that in many places, even though the cost is low, most kids just do not bother to get a license. If such is the case in your area, you will probably want to make it mandatory to have a license in order to enter the Bike-O-Rama. You can arrange with the city department that handles such licenses to have an official on hand at the event to sell bike licenses on the spot.

6.24   SECRETARIES WEEK—April

The National Secretaries Association sponsors this week as a "tribute to secretaries throughout the world for their important role in the professions, industry, and government." And, you know, they've got a point there. You will find that a lot of bosses among your listeners will agree when you conduct this simple promotion.

How It Works

You invite all the bosses in your area to send in a short letter nominating their secretaries as "Centerville Secretary of the Year." The winning secretary is selected by means of a drawing from all those entered. All that is needed is the name of the secretary in a short note of nomination, (not a long letter of recommendation,) on company letterhead, signed by the secretary's boss.

The Prizes

For this contest you should have a fairly noteworthy prize for your top winner. One suggestion is a wardrobe of clothes for spring. Perhaps you may wish to provide the winner with a week's vacation at some nice resort, with a replacement provided to cover the job.

Arrange with an advertiser, such as a florist, to provide a token award to every secretary nominated. For example, a bouquet and a handsome engraved card from the station saluting each individually during Secretaries Week.

Air Salutes

During Secretaries Week you can create a considerable amount of talk by simply saluting on the air those secretaries whose names have been submitted. This can just be a matter of reading the name of the secretary, the name of the boss who submitted the entry, and the name of the company.

Don't Pass This By

On the surface, this may strike you as a somewhat passive promotion, but it contains many advantages. You will be converting a good portion of the work force into listeners. And this promotion will put you on good terms with a very large number of businesspeople and their secretaries throughout your broadcast area. This can be a big bonus the next time one of your salespeople walks in to try to sell some time on your station.

BABY WEEK—April   6.25

If you have a camera store or portrait studio advertiser, here is a tailor-made traffic builder for them, all appropriately tied in with Baby Week. And babies are the most popular photo subjects in America.

How It Works

In recognition of Baby Week you announce the following contest in conjunction with your advertiser: Pictures of your DJs as babies, and as they are now, are mounted in the advertiser's place(s) of business. Listeners are invited to come in and attempt to match them correctly. Entries are deposited at that time. If you wish to complicate it a little bit, you may throw in a couple of extra baby pictures, not of your DJs, and require that the correct ones be selected and matched.

Prizes

Since in all likelihood you will have a number of winners, you should provide for this by either:

1. Having a quantity of duplicate first prizes of a nominal value.
2. Announcing there will be a drawing for a more major first prize in case of ties.
3. A combination of the two wherein all those correctly matching the pictures win a nominal prize, and a drawing is held among these winners for a valuable top prize.

   Since both camera and portrait operations make frequent "free" offers to stimulate business, they might even wish in this case to offer something to everyone entering the contest—such as a roll of film developed free, or a discount or free 5 × 7 portrait for anyone in the entrant's family.

Variations

There are a number of ways you can adapt this idea of matching baby pictures. For example, you can conduct the same contest with one personality, making it a challenge by offering, say, a dozen various baby pictures to choose from, with only one being correct. You may also take the contest in either form and run it in the local newspaper as a mail-in contest. It's an excellent way of publicizing and personalizing your DJs to the public.

6.26   BE KIND TO ANIMALS WEEK—May

Special days and weeks of this type provide you with the opportunity for developing promotions that are a lot of fun for you and your listeners. They give you the hook upon which to hang fun-type ideas. Because they are topical and timely, you will be wise to make extensive use of them throughout the year. And because of their variety, you have the opportunity to reach many segments of your potential audience.

The WZZZ Dog of the Year

Start this promotion at least two weeks in advance of Be Kind to Animals Week so that it winds up during that week.

How It Works

Announce that you are to name a WZZZ Dog of the Year. Listeners are invited to send in their choices for candidates for the title. Each letter should contain the facts as to why the animal should win the award. Portions of the letters are read over the air during the contest.

Judging

The board of judges can include someone from the local chapter of the S.P.C.A., the president of the Humane Society, and so on. Another way to select your winners is to pick three to five finalists and have listeners send in postcard votes.

The Prize

The prize should be a customized doghouse. You can get one of the builder's supply firms that is a regular sponsor to construct the doghouse for you. It should be a fairly elaborate affair, possibly having more than one room. The winner might also receive a year's supply of dog food, a doggie wardrobe from a local pet shop, and so on.

Promoting the Contest

You will have a lot more fun with this contest if you set up a fictional WZZZ dog named Spot. It is at his urging that you stage the contest. Using a gimmick voice, the fictional dog can do your promo announcements for you. These will be known as "Spot" announcements.

The fancy doghouse to be given away should be put on display at the studios. Your DJs can have fun detailing their search for a doghouse architect.

To tie-in with your promotion, the public service spots you broadcast during the period should include a fairly heavy schedule of spots for the Humane Society, the S.P.C.A., and other organizations that have to do with animals.

6.27 MOTHER'S DAY MESSAGE—May

Here is a powerful promotion that you can work out in conjunction with a major radio and television appliance dealer for Mother's Day. If you wish, you can even do a follow-up on it for Father's Day. However, since Father's Day, for some reason, does not carry with it the overall significance of Mother's Day, this will probably not work as well. Give some thought to tying the two days together for the purposes of this promotion and you may end up with something very good.

If possible, try to sell this idea to a national distributor in your area so it can be worked through all of his or her dealers. You will end up with a bigger schedule and the promotion itself will work better. Of necessity, this idea should be presented to an advertiser or advertisers handling a nationally distributed "name" brand of electronic appliances, including tape recording equipment.

How It Works

Through announcements on your station, the advertiser invites everyone to send their mother a *free*, personally recorded message so she can hear her family's voices with a message of love for Mother's Day. All they have to do is to visit the dealer and record the message on the advertised tape recorder.

The dealer then sends the tape to the affiliated dealer nearest to the home of the mother for whom the message is intended. The dealer also sends a card to the mother informing her that there is a personally recorded Mother's Day greeting waiting for her at nearby ABC Radio & TV Appliance Store.

Timing

The campaign should be run sufficiently in advance of Mother's Day to ensure that the messages are delivered in time. This means that the messages should probably be in the mail no later than 10 days before Mother's Day.

The Tape Recordings

The messages themselves are recorded on tape cassettes. Be sure that a note of explanation to the dealer on the other end is included with the tape. And be sure that the card sent to the mother identifies the name and address of the person who recorded the message.

Costs

The dealer will be out a small sum for the cassettes and postage for every person that takes him up on the offer. However, we are sure you can get him to agree that this is a very reasonable price to pay for the opportunity of creating traffic and actually demonstrating his wares to interested potential buyers.

Try for Co-op Money

When presenting this sales idea to dealers or distributors, be sure to suggest that they try to arrange for co-op money from the national organization. This should be readily available, since dealers all over the country will benefit.

MORE MOTHER'S DAY PROMOTIONS—May   6.28

For some reason, in the national mind, Mother's Day is a more serious occasion than Father's Day. There are a number of psychological reasons for this, but we need not go into them here. The point is, you will bring down the wrath of the population on your head if you stage a Mother's Day promotion that might be construed as slighting or facetious. Any promotion should point up the dignity of motherhood.

How It Works—Several Ways

You may wish to do something for Mother's Day as simple as having listeners nominate candidates for the title of Oldest Mother, Youngest Mother, and Mother with the largest family. As ordinary and uninspired as this may sound, it still works well for a Mother's Day promotion.

Mothers Roll Call

A promotion with a little more spread and interest to it is a Mothers Roll Call. Listeners are asked to send in the names of their mothers on a postcard. On Mother's Day, you go on the air with something to the effect: "WZZZ SALUTES THE MOTHERS OF CENTERVILLE, INCLUDING _____" and read three or four of the names. This is continued throughout the day. This is a very simple promotion, easily handled, yet very effective.

Mother Registration

This one will get all of your retail sponsors into the act. First, arrange with as many such sponsors as possible to participate. Then, go on the air to announce that the mothers of your town can be registered at any of these stores. All of the registration slips are put into a drum. A drawing is held on Mother's Day. The winner receives a gift from each of the participating stores. Try to arrange for your mayor, the president of the Chamber of Commerce or some other civic dignitary to draw the winner for you.

You can add some extra suspense to the contest by having listeners who participate mark one of the letters in the word M−O−T−H−E−R on their registration slips. Then the slips are put into separate bins marked with similar letters. A wheel is spun or a preliminary drawing of alphabetical letters is held to determine from which bin the winner will be selected.

If you wish to make it really a big day for your winner, in addition to the prizes from the stores, put a chauffeur-driven car at her disposal for the day and send the winning mother and her entire family out to dinner. You will want to see that she receives a special corsage, of course.

6.29 GIFT BUYER'S GUIDE/MOTHER'S DAY—May

Here is a suggestion to take to a major department store or variety store. The promotion can be used for Mother's Day, or throughout the month of June when many people are faced with the problem of finding gifts for graduates, brides, and for Father's Day.

How It Works

Sell a schedule on the basis of a novel presentation of the spots on the air. Utilize the store's shopping suggestion service, if they have one already in effect. Otherwise, have them set up a specified person to work with you on this promotion.

At intervals throughout the day your disc jockeys place calls to the store and they talk to the store's representative, who then discusses the many gift ideas, and their prices, that the store has available. You will probably want to tape these spots in advance to achieve a better presentation and to keep them under control timewise. This method of presenting the store's message permits a wide variety of products to be mentioned and puts the spotlight on the courteous treatment and service that buyers can expect at this store.

Additional Air Bit

Your personalities can ask listeners to call or write about any specific or unusual gift-buying problems they may have. These can then be worked into the spot announcements. But before you hit the store representatives with any real brain twisters, it is wise to give them advance warning so they can have a chance to work out their answer.

NATIONAL RAISIN WEEK—May

Now for your most magnificent offer of the year, in a tribute to the noble raisin during this special week in its honor, you offer to send a free raisin to anyone writing in and enclosing a stamped, self-addressed envelope.

Another idea is to have your DJs undertake a do-it-yourself raisin-making project. They start with Thompson seedless grapes and a sunlamp and see who can come up with raisins. Or, in connection with a commercial brand of raisins carried in your local supermarkets, you can carry out a raisin recipe contest. Listeners are invited to send in their favorite recipes that include raisins. Those who submit the 10 best recipes receive boxes of raisins as prizes. Follow this up by offering to send copies of the winning recipes to any listeners who care to write in for them. The company you have sold the contest to should bear the cost of printing and mailing.

POLICE WEEK—May

Police Week is in recognition of the contribution the police officers of America have made to our civilization. It's a tribute long overdue, and an ideal peg for an on-air promotion.

How It Works

Your Police Week promotion in its simplest form consists of on-air announcements throughout the week. If your community does not have a huge police force, each announcement can salute an individual policeman, giving his name, rank, and two or three sentences about him. In larger communities you can still select outstanding individuals on the force, or tailor the spots to pay tribute to the entire police force. All of the spots are tagged with an appeal to listeners to take the time to say "hello" and "thank you" the next time they see a police officer.

Depending on how extensive a salute you wish to make out of Police Week, there are a number of additional things you may add to the promotion. You can, for example, tape messages or interviews with various officials, including a message from the chief of police; individual department heads describing their operations, problems, and goals; and a message from the mayor asking the citizens to observe Police Week with a friendly "thank you" to officers. You might also send bits describing their activities in the public interest. These then could be used as individual cut-ins throughout Police Week.

6.32 FUEL DEALER PROMOTION—May

This is a promotion that, by its nature, will work most effectively if pitched on radio. The basis is simple and the public response should be sizable. Also, it is designed to do a job for your fuel dealer account at the slack time of the year.

Start Time

Suggested time for this promotion is May 15 to June 1. You may wish to start a week ahead to get the mail response started before you begin your on-air drawings. The promotion should run for a period of three to four weeks. It can be conducted for as few as two weeks, but it will not sustain itself for a period longer than four weeks.

How It Works

As mentioned above, the promotion is completely simple in its operation; there is nothing complicated or flashy about it. Its only advantage is that it will do a highly effective job of gaining new customers for the fuel dealer involved and put a lot of spots on your station.

Through spot announcements, listeners who use oil fuel are invited to send in postcards with their names, addresses, and telephone numbers. They then have a chance to win free supplies of fuel from the dealer. The winners are drawn and announced on the air. That's all there is to it. You can add the listener hook that, when a person's name is announced, he must call the station within a specified time to qualify for a prize.

Prizes

The prize structure for this promotion should probably be something like this:

- *Top Prize*—a six-month supply of fuel
- *Second Prize*—a three-month supply of fuel
- *Third Prize*—weekly prize of 100 gallons of fuel
- *Daily Prizes*—10 to 25 daily prizes, with each winner receiving 25 gallons of fuel

Advantages

This promotion provides a logical method in which to advertise that this is the time to get your tank filled up to carry you through the summer. With 25 daily winners, in a four-week promotion period there will be 506 winners, therefore, it is likely that a fair proportion will become regular customers. Also, everyone except the top winners will probably have their tanks filled when the prize is delivered. Also, all of the postcard entries go to the dealer and provide the basis for an excellent new customer prospect list.

FATHER'S DAY—June

6.33

Here is a Father's Day promotion that is certain to stir up a lot of talk—and listeners.

How It Works

The promotion should start two weeks ahead of Father's Day, allowing one week of promotion to get entries in and a week to conduct the contest. Listeners are invited to send in the names of their fathers on postcards. Be sure to specify "postcards only" to make handling easy.

Each card should contain the father's first name, middle initial, last name, and address. If he does not have a middle initial, one should be made up by the person sending in the card. The middle initial is simply for the purpose of double-checking. No other information is required. Be sure to tell listeners *not* to send in detailed biographies relating why they think their father is "the most wonderful dad in the world."

All of the postcards received should be placed in a big basket, drum, or some other container. During the Monday through Friday period just prior to Father's Day, one of these cards is drawn from the basket each hour. The DJ on the air reads the name from the card, but not the middle initial. The father whose name is read, or the person who submitted the card, must call the station within a given period of minutes—anywhere from two to five.

The caller then must identify the middle initial as it appears on the card. Each correctly identified card is then set aside and it becomes a finalist for the prize drawing to be held at the end of the week.

Wind-Up

On either Friday or Saturday, you hold a grand drawing to select the WZZZ Father of the Year. Here is one way to pick your winner: You can run a concurrent promotion with the one above to find the man in your listening area who has the most children. This man is given a prize and he is invited down to your studios to draw the winner from the group of finalist cards picked during the week. This gives you a double promotion. The two should be handled and promoted as one. Either promotion will stand by itself without the other.

The Prize

A good prize for the promotion would be an automatic dishwasher so that the winning father will never, under any circumstances, be faced with this chore again. However, the prize need not be this expensive. Regardless of the prize, you will be getting bags full of entries because this promotion gives every person an opportunity to honor his father.

6.34   NATIONAL HUMOR WEEK—June

Assemble a reference library of books containing jokes indexed by categories. There are several volumes of this type available at any library; a good start is *Esar's Comic Dictionary*.

How It Works

Your DJs ask listeners to send in postcards with one-word subjects that they do *not* think there is a joke about. As the subjects come in the DJs read them; for the interesting ones, they read an appropriate joke on that category. Prizes go to the listeners "stumping" your reference library.

Prizes

The prizes are relatively unimportant in this promotion—they may be just about anything. A good prize in keeping with the theme of the promotion is a humorous album.

Additional Twists

When subjects win prizes for "stumping" your joke file, invite listeners to send in any jokes they may know that are about the categories you couldn't provide a joke for. These entries, if applicable, may also win prizes.

6.35   GREAT STONE FACE—June

You may wish to do this promotion on just one afternoon or evening towards the end of National Humor Week, or you can run it for the entire week.

How It Works

Arrange for your afternoon DJ to do his show from the window of a local department store or in a shopping mall's central concourse. Sitting with him is WZZZ's Great Stone Face—probably your morning man, who is apt to be grumpy enough having to get up at that hour every day. A prize of a humorous album (or a humorous book from the store's book department) or something similar goes to anyone who can force a smile or a laugh out of WZZZ's Great Stone Face. Prizes should be of a minor nature, since DJs are a notoriously jolly group and you should have lots of winners. The afternoon DJ does a running play-by-play on the efforts made by onlookers.

Important: You should ballyhoo this event thoroughly for a few days before staging it, and give some people time to work up some really ingenious methods for provoking a chuckle from the Great Stone Face. You should also have a sign at the event explaining the stunt so that passersby will stop and have a go at it.

SALUTE TO SENIORS—June   6.36

Your local jewelers have a big stake in the special retail sales opportunities that come up during the spring. Of particular interest to them are the sales resulting from gifts to graduates—items such as pen and pencil sets, watches, cuff links, and similar personal jewelry gifts have long been top choices as presents to graduates. The following idea, therefore, is a good bet to present to a jewelry store advertiser.

How It Works

A group of the outstanding seniors from the local high school or schools is chosen for a series of short personal taped interviews. They are asked their plans for the future, for instance, whether they are going on to college, directly into business, getting married, and so forth.

Logical candidates are the top scholars, athletes, and activities leaders such as class and school officers. The advertiser then, in effect, sponsors these short recorded tributes to these outstanding young men and women by following each interview with a commercial urging people to shop for graduation gifts at the sponsor's store. These short, interesting interviews with students whose names have become familiar to your entire community will tie the advertiser in as the logical and select place to find appropriate gifts for the graduating seniors.

Store Tie-In

The advertiser ties in with the "Salute to Seniors" by having portraits of these young people displayed in the store window. The portraits can be obtained very reasonably by working with a photographer who realizes the value of having his or her work displayed in a prominent spot. After the promotion the portraits are given to the graduates pictured.

Publicity

Be sure to send a release containing information about the "Salute to Seniors" to the school newspapers, along with a list of those who will be interviewed and what time they will be on the air.

In addition to scheduling this promotion during the day to hit the gift-buyers, give some thought to doing a recap on it during the early evening hours with the idea of hooking in the students to your nighttime shows.

Selecting the Interviewees

There are a couple of simple ways of handling this detail. You can contact the school principals, outline the program, and have them submit appropriate names. Or, you can run a contest to have the students themselves vote on who should be honored. Of course, you can combine the two methods, thus ensuring that the scholars as well at the athletes and others are included.

6.37 SUMMERTIME SAFETY KIT—June

Druggists look with a great deal of pleasure on the summer season as a time for selling vast quantities of suntan lotion, insect repellent, poison ivy lotions, Band-Aids, and everything else associated with outdoor living. Take this idea to a major drugstore or chain to give them the inside track on sales of these items in your area, as advertised on your station.

How It Works

Instead of selling these items individually, the druggist groups a collection of the most common and essential of the summertime home remedies together. He puts these together into a package, along with a small first-aid pamphlet (a number of which are printed for free distribution by the various pharmaceutical houses). The entire package is advertised as the WZZZ Summertime Safety Kit; you make available to your listeners through on-air promos a list of the components that everyone should have on hand for the summer season.

The sale of the kit is then promoted on your station as being available at the XYZ Drug Chain—as cash advertising, of course.

Safety Campaign

An effective way of promoting the availability of the WZZZ Summertime Safety Kit is by tying it in with a campaign of tips, precautions, and safe practices to employ when enjoying outdoor activities. This public service type of campaign is actually sponsored by the drug outlet featuring the Safety Kits. The campaign, naturally, ends with a suggestion to listeners to have one of the kits handy for minor emergencies throughout the summer.

BEACH PATROL—June   6.38

This promotion can be run all summer long and provides the basis for a major sale to a soft drink bottler. It can be switched slightly and sold to a different type of sponsor, but it will work easiest and best with a bottling account.

How It Works

This promotion is very simple. During the summer months members of your air staff, your other staff, or persons hired by you pay visits to the bathing beaches in your area. When they find a person with a bottle or can of the sponsor's product, they give that person a six-pack or more of the product. If this person also has a radio that is tuned to your station, they receive an additional merchandise prize. Essentially, that is all there is to it.

Sell It Big

This can be a very big promotion and your sales effort should reflect this. Naturally, the bottler who gets to participate will have to buy a very large summer schedule on your station. And he should give considerable merchandising support to the "Beach Patrol," too. You should not be hesitant about asking for aisle or shelf display space. You will be giving the promotion and the bottler's product extensive on-air plugs; he should be willing to reciprocate to help make the promotion as successful as possible.

Covering All of the Beaches

You will want to set up a master list of all of the public swimming beaches in your area. With this as a guide, you should then set up a summer-long schedule for your "Beach Patrol" so that all of the beaches will be covered equally on a proportional basis according to the popularity of the beach. There will have to be some adjustment to allow for bad weather, but this can be done as you go along.

Printed Handouts

Whoever is manning your "Beach Patrol" should carry printed handouts with them. These should be distributed as extensively as possible at the various beaches. Working through your sponsor, you will be able, in most cases, to arrange for signs at the beaches calling attention to the "Beach Patrol."

Hype It on the Air

You will want to play up the "Beach Patrol" heavily on the air. Occasionally you will want to plug a specific beach where your "Beach Patrol" is going to be or is at the time you announce it.

Prizes

As mentioned, the people you find with the bottler's product should receive a six-pack or a case of the product. You can arrange to hand out certificates good for the soft drink instead of going to the bother of carrying the product around with you.

The merchandise prizes that go to people who also have your station tuned in on their radios can be almost anything. Cassettes or CDs will work well. But it will be best if you have a fairly wide variety of goods to hand out. Also, if you can possibly set it up, it would be very good to have one major winner each week. The ideal prize for this would be a refurbished soft drink cooler along with a certificate good for a six-month supply of the soft drink.

6.39 SIDEWALK SALE—June

This sales promotion will work to the fullest when it is linked with a shopping center or a specific shopping area so that numerous merchants can be included. Of course, it will produce more spot sales for you, too, when handled in this manner.

The Sidewalk Sale is a natural for the summer months. It is just what its name indicates: a sale that takes place out on the sidewalk. There are many possible variations on the basic theme. We will examine some of them a little later on.

How It Works

Working through the merchants' association at a major shopping center or within a shopping district, you sell the idea of a Sidewalk Sale to be heavily promoted on your station. The merchants move all sale items out onto the sidewalk for the day of the sale, and you are in business.

To be sure that you tie up the advertising dollars to be spent on the affair, you make the promotion "yours" through a contest pitch you will find further on.

Special Features

The Sidewalk Sale promotion can be keyed to specific types of merchandise. There are obvious advantages and disadvantages to handling it in this manner. Some of the possibilities are:

- Barbecue Sale
- Outdoor Living Sale
- Picnic Sale
- Christmas in July Sale
- Scratch and Dent Sale (for floor samples that have been slightly damaged)
- Plus many others

Special Dress for the Merchants

However you handle the approach to this promotion, the merchants involved should be encouraged to wear distinctive dress for the event. They may want to dress as circus clowns, or even as sidewalk pitchmen, complete with flattop straw hats and canes. Maybe dress them in frontier costumes and bill them as Old West Traders. The idea is to give some added flash and excitement to the promotion and almost anything will work.

Remotes

If at all possible, consider doing some remotes from the sale site. This will give you an added talking point when you are asking for the business in the first place.

The Contest

Each of the merchants participating in the Sidewalk Sale provides you with a complete description and the sale price of one of the biggest bargain items he or she will feature in the sale, plus the regular retail price. Each time you promote the event, your disc jockey describes a different item and gives its regular price. He or she then announces that the first person calling in with the correct guess of the sale price wins the item. (You *must* make sure that the merchant has more than one of these "leader" items, and that they will actually be on sale at the price you announce.)

With this contest each merchant gets an individual "plug" and you are constantly pushing the biggest bargains that will be available at the Sidewalk Sale.

Since this is commercial time you are dealing with, you will not want calls coming in over a long period to get a winner. To avoid this, have the disc jockey give clues after a given amount of time has passed with no correct answer.

6.40 NATIONAL SAFE BOATING WEEK—July

Since boating is becoming an increasingly popular pastime in virtually every section of the country, use this week for a concentrated safe boating campaign. There are numerous agencies that will supply you with materials and spots for such a campaign.

Safety Tie-Ins

If you are using the WZZZ Fish Finder promotion, include safe boating tips with your fishing reports. Your weather reports this week, and throughout the summer, can include tips to boaters on wind and weather conditions as they apply to the water.

Rowboat Race

Working in connection with the Coast Guard, Safety Council, and local yacht clubs, stage a rowboat race between your DJs as part of a boating demonstration that will feature safety. Or, on a Saturday or Sunday promote a drive to have all boaters help clear debris from the water in the interest of safety.

6.41 NATIONAL FARM SAFETY WEEK—July

In most markets, a relatively small portion of your audience will find particular significance in this special week, but that portion is a regular and loyal audience. For this reason you should not overlook mentioning Farm Safety Week. To appeal to this early-riser segment of the audience, be sure that you do all spots connected with this week early in the morning.

Special Farm Safety Spots

If you have not received them, request special material from your safety council for use. An excellent way to boost your very early morning audience is to send one of your staff out into the country with a portable tape machine to record some brief bits with local farmers in which they tell what they are doing about safety.

Contest

You may wish to conduct a minor contest (limited to the 5:00 to 6:30 A.M. period) in which you ask for farm safety tips. Or, if you have the CARE Garden promotion going that was suggested in Section 4, work in farm safety bits with it.

NATIONAL INVENTORS' WEEK—July   6.42

For a week prior to and during National Inventors' Week your late-morning DJ calls for suggestions of things that need to be invented. Each day the DJ reads the most interesting suggestions and awards a simple prize of the day to the one chosen best. At the end of the week, the best overall suggestion is awarded a more significant prize. Good prizes for Most-Needed Invention Poll would be a new item or product on the market which your station is selling time for and which the sponsor bills as a "new invention."

Best Invention of the Century Poll

Instead of the above, the disc jockey conducts a poll of opinions as to the most significant invention of the century. The poll is conducted as in the promotion above. You will probably receive suggestions running the gamut from the safety pin to the space shuttle.

DRIVING SAFETY FOR HOLIDAY WEEKEND—July 4   6.43

Keeping on Living Limericks

Radio joins with other media each year during the various holiday seasons to urge motorists to use caution and avoid becoming another casualty of the carnage on the nation's highways. Here is a simple yet effective method of getting more impact into your safe-driving messages, relying to some degree on the increasingly popular theory that you have to "shock" your listeners somewhat to get them to hear. If you have it in your library, use a rhythm background behind these.

There once was a driver named Bill
Who, while trying to pass on a hill,
Met a fast-moving truck
Was unable to duck
And Bill is scattered there still.

A carefree young driver named Fred
Followed close to the car up ahead,
Ended up with a clunk
In the other car's trunk
And from there to a hospital bed.

In a race with a fast-moving train
A driver, not using his brain,
Can win if he's fast,
But it may be his last
'Cause losing can be quite a strain.

With a judgment that's since proved unwise
Tom shouted his claim to the skies:
He could break any rule,
And the misguided fool
Has been missed since the wreck by the guys.

On a holiday outing a friend
Through traffic did weave and did wend,
Passed a car on a curve
Was unable to swerve,
And now I've got flowers to send.

Ignoring the safe-driving folder
Alice grew bolder and bolder,
Increasing her speed
She chose not to heed
Death peering over her shoulder.

Charlie rushed to avoid being late
For a very important first date
Made the journey too fast
It turned out his last
And now it's the date who must wait.

On a ride with a lovely young miss
Friend Arnold tried stealing a kiss,
We hope it was fun
T'was his very last one,

For Arnold's found heavenly bliss.

A traveling chemist named Flynn
Tried mixing whiskey and gin,
Then he got in his car
Headed for the next bar,
And we haven't seen poor Flynn agin.

A message that's simple and terse,
We attempt to relay with this verse,
You must drive with care
Being cautious and fair,
Or your next ride may be in a hearse.

There is many a flower doth wave
O'er the driver who thought he could save
Several minutes or more
With his foot on the floor
And ended spending that time in his grave.

The holiday traffic and such
Didn't bother O'Sullivan much,
Till he made a mistake
By not using his brake
And spent the next year on a crutch.

After drinking you simply can't cope
With the traffic, my friend. Let us hope
The streets you won't roam
Take a taxicab home.
If you must kill yourself, use a rope.

If your temper is getting the best
While you're driving—my friend take a rest,
Do not drive like a fool
Or your anger will cool
In jail—as a permanent guest.

Charlie Racer had a foot made of lead
And he very nearly ended up dead

For his speed caused a wreck
That fractured his neck
Now he's driving a wheelchair instead.

6.44 OPERATION FLAGLIFT—July 4

All too often the true meaning of Independence Day is lost in the fun and fire-
works of midsummer's major holiday. This is a simple goodwill-getter that
serves to bring home a reminder of the tradition of this national holiday.

How It Works

The title explains the pitch of this promotion: WZZZ campaigns to get every
home and business to display the American flag on the Fourth of July. Through
on-air announcements and interviews, and working with civic groups such as
the VFW, Rotary, American Legion, the Armed Services, and Scouts, citizens
are urged to display the flag in honor of this holiday.

Some Ideas

Here are some ideas for expanding and developing Operation Flaglift both on-
air and through civic groups:

- Arrange with an advertiser to offer American flags at cost so that every home
  can have one. These should be flags adequate for mounting outdoors on the
  home, yet at a reasonable price.

- If not already done in your community, work with the Chamber of Commerce on a campaign to have the city streets completely lined with flags on
  The Fourth of July and the day preceding.

- With an organization that has city-wide coverage and a large and active membership, seek to develop a city-wide competition whereby each block seeks to
  have 100 percent participation, with every house displaying a flag. Each
  block achieving this goal is announced on the air.

- Have all of the local scouting organizations join together for a house-to-house
  canvass of the entire city, asking people to sign pledges to display the flag on
  the Fourth of July. This should be done the week prior to the holiday. A close
  check on the number of homes signing is kept and announced on the station.
  An excellent way to add depth to this is to initiate a friendly rivalry with a
  neighboring community to see which can produce the greatest number of
  pledges—or the highest percentage if there is a major discrepancy in size
  between the communities.

NATIONAL CLOWN WEEK—August   6.45

Operating on the old premise that clowns are for kids and kids love clowns, here's a promotion that can build a backlog of goodwill in your area that will last the entire year.

How It Works

In your area there are persons who sell, or in some cases contribute, their talents to serve as clowns for gatherings of children, such as birthday parties or in hospitals. First, you secure the services of two or more of these individuals for the entire week. Then you announce that, as a tribute to National Clown Week, WZZZ is providing Clowns for Kids. A WZZZ clown will pay a cheerful visit to any shut-in youngster whose name, age, and address is submitted by postcard or letter during the week.

INTERNATIONAL CHARACTER DAY—August   6.46

Here is a simple promotion that can be linked with National Clown Week. However, because it is of an entirely different nature than Clowns for Kids, you should not use both.

How It Works

Throughout National Clown Week your listeners are asked to send in their ballots for the Biggest Clown Around. At the end of the week, the "clown" receiving the most votes is named WZZZ's International Character. It is that simple. Nearly everyone has a candidate for whom he would like to cast a negative vote.

NATIONAL SANDWICH MONTH—August   6.47

For this commercially sponsored special month, National Sandwich Month, we propose a readily saleable promotion that will be of very special interest to your mid-morning at-home audience. It's a good bet that some restaurant in your area will recognize this month-long promotion as an ideal way of telling your listeners about its cuisine.

How It Works

During the month of August, in honor of National Sandwich Month, your mid-morning DJ invites listeners to send in their recipes for "something special" in the way of sandwiches to prove that the common sandwich can actually be an exotic meal. Each day a sandwich recipe is selected from the entries and given to the chef at the restaurant sponsoring the promotion.

With the phone line open so your listeners can hear, the DJ reads the recipe to the chef. The completed work of art is delivered so that it can be consumed while the DJ is on the air. Each entry selected entitles the person sending it in to a free dinner or luncheon for two at the sponsoring restaurant.

6.48   NATIONAL AVIATION DAY—August

The skies over America have filled with private planes of every size and shape. Thousands of men and women all over the country are learning to fly. The public is becoming more interested in flying every day. Here's a promotion for National Aviation Day that will give you a good program feature capitalizing on this interest, and it should be readily saleable to the nearest airport-flying school operation in your area.

How It Works

Basically the idea is that on National Aviation Day, or for the weekend, WZZZ promotes a private plane show and open house at the airport. Publicized strongly in advance, the open house features models of all of the new light planes that can be obtained, a drawing for free scenic flights over the city, plus a special "stunt" feature attraction staged by one of your disc jockeys. You may go even further and arrange some stunt flying demonstrations or parachute-jumping to lend an air-show atmosphere.

The Buildup

The advance promotion for this event is handled by having one of your disc jockeys start taking flying lessons from the flight school some time in advance of National Aviation Day. The feature attraction at the open house is your erst-while student's first solo flight, during which he broadcasts his comments and observations and flight routine. During the lesson period your DJ gives daily progress reports on his flight training and experiences.

6.49   NATIONAL BAREFOOT FREEDOM WEEK—September

Here are a couple of "stunt"-type promotions that will permit amusing acknowledgement of this unique special week.

How It Works

Run an ad in the local newspaper with a large picture of the bare feet, from about mid-calf down, of five of your DJs. The copy should identify the DJs whose feet are in the picture, but not in the order in which they appear.

Invite listeners to tear out the ad, identify the feet in correct order, and mail it in. Your DJs can give "clues" on the air, such as: "I wear a size 13D shoe and have a corn on one of my toes." The prize can be anything from a year's supply of corn pads to new shoes.

CARAVAN OF NEW CARS—September   6.50

Come fall and new car advertising becomes a major item. Here is a promotion that will make sure you get the bulk of this advertising, and at the same time give you an excellent opportunity for station publicity.

How It Works

Most of the new models of American cars come on the market within a period of a few weeks in the fall. Working in advance through the dealers and dealer organizations in your area, arrange to stage a Caravan of New Cars to give the public the opportunity to see all of the new models at one place and time. You will wish to schedule the event for a Saturday.

Give the event plenty of advance publicity on the air. Once the event is set, get your salespeople out making those calls to tie in that extra business. You will find the car dealers generally enthusiastic about this promotion. To stave off any bickering, limit them to one sign of a standard size on each side of the cars entered in the caravan.

Put Some Hoopla in the Caravan

Arrange for a parade of all of the new cars through town. You will want to have your air personalities riding in the cars. If you have a news van, it should lead the parade. In addition, give some thought to doing a remote on the Caravan.

If there is room for it, have the parade and the cars go on display outside your station. Otherwise, pick a central area. If yours is a big city, you might want to arrange for the Caravan to appear at two or three of the major shopping centers, thus getting the widest possible coverage.

Selling the Caravan

Just that your station is interested enough in the car dealers to stage the Caravan of New Cars should attract the bulk of the new car advertising, but get your salespeople working at it actively. Make certain that they point out that the dealers with spots on the air will create the greatest impact on the car-buying public who will come out to view the Caravan.

Putting in a Real Hook

If you really want to get thousands of people out for the Caravan, try this: At the conclusion of the caravan, get the dealers to go together and agree to sell one of the new cars for $1.00. The cost should be spread among all of the dealers. The car to be sold should be determined by drawing the name of that car from a fishbowl.

The person who gets to buy the car for $1.00 is also determined by a drawing. To be eligible, a person must first listen to a sales pitch from one of the dealer representatives with the Caravan who will then give that person a numbered card.

A word of caution: If you try this, be sure there are plenty of police officers on hand to control the crowds. You will need them.

6.51 NATIONAL LETTER WRITING WEEK—October

Here is a sort of a reverse-popularity poll that will let your disc jockeys and your listeners have some good fun during National Letter Writing Week. There is little or no commercial flavor to this special week. So, in recognition (of sorts) of National Letter Writing Week, you invite listeners to choose the WZZZ Pen Pal from among your disc jockeys. Listeners are asked to write a letter, which counts as a vote, to their favorite WZZZ DJ; however, the reason that your DJs will be plugging their fellow workers rather than themselves is that the DJ receiving the most mail must personally answer all of it.

Incentive

The possibility of receiving a personal answer to their letter from a disc jockey does not motivate too many people, but the idea of making a DJ work will. Since none of your air personalities will relish the idea of having to answer personally several hundred or even thousand letters, they will go to great lengths to devise reasons why the other DJs should be voted the most popular. It will be an amusing bit as the disc jockeys decry their own talents to build up effusively the merits of their cohorts.

6.52 FIRE PREVENTION WEEK—October

Few of the "special" weeks throughout the year are more deserving of your station's support than National Fire Prevention Week—and few organizations are more cooperative than your local fire department.

DJ's Fire Prevention Check

Each day of Fire Prevention Week a fire inspection team from the fire department accompanies a different DJ to the DJ's home and conducts a check for possible fire hazards. The visit is made with the parties coming and going in a fire engine and attracting as much outside attention as possible. As the team conducts the check, the inspector notes the fire hazards (and every home has them) in a discussion with the DJ. This interview-exchange is recorded and used on the air.

Dramatize Fire Rescues

An additional "gimmick" that can do a lot to dramatize Fire Prevention Week and the services and efficiency of your local Fire Department can be staged if there is a practice fire tower available. With as much fanfare and as many prior announcements as possible, one of your DJs becomes the object of a practice "rescue" from the tower. A remote unit (or tape if you wish to delay this) is set up on the top of the tower. The DJ does the play-by-play, as an "emergency call" is placed to the fire hall. Firemen rush to the scene, raise ladders, and come to the rescue of your DJ. As the disc jockey is "rescued" and can no longer handle the commentary, a newsperson on the ground takes over. Or if your news department has a hand-held unit or cellular telephone, have your rescued DJ give a play-by-play all the way through the rescue operation. Perhaps a large live audience can be promoted for this event, with fire prevention pamphlets handed out to the crowd.

Junior Fire Marshal Corps

This promotion is directed primarily at the elementary school-age children in your listening area—and obliquely, but forcefully, at their parents. In fact, you will require parents' cooperation, but since the objective of the promotion is fire safety education, they will be willing to give you all the help they can.

The whole idea is this: On the first day of Fire Prevention Week every elementary school youngster in your area is designated a "WZZZ Junior Fire Marshal." They are presented also with a WZZZ Junior Fire Marshal badge or card, or both, plus a list of fire prevention rules provided by the Fire Department. Each set of rules carries a space for the name of the youngster and the signature of the parent.

Make It a Party

The capper to the entire promotion comes in the form of a gigantic party for the youngsters the following weekend. The theme again is to educate them to fire prevention procedures.

In October, weather can be a factor that may make it mandatory to hold this gathering inside. Should this be the case, it can take the form of a movie party, a feature of which is a film or talk on fire prevention. Weather permitting, an outdoor gathering can be held, with the youngsters seeing a demonstration of fire equipment and possibly given a ride on a fire engine. The "ticket of admission" for the event is the parent's signature on the fire prevention tip sheet.

Lots of Help

We have outlined a very simple idea. Because of its effectiveness and good purpose, you can probably find any number of individuals and firms willing to participate in the effort. For example, a local theater might donate the site and facilities for the party. A union might contribute the necessary technical help. Refreshments could well be donated by still other commercial firms.

On-Air Bits

Use some of the children for short taped bits to plug fire prevention. Such little sequences can go like this:

Anncr: HERE, NOW, IS A FOURTH-GRADER FROM THE HORACE MANN SCHOOL:

Jimmy: THIS IS JIMMY JONES. I'M A WZZZ JUNIOR FIRE MARSHAL. I'VE CHECKED OUR BASEMENT TO MAKE SURE THERE ARE NO PILES OF RUBBISH THAT CAN CAUSE A FIRE. YOU SHOULD, TOO, BECAUSE MOST FIRES ARE THE RESULT OF CARELESSNESS.

6.53 NATIONAL PASS THE LAUGH WEEK—October

Here is a simple "fun" promotion you can work through one of your advertisers that will create store traffic and provide you with an effective and amusing promotion to run throughout "National Pass the Laugh Week."

How It Works

A tape recorder is set up in a booth in the store or business place of your advertiser. Listeners are invited to come and "pass the laugh" by recording the sound of their own laughter. Their names and addresses are recorded carefully to *properly* identify each laugh.

The collective chuckles are then aired at random on WZZZ throughout the week from the tapes made at the store. Any person who hears his own laugh broadcast on WZZZ, and calls the station and identifies it within three minutes, wins a simple prize, either provided by the advertiser, or by WZZZ in the form of a "comic" record or tape.

Peoples' efforts to record a distinctive laugh that they can identify when they hear it on WZZZ will provide you with some highly entertaining sounds, but a note of caution: Be *sure* there is no slip-up in correctly identifying each laugh so that when the person calls you can be positive as to your identification. Be sure also to announce the names of the laughers if they fail to call within the time limit.

NATIONAL DOUGHNUT WEEK—October   6.54

There are a number of simple suggestions you can use to make a sales tie-in with the commercial flavor of National Doughnut Week. Here are several for you to take to potential sponsors so that you both may take advantage of the promotional opportunities of this week.

Baker's Dozen

A large bakery or chain of bakeries make their customers a special "bakers dozen," thirteen for the price of twelve, or a "two dozen for the price of one" offer on doughnuts throughout the week. Each day a different variety of doughnuts is offered on the "special." The promotion is advertised to the fullest, of course, on WZZZ.

Open House

The great national snack, coffee and doughnuts, is the enticement at the open house at WZZZ. Your disc jockeys are the hosts and the public the guests as specific brands of coffee and doughnuts are featured. To add to the interest, a portable "doughnut vat" can be set up and the doughnuts made right on the spot.

The same "coffee and doughnuts" promotion can be staged even more effectively at a bakery, or better yet, at a supermarket that has a coffee bar and bakery as part of its operation. Again, one or more of your on-the-air personalities may host, or better yet, you can conduct a remote operation from the site of the coffee break, constantly inviting listeners to drop in for coffee and doughnuts.

Advertiser Goodwill

WZZZ treats all of the advertising agencies and your major advertisers in Centerville to a coffee break with doughnuts in recognition of National Doughnut Week. As well as being a nice goodwill impression to these valuable friends, it shows them that WZZZ is on the ball in recognizing the commercial promotion activities outside of the broadcasting industry. Arrangements are made with a caterer for the hot coffee and doughnuts to be delivered to the offices, compliments of WZZZ. One of your personalities may go in person with the coffee and doughnuts to present the station's treat.

6.55 HALLOWEEN PRIZE PUMPKINS—October 31

Halloween calls for a special promotion of some type and you are anxious to get away from the haunted-house bit that has been so overworked. Here is a promotion that is good, clean fun. It will create a great deal of talk and excitement, and it will do a lot of long-range good in building your audience.

How It Works

Get 500, 1,000 or 2,000 small pumpkins, each about the size of a cantaloupe. The number of pumpkins you will use will be determined by the size of your market. To each pumpkin attach a slip of paper stating that this is a WZZZ Prize Pumpkin and if the finder brings it to your station before midnight, he or she will receive the prize indicated on the slip. (The best way to attach the slips of paper is to staple them on. Tape is just not satisfactory for the job.)

Then, just after dark on Halloween have the pumpkins set out in every part of your city. Arrange for several crews of your people, working two to a car, to do the job quickly. The pumpkins should not be hidden because you want them found. Just set them out on parking strips, by telephone poles, and so forth.

The Prizes

This promotion does not require prizes of any great value. The great bulk of the prizes can be simply cassettes or CDs. Every person bringing in a pumpkin should receive two records or CDs and an apple. You can get the apples through your local Apple Commission, a wholesale house, or a retail produce outlet. They will be glad to provide them for the publicity.

You should have about 25 or more bigger prizes, but, as indicated above, these need not be of great value. Be sure you state on the slip attached to the pumpkin what each prize will be so that no one can complain.

Getting the Greatest Value from This Promotion

Once you have set out the pumpkins, have enough personnel on hand at the station to handle the crush of people bringing the pumpkins in. You will be amazed at the return. Have things set up so that the people bringing in the pumpkins (and they will not all be children by any means) can take a quick tour of your station. Remember, once they have had a chance to see your operation, they will feel that they really know you and will be much more likely to tune you in.

If you have them, hand out printed pieces about your station. The beauty of this pumpkin promotion is that, while your on-the-air publicity will send your regular listeners out looking, you will also reach thousands of people who may never even have heard of your station before.

NATIONAL TIE WEEK—October   6.56

This is a happy-type promotion that has a very strong built-in sales hook. Take this idea to a major local dry cleaner or chain of dry-cleaning establishments. It not only provides good publicity and promotion for such an advertiser, but it can be the basis of a great deal of future business for him.

How It Works

The promotion is simply this: In recognition of National Tie Week, WZZZ and Acme Cleaners are conducting the Great Tie Swap. Listeners are invited to send to the station any old tie that is around the house. They can send in as many as they want, but each must be mailed separately. In return, they will receive another tie. All ties sent in will be cleaned by Acme Cleaners. No satisfaction is guaranteed—except with the dry cleaning.

In conjunction with the promotion, Acme offers several dry-cleaning specials, including one on ties.

Handling

The simplest method for handling the ties is to ask that those sending in a tie include a stamped self-addressed envelope. The ties are then sent out after cleaning, selected at random. Naturally, publicity stuffers should be included for both the station and the cleaning establishment. The major fault with this method is that a tie does not fit very well in an average envelope and it is apt to arrive crumpled. This does not show the Acme service to the best advantage.

Some Alternatives

- You can ask each listener to include 50 cents postage and packing when they send in a tie.
- You can request two first-class stamps to be sent in with each tie. The cleaner then absorbs the packaging cost.
- You can talk the dry cleaner into absorbing all of the return mailing cost as part of his contribution to the promotion.

On-Air Publicity

Here are a few lines you can use to publicize the stunt on the air:

IF YOU'RE FIT TO BE TIED . . . STAY TUNED FOR THE GREAT WZZZ TIE SWAP.

* * * *

JOIN THE GREAT WZZZ TIE SWAP . . . IT'S YOUR CHANCE TO GET RID OF THOSE HORRIBLE TIES YOU RECEIVE AS CHRISTMAS AND BIRTHDAY PRESENTS.

* * * *

IT'S AN EYE FOR AN EYE . . . A TOOTH FOR A TOOTH . . . AND TIE FOR A TIE WHEN YOU JOIN THE GREAT WZZZ TIE SWAP. COMING SOON, SO STAY IN TUNE.

Additional Tie-In (pun intended)

You also have the opportunity of linking a department store with this promotion. Simply have such a store offer a new tie to the person sending in an old tie which wins in these categories:

- Worst-looking tie
- Shortest tie
- Oldest-looking tie
- Most varicolored tie
- Loudest-colored tie
- Narrowest tie
- Most sedate tie
- Widest tie
- Longest tie
- Worst hand-painted tie

6.57   ELECTION PROMOTIONS—November

These promotions are geared for use around election time. Rather than give you a single promotion idea to use for this period, we have included a large group of ideas with the thought that you may well wish to use more than one of them.

In maintaining your public service image in the community, there are many things you can do to create a greater impact than merely relying on public service announcements. In your on-air plugs for these promotions be sure that you give emphasis to the election coverage that your station will be carrying. Have the spots plugging your promotions recorded by the person who will head the election coverage.

Rides to the Polls

As an incentive to get voters out on election day, various organizations, both partisan and nonpartisan, in many parts of the country set up a service providing rides to the polls for voters who could not otherwise get out and vote. Often groups such as the Young Republicans, Young Democrats, and the League of Women Voters will even provide baby-sitter service for the time it takes a parent to go to the polls and vote.

Offer WZZZ as the clearing house for these services, and use your airtime to promote them. If necessary, set up a special line to handle the calls. The organizations you are working with will provide the labor.

Voters' Information Service

As a public service set up a special Election Day telephone information service. Arrange a special number that you publicize on your air and wherever else possible. Have two or more people covering the phones at all times prepared to answer questions on location of polls, times they are open, what is on the ballot, and so forth.

Promote your information service to the hilt. Ninety-five percent of the effectiveness of this promotion is gained from the fact that people are aware you are doing it. You may or may not have a large volume of calls, but that is immaterial as long as you demonstrate to the people your willingness to serve.

Pennies for Political Posters

This promotion is about as simple as any you can run. On the day after election day you announce that, as the WZZZ contribution to the election campaign, and to further the city's cleanup campaign, you will pay five cents for each political poster brought to the station. A companion announcement states that you will stage a giant bonfire the following Friday to burn all of the posters. (Make sure that this date does not conflict with a major local football game.)

In the "Christmas Tree Bonfire" promotion in section 2 of this book you will find details for a similar promotion which can be applied here.

WZZZ Poll Cat

In many areas it is common practice to give persons who have voted some item or symbol to wear that indicates they have visited the polls. If your local authorities will permit it (and there's no reason they should not, but be sure to check first), you can capitalize on this practice to make every voter a promoter of WZZZ.

Have printed an appropriate quantity of stickers of the type that can be merely applied to a lapel or coat and will stay, yet can be easily removed (called "pressure-sensitive" paper). They should be reasonably small and done in good taste. The copy should read: "I'm a WZZZ Poll Cat—I've Voted, Have You?"

Soapbox Marathon

In spite of the fact that most Americans would be willing to risk or even to give their lives to protect their right to vote, many must be urged to take advantage of their right. To help get a record turnout at the polls in your area, the WZZZ disc jockeys announce that they are going to stage a soapbox marathon urging people to go to the polls on Election Day. Pick the most heavily trafficked and conspicuous corner downtown. Your DJs, in shifts, mount the soapbox to urge citizens to vote. The talkathon continues until the polls close.

Other Promotions

In other sections of this book you will find election promotions you may wish to use at this time: In the Contest Section see "Election Contest," and in the Outside Stunt section see "Election Bet Payoffs."

6.58   YOUTH APPRECIATION WEEK—November

More often than not the good things done by youngsters, particularly teenagers, are far overshadowed by the criticism leveled against them. Why not take advantage of "Youth Appreciation Week" to salute the fine young people of your area and tell of some of the noteworthy projects the youngsters have undertaken.

Each day of Youth Appreciation Week select one or more of the goodwill projects undertaken by local teenagers for a WZZZ Salute. It may be a local muscle-car club's safe and courteous driving campaign, a "get out the vote" drive conducted by local youngsters, a school club's sponsorship of a party for disadvantaged children, or many other things. Conduct interviews with the youngsters responsible. Have them tell what they did and why—and talk to the people who benefitted from their generosity.

Grand Climax

Stage a city-wide free dance for all local teenagers. It should be emceed by your disc jockeys.

NATIONAL PROSPERITY WEEK—November 6.59

Throughout the years there have been developed various phrases describing so-called "symbols of prosperity." The two most memorable are, of course, "two chickens in every pot" and "two cars in every garage."

How It Works

Listeners are asked to mail in their idea of what constitutes modern-day prosperity. On a postcard they send in a short phrase symbolizing prosperity to them, such as "two planes in every pasture," or "two VCRs in every family room." At the end of the week judges select the cleverest and most original phrase to receive a prize.

A good suggestion for a first prize would be a radio for every room of the winner's house. Being able to listen to WZZZ throughout the home is definitely a symbol of prosperity.

SALUTE TO HOMEMAKERS WEEK—November 6.60

Let's not forget the homemakers. You had better not; they make up the bulk of your daytime listeners. Instead of suggesting an elaborate promotion, we are recommending that you pay a simple tribute to as many of them as possible during the week.

How It Works

The week prior to Salute to Homemakers week, all listeners are invited to send in the names, addresses, and phone numbers of homemakers deserving recognition. Then, during the week of the salute, names are drawn at random from those sent in. The names are drawn as frequently as possible throughout the day so that as many winners as possible are selected. The names are announced on the air and each receives a flower from a local florist.

6.61   SOUNDS OF SANTA—December

There is undoubtedly one, or more, Santa Claus seated in the department store Toyland in your city interviewing youngster after youngster on his or her wishes for Christmas—and asking if he or she has been bad or good. These exchanges between awed, and sometimes skeptical, youngsters and good old St. Nick can constitute some bright air bits.

How It Works

A microphone is hidden in Santa's beard to pick up his conversations with various children as they confide in him what they want for Christmas. The mike feeds into a tape recorder. You screen the tapes and play them back later.

A possible variation on this same theme would be to simply have one of your DJs or newspeople take a tape recorder to a daycare center or grade school and interview a group of the children as to what they want for Christmas.

6.62   SANTA CLAUS CARS—December

Each year an increasing number of people accept the idea of giving a good used car for Christmas, often to a teenage member of the family so that the folks can retain use of their own car. Here is an idea to pass on to a car dealer that may give him the jump on his competitors. (And do not overlook the possibility of pitching this to new car dealers, too.)

How It Works

Here is the bonus your promotion offers: With the purchase of a Christmas Car Special, the dealer will have the car delivered to the purchaser, by Santa Claus. St. Nick will drive up in the car as a surprise right on the dot Christmas Eve or Christmas morning. In the case of new cars, you might even offer to deliver it gift-wrapped with a big ribbon around the car.

All the dealer has to do is make arrangements for a Santa in costume to be on duty to deliver the cars, and for a pickup car to take the old gent back to the lot. If business goes good, he might require a flock of Santas on duty Christmas Eve. But he is not going to complain. Think of the cars he's selling!

The Spots

The spot announcements advertising this special Christmas offer should probably incorporate the voice of Santa telling the public of the service he is going to perform for the lucky people who buy a car now.

MERRY CHRISTMAS TO ALL—December   6.63

About a week and a half before Christmas, WZZZ starts wishing Merry Christmas to individuals in your listening area. These greetings simply should be dropped in about 5 to 10 an hour. The message should be nothing more than: "WZZZ wishes Merry Christmas to Mrs. Mary Jones of 5521 Elm Street." That's all.

Use the names of people who have entered previous contests or promotions. Be sure that you include the names of sponsors and their families. The pleasant part of this simple little promotion is that a short time after you start it you will begin receiving calls from listeners requesting that the station air a greeting to a friend or relative. Very little airtime will be used.

CHRISTMAS STOCKING SALE—December   6.64

Here is another promotion keyed to a major appliance dealer and timely to the Christmas season. Again, it has the advantage of being good business for your advertiser while offering a very satisfying appeal to his customers.

How It Works

The pitch, as advertised on your station, is that the dealer gives a giant six-foot Christmas stocking stuffed with $75 to $100 worth of toys with the purchase of each major appliance—provided there is no trade-in. The appeal, of course, is to buy the appliance for the spouse and get the toys for the kids as a bonus.

Dealer's Delight

Your advertiser should be able to offer a fine selection of good toys, retailing for $75 to $100, for about a third of that cost wholesale if he makes the right arrangements. Naturally, this means that a department store or other store that also carries toys is going to find this promotion particularly appealing. The dealer will find himself closing deals where he would have to offer twice that amount for a worthless trade-in, because he is relieving the customer of the necessity to go out and make a whole group of purchases for the kids. It is simple, direct, and practical.

The "no trade-in" aspect of the promotion will be especially appealing to the merchant. He is not going to find himself saddled with a trade-in that he will later have to dispose of, probably at a loss.

The Stockings

The stockings of toys should be made up in advance because it will produce too many headaches if the customers are allowed to pick and choose from among the toys. The stockings should be made up in age groups so the customer can select one containing toys suitable for his child. Some half-size stockings should also be made up so a customer with, say, children aged 10 and 5 can get one of the smaller-sized stockings for each child.

6.65 SHOPPING NIGHT, FOR MEN ONLY—December

Here is another promotion keyed to the Christmas shopping season. This one is tailor-made for a large department store or shopping center. Take them this idea and bring home a nice sale as they advertise the promotion on your station.

How It Works

The average male has more difficulty coming up with gift ideas than the average female shopper. But during the Christmas shopping it becomes out of the question. With this in mind, here is the benevolent gesture your advertiser makes to the males of the community—with much fanfare on your station. On a given night before Christmas the store designates a "Men Only" night. On that evening the store is open to males only. No women admitted after 6:00 P.M. This will take considerable advance publicity.

The Trimmings

From the basic idea stated above you add the trimmings. Additional features you can incorporate include: free coffee for the men while shopping, special printed lists of gift suggestions, and helpful salespeople acting as gift consultants to the men shoppers.

The store might consider something as extensive as this: They provide forms for the men to fill out to indicate the age, color of hair, sex, and so forth, of the person for whom they are buying a gift, along with an approximate amount to be spent. This is then processed and a gift list produced to suit the shopper's needs.

6.66 GREAT TOY TRADE-IN—December

Here, again, is a goodwill-building promotion for both your station and some discerning advertiser. And it should result in a nice cash return for both parties. It ties right into the spirit of the season, and also into the selling spirit most merchants are imbued with at Christmastime.

How It Works

Undoubtedly in your community there are one or more agencies or organizations that annually collect toys for distribution to needy children at Christmas. On behalf of such a group you make arrangements to conduct the "Great Toy Trade-In."

The cosponsor is a local merchant. On a given day (or days) during the Christmas buying season the retailer announces through spots on your station that he or she will accept trade-ins on toys. There will be a 10 percent discount offered on the purchase of any new toy if accompanied by a used toy "trade-in." The trade-ins are turned over to the charity organization for distribution to needy youngsters.

The Cosponsor

The cosponsor of the "Great Toy Trade-In" may be an outlet dealing exclusively in toys, or it may be a department store or variety store. Do not overlook the possibility of working this out with a drugstore chain, since most of them get into the toy business in a big way during the Christmas season. You might even be able to sell it to the entire downtown merchants association, or a similar organization, as an area-wide promotion.

The greatest benefit will probably be gained by an advertiser such as a department store, variety store, or drugstore that can take advantage of the traffic created by this promotion to sell other wares. We suggest that you look in this direction first for a cosponsor. An advertiser carrying a variety of products can easily write off the discounts on the toys through the increased store traffic and sales in other departments.

Since you are talking about cosponsorship with the station, an important selling point will be the promotion spots they will be airing in connection with the stunt.

The Toys

The promo spots for the "Great Toy Trade-In" should ask for toys in "fair" condition or "working order." To avoid any misunderstanding, however, the store will probably decide to accept any toy as a suitable trade-in. There possibly will be a few people who bring items that are virtually junk, but it is hard to be too choosy when accepting items for charity, even though in this case you are offering a value in return.

The Discount

The store can offer a straight discount of 10 percent (or some other suitable figure), or it might add a little more flash and excitement to this phase of the promotion. The store can offer the public a chance to pick its own discount, ranging from 2 percent to 50 percent. In this case, the store would get a big box containing cards with numbers on them. A person bringing in a trade-in and making a purchase is then allowed to select one of these cards. The number on the card indicates the percentage of the discount.

Followthrough

Do not overlook any opportunities to capitalize on this goodwill-builder by following the toys as they go to the youngsters. Be on the lookout for picture possibilities as the toys are turned over to the charity organization, and as the organization delivers the toys.

Timing

We suggest that you try to put this promotion into effect at an early date. Stores are anxious to get shoppers in as soon as possible, and they won't consider an idea like this during the final selling days prior to Christmas.

6.67 CHRISTMAS CARD DISCOUNTS—December

The week between Christmas and New Year's is a slow period for most radio stations, too. Here is a promotion that will permit some merchant to bolster his sales during this week through advertising on your station. It also takes advantages of the Christmas decorations the merchant will still have up at this time.

How It Works

Your advertiser decorates one of the large Christmas trees he or she has erected in the store with dozens—or hundreds—of Christmas cards or gift cards in envelopes, all sealed. Each sealed envelope contains a note that indicates a discount ranging from 2 percent to 30 percent. After making a purchase, a customer is permitted to select one of the envelopes from the tree and receives the discount indicated.

What Merchandise?

Your merchant will not wish to make this a blanket offer in most cases; the promotion can be limited to specific departments within the store, or it can be limited to specific items that are called to the attention of the public through spot announcements on your station, as well as signs throughout the store. This will work very effectively if limited to Christmas-type merchandise that the store is anxious to move so it will not have to put it in storage until the following year.

Additional Gimmick

As an additional bonus, certain of the cards on the tree may have a note inside that, instead of giving a discount, permits the customer to select a special gift from among the pile of packages heaped around the base of the tree.

SANTA CALLING—December 25   6.68

This is a very simple but rewarding promotion. And you can be sure that the "guest Santas" referred to below will get as much enjoyment out of it as the children will.

How It Works

Little children have a wonderful implicit faith in the reality of Santa Claus. If you have forgotten this, watch a department store Santa at work sometime. This is a promotion to help bring Santa home to children on a very personal level.

Your station announces that it has set up a special telephone line for the use of Santa Claus on the days just before Christmas. Any parent who wishes to have Santa call his child before bedtime can write to the station and you will see that the call is made. In this particular way your station becomes a real Santa's Helper. Those of you with stations in major markets may decide at this point that it will be impossible for you to handle this promotion because of the physical load involved. But read on—there are ways.

Guest Santas

The group of people acting as your guest Santas and making the calls will be necessarily composed of men. One method to provide the manpower for this is to arrange for one or more men's lodges or clubs to take on the project. The members of any such organization should be anxious to cooperate with you on this. Working through a club or lodge is probably the best way to handle it because you can contact them on a direct basis and relieve yourself of the need to talk about it on the air.

The other way to line up Santas is through on-air announcements. Ask that any men who wish to become a WZZZ guest Santa Claus and make some children happy by making a few telephone calls should contact your station. You can be relatively free in what you say in such announcements because children young enough to believe in Santa Claus are probably not going to understand what you are saying here anyway, or at least they won't relate it to the other part of the promotion.

The Children

When asking parents to write in to register their children to receive a call from Santa, specify that the children should be between the ages of three and six. Children younger than this will probably be bewildered by this type of call, and the older ones are sophisticated enough to see through it. Parents should be asked to send some specific information about the child ". . . so that Santa will be sure to get everything right." Parents should also be asked to indicate a half-hour period during which it is best for Santa to call.

State in your on-air promos that all requests for Santa calls must be in your hands no later than December 20 to be sure that the names get on Santa's list. You will require this much time in advance to handle the distribution of names to your guest Santas. But be sure that station personnel or someone else takes care of any late entries because the parent may have told the child that Santa will be calling. The early deadline is just to limit the number of late entries.

Number of Calls per Santa

If possible, you will want to limit the number of calls to be made by each guest Santa to five or six. This many calls can be handled easily. Any more than this could create some problems. In distributing the call information to your guest Santas, you want to make certain that the group given to any one individual does not all request calls within the same half-hour period. Your guest Santas can get information they need from the parents' letters, so you should simply turn over the actual letters to them to keep things simple.

Format

To make sure that things are handled properly, you will want to provide each of your guest Santas with a format of what he should say to the children on the phone. This will make it easy for the men cooperating with you to do the most effective kind of job. Your format can be something like this:

> Hello, (name of child), this is Santa Claus calling. Your mommy and daddy have told me that you've been a good girl (or boy) most of the time this year. And so I'm going to be coming by your house later with all sorts of presents for you. Will you like that (name of child)? (Child gets to talk here.) I've got a great sackful of toys and presents for all the good little boys and girls. And I'll be around tonight to put them under the Christmas tree for you.

But if I am going to do that for you, I want you to do something for me. I want you to go to bed when mommy asks you to tonight—and go right to sleep. Because I can only come to your house after you're asleep. Will you do that for me (name of child)? Will you go right to bed and to sleep tonight? I've got to go now and make sure the elves have everything ready. So, Merry Christmas (name of child).

Ask your guest Santas to stick fairly close to the format you have given them. You should also tell them that, if the parent's letter tells of any specific toys that the child will be receiving, they might work this in on the basis of: "I know you've been wanting a red wagon, Johnny, so I'm going to dig down deep in my bag and see if I can't find one just for you."

Regardless of how you arrange for your guest Santas, impress on everyone connected with this promotion that *all* calls must be made. There could be nothing worse than a child sitting by the telephone on Christmas Eve, waiting for a call from Santa—and the call never comes. Even a single instance of this happening will mean that you have a bad promotion because you will have broken faith with a child.

Store Tie-In

In addition to handling requests for Santa Claus at the station, you may also wish to make a tie-in with a local store or group of stores. This means that you would make it possible for a parent to register his child for a Santa call in the toy department of the store. The store can set up a special booth to take care of this registration. In this way you can be sure of getting all of the specific information you need on the child by having a regular form for the parent to fill in. Any store should be happy to provide this service because it is an excellent way for them to create more traffic.

SANTA CLAUS IS COMING TO TOWN—December   6.69

Here's a simple on-air promotion that will prove enjoyable to both young and old in your listening audience. It will keep them tuned in throughout the important two weeks prior to Christmas.

How It Works

About two weeks before Christmas, WZZZ starts carrying frequent capsule reports on the activities of Santa Claus up at the North Pole as he gets ready for the Christmas Eve ride to Centerville. Throughout this activity period, WZZZ broadcasts bulletins updating Santa's progress.

Have on-the-spot reporters give details of the preparations at the North Pole. You can also have reports phoned-in from checkpoints in Alaska, Canada.

Santa Readies for Christmas

Later in this section you will find a number of sample progress reports on Santa's activities getting ready for his Christmas visit. We suggest you use these and also make a number of your own. Localize the suggested reports whenever possible, working in the names of local persons and places. These bulletins may be read by your disc jockeys as received from your "North Pole correspondent," or can be played as though they were phoned in from stringers.

Santa's Travel Checkpoints

You may take either of two approaches to the checkpoint reports called in as Santa flies from the North Pole to Centerville. They should be in the form of phone reports from various points on Santa's route, and you may produce them all yourself. Or, you can actually place phone calls to places, such as other radio stations, the Coast Guard, and Air Force. They will be glad to take part in the fun and give you a detailed report of a "sighting."

Either method is effective when done with care. In both cases, however, make all of the preparations and recordings well in advance. Have them on a master tape, plus carefully labeled carts, so that they can be used easily and in proper sequence.

Welcome Santa

As Santa nears, ring in some (pretaped) phone calls from the governor, mayor, and other local notables welcoming the visitor and wishing him well. Perhaps the DJs could place calls to local youngsters, getting their reaction to the impending arrival of the beloved elf. (These might be taped in advance to make sure you get some good ones on the air.)

Sometime in the early or mid-evening of Christmas Eve, the bells on Santas reindeer or their hoofbeats are heard on WZZZ and your listeners will know that St. Nick has arrived.

Progress Reports—On-Air Copy

WITH JUST TWO WEEKS LEFT UNTIL CHRISTMAS, SANTA HAS PUT ON AN EXTRA SHIFT OF ELVES, AND THEY'RE WORKING AROUND THE CLOCK MAKING TOYS. A SPOKESPERSON FOR SANTA'S WORKSHOP SAYS THAT WHILE PRODUCTION IS BEHIND LAST YEAR AT THIS TIME, THERE IS NO DANGER OF THE ELVES NOT MEETING THE DECEMBER 24TH DEADLINE.

* * * *

SANTA CLAUS TOOK HIS REINDEER OUT ON A TRIAL RUN TODAY IN PREPA-
RATION FOR THE BIG FLIGHT CHRISTMAS EVE. SANTA SAID THE REINDEER
WERE A BIT WILD AFTER THEIR REST SINCE LAST CHRISTMAS, BUT WILL
SOON BE BACK IN CONDITION. HE PLANS TO HAVE ANOTHER TRIAL FLIGHT,
THIS TIME WITH A FULL SLED, LATER IN THE WEEK.

* * * *

SANTA TODAY NOTIFIED THE U.S. AND CANADIAN AIR FORCES TO BE ON
THE LOOKOUT FOR HIS SLED ON CHRISTMAS EVE. HE SAID HE HOPED
THERE WOULD BE NO RECURRENCE OF THE INCIDENT LAST YEAR WHEN HE
WAS TAILED BY SURVEILLANCE AIRCRAFT. HIS WHISKERS WERE SINGED BY
THE JET ENGINE'S EXHAUST, AND THE REINDEER WERE JITTERY FOR THE
WHOLE FLIGHT.

* * * *

SANTA CLAUS IS DOWN WITH A SLIGHT COLD TODAY, BUT THE WORK CON-
TINUES AS THE ELVES GET READY FOR CHRISTMAS. MRS. CLAUS SAYS THAT
SHE IS SURE SANTA WILL BE BACK ON HIS FEET AGAIN TOMORROW AND PER-
FECTLY WELL BY CHRISTMAS EVE. SANTA IS USING HIS TIME IN BED TO
STUDY THE CENTERVILLE STREET MAPS TO BE SURE HE MAKES ALL DELIV-
ERIES.

* * * *

SANTA REPORTS THAT HE IS MAKING A SPECIAL STUDY OF ALL GIRLS' AND
BOYS' BEHAVIOR FROM NOW UNTIL CHRISTMAS. HE HOPES NONE OF THEM
ARE BAD BECAUSE HE ALREADY HAS HIS GIFT LIST MADE OUT AND HE
WOULD HATE TO CHANGE IT. HE RECEIVED A SPECIAL REQUEST TODAY
FROM _____ OF CENTERVILLE FOR A _____ AND HE IS
ADDING THIS TO HIS LIST.

"MERRY CHRISTMAS" IN MANY TONGUES—December   6.70

If there is a college or university in your area, or some other place where there
are a number of people from different lands, arrange to have representatives
from the various nations record a brief Christmas greeting in their native
tongues. Most will be happy to cooperate. This provides a simple and interesting broadcast item that promotes the international spirit of Christmas.

If you'd like your DJs to take a whack at it themselves, we've dug out the following international holiday greetings. You'll have to struggle through the pronunciation with our minimal phonetic renditions. Maybe your listeners can call in and help you get it right.

Different Ways to Say "Merry Christmas"

Chinese	*Kung Ho Shen Tan*
Czech	*Vesele Vanoce*
Dutch	*Vrolijk Kertmis*
Esperanto	*Gojan Kristnaskon*
French	*Joyeux Noel*
Finnish	*Hauska Joulua*
Greek	*Kala Hrystouchena*
German	*Fröhliche Weinachten*
Hungarian	*Boldog Karacsony Unnep*
Norwegian	*Glad Jul (or Gladilig Jul)*
Polish	*Wesolych Swiat*
Portuguese	*Feliz Natal*
Spanish	*Feliz Navidad*
Swedish	*God Jul*

6.71   HOLIDAY PACKAGE—December 25

This is a sales promotion that can create more goodwill, and subtly, do a more effective selling job than anything we have come across in a long time. Basically, it works like this: You contract with a major sponsor to sell him your entire programming schedule for from one to five holidays. This means he will be the exclusive sponsor on those days. The best holidays to sell are:

- Christmas
- New Year's Day
- Easter Sunday
- Fourth of July
- Thanksgiving Day

For his money the sponsor receives store mention every 15 minutes throughout the day: THIS CHRISTMAS DAY OF UNINTERRUPTED MUSIC IS BEING BROUGHT TO YOU BY GARSON'S DEPARTMENT STORE, 111 MAIN STREET.

Give fairly heavy promotion to the event during the three to four days prior to the holiday, and be sure that the sponsor promotes it heavily in his store. The effect of this holiday package of uninterrupted music will reflect favorably on both the sponsor and the station. Most of these holidays are days on which you will be carrying a minimum of sponsored time anyway. Your sponsored newscasts will not conflict if the sponsor adapts his commercials to the programming pattern of the day (which he will probably be doing anyway).

Keep in mind that the holiday package will work better if all of the holidays are sold to a single sponsor. Such sponsorship carries with it a quality image that is difficult to achieve in any other way.

Because of the nature of the days involved, you can price this package most attractively. You will have to work far in advance to make sure that the time is kept clear. Be sure that your salespeople point out to potential sponsors the heavy holiday radio listening, both in-home and out-of-home. Be sure to keep a tally sheet of complimentary phone calls to show to the sponsor.

CAUTION COFFEE/CAB SERVICE—December 31   6.72

Despite the warnings and the pleas directed toward the public not to mix drinking and driving on the holidays, especially New Year's Eve, there will still be any number of drivers on the road groggy from either lack of sleep, too much alcohol, or a combination of both. You will score goodwill points in the community with this simple gesture.

For Tired Traveler

To help make alert drivers out of New Year's Eve celebrants, WZZZ offers a free cup of coffee to anyone stopping at a certain restaurant or drive-in, or group of them, between 9:00 P.M. and 3:00 or 4:00 A.M. The invitation is announced throughout the week prior to the holiday.

Community Cab Service

For those drivers who have been "into their cups" and are in no shape to drive, WZZZ can work a deal with one or more local cab companies to provide safe rides home. This encourages good community relations, visibility for the cab company, and helps promote highway safety.

The cab company donates the rides in exchange for free commercial time on WZZZ. Obviously, the free spots would run during the week before the holiday, mentioning the cab company's involvement in the free-ride home promotion.

Station Anniversary Promotions

YOUR AUDIENCE IS INTERESTED IN YOUR STATION. NOT JUST THE RECORDS YOU play or the news you collect, but *you*. After all, your station and your air personalities are invited into the cars and living rooms (even bathrooms) of your listeners every day. You have achieved an intimacy that is like a primary-level friendship.

As with any close friend, your listeners (at least some of them) want to know about your station. As your broadcast operation matures and passes milestones, these are causes for celebration and on-air hoopla.

The following ideas take your station's natural milestones and turn them into opportunities for further publicity and promotion without going into great detail on any one of them. This section contains suggestions for dozens of anniversary promotions, with a great many additional variations. A good number of these are original, but we freely admit that many of these promotions have been used by stations before. A few have had quite extensive use.

We feel that this section will be of the greatest value to you by giving you a very large group of promotions. This way, when your anniversary date rolls around, you will have the widest possible choice available. If such a group of anniversary ideas has been gathered together before, we have never come across it.

For the purpose of simplicity, we have arbitrarily used the twentieth anniversary as the basis for all these promotions. You can easily adapt all of them to suit the actual number of years that applies to your station.

7.1 TRADITIONAL ANNIVERSARIES

There are a large number of promotions—or parts of promotions—that can be built around the materials traditionally associated with anniversaries. Here is a standard list of such items:

- *First*—paper
- *Second*—cotton
- *Third*—leather
- *Fourth*—fruit and flowers
- *Fifth*—wood
- *Sixth*—sugar/candy or iron
- *Seventh*—woolen or copper
- *Eighth*—bronze or pottery
- *Ninth*—willow or pottery
- *Tenth*—tin or aluminum
- *Eleventh*—steel
- *Twelfth*—silk or linen
- *Thirteenth*—lace
- *Fourteenth*—ivory
- *Fifteenth*—crystal
- *Twentieth*—china
- *Twenty-fifth*—silver
- *Thirtieth*—pearl
- *Thirty-fifth*-coral
- *Fortieth*—ruby

MERCHANTS CELEBRATE YOUR BIRTHDAY 7.2

Perhaps the most pleasant kind of promotion to stage calling attention to your station anniversary is one that also turns a healthy profit. Here is one that can do just that—and do a tremendous job for a group of merchants, too.

How It Works

Your station invites all of the downtown merchants to participate in the station's birthday celebration. Each advertiser is offered a special Birthday Bonus Package of spots at a low rate. The number of spots in the package should equal the number of years you have been on the air. The spots, of course, advertise the individual retailer, but each is tagged with a line urging people to shop downtown on your birthday. The advertisers tie in with special birthday sales and offers, and use "20" as often as possible in their prices.

There are unlimited ways your advertisers can take advantage of the birthday party theme: special sales, party favors for the kids, free coffee and cake to patrons, special twenty-cent parking rates in downtown lots, twenty-cent surprise "Grab bags" in stores, containing unidentified merchandise, and free gift wrapping.

You should be doing your broadcasts out in the open where the public can see you, perhaps have a parade to start things out right, with appearances in all of the stores by your personalities. The idea is a gigantic downtown sale with your station anniversary as the theme that ties the whole thing together.

ADVERTISER ANNIVERSARY CAKES 7.3

Just because it is your station's birthday, do not overlook the blessings to be gained by giving rather than receiving. You will want to call the attention of your advertisers to the fact that you are celebrating your twentieth year of serving them and the community.

How It Works

Have a salesperson who handles the account drop in on each of your important agencies and advertisers to deliver a birthday cake for their enjoyment. You may also wish to arrange for coffee to be delivered at the same time so that each place can have a little birthday party in your honor.

7.4   ANNIVERSARY LETTER

All too often, the cycle of selling ad time and bringing in business for your sponsors gets dull. Your station's anniversary is a good time to breathe some life back into your relationship with sponsors.

How It Works

On the occasion of your anniversary, make up a list of advertisers whose business you have enjoyed over a period of time, say, two or more years. (Or you can simply use all of your advertisers.) To these firms send a letter similar to the following:

Mr. Edward Jones
Main Street Pharmacy
1600 Main Street
Centerville

Dear Ed:

May 5th is WZZZ's twentieth birthday.

Next Saturday will mark the start of our twenty-first year of serving Centerville, its citizens, and our advertisers.

We would like to take the occasion of our anniversary to extend our thanks to you for helping make WZZZ's past twenty years possible. It is only through the support of advertisers such as yourself that WZZZ Radio has been able to bring Centerville top entertainment, information, and service.

We know that you, too, have profited from the advertising you have placed on WZZZ. Our wish at this time is to thank you for that business, and to express hope that we may serve you frequently in the years to come.

Sincerely,

Mike Jones
General Manager, WZZZ

7.5   RECREATE THE DAY AND YEAR

This promotion involves a considerable amount of work, but if you handle it properly, the results can be some outstanding programming.

How It Works

The idea is to carry your listeners back to the time when the station went on the air 20 years ago. Some of the material you use will apply to the specific day you started, but the bulk of it will, of necessity, have to apply to the year as a whole. All of your music on the anniversary date will be from the year of your station's start.

Your regular newscasts will have to stay pretty much as usual. But you can prepare special newscasts relating to the events of the year when you went on the air and schedule these for 15 minutes after the hour.

If you can get hold of any special recorded material from the year, use it. Dig back in your own files, or go to the files of the newspaper, and work up a list of prices from the year when you started. This will provide some amusing (or maybe not so amusing) comparisons for your listeners. If your library or archives contains recordings of your old station promo jingle packages, use those as well. Sponsors may also enjoy running real commercials using old-style jingle packages.

Dress the Part

If you are planning any outside events or remote broadcasts for the day, dress your disc jockeys and newspeople up in garb from the period. The idea is, through music, news, and other things, to recreate the feeling of the time when you first went on the air: what the people were thinking, talking about, and listening to. If you put in the effort to do it right, the result can be extremely gratifying for everyone concerned.

RADIO STATION OPEN HOUSE   7.6

Milestones are meant to be celebrated with your friends. Why not have the listeners stop by for a visit?

How it Works

For your anniversary you can hold an open house at the station and invite the public. This provides you with an excellent opportunity to expose your personalities, show off your facilities, and give the townspeople a chance to get to know all of you personally (which will mean that they will become unshakable listeners).

Naturally, you will want to serve some sort of simple refreshment, and you should have everyone attending register for a series of prize drawings to be held throughout the day. A natural prize would be radios. In addition, give everyone a chance to tour the station. If your station staff is limited, you may have to bring in some outsiders to help out as guides. You may want to call on the spouses of employees to do this, with a big station party to follow in the evening.

As is true with many of the promotion ideas suggested here, you can group a number of the other ideas in this section within the open house format and come up with an even bigger stunt.

7.7 SONG CONTEST

For this promotion, get your listeners to help you. Surely some nostalgia buffs can help you recreate the day you went on the air.

How It Works

In advance of your anniversary date you announce a contest inviting listeners to send in lists of songs published or popular in the year you started on the air. The longest correct list wins the prize, which, in this case, might be a group of record albums or CDs.

The winner can also be given a chance to pick his five favorite songs from his list. These would be played as a group on your anniversary date and the winner interviewed. You can also build a listener hook into your contest promos by tagging each spot with the names of four or five possible songs.

7.8 CELEBRITY GREETINGS

For your birthday celebration you will want to line up in advance a sizable group of anniversary greetings from public officials and celebrities for use on the air. Work in advance to have as many recording artists as possible to do these for you. You will also want tapes from the mayor, the governor, city councilmen, Senators, Congressmen, president of the Chamber of Commerce, and as many other prominent people as possible.

Since you will wish to use a large quantity of these, be sure that the greetings are kept as short as possible. Therefore, do not leave it up to the discretion of the person who is doing the tape for you. Give him some suggested copy that runs just a couple of sentences.

7.9 PUBLIC GREETINGS

You may want to use a slight twist in addition to the celebrity greeting bit that will involve the general public as well. Have advertisers who carry tape recording equipment set up a machine in their store. A large sign should inform the public (and you will want to talk about it on the air, too) that they can record a short birthday greeting to your station that will be used on the air on your anniversary date.

Each person should identify himself by name and address or place of business. It is a good idea to provide suggested copy, and be sure to monitor the tapes closely before airing to make certain some joker has not slipped in profanity or some other inappropriate remark.

IDENTIFY THE CELEBRITY 7.10

If you arrange for a large group of taped greetings from famous celebrities, here is a way you can get some additional mileage out of it. Suppose you have a taped greeting that goes: "Hi, this is Kenny Rogers saying happy twentieth birthday to Radio WZZZ in Centerville. Keep up the good work, fellows."

Dub all of these spots off and delete the name of the person who made the spot. Then, a week or two weeks prior to your anniversary start a contest using these dubbed tapes. The idea is to have listeners identify the voices of the stars. You can do this by using one spot and continue to air it once every 15 or 30 minutes until a listener calls in with the correct identification. Or, you can use one a day and ask listeners to send in postcards.

The winner for each day is then drawn from the correct entries. Or you can use a number of different celebrity spots each day with your winner being the person who identifies the most voices. This last bit can be conducted on a daily basis or for the entire period of your advance promotion or a combination of the two. No matter which way you go, all of the original spots containing the celebrities' names should be used on your birthday.

PROCLAMATION BY MAYOR 7.11

As an adjunct to some of the other things you will be doing on your birthday, you should have little difficulty arranging for the mayor to issue a proclamation declaring that date "WZZZ Radio Day in Centerville." He and the city council both should be anxious to commend you for the outstanding job you have done for the community over the years.

Naturally you will want to use this declaration on the air. If possible, try to have the mayor tape record the declaration for you.

7.12 ANNIVERSARY YEAR CONTEST

The idea here is to arrange a prize, or prizes, associated with the number of years you have been on the air—in this case, 20. Therefore, your prize can be 20 dollars, a group of 20 small prizes all given to a single winner, 20 different prizes given to twenty different winners, or multiples of these.

There are any number of contest possibilities you can use to award such prizes:

- A simple postcard entry contest with the winner or winners selected by a random drawing.
- Entries in exactly 20 words on "WZZZ has given me twenty years of pleasure because . . . ".
- During the 20 days immediately prior to your anniversary, you give a word each day from a secret anniversary message. The words are not given in the order they are used in the secret message. The first person to come up with the correct complete message is your winner. Earliest postmark determines the winner. You can add excitement by using the secret message for the first time on the air on your anniversary day and announcing the winner, or winners then.

7.13 ANNIVERSARY CARD CONTEST

Invite your listeners to send greetings to the station on the occasion of your twentieth anniversary. This becomes the basis for yet another audience participation promotion.

How It Works

On your station's birthday, one of these greetings from a listener is selected at random every 20 minutes (the time interval corresponds to the number of years you have been on the air). The greeting is read. If the person who sent it in calls the station and correctly identifies himself within five minutes, he or she wins a prize. Since you will be reading the greetings on the air, eliminate lengthy dissertations by specifying that the greetings be limited to 20 words or less.

You will undoubtedly be holding an open house on your anniversary, having in a group of celebrities or local dignitaries or businessmen, or at least having some extra people around the station on your birthday. Therefore, if you conduct any contests that involve drawings, be sure to have these outsiders do the drawings for you.

GASOLINE GIVEAWAY

A good way to spotlight your anniversary and promote the span of years during which you have been serving the community is to run a simple little contest such as the Gasoline Giveaway. It also provides the basis for a good commercial tie-in with one of your oil company accounts.

If your station has been on the air less than 15 years, you had better skip this one because you will have too large a number of winners. However, we do outline below a variation that makes this adaptable to any station anniversary, no matter how few years you have been on the air. Also, since the promotion deals with the model year of cars, it will not work if you went on the air during the war years. No cars were produced for civilian consumption during the war years of 1943 to 1945.

How It Works

Announce that, as part of your birthday celebration, you will give gasoline to anyone driving an automobile manufactured in the year that your station went on the air. People having such cars bring them to the station where they are checked and a certificate for the gasoline is presented.

The amount of gas to be given is variable. It can be five gallons, a tankful, or the number of gallons corresponding to the number of years you have been on the air. The winners present the certificate to one of the chain of gas stations cooperating with you on the promotion to collect.

Unless you have people come to the station to receive their certificates, you might have some difficulty. If you permit them to go directly to the gas stations, there will certainly be several who will go all over town collecting gas at each of the participating stations.

Instead of gasoline, you can offer a free car wash as a prize. Offering tune-ups or cooling/air conditioning system checkups are other possibilities.

It is a good idea to include an additional gimmick in this promotion to give it more importance. Offer a special big prize to the person who has actually owned a car from the specified year for the longest time. Owners must bring along their titles of ownership to establish priority for this prize.

If your station has been on the air a relatively short time, you do not want to offer a tankful of gas to the driver of every car of recent make. There will be too many of them. But the promotional approach can still be used. You can offer some small award to everyone bringing a car from the right year to the station. They are then registered and a drawing is held to select the winner of the major prize you will be giving away.

7.15   BIRTHDAY AWARDS

Invite each of your listeners who has a birthday falling on the same day as your station anniversary to register at the station. Naturally, they must bring some proof with them. And you may want to make it possible for them to register at the stores of some of your sponsors.

There are a number of things you can do to honor these people:
- You can salute them on the air on your mutual birthday.
- You may want to have them cut spots for you saying something like: "This is Charles White—and I'm celebrating my birthday with WZZZ on May 15th."
- Give some thought to having a special birthday luncheon to which these people are invited.
- You can give each one a small gift, with a special large award to the one born closest to the exact time your station went on the air.
- Through one of your bakery accounts, you can arrange to have a birthday cake sent to each person sharing your birthday.
- You should try to get all of them together for pictures that will make excellent publicity shots for you.
- Present a special award to anyone born on the day you went on the air.

7.16   ANNIVERSARY AWARDS

With the previously mentioned promotion in mind, you can do similar things for any listener who is celebrating an anniversary of any type that corresponds timewise to yours. Depending on the size of your market and how extensively you want to go into this, you can include people whose twentieth anniversary falls in the same year as yours, or within the same month, the same week, or the same day.

These anniversaries to be honored can include:
- wedding anniversaries
- business anniversaries
- employment anniversaries
- school class anniversaries
- civic or government holidays

7.17   TWENTY YEARS OF PROGRESS

This promotion, and some of the others included in this section, will take more airtime than you will want to devote to it in a single day. But remember, you can just as easily establish an anniversary week or an anniversary month for your station.

How It Works

The idea here is to relate your station's 20 years of progressive broadcasting to the general events and progress of the period. It will provide amazingly interesting and informative listening. This should be done on a national and international scale, with particular emphasis on the local aspects and applications of the subjects covered. You may wish to take up a single subject each day for the 20 days prior to your anniversary.

Well in advance, go to work lining up a group of prominent authorities in the fields to be covered. They should prepare five-minute discussions that cover as completely as possible the history of their particular fields during the past 20 years. This should be a generalized report on what has actually happened over the 20-year span, with selected points of reference within your community or area. This is going to take considerable work on the part of the authorities involved. Give them plenty of advance notice so that they will have time to do the job right.

Here is a suggested list of subjects that can be covered within this format:

- Communications
- Recreation
- Entertainment
- Chemistry
- Physics
- Government
- Literature
- Art
- Transportation
- Medicine
- Clothing
- Merchandising
- Food
- Major architecture
- Housing
- Military arms
- Labor
- Industry
- Farming
- International relations

Since this project will result in a 20-year historical report with local applications, give serious thought to having the entire series reprinted. If you do such a booklet, make an effort to include historical photos.

Many of your listeners will be anxious to receive copies. The booklet should be of special interest to the schools in your area and you should make it available to them for classroom use. All of the businesspeople in your area will want to have a copy. Of course, copies should also be given to the public libraries. And you should certainly use it as a progress report on your area, with copies going to national time-buyers and other key people throughout the country. If you handle this entire project properly, it can be the most rewarding anniversary promotion you conduct.

7.18   FUTURE FORECAST

Here is an idea that can be used as a separate project, or as a supplement to the "Twenty Years of Progress" promotion.

How It Works

On the basis of the same or a similar list of subjects, you invite 20 distinguished authorities to make educated predictions as to what conditions will be like 20 years in the future. Depending on how you wish to handle it, you may or may not wish to have the same person act as a historical reporter and predictor of the future within his or her own special field of endeavor. At any rate, the coupling of the past and future treatment of each subject should make highly interesting listening.

7.19   TIME CAPSULES

There is always considerable public interest in the placing of time capsules containing examples of current living and comments on current events. Here is a way to create interest and listening, not only when the time capsules are buried, but also for a long period of time afterwards.

Prepare and bury, with considerable fanfare and ceremony, a group of 20 time capsules. One of these will be dug up and opened each year on the occasion of your station anniversary. Because of the possibility of pranksters tampering with them, you may wish to have your time capsules placed in a bank vault or some other similarly safe place.

The first 19 of the capsules should contain predictions of events or advances to have taken place by the year each capsule is opened. These can be predictions made by the authorities who cooperated with you on the "Future Forecast" promotion outlined earlier. Or they can be prepared by a separate group of knowledgeable individuals. The twentieth capsule should contain a similar set of predictions. It should also contain a detailed report on local, national, and international conditions as they exist today when the capsule is buried. The 20 categories listed before can provide this basis for this discussion of current things. Naturally, this should be a "sound" report on tape.

Each year when one of your time capsules is opened its contents will be used on the air. The predictions will be balanced against the events which have actually happened.

TIME CAPSULE CONTEST   7.20

There is a very interesting contest that can be a lot of fun when used in connection with your time capsule promotion. This will work best if used in conjunction with the opening of your first time capsule one year from now. It is highly doubtful that it can be set in motion now for use at the opening of your second or third time capsule.

How It Works

In connection with your anniversary and the burying of your time capsules, you announce that you are going to place a series of questions in the capsule, too. These are questions about things that will happen during the coming year. Listeners are invited to send in their predictions as to the answers of these questions. All entries must be at the station by your anniversary day, since the entries will be buried along with the capsule to be dug up and judged one year from now.

Use Entry Blanks

To simplify matters, and provide a good commercial tie-in, have entry blanks containing the questions available at certain of your sponsors' stores. You will have a limited time in which to judge the entries when you dig them up in a year if you are to announce your winner on the same day you bring out your time capsule, so you will make matters easy for yourself if you have a standard form for the entries.

Set up your questions so that participants can give specific answers. Avoid questions that require a judgment or a point of view. Your winner will be the person with the greatest number of correct answers. Be sure to specify one of the questions as a tie-breaker. This can be a question that asks what the temperature will be at noon on your anniversary one year from now, as announced on your station. If you have more than one person with the same number of right answers, the one coming closest to the right temperature wins.

The answers to some of the questions you ask will be provided before the year is out. When this happens, be sure to announce on the air that this was one of the questions sealed in your time capsule.

Prizes

The prize you offer should be scaled so that if your winner gets all of the answers right, he receives a huge prize. The value of the prize is then reduced for each wrong answer on the winner's entry. Since it is a virtual impossibility for anyone to have all of the answers right, you can offer a fantastically big prize to anyone who is 100 percent correct.

If you are offering a cash prize (which is a good idea), you can probably get it insured by Lloyds. And if you start with a gigantic prize and then work down the scale, be sure to specify that only one entry to a person will be allowed and that all duplicate entries will be thrown out. You can make double-checking on this easier if you sort out the entries alphabetically before you bury them.

Possible Questions

Here are some suggestions for questions you may want to include. Be sure that a number of your questions relate to things that will happen locally during the year:

1. What will the temperature be at 12:00 noon on May 19 (year), as announced on WZZZ?
2. What recording artist will have the Number 1 record, as reported on the WZZZ Hit List, on May 15 (year)? (Use a question like this only if yours is a Top 40 operation.)
3. What party will win the mayor's race for your town?
4. What teams will be in the World Series?
5. What teams will play in the Rose Bowl? (or the bowl game nearest to you)
6. Who will receive Oscars as the best actor and the best actress in the (year) Academy Awards?

(On questions such as the above three, allow 50 percent credit for each correct part.)

7. In what year will the first man walk on Mars?
8. How may local (or statewide) traffic deaths will there be in the next twelve-month period?
9. What will be the highest temperature for the year?
10. What will be the lowest temperature for the year?
11. Which U.S. political party will control the White House? (Use this only for longer-term time capsules.)

Merchants' Milestones

HERE ARE SOME IDEAS THAT FOCUS ON MERCHANTS AND SPECIAL OCCASIONS that arise in their businesses. It's never too early for your sales staff to plan ahead for these milestones. Each client should provide you with profile information about when the business was first established, when branch stores were opened, and so forth.

When a sponsor comes up with a promotion like this himself, you will only get a small piece of the advertising budget. And if you depend on the sponsor for ideas, rather than coming up with them yourself, then you only deserve a small part of the budget. Instead, identify a possible milestone promotion for each sponsor at least a year or two in advance. This will give both you and your client plenty of time to plan ahead for an effective campaign. Plus, you'll be at the head of the line for your client's advertising dollars.

8.1   OPEN FOR ALTERATIONS

Occasionally one of the retail businesses in your area will close for a period of days or weeks while the store is undergoing major alterations for expansion. Even though the firm is technically "out of business" for a short while, here is a way that they can keep in touch with their customers and have the whole community waiting for their reopening.

How It Works

Through a series of progress reports broadcast several times daily throughout the process all building toward the grand reopening, the store opens their entire remodeling operation to the public. Either through the use of taped interviews from the site or phone calls, your disc jockeys talk daily with the store manager, and the job foreman or contractor. They report on the step-by-step progress of the job: problems, details, plans for the day, and so on. With these reports, you also remind the listeners each time of the grand reopening.

If space and circumstances permit, the store sets aside an area equipped with benches as a "sidewalk superintendent" viewing site, and constantly invites people down to see the remodeling in progress. Perhaps the store will even go to the extent of offering a free cup of coffee to watchers.

Construction Contest

Perhaps you can also sell the store on the idea of running a contest in conjunction with the progress reports, with a grand prize going to the person who most accurately estimates the total number of man-hours involved in the entire remodeling process or some other estimate based on a phase of the work.

Keep It Interesting

The whole idea of this promotion is to keep the store in touch with its customers and potential customers even though it is closed for a period. It will also arouse curiosity among listeners so that they will want to see the finished product. Therefore, it is important that you keep the progress reports as interesting as possible and draw your listeners right into the project, perhaps by asking them to send in recommendations on colors or materials (which never need to be followed).

If the work sticks on one phase of construction for several days and there is little news to report, there are undoubtedly many other facts about the new store and plans for the future that can be worked into the short broadcasts. The reports themselves should be standard 60-second spots.

The Grand Opening

Once you have sold the "Open for Alterations" idea to a sponsor who is remodeling, you are naturally going to get the bulk of his advertising budget for the reopening. You should have something going for you in this phase of the project as well.

The approach here is to make certain that your station gets all or virtually all of the advertising budget. Keep this in mind when you are working out the details of any sales promotion.

STORE RELOCATION CLEARANCE SALE 8.2

Periodically, a retail store in your market moves to a new location or opens a new outlet. This is a fairly high-powered sales promotion you can pitch to sew up most of his advertising dollars for the switch.

If the store is moving its location, one problem it faces is to sell as much of its on-hand merchandise as possible to avoid the cost of transporting it to the new store. An extra advantage of this sales promotion is that if an additional outlet is being opened, this gives the store an excellent reason for running a sale at the original location (or locations) before the new opening.

How It Works

You arrange to have "bidding checks" printed for the store. If you face much competition at all, have these printed at your own cost. These can be handled quite inexpensively. Furthermore, by having them printed yourself, you can get your call letters on the "bidding checks" and, thus, keep the promotion tied exclusively to your station.

The spot announcements you carry will tell listeners that with each purchase they make at the old store they will receive an equal value in "bidding checks." The store will undoubtedly have certain merchandise that it is particularly anxious to move. These should be promoted as double-value items and double the amount of "bidding checks" should be given to people who purchase such items.

The Auction

The new store location is then opened with an all-day auction. The bidding checks are used to bid on all of the merchandise offered.

You may want to try to sell some remote from the new store location on the day of the auction. You may even wish to go so far as to arrange for your air personalities to act as auctioneers during part of the special sale.

Advantages

There are a number of obvious advantages to the store in a promotion such as this: It will build traffic at the old location and move merchandise. The auction will attract huge crowds to the new store location. Naturally, the promotion can be successful only if the store owner or manager purchases a heavy enough schedule on your station to do the job right.

Bidding Checks

Things will work better if your bidding checks have a point value rather than a money value. Thus, a $1.00 purchase gets 100 points, a $5.00 purchase 500 points, and so on. In this way, when the auction is held, the amount bid on the items will be higher since the customers will not be thinking in terms of dollars. It might even be better to have a $1.00 purchase receive 1 point.

8.3   LAUNDROMAT OPENING

There are thousands of self-service laundry facilities throughout the United States and Canada, and they are appearing in an increasing number of other countries as well. The next time one is going to open in your area, take this idea to the owner. It will pay off for both of you.

How It Works

On the opening day of the laundromat, your disc jockeys (with some helpers hired by the laundry management) will do everyone's wash. The station (actually the laundry) picks up the tab.

In other words, plug the daylights out of giving away a free wash and dry on opening day, with your disc jockeys on hand in rotating shifts for added excitement. In addition, run an on-air contest in connection with the opening.

Keep in Mind

Besides the free wash and dry, the coin-op laundry should also offer free coffee and doughnuts. This is particularly important because you will have people lined up waiting their turns. Also, it should be clearly stated that you can handle on a free basis only two washer loads for each customer.

The Contest

Tied in with your advance publicity of the laundry opening, you announce a contest. The winner will be the person who sends in a postcard with the closest estimate to the actual number of loads of wash processed by your disc jockeys at the laundromat on the opening day. Entries, of course, must be postmarked by midnight the day before.

You might vary the contest and have listeners try to guess the total number of pounds of wash that will be handled. Or, you can have an alarm clock set. When it goes off, a number is drawn and the person with wash in the machine bearing that number is your winner.

The prize can be cash. Or it can be one, three, or six months' free laundry service at the new laundromat.

REBATE DAYS   8.4

This promotion will work best for a merchant who deals in fairly high mark-up tickets—furniture, appliances, and jewelry stores are ideal. Because of the scope of the promotion, the first time you pitch this, you are going to have to find a merchant with enough courage to undertake it. Once you have established the success pattern that will most assuredly follow, you will have no problem in subsequent years. As a matter of fact, this is a promotion that will improve each year that it is run. Do not overlook the possibility of pitching this to a whole suburban shopping mall or a whole downtown shopping district. Although we talk here in terms of a single store, the approach is the same when applied to a whole group of stores.

How It Works

A month-long period is set aside by the store as "Rebate Days." It is promoted with the heaviest possible schedule of spot announcements. Every cash register receipt is automatically dated. People making purchases on credit terms also receive dated sales slips. Everyone who buys anything at the store during "Rebate Days" is told to hold onto his or her receipt.

At the end of the month-long promotion, one day of the month is selected by a drawing. Everyone who brings in a sales receipt bearing the date selected receives a complete refund. (If your merchant wishes to hedge some, he or she can offer a 50 percent rebate, but a full rebate is preferable.) Check the sales tax regulations in your state. In most states the store will only be able to rebate the purchase price of the item, with the tax still going to the state.

On the day the "Rebate Day" is selected, the store involved should stay open from 9:00 A.M. to 9:00 P.M. A prominent local citizen should make the selection by a random drawing. This can be done at your studios or, better, during a remote from the store. The drawing should be held shortly after the store opens for business.

When Are Receipts Redeemable?

The winning receipts should be redeemable only on the day that the "Rebate Day" is selected. The store should be encouraged to conduct a special sale on this day. In most cases, a Saturday is a natural day for this.

In any case, it should be on a day other than one on which the store is normally open until 9:00 P.M. This makes the positive results of doing the promotion more obvious to your sponsor.

Spot Announcements

Work with the store to develop recorded spot announcements for use during this campaign. If the announcements are not recorded, there should be at least a special intro developed to precede the live spots.

A part of the package deal you may wish to arrange is for some of your personalities to appear at the store during the month. Also, there are innumerable gimmicks you can develop built around the "rebate" idea that will help create additional excitement about the "Rebate Days."

8.5   BALLOON BARGAINS

This is a promotion that will not only pull crowds into a store, it will create sales as well. Take this idea to the manager of a department, appliance, or furniture store. Naturally, he or she is going to tell customers about it on your station.

How It Works

For this special sale the ceiling of the store is covered with helium-filled balloons. Each balloon is anchored by a string tied to the counters around the store. In the balloons are slips of paper containing special offers such as those outlined further on. With a purchase, the customer gets to select any balloon and pull it down. Whatever is on the slip of paper inside applies to the purchase.

How Wide the Application?

The extent to which the balloon bargains apply is entirely up to the store using the promotion. If it is a complete storewide sale or an opening sale, the balloons can be used with every purchase of one dollar (or two or five dollars) or more. Or the balloon bargains can be used to apply to specific sale merchandise. The gimmick will work effectively either way.

Discount Specials

One of the ways in which this promotion can be used is to have each slip in a balloon contain a percentage discount. The percentages of discount should range from 5 percent to 50 percent or higher. The customer receives whatever discount is printed on the slip.

If the Discount Specials approach is used, the breakdown of slips should follow a pattern similar to this one on the basis of five hundred balloons:

- 10 balloons @ 50%
- 10 balloons @ 45%
- 10 balloons @ 40%
- 15 balloons @ 35%
- 25 balloons @ 30%

- 50 balloons @ 25%
- 80 balloons @ 20%
- 100 balloons @ 15%
- 100 balloons @ 10%
- 100 balloons @ 5%

Play Money Specials

In this case the balloons contain "play money" in various denominations. The amount indicated by the play money is deducted from the amount of the customers purchase. The balloons can be departmentalized, with one set used for purchases up to $5.00, another for purchases up to $10.00, another for the up to $25.00 tickets, and so forth.

If the promotion is used solely in connection with major appliances or furniture, the "play money" can be used either to apply on the actual purchase, or can be applied to the purchase of another appliance or furniture piece.

The store can publicize this event through all their advertising channels.

A Note of Caution

When you break a balloon containing a slip of paper, there is a very good chance that the slip of paper will go flying halfway across the store. To prevent this, each counter in the store should be supplied with a quantity of large plastic bags and some long hat pins. After the customer has selected his balloon and pulled it down, the balloon is then placed in the plastic bag and the customer breaks the balloon by sticking the hat pin through the plastic bag. Be sure to use clear plastic bags so the customer can be sure that his or her sales slip is not switched for one of a low denomination.

In Conclusion

Letting the customer make his own choice for a chance at a substantial savings—and at least a savings of some amount—will prove a very effective method of building traffic for a store. A good-quality balloon should be used for this promotion. If gas-filled balloons are used, the promotion cannot be continued indefinitely with the same set of balloons. Over a period of time the loss of gas will cause the balloons to shrivel and fall.

8.6   GIFT CERTIFICATE SPECIALS

This promotion is structured similarly to the previous one. The balloons in this case contain gift certificates in various denominations. Or the gift certificates can be in the form of various discounts on specific items of merchandise. One advantage of using this approach is that there is a good chance the customer will come back to the store a second time in order to use the gift certificate. If you wish to assure this, the gift certificate can be post-dated to be good during the following week.

8.7   FASHION REPORT

This is a promotion with which you can have a lot of fun on the air. You can turn it into a very effective sales tool for a major advertiser as well.

How It Works

One or more of your air personalities becomes a fashion expert for a department store or women's clothing shop and reports on the latest in women's fashions. Instead of praising and describing the fashions from prepared copy, however, your DJ describes the fashions, fashion trends, and specific buys available in his or her own words. With no knowledge of the descriptive jargon applied to women's fashions, your air personality should provide an interesting and amusing report.

Be sure that the commentary, however inept it may be, is still favorable to your advertiser's wares.

Additional Mileage

To get a bit extra out of this stunt, have the store set up a special fashion show in honor of your Fashion Expert. The public should be invited. Your DJ will have a post of prominence. The descriptions of the fashion show can be pretaped for use at the show as well as on the air, or they can be done live and the whole thing taped or used on the air live.

OUR PAINT IS A WORK OF ART   8.8

This is a promotion that you can sell to one of the major paint companies in your area—and every area has a fair number of them. They are not frequent radio advertisers, in part because we do not give them enough reasons to become so. Here is a promotion that will do just that, and keep them coming back again and again.

How It Works

You arrange a promotion with a paint company that has a number of outlets. It is a painting contest—an art contest—open to both amateur and professional artists. The idea is that the contestants do their paintings in the household paints of the company you are advertising.

The promotion lends itself ideally to widespread publicity in many directions: locally, regionally, and, possibly, nationally—certainly it can be plugged through the national trade publications of the paint industry. A great line around which to build such a promotion is: "ABC Paints Are a Work of Art."

What Happens

Through advertising on your station, the public is invited to participate in an art contest. They can submit entries in any painting technique. There is only one basic requirement: the paints used in these works of art must be the household paints of the advertising company.

No entry blanks are necessary. The only thing is that all entries must be turned in to one of the participating stores—for display, naturally.

As an additional part of this promotion, it might be a good idea to have each store put up a large canvas with paints and brushes available upon which anyone coming into the store can add his or her brush strokes, thus making a composite picture.

Judges

Since you are going to have two different categories of entries—amateur and professional—you will want to have two different categories of judges:

1. Legitimate art authorities for judging those entries which are, obviously, in the real art area.

2. Have professional house painters judge all of the other entries.

Prizes

For the professionals this must be a cash award. The paintings will be placed on a permanent rotating display at the various paint stores involved. Eventually they will be given to a local museum. For the amateur artists the top prize should be enough paint to do the inside or outside of a house. Secondary prizes should be enough paint to do various rooms in a house.

8.9 THE WZZZ MYSTERY RADIOS

This is a very simple, short-term promotion that will generate a lot of listener interest. More important, it vividly will demonstrate to any group of retail merchants just how effective your station is in reaching and motivating the listening audience.

The purpose of this promotion is to provide the graphic reasons you need to convince local non-sponsoring merchants that they should be advertising on your station.

How It Works

Place a number of portable radios in various stores and places of business around town. You should set up at least 10 radios, preferably many more. These radios are to be kept tuned to your station during the store hours on the day of the promotion.

To have a chance to win one of these radios all a person has to do is ask the store owner or clerk, "Is this a WZZZ Mystery Radio?" Such a person is then given a simple entry form to fill out and leave at the store.

Since the radios may be anyplace in town, listeners are encouraged to ask the question whenever they spot a radio in any place of business. Certainly, they can tell their friends to go in and register, but in doing so they lessen their own chances of winning the radio.

Picking Winners

The registration slips from each store are turned in to the station. Throughout the following day, individual winners are selected by drawing and announced over the air. Winners are told that they can receive their radios by going to the store where they registered and identifying themselves.

Use It as a Sales Tool

Participating stores for this promotion should be lined up from the list of those potential advertisers who in the past have not believed in the effectiveness of your station. The only requirements on their parts is a willingness to be shown, and a willingness to have a heavy traffic load come to their places of business. Handled properly, this should create a fine impression for your station.

Ensuring Success

To ensure the success of this promotion, and add more of a listening hook, you may wish to give some clues as to the location of the WZZZ Mystery Radios. Such clues can be in the form of naming the types of stores in which the radios are located. You may also want to specify certain areas where listeners can find the radios.

An Alternative

Instead of having people register for a chance to win one of the WZZZ Mystery Radios, you may wish to have the first person to ask be the winner. This is not nearly as strong as the other method though.

Another Alternative

An easy twist on the above-mentioned promotion is this: Specify the exact locations of the various radios to be given away. Any person can win one of these radios by being in the store having such a radio when you play a recognized sound tone on your air. Then they must still ask, "Is that a WZZZ Mystery Radio?" in order to win.

SECTION

9

On-Air Themes

T HE ON-AIR THEME SECTION IS INCLUDED IN THIS BOOK TO PROVIDE YOUR DISC jockeys with a logical group of talking points. The idea here is the effective projection of a programming image. There are many additional promotions that can be associated with these themes. You will find some specific suggestions along this line included in other sections.

This material is not designed to be used to the exclusion of all other on-air promos. It should be interwoven with the other things you are using. This simply provides you with the basis for setting up a generalized theme to cover a given period of time—generally three months. This is then broken down into monthly segments of a more specific nature. It sets up a track for you to run on, keeps what is being said on your air within a consistent mold, and lets you hammer home, in the most effective way, the listenability factor.

9.1 HAPPY PROMOS

Happy Habit

GET THE HAPPY HABIT . . . THE HAPPY LISTENING HABIT THAT IS YOURS WHEN YOU STAY TUNED TO WZZZ—RADIO 460—CENTERVILLE.

WZZZ MUSIC IS HABIT FORMING . . . HAPPY HABIT FORMING, THAT IS. WZZZ—RADIO 460, CENTERVILLE.

ONE HABIT YOU'LL NEVER WANT TO BREAK . . . THE HAPPY HABIT OF WZZZ RADIO.

GET THE WZZZ RADIO HABIT. IT'S A HAPPY HABIT—YOU'LL BE HAPPY YOU HAVE IT.

WZZZ RADIO . . . THE BEST SOUND AROUND . . . IT'S HAPPY HABIT FORMING.

YOU'LL NEVER REGRET IT WHEN YOU GET IT. WHAT? THE HAPPY HABIT OF WZZZ.

LISTENING IS A HABIT . . . BUT LISTENING TO WZZZ IS A HAPPY HABIT. GOT IT? GET IT.

MUSIC IS A HABIT . . . BUT WZZZ MUSIC IS A HAPPY HABIT. GOT IT? GET IT.

WITHOUT IT? GET WITH IT. THE HAPPY HABIT OF WZZZ.

THE HAPPY HABIT OF WZZZ MUSIC IS GOOD FOR WHAT'S BEEN BOTHERING YOUR EAR.

GOT THE HAPPY HABIT? THE HAPPY HABIT IS THE WZZZ HABIT. GET IT.

THERE'S MORE FUN IN YOUR LISTENING DAY WHEN YOU GET THE HAPPY HABIT OF WZZZ.

MUSIC AND FUN GO TOGETHER TO MAKE A HAPPY HABIT ON WZZZ.

Happy People

JOIN THE HAPPY PEOPLE. KEEP YOUR RADIO DIAL SET ON 460—WZZZ, THE HAPPY SOUND.

HAPPY PEOPLE HAVE THE HAPPY HABIT OF WZZZ. GET WITH THE HAPPY PEOPLE AT RADIO 460.

IN CENTERVILLE, THE HAPPY PEOPLE LISTEN TO WZZZ.

BLUE MONDAY? THERE'S A CURE WHEN YOU JOIN THE HAPPY PEOPLE ON WZZZ.

IT IS POSSIBLE TO BE HAPPY WITHOUT LISTENING TO WZZZ . . . BUT WHY DO THINGS THE HARD WAY?

WZZZ—RADIO 460—WHERE WE PLAY NOTHING BUT "MUSIC TO BE HAPPY BY."

TURN ON A SMILE WITH YOUR RADIO DIAL. TUNE RADIO 460—AND JOIN THE HAPPY PEOPLE.

HAPPY IN THE HOME—CAREFREE IN THE CAR. HAPPY PEOPLE TUNE TO WZZZ.

WZZZ MUSIC—IT'S THE THEME SONG OF THE HAPPY PEOPLE ON WZZZ.

AT WORK OR AT PLAY—THE HAPPY PEOPLE STAY WITH WZZZ, RADIO 460.

AMONG HAPPY PEOPLE—IT'S WZZZ RADIO 20 TO 1.

GET WITH THE HAPPY PEOPLE—ENJOY THE FUN AND MUSIC OF WZZZ—RADIO 460.

WZZZ—RADIO 460—WHERE HAPPY PEOPLE HAVE A HAPPY HABIT.

WHAT? ME WORRY? DON'T BE SILLY. I'M ONE OF THE HAPPY PEOPLE LISTENING TO WZZZ.

Happy Sound

THE HAPPY SOUND IS THE BEST SOUND AROUND. IT'S THE SOUND THAT'S FOUND ON WZZZ.

STAY TUNED TO RADIO 460. YOU'VE FOUND THE HAPPY SOUND OF WZZZ.

HAPPY PEOPLE GO STEADY WITH THE HAPPY SOUND OF WZZZ.

BETTER MUSIC IS FOUND—IN THE HAPPY SOUND OF WZZZ.

TREAT YOUR EARS TO THE HAPPY SOUND—THE SOUND OF WZZZ.

GOOD MUSIC ABOUNDS—ON RADIO 460—THE HOME OF THE HAPPY SOUND.

YOU'VE FOUND THE HOME OF THE HAPPY SOUND—WZZZ.

AROUND THE HOME—AROUND THE TOWN—AROUND THE CLOCK . . . WZZZ BRINGS YOU THE HAPPY SOUND.

LOOKING FOR HAPPY LISTENING? TRY THE HAPPY SOUND OF WZZZ.

9.2   RADIO ON THE GO PROMOS

It's Portable

WZZZ—IT'S PORTABLE.

DON'T MISS THE FUN OF SUMMER RADIO. TAKE WZZZ WITH YOU ON YOUR PORTABLE.

THE LIGHTEST SOUND ON THE SUMMER AIR. WZZZ—IT'S PORTABLE.

WZZZ—WITH THE SUMMER SOUND THAT'S LIGHT AS A FEATHER. IT TICKLES YOUR EAR—AND IT'S PORTABLE.

DON'T MISS A NOTE OF THE MUSIC—DON'T MISS A SECOND OF THE FUN.

PUT THE LIGHT SUMMER SOUND OF WZZZ ON YOUR PORTABLE RADIO.

WZZZ—THE LIGHT SUMMER SOUND SPECIALLY STYLED FOR PORTABLE LISTENING.

THE LIGHTEST THING YOU CAN CARRY—WZZZ ON YOUR PORTABLE RADIO.

RIDE A COCK HORSE TO BANBURY CROSS, TO SEE A FINE LADY ON A FINE HORSE. WITH WZZZ ON HER PORTABLE SHE KNOWS, SHE SHALL HAVE MUSIC WHEREVER SHE GOES.

THIS IS IT. YOU'VE FOUND THE PORTABLE SOUND ON WZZZ.

PICK WZZZ UP ON YOUR PORTABLE RADIO AND DISCOVER FOR YOURSELF WHAT LIGHT SUMMER LISTENING CAN BE.

WZZZ—BREWERS OF LIGHT SUMMER LISTENING. AS EASY TO CARRY WITH YOU AS YOUR PORTABLE.

LIGHT AS A FEATHER IN SUMMER WEATHER. WZZZ ON YOUR PORTABLE RADIO.

PORTABLE PLEASURE ON YOUR PORTABLE RADIO WITH PORTABLE WZZZ.

IN THE SUMMERTIME, GET TOGETHER WITH THE PORTABLE PLEASURE OF WZZZ.

WON'T CURE POISON IVY—BUT WON'T CATCH IT EITHER. WZZZ—PORTABLE PLEASURE ON SUMMER TRAVELS.

WON'T SOOTHE SUNBURN, BUT IT'S REFRESHING TO THE EARS. THE PORTABLE PLEASURE OF WZZZ.

CAN'T CATCH FISH, BUT ATTRACTS FISHERMEN. THE PORTABLE PLEASURE OF WZZZ.

ANTS AT YOUR PICNIC? ENTERTAIN THEM WITH THE PORTABLE PLEASURE OF WZZZ.

CAN'T BEAT THE HEAT, BUT IT'S REAL COOL LISTENING. THE PORTABLE PLEASURE OF WZZZ.

Car Radio Companion

THERE ARE MORE SMILES TO THE MILE WITH WZZZ ON YOUR CAR RADIO DIAL.

IF YOU'RE LOOKING FOR AN AUTOMOBILE ACCESSORY TO PUT THE FUN BACK INTO SUMMER DRIVING, TRY WZZZ ON YOUR CAR RADIO DIAL.

WHEN YOU TRAVEL, THE SMARTEST THING TO TAKE WITH YOU IS WZZZ ON YOUR CAR RADIO.

THIS SUMMER, TAKE THE FUN OF WZZZ WITH YOU ON YOUR CAR RADIO.

WZZZ—THE IDEAL COMPANION FOR SUMMER DRIVING.

YOU DRIVE RELAXED WHEN YOU DRIVE WITH WZZZ ON YOUR CAR RADIO.

THIS SUMMER TRAVEL THE HAPPY HIGHWAY—WITH WZZZ ON YOUR CAR RADIO.

WHEREVER YOU GO THIS SUMMER, DON'T START WITHOUT WZZZ ON YOUR CAR RADIO.

THE SHORTEST, MOST PLEASANT DRIVE YOU CAN TAKE IS THE ONE WITH WZZZ ON YOUR CAR RADIO.

TRAFFIC TROUBLES? SELECT THE SOOTHING SOUND OF WZZZ ON YOUR CAR RADIO.

WZZZ ON YOUR CAR RADIO MAKES ANY ROAD THE ROAD TO HAPPY LISTENING.

IF YOU PUT YOURSELF IN THE DRIVER'S SEAT, PUT WZZZ ON THE CAR RADIO.

WZZZ ON YOUR CAR RADIO PAYS FOR ITS PASSAGE—WITH PLEASURE.

THE SONG OF THE OPEN ROAD IS THE HAPPY SOUND OF WZZZ ON YOUR CAR RADIO.

WZZZ ON YOUR CAR RADIO—WHEN YOU CARE ENOUGH TO TUNE THE VERY BEST.

DRIVE YOURSELF HAPPY, WITH WZZZ ON YOUR CAR RADIO.

Goes Where You Go

SUMMERTIME IS TRAVEL TIME, AND WZZZ GOES WHERE YOU GO.

TAKE WZZZ WITH YOU WHEREVER YOU GO THIS SUMMER.

THIS SUMMER, WHEREVER YOU GO, WZZZ GOES WITH YOU.

ON THE MOVE THIS SUMMER? WZZZ GOES WHERE YOU GO.

EVERYWHERE YOU GO, WZZZ GOES WITH YOU.

PUT WZZZ ON YOUR SUMMER ITINERARY—AND WZZZ IS EVERYWHERE.

WHEREVER YOU GO, WZZZ IS THE EASIEST THING YOU CAN TAKE WITH YOU.

FOR MEN AND WOMEN ON THE GO—IT'S WZZZ RADIO.

AT HOME OR AWAY—NIGHT OR DAY—WZZZ IS AS NEAR AS YOUR RADIO. IT GOES WHERE YOU GO.

WHEREVER YOU GO, MAKE WZZZ YOUR SUMMERTIME TRAVELING COM-PANION.

WZZZ INVITES YOU TO BRING US ALONG ON YOUR SUMMERTIME TRAVELS.

YOU'VE FOUND THE SOUND PROMOS   9.3

LOOKING FOR THE SOUND OF MUSIC? THIS IS WZZZ. YOU'VE FOUND THE SOUND.

LOOKING FOR THE SOUND OF ACCURATE NEWS? THIS IS WZZZ. YOU'VE FOUND THE SOUND!

LOOKING FOR THE SOUND OF FAMILY ENTERTAINMENT? THIS IS WZZZ. YOU'VE FOUND THE SOUND!

LOOKING FOR THE SOUND OF FRIENDLY RADIO? THIS IS WZZZ. YOU'VE FOUND THE SOUND!

HOLD IT! DIAL NO FURTHER! YOU'VE FOUND THE SOUND OF WZZZ!

THE DIAL'S RIGHT ON 460. YOU'VE FOUND THE SOUND OF WZZZ.

YOUR HUNTING'S OVER. YOU'VE FOUND THE SOUND OF MUSIC, NEWS, WEATHER AND FUN—WZZZ.

WELCOME TO WZZZ. YOU'VE FOUND THE SOUND THAT WILL BRIGHTEN YOUR DAY, CHEER YOUR EVENINGS.

DIAL TWISTERS ATTENTION! LOOKING FOR GOOD MUSIC ALL DAY LONG? THE BEST IN NEWS! YOU'VE FOUND THE SOUND RIGHT HERE ON WZZZ!

DAY SEEMS TO BE BOUNCING RIGHT ALONG? SURE! YOU'VE FOUND THE SOUND ON WZZZ!

NIGHTS SEEM TO BE BRIGHTER THAN USUAL? SURE! YOU'VE FOUND THE SOUND ON WZZZ!

AFTERNOON HOUSEWORK SEEMS LIGHTER THAN BEFORE? SURE! YOU'VE FOUND THE SOUND ON WZZZ!

TRAFFIC HEAVY, BUT YOU DON'T CARE? WHY SHOULD YOU? YOU'VE FOUND THE SOUND ON WZZZ!

GREAT DAY IN THE MORNING? SURE! YOU'VE FOUND THE SOUND ON WZZZ!

SEEM LIKE A RELAXING EVENING? IT IS! YOU'VE FOUND THE SOUND ON WZZZ!

LOOKING FOR THE HAPPY SOUND? THIS IS WZZZ. YOU'VE FOUND THE SOUND.

LOOKING FOR THE SOUND THAT ENTERTAINS YOU ALL DAY LONG—ALL NIGHT TOO? THIS IS WZZZ. YOU'VE FOUND THE SOUND.

LOOKING FOR THE BRIGHTEST SOUND AROUND? THIS IS WZZZ. YOU'VE FOUND THE SOUND.

LOOKING FOR THE SOUND THAT PUTS THE FUN INTO RADIO LISTENING? THIS IS WZZZ. YOU'VE FOUND THE SOUND.

LOOKING FOR THE SOUND OF CENTERVILLE? THIS IS WZZZ. YOU'VE FOUND THE SOUND!

NINE OUT OF TEN   9.4

NINE OUT OF TEN MAILMEN KEEP POSTED WITH WZZZ.

FIVE OUT OF SIX TAXI DRIVERS ENJOY THE FARE ON WZZZ.

TWENTY-TWO OUT OF TWENTY-THREE DEEP-SEA DIVERS FIND TREASURE ON WZZZ.

SEVENTY-SEVEN OUT OF SEVENTY-EIGHT FORTUNE TELLERS PREDICT SUN-SHINE ON WZZZ.

FORTY-TWO OUT OF FORTY-THREE STARGAZERS LOOK TO WZZZ.

SEVENTEEN OUT OF EIGHTEEN MATHEMATICIANS ADD UP THE FUN ON WZZZ.

TEN OUT OF ELEVEN CHEMISTS FIND THE PERFECT SOLUTION ON WZZZ.

FOURTEEN OUT OF SIXTEEN RACE DRIVERS TURN TO WZZZ.

FIFTY-THREE OUT OF FIFTY-FOUR WATCHMAKERS SET THEIR DIALS ON WZZZ.

ONE HUNDRED OUT OF ONE HUNDRED AND ONE SKYDIVERS JUMP FOR JOY WITH WZZZ.

TWO OUT OF THREE POLITICIANS GIVE THEIR VOTE TO WZZZ.

EIGHT OUT OF NINE HALFBACKS GET THEIR KICKS FROM WZZZ.

THIRTY-FOUR OUT OF THIRTY-FIVE ELEVATOR OPERATORS GET A RISE OUT OF WZZZ.

FOUR OUT OF FIVE COWBOYS STAY IN RANGE OF WZZZ.

SIXTY-THREE OUT OF SIXTY-FOUR PANCAKE MAKERS FLIP OVER WZZZ.

THIRTEEN OUT OF FOURTEEN PHOTOGRAPHERS LIKE THE DEVELOPMENTS ON WZZZ.

NINETEEN OUT OF TWENTY PROSPECTORS DISCOVER A FORTUNE IN FUN ON WZZZ.

SIXTY-SEVEN OUT OF SIXTY-EIGHT TRACKMEN LIKE THE RECORDS ON WZZZ.

TWENTY-THREE OUT OF TWENTY-FOUR BRIDES LIKE THE RECEPTION ON WZZZ.

TWO-HUNDRED AND ONE OUT OF TWO-HUNDRED AND TWO MAGICIANS MAKE TROUBLES DISAPPEAR WITH WZZZ.

FOUR OUT OF FIVE BALLOONISTS SETTLE ON WZZZ.

EIGHTEEN OUT OF NINETEEN DECORATORS BRIGHTEN THEIR DAY WITH WZZZ.

SEVENTY-ONE OUT OF SEVENTY-TWO LOCKSMITHS HAVE FOUND THE KEY TO PLEASURE ON WZZZ.

NINETY-NINE OUT OF ONE-HUNDRED AND ONE BUS DRIVERS TAKE THE ROUTE TO FUN ON WZZZ.

TWENTY-THREE OUT OF TWENTY-FIVE MODELS STAY IN FASHION WITH WZZZ.

FIFTEEN OUT OF SEVENTEEN ARCHERS HIT THE TARGET WITH WZZZ.

SEVEN OUT OF EIGHT PILOTS ARE KEPT IN THE CLOUDS WITH WZZZ.

THIRTY-THREE OUT OF THIRTY-FIVE ARCHITECTS FIND A DESIGN FOR GOOD LIVING ON WZZZ.

FORTY-ONE OUT OF FORTY-FOUR SHARPSHOOTERS HAVE HIT THE SPOT ON WZZZ.

NINE OUT OF TEN PRIZE FIGHTERS GET A WALLOP OUT OF WZZZ.

EIGHTEEN OUT OF TWENTY CARPENTERS HIT THE NAIL ON THE HEAD WITH WZZZ.

NINE OUT OF TEN RAILROAD MEN STAY ON THE RIGHT TRACK WITH WZZZ.

TWENTY OUT OF TWENTY-FIVE WAITRESSES GET THEIR BEST TIPS ON WZZZ.

FOURTEEN OUT OF FIFTEEN STUDENTS MAKE THE GRADE WITH WZZZ.

THIRTY-THREE OUT OF THIRTY-FIVE CAN-CAN DANCERS GET THEIR KICKS WITH WZZZ.

THIRTEEN OUT OF FIFTEEN GARDENERS SAY THEY DIG IT THE MOST—WZZZ.

SEVENTEEN OUT OF TWENTY CASHIERS FILL THE BILL WITH WZZZ.

FOUR OUT OF FIVE SHOE SALESMEN STAY IN STEP WITH WZZZ.

NINE OUT OF TEN BALLERINAS KEEP ON THEIR TOES WITH WZZZ.

TEN OUT OF TWELVE MULES GET A KICK OUT OF WZZZ.

NINETY-SIX OUT OF ONE HUNDRED PATIENTS SAY IT'S JUST WHAT THE DOCTOR ORDERED—WZZZ.

FORTY-SEVEN OUT OF FIFTY DENTISTS SAY IT'S SO PAINLESS—WZZZ.

NINE OUT OF TEN DIAMOND CUTTERS ARE DAZZLED BY WZZZ.

EIGHTEEN OUT OF TWENTY BAKERS GET A RISE OUT OF WZZZ.

SEVEN OUT OF EIGHT HOSTESSES KEEP GOOD COMPANY WITH WZZZ.

FIVE OUT OF SIX BOWLERS KEEP ROLLING WITH WZZZ.

NINETEEN OUT OF TWENTY GOLFERS KEEP IN THE SWING WITH WZZZ.

NINE OUT OF TEN MARTIANS STAY OUT OF THIS WORLD WITH WZZZ.

TWENTY-EIGHT OUT OF THIRTY FISHERMEN HAVE CAUGHT THE BIG ONE ON WZZZ.

SIX OUT OF SEVEN NEEDLE MAKERS GET THE POINT WITH WZZZ.

9.5 "THE FASHION IS WZZZ"

THIS SPRING, EVERYWHERE YOU LISTEN . . . THE FASHION IS WZZZ.

THE FASHION IS WZZZ . . . STYLED IN SOUND FOR CENTERVILLE LISTENING PLEASURE.

WEARS WELL, DRESSES UP THE DAY . . . BECAUSE THE FASHION IS WZZZ.

THE FASHION IS WZZZ . . . PATTERNED FOR YOUR PLEASURE 24 HOURS DAILY.

LEADING THE STYLE PARADE . . . THE FASHION IS WZZZ.

THE FASHION IS WZZZ . . . FIRST IN CENTERVILLE WITH THE NEW SOUND.

A FASHION HIT! THE SMOOTH LINES OF WZZZ, CENTERVILLE!

THE SMART SET IS YOUR RADIO SET . . . WHEN IT'S TUNED TO WZZZ, CEN-TERVILLE.

THERE'S NO WASTE ON 460 . . . BECAUSE THE FASHION IS WZZZ.

PERFECT DIMENSIONS FOR GOOD LISTENING: FOUR . . . SIX . . . OH. THE FASHION IS WZZZ.

THE FASHION IS WZZZ . . . NEW COLOR, NEW DASH, NEW ELEGANCE.

CENTERVILLE'S MODEL STATION . . . BECAUSE THE FASHION IS WZZZ.

LISTEN TO THE SHAPE OF THINGS TO COME ON CENTERVILLE'S FASHION-ABLE STATION, WZZZ, 460.

THE FASHION IS WZZZ . . . A PERFECT BLEND OF LIGHT LISTENING AND MEMORABLE PROGRAMMING.

LOOK FOR THE FASHION LABEL ON YOUR DIAL: 460 AND THE NEWEST, BRIGHTEST SOUND FROM WZZZ.

IT'S CUSTOM-BUILT FOR YOUR LISTENING PLEASURE . . . THAT'S WHY THE FASHION IS WZZZ.

IT'S THE MOST FASHIONABLE SOUND IN TOWN . . . WZZZ, OF COURSE . . . THE FASHION IS WZZZ.

YOUR EARS ARE ALWAYS WELL-GROOMED WHEN YOU KEEP THEM IN TUNE WITH THE STYLISH SOUND OF WZZZ IN CENTERVILLE, THE FASHION IN SOUND IS WZZZ.

IN CENTERVILLE, THE FASHION IN SOUND IS WZZZ . . . STYLED BY THE LEADING DESIGNERS OF HAPPY LISTENING RADIO.

NURSERY RHYMES   9.6

Because these promos are in the form of nursery rhymes that often use the call letters as the rhyming element, it is not possible to supply ones that will work unchanged for all of you. However, with very little effort they can be adjusted to fit your station. In the examples, we have arbitrarily used the call letters KABI.

Production

All of the examples require two voices. Select the two best character voices you have at the station to cut these.

Anncr 1: HICKORY, DICKORY, DOCK . . . THE MOUSE TURNED ON THE RADIO CLOCK.

Anncr 2: KABI WAS THE ONE WHERE HE LISTENED FOR FUN.

Anncr 1: HICKORY, DICKORY, DOCK.

Anncr 2: NICE MOUSIE.

* * * *

Anncr 1: LITTLE MISS MUFFET SAT ON A TUFFET LISTENING TO KABI.

Anncr 2: ALONG CAME A SPIDER AND SAT DOWN BESIDE HER TO HEAR THE GOOD MUSIC GO BY.

Anncr 1: WHAT ABOUT THE CURDS AND WHEY?

Anncr 2: THEY DON'T HAVE THOSE ON KABI.

* * * *

Anncr 1: JACK SPRAT COULD EAT NO FAT—HIS WIFE COULD EAT NO LEAN.

Anncr 2: BUT KABI GAVE THE TWO OF THEM A MUSICAL DIET SUPREME.

Anncr 1: AH, ME,—HUNGRY BUT HAPPY WITH KABI.

* * * *

Anncr 1: LITTLE JACK HORNER SAT IN A CORNER EATING HIS CHRISTMAS PIE.

Anncr 2: TUNED 4-6-0 ON HIS RADIO AND SAID, "MY STATION'S KABI."

Anncr 1: WHICH IS A LOT BETTER THAN A STICKY OLD PLUM ON YOUR THUMB.

* * * *

Anncr 1: OLD MOTHER HUBBARD WENT TO THE CUPBOARD TO LISTEN TO KABI.

Anncr 2: THE MUSIC SHE FOUND WAS THE SORT OF A SOUND THAT MADE HER FEEL HAPPY AND SPRY.

Anncr 1: THAT DIDN'T HELP HER POOR, HUNGRY DOG, THOUGH.

* * * *

Anncr 1: THERE WAS A LITTLE GIRL, WHO GAVE HER DIAL A TWIRL TO LISTEN TO KABI.

Anncr 2: FOR WHEN SHE WAS GOOD HER MOTHER SAID SHE COULD.

Anncr 1: BUT WHEN SHE WAS BAD, SHE WAS STILL HORRID.

* * * *

Anncr 1: MARY HAD A LITTLE LAMB WHO LISTENED TO KABI.

Anncr 2: AND EVERYWHERE THE LITTLE LAMB WENT HAPPY MUSIC WAS ALWAYS CLOSE BY.

Anncr 1:   AND NOW MARY FOLLOWS THE LAMB.

* * * *

Anncr 1:   THREE LITTLE KITTENS LOST THEIR MITTENS AND THEY BEGAN TO CRY.

Anncr 2:   TILL THEY WERE CHEERED BY THE HAPPY SOUND THAT'S ALWAYS ON KABI.

Anncr 1:   AND THEIR MOTHER COULDN'T COMPLAIN ABOUT THAT, NOW, COULD SHE?

* * * *

Anncr 1:   OLD KING COLE WAS A MERRY OLD SOUL AND A MERRY OLD SOUL WAS HE.

Anncr 2:   BECAUSE HE FOUND THE KABI SOUND WAS THE WAY TO LIVE HAP-PILY.

Anncr 1:   AND THOSE THREE FIDDLERS OF HIS—THEY LISTENED, TOO.

* * * *

Anncr 1:   LITTLE BO PEEP HAS LOST HER SHEEP—AND THEY WON'T ANSWER HER CRY.

Anncr 2:   THE SHEEP THAT'RE MISSIN' NOW ONLY LISTEN TO THE SOUND OF KABI.

Anncr 1:   AND SO DOES BO PEEP—WHICH IS WHY SHE ISN'T REALLY LOOK-ING FOR LOST SHEEP.

* * * *

Anncr 1:   JACK AND JILL WENT UP THE HILL—LISTENING TO KABI FOR LAUGHTER.

Anncr 2:   JACK FELL DOWN AND BROKE HIS CROWN—AND JILL CAME TUM-BLING AFTER.

Anncr 1:   BECAUSE JACK HAS THE PORTABLE RADIO.

Anncr 2:   AND I SUPPOSE JILL JUST COULDN'T STAND TO LEAVE THE HAPPY SOUND OF KABI.

* * * *

Anncr 1: SIMPLE SIMON MET A PIE-MAN WHILE LISTENING TO KABI.

Anncr 2: SAID THE PIE-MAN, A KABI-MAN, "YOU'RE NOT SO SIMPLE, SIMON."

Anncr 1: WHICH JUST GOES TO PROVE THAT, IN CENTERVILLE, ALMOST EVERYONE LISTENS TO KABI.

Anncr 2: I THOUGHT IT PROVED THAT GREEN APPLE PIES ARE THE MOST POPULAR.

* * * *

Anncr 1: HUMPTY DUMPTY SAT ON A WALL.

Anncr 2: HUMPTY DUMPTY HAD A GREAT FALL.

Anncr 1: AND ALL THE KING'S HORSES AND ALL THE KING'S MEN

Anncr 2: STARTED LISTENING TO RADIO AGAIN.

Anncr 1: BECAUSE, YOU SEE, HUMPTY FELL FOR THE BIG SOUND OF MUSIC ON KABI—RADIO 460.

Anncr 2: BUT, THEN, DOESN'T EVERYONE?

* * * *

Anncr 1: THERE WAS AN OLD WOMAN WHO LIVED IN A SHOE.

Anncr 2: SHE HAD SO MANY CHILDREN SHE DIDN'T KNOW WHAT TO DO.

Anncr 1: SO SHE JUST SET THE DIAL FOR 4-6-0.

Anncr 2: AND MADE THEM ALL HAPPY WITH KABI RADIO.

Anncr 1: THEY STILL HAD TO GO TO BED HUNGRY.

Anncr 2: BUT THEN YOU CAN'T HAVE EVERYTHING.

9.7 MORE AND MORE

These are short promos with enough of them provided here so that they can be used with considerable frequency on the air. The short spots should have a brief musical opener to set them up and conclude with one of your short station jingle closes that give your call letters musically.

MORE AND MORE WAGON MASTERS LISTEN TO THE GOOD SOUNDS OF WZZZ RADIO . . . BECAUSE IT KEEPS THINGS ROLLING.

MORE AND MORE TENNIS PLAYERS LISTEN TO THE GOOD SOUNDS OF WZZZ RADIO . . . BECAUSE THEY GO FOR THAT LOVE SET.

MORE AND MORE BOWLERS LISTEN TO THE GOOD SOUNDS OF WZZZ RADIO . . . BECAUSE IT'S RIGHT DOWN THEIR ALLEY.

MORE AND MORE BASEBALL PITCHERS LISTEN TO THE GOOD SOUNDS OF WZZZ RADIO . . . BECAUSE IT'S ON THE BALL.

MORE AND MORE GARDENERS LISTEN TO THE GOOD SOUNDS OF WZZZ RADIO . . . BECAUSE IT GIVES THEM THE LATEST DIRT.

MORE AND MORE HAIRDRESSERS LISTEN TO THE GOOD SOUNDS OF WZZZ RADIO . . . BECAUSE THE QUALITY IS SO PERMANENT.

MORE AND MORE MERMAIDS LISTEN TO THE GOOD SOUNDS OF WZZZ RADIO . . . BECAUSE IT KEEPS THEM IN THE SWIM OF THINGS.

MORE AND MORE AUSTRALIAN KANGAROOS LISTEN TO THE GOOD SOUNDS OF WZZZ RADIO . . . BECAUSE IT IS REALLY JUMPING.

MORE AND MORE MARTIANS LISTEN TO THE GOOD SOUNDS OF WZZZ RADIO . . . BECAUSE IT'S OUT OF THIS WORLD.

MORE AND MORE BATTERY MAKERS LISTEN TO THE GOOD SOUNDS OF WZZZ RADIO . . . BECAUSE IT GIVES THEM A CHARGE.

MORE AND MORE AIRLINE PILOTS LISTEN TO THE GOOD SOUNDS OF WZZZ RADIO . . . BECAUSE IT'S REALLY FLYING.

MORE AND MORE PIZZA-MAKERS LISTEN TO THE GOOD SOUNDS OF WZZZ RADIO . . . BECAUSE IT REALLY FLIPS.

MORE AND MORE SERVICE STATION OPERATORS LISTEN TO THE GOOD SOUNDS OF WZZZ RADIO . . . BECAUSE IT'S A REAL GAS.

MORE AND MORE CARPENTERS LISTEN TO THE GOOD SOUNDS OF WZZZ RADIO . . . BECAUSE IT'S ON THE LEVEL.

MORE AND MORE CONVICTS LISTEN TO THE GOOD SOUNDS OF WZZZ RADIO . . . BECAUSE IT'S FREE.

MORE AND MORE ATHLETES LISTEN TO THE GOOD SOUNDS OF WZZZ RADIO
. . . BECAUSE IT BREAKS ALL RECORDS.

MORE AND MORE MUSICIANS LISTEN TO THE GOOD SOUNDS OF WZZZ
RADIO . . . BECAUSE IT'S NOTED.

MORE AND MORE FIRECRACKERS LISTEN TO THE GOOD SOUNDS OF WZZZ
RADIO . . . BECAUSE THEY GET A BANG OUT OF IT.

MORE AND MORE CHEFS LISTEN TO THE GOOD SOUNDS OF WZZZ RADIO . . .
BECAUSE IT'S ALWAYS IN GOOD TASTE.

MORE AND MORE COYOTES LISTEN TO THE GOOD SOUNDS OF WZZZ RADIO
. . . BECAUSE IT'S SUCH A HOWL.

MORE AND MORE ASTRONAUTS LISTEN TO THE GOOD SOUNDS OF WZZZ
RADIO . . . BECAUSE IT REALLY PUTS THEM IN ORBIT.

MORE AND MORE UPHOLSTERERS LISTEN TO THE GOOD SOUNDS OF WZZZ
RADIO . . . BECAUSE IT COVERS EVERYTHING.

MORE AND MORE SLEEPWALKERS LISTEN TO THE GOOD SOUNDS OF WZZZ
RADIO . . . BECAUSE IT IS THE DREAMIEST.

MORE AND MORE NEWSPAPERMEN LISTEN TO THE GOOD SOUNDS OF WZZZ
RADIO . . . BECAUSE IT'S ALWAYS UP-TO-THE-MINUTE.

MORE AND MORE TRAVELERS LISTEN TO THE GOOD SOUNDS OF WZZZ
RADIO . . . BECAUSE IT'S ALWAYS ON THE GO.

MORE AND MORE AIRLINE MECHANICS LISTEN TO THE GOOD SOUNDS OF
WZZZ RADIO . . . BECAUSE IT CHECKS OUT.

MORE AND MORE NUCLEAR PHYSICISTS LISTEN TO THE GOOD SOUNDS OF
WZZZ RADIO . . . BECAUSE IT BREAKS THEM UP.

MORE AND MORE SHIPPING CLERKS LISTEN TO THE GOOD SOUNDS OF
WZZZ RADIO . . . BECAUSE IT SENDS THEM.

MORE AND MORE DITCH-DIGGERS LISTEN TO THE GOOD SOUNDS OF WZZZ
RADIO . . . BECAUSE THEY HAVE THEIR PICK.

MORE AND MORE ROOSTERS LISTEN TO THE GOOD SOUNDS OF WZZZ RADIO
. . . BECAUSE IT'S REALLY SOMETHING TO CROW ABOUT.

MORE AND MORE SHOEMAKERS LISTEN TO THE GOOD SOUNDS OF WZZZ RADIO . . . BECAUSE IT LETS THEM GET AWAY FROM THE AWL.

MORE AND MORE GARBAGE MEN LISTEN TO THE GOOD SOUNDS OF WZZZ RADIO . . . BECAUSE IT GETS THEM OUT OF THE DUMPS.

MORE AND MORE POLITICIANS LISTEN TO THE GOOD SOUNDS OF WZZZ RADIO . . . BECAUSE IT LEAVES THEM SPEECHLESS.

MORE AND MORE MULES LISTEN TO THE GOOD SOUNDS OF WZZZ RADIO . . . BECAUSE THEY GET A KICK OUT OF IT.

MORE AND MORE TRACK STARS LISTEN TO THE GOOD SOUNDS OF WZZZ RADIO . . . BECAUSE THEY LIKE TO KNOW ABOUT THE LATEST RECORDS.

MORE AND MORE CATTLE RANCHERS LISTEN TO THE GOOD SOUNDS OF WZZZ RADIO . . . BECAUSE THEY NEVER GET A BUM STEER.

MORE AND MORE WATCHMAKERS LISTEN TO THE GOOD SOUNDS OF WZZZ RADIO . . . BECAUSE IT WORKS AROUND THE CLOCK.

MORE AND MORE SUNBATHERS LISTEN TO THE GOOD SOUNDS OF WZZZ RADIO . . . BECAUSE IT REALLY SHINES.

MORE AND MORE CIRCUS CLOWNS LISTEN TO THE GOOD SOUNDS OF WZZZ RADIO . . . BECAUSE IT'S SO MUCH FUN.

MORE AND MORE BABIES LISTEN TO THE GOOD SOUNDS OF WZZZ RADIO . . . BECAUSE IT'S HOWLING.

MORE AND MORE BRIDGE PLAYERS LISTEN TO THE GOOD SOUNDS OF WZZZ RADIO . . . BECAUSE IT'S SUCH A GOOD DEAL.

MORE AND MORE FISH LISTEN TO THE GOOD SOUNDS OF WZZZ RADIO . . . BECAUSE THERE'S NO CATCH TO IT.

MORE AND MORE POLICEMEN LISTEN TO THE GOOD SOUNDS OF WZZZ RADIO . . . BECAUSE IT REALLY COVERS THE BEAT.

MORE AND MORE STATISTICIANS LISTEN TO THE GOOD SOUNDS OF WZZZ RADIO . . . BECAUSE IT ADDS UP.

MORE AND MORE OPTOMETRISTS LISTEN TO THE GOOD SOUNDS OF WZZZ RADIO . . . BECAUSE IT'S THE GREATEST SPECTACLE ON RADIO.

MORE AND MORE RECORD MANUFACTURERS LISTEN TO THE GOOD SOUNDS OF WZZZ RADIO . . . BECAUSE IT'S IN THE GROOVE.

MORE AND MORE SOFT-DRINK BOTTLERS LISTEN TO THE GOOD SOUNDS OF WZZZ RADIO . . . BECAUSE IT'S GOT THE LATEST POPS.

MORE AND MORE BARBERS LISTEN TO THE GOOD SOUNDS OF WZZZ RADIO . . . BECAUSE IT'S SUCH SHEAR PLEASURE.

MORE AND MORE SURGEONS LISTEN TO THE GOOD SOUNDS OF WZZZ RADIO . . . BECAUSE THE DISC JOCKEYS ARE SUCH CUT-UPS.

MORE AND MORE ELECTRICIANS LISTEN TO THE GOOD SOUNDS OF WZZZ RADIO . . . BECAUSE IT'S A LIVE WIRE.

MORE AND MORE SQUIRRELS LISTEN TO THE GOOD SOUNDS OF WZZZ RADIO . . . BECAUSE IT'S SO NUTTY.

MORE AND MORE ELEVATOR REPAIRMEN LISTEN TO THE GOOD SOUNDS OF WZZZ RADIO . . . BECAUSE IT GIVES THEM A LIFT.

MORE AND MORE WEATHER FORECASTERS LISTEN TO THE GOOD SOUNDS OF WZZZ RADIO . . . BECAUSE IT'S SO UNPREDICTABLE.

MORE AND MORE FARMERS LISTEN TO THE GOOD SOUNDS OF WZZZ RADIO . . . BECAUSE IT IS SO DOWN TO EARTH.

MORE AND MORE BEEKEEPERS LISTEN TO THE GOOD SOUNDS OF WZZZ RADIO . . . BECAUSE IT'S A HONEY.

MORE AND MORE GAMBLERS LISTEN TO THE GOOD SOUNDS OF WZZZ RADIO . . . BECAUSE IT'S A WINNER.

MORE AND MORE JUDGES LISTEN TO THE GOOD SOUNDS OF WZZZ RADIO . . . BECAUSE IT HAS CONVICTIONS.

MORE AND MORE BASEBALL PLAYERS LISTEN TO THE GOOD SOUNDS OF WZZZ RADIO . . . BECAUSE IT'S A HIT.

MORE AND MORE ASTRONAUTS LISTEN TO THE GOOD SOUNDS OF WZZZ RADIO . . . BECAUSE IT'S WAY OUT.

MORE AND MORE SHOE REPAIRMEN LISTEN TO THE GOOD SOUNDS OF WZZZ RADIO . . . BECAUSE IT HAS SOLE.

MORE AND MORE WAITRESSES LISTEN TO THE GOOD SOUNDS OF WZZZ RADIO . . . BECAUSE IT HAS GOOD TIPS.

MORE AND MORE DRESSMAKERS LISTEN TO THE GOOD SOUNDS OF WZZZ RADIO . . . BECAUSE IT HAS SUCH A NICE PATTERN.

MORE AND MORE RAILROAD ENGINEERS LISTEN TO THE GOOD SOUNDS OF WZZZ RADIO . . . BECAUSE IT'S ON THE RIGHT TRACK.

MORE AND MORE FIREMEN LISTEN TO THE GOOD SOUNDS OF WZZZ RADIO . . . BECAUSE IT'S REAL HOT.

MORE AND MORE MATHEMATICIANS LISTEN TO THE GOOD SOUNDS OF WZZZ RADIO . . . BECAUSE IT REALLY COUNTS.

MORE AND MORE BANKERS LISTEN TO THE GOOD SOUNDS OF WZZZ RADIO . . . BECAUSE THERE IS SO MUCH INTEREST.

MORE AND MORE DIPLOMATS LISTEN TO THE GOOD SOUNDS OF WZZZ RADIO . . . BECAUSE IT STAYS AT THE SUMMIT.

MORE AND MORE RIFLEMEN LISTEN TO THE GOOD SOUNDS OF WZZZ RADIO . . . BECAUSE IT'S ALWAYS ON TARGET.

MORE AND MORE BILL COLLECTORS LISTEN TO THE GOOD SOUNDS OF WZZZ RADIO AT NIGHT . . . BECAUSE THEY GET THE LATE CHARGE.

MORE AND MORE SCUBA DIVERS LISTEN TO THE GOOD SOUNDS OF WZZZ RADIO . . . BECAUSE IT GETS THEM DOWN DEEP.

MORE AND MORE KNIFE SHARPENERS LISTEN TO THE GOOD SOUNDS OF WZZZ RADIO . . . BECAUSE IT'S SO SHARP.

MORE AND MORE ARCHITECTS LISTEN TO THE GOOD SOUNDS OF WZZZ RADIO . . . BECAUSE IT'S DESIGNED FOR GOOD LISTENING.

MORE AND MORE PRIZE FIGHTERS LISTEN TO THE GOOD SOUNDS OF WZZZ RADIO . . . BECAUSE IT PACKS SUCH A WALLOP.

MORE AND MORE STAMP COLLECTORS LISTEN TO THE GOOD SOUNDS OF WZZZ RADIO . . . BECAUSE IT GETS IN EVERY LICK.

MORE AND MORE TEACHERS LISTEN TO THE GOOD SOUNDS OF WZZZ RADIO . . . BECAUSE IT MAKES THE GRADE.

MORE AND MORE DRESS DESIGNERS LISTEN TO THE GOOD SOUNDS OF WZZZ RADIO . . . BECAUSE IT'S ALWAYS IN STYLE.

MORE AND MORE CASHIERS LISTEN TO THE GOOD SOUNDS OF WZZZ RADIO . . . BECAUSE IT FILLS THE BILL.

MORE AND MORE CLEANERS LISTEN TO THE GOOD SOUNDS OF WZZZ RADIO . . . BECAUSE IT HITS THE SPOT.

MORE AND MORE GARDENERS LISTEN TO THE GOOD SOUNDS OF WZZZ RADIO . . . BECAUSE THEY DIG IT THE MOST.

MORE AND MORE JET PILOTS LISTEN TO THE GOOD SOUNDS OF WZZZ RADIO . . . BECAUSE IT'S THEIR SPEED.

MORE AND MORE BALLERINAS LISTEN TO THE GOOD SOUNDS OF WZZZ RADIO . . . BECAUSE IT KEEPS THEM ON THEIR TOES.

MORE AND MORE PATIENTS LISTEN TO THE GOOD SOUNDS OF WZZZ RADIO . . . BECAUSE IT'S JUST WHAT THE DOCTOR ORDERED.

MORE AND MORE NAVY CAPTAINS LISTEN TO THE GOOD SOUNDS OF WZZZ RADIO . . . BECAUSE IT'S SO ADMIRABLE.

9.8   ANSWER TIME

These are strictly fun promotions. Put some effort into the production element for the best effect. Also, rotate the names of your air personalities and news-casters through these in the spots indicated, and include the names of as many nearby communities as possible.

Produce a standard open and close to simplify your production problems. Below is the overall format for the spots, followed by drop-in copy which can be included in the additional promos.

The Format Shell

SFX: (big fanfare opening)

Anncr 1:   IT'S QUESTION AND ANSWER TIME!

SFX: (more fanfare bridge)

Anncr 1: ONCE AGAIN, IT'S TIME TO GET TO KNOW WZZZ. TIME TO ANSWER THE QUESTIONS THAT YOU, OUR LISTENERS, HAVE ASKED US. AND WHAT IS THE QUESTION TODAY?

Anncr 2: MR. HARRY AARDVARK OF (town) ASKS WZZZ, "HOW DOES (personality) HAVE TIME TO READ SO MANY BOOKS?"

Anncr 3: MR. AARDVARK, IF YOU READ THE SAME BOOKS (personality) DOES, IT WOULDN'T TAKE YOU LONG EITHER. I MEAN— "THE DOG'S NAME IS SPOT. SEE SPOT RUN. RUN SPOT RUN."

SFX: (big closing fanfare)

Suggested Questions and Answers

Anncr 2: MISS SAMANTHA FRUMP OF (town) ASKS WZZZ, "HAS SUCCESS AFFECTED (personality)?"

Anncr 3: NO, MISS FRUMP, IT HASN'T—UNLESS YOU HAPPEN TO THINK THAT GARDENING IN A SEQUINED JACKET AND TAP SHOES ARE UNUSUAL.

* * * *

Anncr 2: MISS CORDELIA SCHLAMP OF (town) ASKS WZZZ, "DOES (personality) HAVE TROUBLE GETTING SHOES TO FIT HIS BIG FEET?"

Anncr 3: NO, MISS SCHLAMP, (personality) NEVER HAS TROUBLE GETTING SHOES TO FIT HIS BIG FEET. (Personality) HAS NEVER WORN SHOES.

* * * *

Anncr 2: MR. AMBERCROMBIE HEATHERWEIGHT OF (town) ASKS WZZZ, "DOES (personality) REALLY SPEND HIS SPARE TIME WATCHING SUN BATHERS?"

Anncr 3: MR. HEATHERWEIGHT, (personality) SPENDS SO MUCH TIME AT THE BEACH, HE HAS HAD TO JOIN THE LOCAL LONGSHOREMAN'S UNION."

* * * *

Anncr 2: MISS DESDEMONA SWARTZ OF (town) ASKS WZZZ, "DOES (personality) EVER GET LONELY ON HIS ALL-NIGHT SHIFT AT WZZZ WITH NOBODY AROUND?"

Anncr 3: DON'T TELL ANYONE, MISS SWARTZ, BUT (personality) BELONGS TO

THE ONLY AFTER-HOURS CLUB IN TOWN WITH A CATERING SER-VICE.

* * * *

Anncr 2: MR. FARLEY FRANGIPANI OF (town) ASKS WZZZ, DOES "WZZZ EVER TAKE SIDES ON AN ISSUE?"

Anncr 3: YES, MR. FRANGIPANI, WE OFTEN TAKE SIDES. USUALLY, WE'RE ON THE OUTSIDE.

* * * *

Anncr 2: MISS DEBBIE DONGLEWHANGER OF (town) ASKS WZZZ, "DO THE WZZZ NEWSMEN HAVE PRESS CARDS?"

Anncr 3: YES, MISS DONGLEWHANGER, THEY DO. BUT THEY STILL WEAR WRINKLED SUITS.

* * * *

Anncr 2: MRS. MAZIE MUDD OF (town) ASKS WZZZ, "WHAT ARE (personality's) BIGGEST PROBLEMS?"

Anncr 3: WELL, MRS. MUDD, I'D SAY—TO KEEP THE MONEY COMING IN AND HIS HAIR FROM FALLING OUT.

* * * *

Anncr 2: MR. FERRIS BORNSWAGLE OF (town) ASKS WZZZ, "IS (personality) REALLY MODEST?"

Anncr 3: WELL, MR. BORNSWAGLE, (personality) IS THE ONLY GUY AROUND HERE WHO BLUSHES—OR NEEDS TO.

* * * *

Anncr 2: MRS BERTHA DIDDLEWORT OF (town) ASKS WZZZ, "IS (personality) HEN-PECKED?"

Anncr 3: ALL I CAN SAY, MRS. DIDDLEWORT, IS THAT HE CACKLES IN HIS SLEEP AND CROWS EVERY MORNING AT SUNUP.

* * * *

Anncr 2: MR. BRUCE GAGGLE OF (town) ASKS WZZZ, "HAD (personality) EVER BEEN IN TROUBLE WITH THE LEGAL AUTHORITIES?"

Anncr 3: NO, MR. GAGGLE, HE HASN'T . . . IN SPITE OF THE FACT THE ONLY LAW (personality) OBSERVES IS THE LAW OF GRAVITY.

* * * *

Anncr 2: MRS. BRUNHILDE MUGGLEBOTTOM OF (town) ASKS WZZZ, "SOMEONE ONCE SAID (personality) IS A BRAGGART. I WANT TO KNOW IF THIS IS TRUE."

Anncr 3: LET'S PUT IT THIS WAY, MRS. MUGGLEBOTTOM . . . WITH (personality) IT IS NO SOONER DONE THAN SAID.

* * * *

Anncr 2: MR. TIMOTHY NANCE OF (town) ASKS WZZZ, "WHAT HAPPENED TO (personality) IN THE HOSPITAL RECENTLY?"

Anncr 3: A MINOR OPERATION, MR. NANCE . . . AND THEY HAD TO GIVE HIM ETHER TWICE. ONCE BEFORE THE OPERATION, AND AGAIN AFTERWARD TO STOP HIM FROM TALKING ABOUT IT.

* * * *

Anncr 2: MISS ALVERDA TALLYWHACKER OF (town) ASKS WZZZ, "DO THE WZZZ DISC JOCKEYS MAKE MUCH MONEY?"

Anncr 3: WELL, LET'S PUT IT THIS WAY, MRS. TALLYWHACKER . . . THEY GENERALLY CASH THEIR PAY CHECKS ON A CITY BUS.

* * * *

Anncr 2: MRS. EMMA POTTYTROTTER OF (town) ASKS WZZZ, "DOES WZZZ NEWS DIRECTOR (personality) EVER GET NERVOUS BEFORE DOING A NEWSCAST?"

Anncr 3: I'LL LET YOU DRAW YOUR OWN CONCLUSIONS, MRS. POTTYTROTTER. EVERY TIME (personality) READS A NEWSCAST, HE MIXES A CAN OF PAINT AT THE SAME TIME.

* * * *

Anncr 2: MR. PERCY PRANGPRONGER OF (town) ASKS WZZZ, "I'VE HEARD

THAT SOME OF THE JOKE MATERIAL THAT (personality) USES IS NOT ORIGINAL. IS THAT TRUE."

Anncr 3: MR. PRANGPRONGER, (personality) HAS LIFTED MORE STUFF THAN OTIS ELEVATORS.

* * * *

Anncr 2: MR. ORVILLE CRUDHITE OF (town) ASKS WZZZ, "IS (personality) REALLY CONCEITED?"

Anncr 3: THAT'S A RATHER RUDE QUESTION, MR. CRUDHITE. NO, (personality) IS NOT CONCEITED . . . . UNLESS YOU CONSIDER IT CONCEITED TO SEND YOUR MOTHER A LETTER OF CONGRATULATIONS ON YOUR OWN BIRTHDAY.

* * * *

Anncr 2: MRS. HARRIET JONGSWORTHY OF (town) ASKS WZZZ, "I HAVE HEARD (personality) DESCRIBED AS A PRIZE-WINNING DISC JOCKEY. WHAT DOES THAT MEAN?"

Anncr 3: WELL, MRS. JONGSWORTHY, (personality) ONCE WON A PRIZE FOR LAZINESS WHEN HE TRIED TO CLIMB A BARBED WIRE FENCE WITHOUT TAKING HIS HANDS OUT OF HIS POCKETS.

* * * *

Anncr 2: MR. MALROY WAGLESTAFF OF (town) ASKS WZZZ, "DOES (personality) REALLY LIVE IN (fancy section of town)."

Anncr 3: WELL, MR. WAGLESTAFF, WE ALL HAVE TO LIVE SOMEWHERE.

* * * *

Anncr 2: MRS. EUGENIE BOTTLEDORF OF (town) ASKS WZZZ, "IS (personality) GETTING FAT?"

Anncr 3: WELL, MRS. BOTTLEDORF, (personality) IS PUTTING ON A LITTLE WEIGHT . . . . BUT I GUESS WE SHOULDN'T HAVE FUN AT HIS EXPANSE.

* * * *

Anncr 2: MR. MYRON CRONFARDLE OF (town) ASKS WZZZ, "WHEN DOES

THE WZZZ ALL-NIGHT MAN (personality) GET ANY SLEEP.

Anncr 3: I SEE, MR. CRONFARDLE, THAT YOU HAVEN'T LISTENED TO (personality's) SHOW LATELY.

* * * *

Anncr 2: MR. CLARENCE DORFDIRKER OF (town) ASKS WZZZ, "DOES NEWS-MAN (personality) REALLY HAVE A DOG THAT BARKS DURING HIS NEWSCAST?"

Anncr 3: NO, MR. DORFDIRKER—(personality) JUST HAS A STOMACH PROBLEM.

* * * *

Anncr 2: MRS. SERVERINO ZUGMAN OF (town) ASKS WZZZ, "IS (personality) A VERY WELL-LIKED PERSON?"

Anncr 3: HE DOESN'T HAVE AN ENEMY IN THE WORLD—ALL HIS FRIENDS HATE HIM.

* * * *

Anncr 2: MR. WILBERT SPITTOONYA OF (town) ASKS WZZZ, "I WANT TO CONFIRM A RUMOR THAT (personality) IS HOMELESS."

Anncr 3: NO, MR. SPITTOONYA—HE'S JUST HOME LESS THAN MOST OF US.

* * * *

Anncr 2: MR. OSCAR LAMPREY OF (town) ASKS WZZZ, "IS YOUR ALL-NIGHT DISC JOCKEY (personality) REALLY A GOOD SALESMAN?"

Anncr 3: LET'S EXPLAIN IT THIS WAY, MR. LAMPREY—(personality) SOLD HIS WIFE ON THE IDEA SHE LOOKS FAT IN A FUR COAT.

* * * *

Anncr 2: MR. ANSELMO OGLETHORPE OF (town) ASKS WZZZ, "DO THE WZZZ DISC JOCKEYS LISTEN TO RADIO IN THEIR SPARE TIME?"

Anncr 3: NO, MR. OGLETHORPE. MOST OF THEM DON'T HAVE THE TIME. THEY ARE TOO BUSY GOING TO NIGHT SCHOOL TAKING COURSES IN RADIO ANNOUNCING.

SECTION

10

Quickie Humor Material

HERE'S SOME GOOFY STUFF TO DROP IN HERE AND THERE. TO HELP YOU FIND A line apropos to a given situation, we've broken the collection down into several general categories.

10.1 ON THE JOB

The most difficult part of getting to the top of the ladder is getting through the crowd at the bottom.

One way to succeed is to make hay out of the grass growing under other folk's feet.

If you can keep your head in the midst of all this confusion, you simply do not understand the situation.

The great genius is a person who can do the average thing when everybody else is going crazy.

Work fascinates me. I can sit and look at it for hours.

Dog tired last night? Maybe you've been growling too much during the day.

Mistakes will happen. But must you give them so much help?

Samson had the right idea about advertising. He took two columns and brought down the house.

Keep your eye on the ball, your shoulder to the wheel, your ear to the ground. Now, try to work in that position.

Anything worthwhile is worth doing for money.

The person who falls down on the job is much more likely to succeed than the one who lies down on the job.

Asking the boss for a raise is a patriotic duty—the government needs the additional taxes.

A person who knows all the answers has probably been asked all the questions.

Architects cover their mistakes with ivy. Drivers cover theirs with sod. And young brides cover theirs with mayonnaise.

LOVE AND MARRIAGE 10.2

Definition of a kiss: nothing divided by two.

Your knowledge of love depends on the way you grasp your subject.

Stealing a kiss may be petty larceny, but sometimes it is grand.

When billing and cooing results in matrimony, the billing always comes after the cooing.

A wise husband never forgets his wife's birthday. He merely forgets which one it is.

With so many divorces these days, it's getting hard to tell who's whose.

A little flattery now and then makes husbands out of single men.

Fellows who drive with one hand are headed for a church aisle. Some will walk down it. Some will be carried.

Never underestimate a woman—unless you're guessing her age.

The best way to get your husband to listen to what you say is to talk in your sleep.

Here's some advice for married couples: It takes horse sense and stable thinking to stay hitched.

For every woman who makes a fool out of a man, there is another one who makes a man out of a fool.

A woman never knows what kind of husband she doesn't want—until she marries him.

The best cure for love at first sight is to take a second look.

A bachelor is a man who believes that one can live as cheaply as two.

RAISING KIDS 10.3

The trouble with college is that professors don't recognize ability and the students don't possess it.

The younger generation would probably turn out better if they turned in earlier.

Science cannot abolish sleep—but babies can.

A father is afraid all young men want to marry his daughter; a mother is afraid they don't.

Today, a switch in the modern home regulates everything but the children.

Children are a great comfort in your old age—and they help you get there faster, too.

Out of the mouths of babes come those words we should have been more careful about using in front of them.

The baby that's a healthy pink may also be a loud yeller.

Do you suppose one reason why so many kids are on the streets at night is because they are afraid to stay home alone?

An alarm clock is a small device for waking up people who have no children.

A good little boy will wash up when asked and dry up when told.

Today's children don't even believe the stork brings baby storks.

Children are natural mimics. They act like their parents in spite of every attempt to teach them good manners.

10.4   GETTING ALONG WITH OTHERS

If we could see ourselves as others see us, some of us would see things we'd find hard to believe.

The man who monopolizes the conversation usually monotonizes it.

We don't mind the ups and downs in life—it's the jerks that bother us.

Never waste household scraps. Open the windows and let the neighbors hear them.

Every married man should forget his mistakes. There is no sense in two people remembering the same thing.

The bridge player who is absent from the game gets the most slams.

Don't you hate people who talk behind your back—especially at the movies?

The only law that everyone observes is the law of gravity.

Whatever happens—there is always someone who knew it would.

Discretion is what comes to a man when he is too old for it to do him any good.

Don't tell your troubles to others: Most of them don't care a hang, and the rest are glad that it happened to you.

It is impossible to make a sound argument without making a lot of noise.

The trouble with people who lose their tempers is that they keep finding them again.

My best is none too good. So, don't bring out the worst in me.

Two things are hard on the heart: Running up hill and running down people.

Tact is the art of making people feel at home when you wish they were.

Everything is funny as long as it is happening to somebody else.

Truly the easiest way to save face is to keep the lower half shut.

The reason a dog has so many friends—his tail wags instead of his tongue.

One of the best things to have up your sleeve is a funny bone.

A soft answer may turn away wrath, but a good punch in the nose ends the matter then and there.

Did you ever notice how many people there are who always reach for the stool when there's a piano to be moved.

LOSER LINES   10.5

Time wounds all heels.

A kleptomaniac is one who helps himself because he can't help himself.

Two of the best known finishes for automobiles are lacquer and liquor.

If we could see ourselves as others see us—one thing we'd need is an introduction.

The trouble with trouble is that it usually starts out as fun.

If ignorance is bliss, why aren't there more happy people?

What lazy people need is a kick in the seat of their can'ts.

The person who is always kicking is often left without a leg to stand on.

Don't go around saying the world owes you a living—it was here first.

A conscience is that little voice that tells you you'd better start figuring out an alibi.

Some people apparently go through life pushing doors marked "Pull."

After all is said and done—more is said than done.

A diet is something to take the starch out of you.

No one is entirely useless. Even the worst of us can serve as horrible examples.

Most of our troubles in life come from our mouth: We eat too much, we drink too much, and we talk too much.

There are two kinds of egotists: Those who admit it, and the rest of us.

Most men have two sides to them: the side their wives know—and the side they think their wives don't know.

Eat, drink, and be merry—and tomorrow you'll wish you were dead.

10.6 PUBLIC SERVANTS

History shows that most kings deserve to be crowned.

A lawsuit is the clothing worn by a policeman.

A good speech has a good opening and a good ending; both of which are kept very close together.

A statesman thinks he belongs to the state, but a politician thinks the state belongs to him.

A street is something torn up by fast drivers and slow contractors.

SERVICES RENDERED

The servant problem wouldn't hurt the U.S. if it would settle its public servant problem.

If you plan to be a dentist, start saving up old magazines.

Spaghetti should not be cooked too long, at least not over three feet.

A true salesman knows how to make someone itch where the salesman wants to scratch.

WORDS TO THE WISE

Think: It may be a new experience.

People who look through keyholes don't see much to speak of.

Most people would turn over a new leaf if they could tear out some of the old pages, too.

If you get gloomy, just take an hour off and sit and think how much better this world is than Hades. Of course, it won't cheer you up much if you expect to go there.

Even the laziest sailor never has grass growing under his feet.

Many people can rise to the occasion, but few know when to sit down.

Procrastination is the art of keeping up with yesterday.

If you burn the candle at both ends, you'll make both ends meet.

Better to sit in the back row and be discovered than sit in the front row and be found out.

Discussion is the better part of valor.

An optimist is a guy that has never had much experience.

A man thinks he amounts to a great deal. But to a flea or a mosquito a human being is merely something good to eat.

Man is the only animal that blushes—or needs to.

Conscience is something that feels terrible when everything else feels great.

One good thing about telling the truth is that you don't have to remember what you said.

People who think the hometown newspaper doesn't print all the news should be thankful it doesn't.

The bees got their governmental system settled millions of years ago—but the human race is still groping.

Never be boastful—someone may come along who knew you as a child.

When we have to swallow our own medicine, the spoon always seems too big.

Humans, like horses, can't kick and go forward at the same time.

It's always the better policy to speak the truth—unless you happen to be an exceptionally good liar.

A neck is something which, if you don't stick it out, you won't get in trouble up to.

A garden is something most men prefer to turn over in their minds.

Be careful when you demand justice. You might get it.

Most troubles are caused by too much bone in the head and not enough in the back.

The bigger the vacation, the harder the fall.

If you want to be a self-made person, don't leave out any of the working parts.

DRIVING AND TRAVEL TIPS 10.9

Auto accidents most often occur when the man at the wheel refuses to release his clutch.

Some cause happiness wherever they go—others whenever they go.

It may be all right keeping up with the Joneses, but only a fool would attempt to pass the Smiths on a hill.

How can anyone expect life to begin at 40 if he drives 60 at 20.

Judging from statistics, front-seat drivers aren't so smart either.

CHANGING TIMES 10.10

If Patrick Henry thought taxation without representation was bad, what would he think of it today *with* representation.

A man is an old-timer when he can remember when the only problem about parking was getting the girl to agree to it.

If brevity is the soul of wit, then women's bathing suits are getting funnier and funnier.

Middle age is the period where you look back on your mistakes and wish you could repeat them.

There are just two things a man can count on these days: his fingers and his toes.

A man hopes that his lean years are behind him—a woman hopes hers are ahead.

When a man reaches middle age it isn't the age that matters as much as the middle.

After you're no longer a member of it, the younger generation looks pretty bad.

If you want to make light of your age, put candles on your birthday cake.

10.11   MONEY TALKS

Absence conquers love, but not when money is the thing that's absent.

The rich man suffers from laryngitis, but the poor man suffers from a cold.

When we were kids, 10 cents was big money. How dimes have changed.

If you run into debt with your shoemaker, you can't call your sole your own.

Time is money, but just try to deposit it.

A small salary isn't so hard to live on if you don't spend too much of it trying to keep it a secret.

A salesman sometimes needs to have the wind taken out of his sales.

When you think of the government debt the next generation must pay off, no wonder a baby yells when it's born.

Money may not buy happiness, but you can certainly purchase a change of misery for it.

When your outgo exceeds your income, it won't be too long before your upkeep becomes your downfall.

Success is the ability to make more money to meet obligations you wouldn't have if you didn't make so much money.

Love makes the world go around, but cold cash brings it to a grinding halt.

It's more blessed to give than to receive—besides, it's deductible.

Despite inflation, a penny for most people's thoughts is still a pretty fair price.

In every university there are many young men who diligently are working their dads through college.

A dairyman owes all he is to udders.

It may be true that George Washington never told a lie—but there were no income taxes then.

The only way to double your money is to fold it and put it in your hip pocket.

LEISURE TIME   10.12

Three-fourths of the earth's surface is water and the other one-fourth is land. Therefore, it is logical that man should spend three times as much time fishing as he does plowing.

Every man needs a certain amount of leisure time. How else could his wife get the lawn mowed?

Caution is a great asset in fishing, especially if you are the fish.

THE NATURE OF THE BEAST   10.13

A million years ago, nature didn't know we were going to wear glasses; yet look at the way she placed our ears.

A dachshund makes a good family dog because all the members of the family can pet him at the same time.

A man who sits in a swamp all day waiting to shoot a duck will kick if his wife has dinner 10 minutes late.

A reasonable number of fleas is good for a dog; it keeps him from brooding over being a dog.

Some people are known by their deeds; others by their mortgages.

No wonder a hen gets discouraged; she can never find things where she laid them.

The only two who can live as cheaply as one are a flea and a dog.

If you take a cigar out of a cigar box, the cigar box will become a cigar lighter.

If a black cat crosses the path of a car, it's a lucky cat.

MORE DAFFYNITIONS   10.14

accordion—an instrument invented by the man who couldn't decide how big the fish was that got away.

acquaintance—a person we know well enough to borrow from but not well enough to lend to.

acrobat—the only person who can do what everybody else would like to do: pat himself on the back.

kangaroo—a very jumpy animal because it is usually left holding the bag.

moth—a most economical insect because it eats nothing but holes.

mustache—the only thing that keeps many a man from being a bare-faced liar.

self-made man—one who would have done better by letting out the contract.

sleepwalker—one who gets his exercise and sleep at the same time.

belly laugh—mirthquake.

language—the art of concealing thought.

synonym—it's a word you can use if you can't spell the word you want.

stork—a bird with a big bill.

cannibal—one who lives in the uninhibited parts of the earth.

another definition of a cannibal—a person who shows his hospitality by constantly having people for dinner.

car—an invention to take both drivers and pedestrians off their feet.

diplomacy—the art of letting someone else have your way.

census taker—one who goes from door to door increasing the population.

SECTION

11

Station
Identification

YOUR STATION IDENTIFICATION IS YOUR STATION'S IDENTITY! IT SHOULD reveal something about who you are and what your listeners can expect from you. In this section, we hope to spark your imagination with a variety of suggestions for dressing up the obligatory "WZZZ, Centerville" announcement. (Remember, though, you must say "WZZZ, Centerville" without sandwiching other stuff between the call letters and your city of license.)

11.1 STATION IDs WITH AN INTERNATIONAL FLAVOR

These IDs play on the keen interest listeners have in other countries of the world . . . daily news, headlines, an increased public interest in foreign languages combine to create interest in your station ID series for the coming period.

The format is simple, and the attention-getting element high. In each example in this section, you will find a sentence in either German, French, or Spanish, coupled with an English statement giving your call letters and city. These countries were chosen because they represent the three most popular "live" languages (other than English) known today. Chances are your own staff members know how to pronounce correctly one or more of the three languages represented here. If possible, you probably would find it advantageous to have each foreign lead-in taped, with the English tag delivered by the board announcer. On the other hand, a great deal of light fun could result from an "unschooled" reading of the lines.

The French and German sayings are as famous in their respective countries as "What this country needs is a good five-cent cigar" is in ours. To provide contrast, the Spanish sayings are beginning exercises for college students of Spanish.

The Multilingual IDs

Le naturel est le sceau du genie.
(Naturalness is the seal of genius.)
. . . any way you say it, (town) listeners like the *natural* sound of WZZZ, Centerville.

Le onde entier est notra ville.
(The whole world is our town.)
. . . in French, Italian, or Spanish, WZZZ is proud to serve the people of this area—WZZZ, Centerville.

Allein zu tragen dieses Glück und Elend vermag ich nicht.

(Alone I cannot bear this bliss and woe.)
. . . in any language, more (town) listeners share the fun and drama on WZZZ, Centerville.

Da geh ich lieber ins Wirtshaus.
(I would rather go back to the inn.)
. . . even in German, it says good times are found wherever there's WZZZ, Centerville.

Escuchen ustedes bien.
(Listen carefully.)
. . . this is WZZZ, Centerville . . . the station that listens to people.

Voy a pasar lista.
(I am going to call the roll.)
. . . whenever the roll is called, more listeners are tuned to WZZZ, Centerville.

C'est dans les grands dangers qu'on voit un grand courage.
('Tis in great perils that great valour's shown.)
. . . perhaps the way the French would say; stay tuned for the latest news on WZZZ, Centerville.

Addressex-voux aux jeunes: ils savent tout!
(Ask the young people: they know everything!)
. . . that's right! People who are young in heart know good listening on WZZZ, Centerville.

Con mucho gusto.
(Gladly; with great pleasure.)
. . . Even in Spanish, listeners dial WZZZ, Centerville with pleasure.

Tenemos tanto gusto en hablar.
(We are so glad to speak.)
. . . another way of saying, this is WZZZ in Centerville.

Quien temprano se levanta tiene una hora mas de vide, y en su trabajo adelanta.
(He who rises early has one more hour of life, and progresses in his work.)
. . . or, to put it in a different way, join the morning crowd everyday right here on WZZZ, Centerville.

Das ist gesprochen wie ein Mann!

(That's spoken like a man!)

. . . another satisfied listener of WZZZ, Centerville.

Der ist beglückt, der sein darf, was er ist!
(He is happy who dares to be what he is!)

. . . and the universal pleasures of good radio listening are found right here on WZZZ, Centerville.

Le monde est le livre des femmes.
(The world is woman's book.)

. . . the French know the secret: WZZZ, Centerville.

11.2 ADVERTISING SLOGANS

All of these IDs in this first part are built around actual advertising slogans—both old and new. They achieve an added impact because of this fact. If there are local or regional slogans in your area, you will do well to adapt them for use, too.

IF IT'S WZZZ—IT'S GOT TO BE GOOD.

YOU CAN HEAR THE DIFFERENCE—ON WZZZ.

WZZZ—ALWAYS AN ADVENTURE IN GOOD LISTENING.

IN CENTERVILLE—ALMOST EVERYONE LISTENS TO WZZZ.

YOU CAN BE SURE—IF IT'S WZZZ.

WZZZ DISC JOCKEYS—OUTSTANDING—AND THEY ARE WILD.

WZZZ—ALWAYS GOOD TO THE LAST NOTE.

WZZZ—NOW FORTIFIED WITH GM 4-60—GOOD MUSIC AT THE 4-60 SPOT—FOR EVEN GREATER LISTENING PLEASURE.

WZZZ—IT SATISFIES.

THE GREAT ONE—WZZZ.

THE SIGN OF GOOD TASTE—AND SOUND—WZZZ.

WHERE THERE'S LIFE—THERE'S WZZZ.

TRY WZZZ—THE LIGHT ENTERTAINMENT.

NATURALLY BETTER—BECAUSE IT'S BETTER NATURALLY—WZZZ.

DON'T MISS THE FUN OF RADIO—TUNE WZZZ.

AT WZZZ—ENTERTAINMENT IS OUR MOST IMPORTANT PRODUCT.

GET RELIEF—FAST—FAST—FAST—WITH WZZZ.

I FEEL GREAT—WZZZ DOESN'T UPSET MY EAR.

HE'S A NATURAL—HE LISTENS TO WZZZ.

DID YOU KNOW—CONCENTRATED WZZZ LISTENING CAN BURN A HOLE IN THE BLUES?

WZZZ—WITH GM 4-60—THAT'S GOOD MUSIC AT THE 4-60 SPOT—KEEPS YOUR EAR GROOMED ALL DAY—THE GOOD MUSIC WAY.

WZZZ SOUNDS GOOD—LIKE RADIO SHOULD.

FOR MEN OF DISTINCTION—LADIES, TOO—IT'S WZZZ.

NOTHING DOES IT—LIKE WZZZ.

JUST ONE EASY APPLICATION—THAT'S ALL . . . WZZZ—PROVED COMPLETELY EFFECTIVE EVEN IN THE SEVEREST CASES OF THE BLUES.

MMMMMMMMMMM, GOOD. WZZZ.

THERE'S NOTHING NEWER IN THE WORLD—WZZZ.

I'D WALK A MILE—TO LISTEN TO WZZZ.

IT'S ALWAYS A PLEASURE—ON WZZZ.

EVERYBODY'S RADIO—BECAUSE IT SOUNDS SO GOOD—WZZZ.

FOR A NEW KIND OF LISTENING—DEEP DOWN—WHERE ENTERTAINMENT BEGINS—WZZZ.

WAKE UP REFRESHED—WITH WZZZ.

RADIO IS OUR BUSINESS—OUR ONLY BUSINESS—AT WZZZ.

JUST FOR FUN—WZZZ.

YOU LIKE IT—IT LIKES YOU—WZZZ.

WHAT DO DOCTORS DO? THEY LISTEN TO WZZZ.

AREN'T YOU GLAD YOU LISTEN TO WZZZ? DON'T YOU WISH EVERYBODY DID?

WZZZ—THE RADIO STATION LISTENERS RECOMMEND MORE OFTEN THAN ANY OTHER.

11.3 LISTENER IDs

We're suggesting something a little different in the way of station IDs here. These are going to take some work on your part, but the result should be worth the effort. Each of the IDs suggested here should be recorded by a different listener. This will provide you with a multitude of authentic-sounding voices doing testimonials for you.

SURE, I LISTEN TO WZZZ. DOESN'T EVERYBODY?

WZZZ—THAT'S MY KIND OF RADIO STATION.

MY RADIO DIAL HAS HAD A LOVE AFFAIR WITH WZZZ FOR YEARS.

WHEN I WANT THE NEWS—UP TO THE MINUTE—I TURN TO WZZZ.

THEY PLAY MY KIND OF MUSIC ON WZZZ.

AT HOME OR IN THE CAR—WZZZ IS ALWAYS WITH ME.

(Child's voice) I WAS SEVEN YEARS OLD BEFORE I FOUND OUT THERE WAS ANY OTHER STATION BESIDES WZZZ.

OF COURSE I LISTEN TO WZZZ. I WOULDN'T LISTEN ANY OTHER WAY.

WZZZ—THAT'S WHERE THE NEWS BREAKS FIRST.

AT OUR HOUSE, WZZZ GOES ON WITH THE TOAST—AND STAYS ON ALL DAY.

WZZZ—THAT'S THE STATION THAT PUT FUN BACK INTO RADIO LISTENING.

WZZZ JUST SEEMS TO BRIGHTEN UP THE DAY. THAT'S WHY WE LISTEN.

SURE, WE'VE GOT THE WZZZ HABIT AT OUR HOUSE. IT'S ONE OF THE BEST HABITS WE HAVE.

WZZZ JUST SORT OF COMES NATURALLY. GOOD LISTENING—ALL THE TIME—THAT'S WHAT DOES IT.

OUR DIAL STAYS SET ON WZZZ. WE WOULDN'T HAVE IT ANY OTHER WAY.

WZZZ EVEN MAKES AN OLD MORNING GROUCH LIKE ME WANT TO GET UP AND LIVE.

IT'S EASY ON THE EAR. THAT'S WHY WE LISTEN TO WZZZ.

WZZZ JUST SEEMS TO GO WITH OUR PATTERN OF LIVING. WE LIKE IT.

I WANT RADIO AT ITS LISTENABLE BEST. I GET IT WITH WZZZ.

SPECIALIST IDs   11.4

I'M A CHAMPION RACE DRIVER AND I SAY WZZZ SIMPLY CAN'T BE BEAT.

I'M A DOGCATCHER AND I SAY WZZZ IS HUMANE TO THE EAR.

I'M A DEEP-SEA DIVER AND I SAY WZZZ EVEN SOUNDS GOOD AT 25 FATHOMS.

I'M A JET PILOT AND I SAY WZZZ SOUNDS EVEN BETTER AT 40,000 FEET.

I'M A VIOLIN-MAKER AND I SAY NOTHING COMPARES TO THE SWEET SOUND OF WZZZ.

I'M A COLLEGE PROFESSOR AND I SAY WZZZ APPEALS TO ALL CLASSES.

I'M AN ARCHAEOLOGIST AND I SAY WZZZ BELONGS TO ALL AGES.

I'M A PARIS FASHION EXPERT AND I SAY WZZZ IS IN VOGUE THIS SEASON.

I'M A BUILDING INSPECTOR AND I SAY WZZZ BELONGS IN YOUR HOME.

I'M A FLAGPOLE SITTER AND I SAY WZZZ TOPS THEM ALL.

I'M A DANCE INSTRUCTOR AND I SAY WZZZ OUT-STEPS ANY OTHER SOUND AROUND.

I'M AN ELECTRONIC ENGINEER AND I SAY WZZZ IS EASY TO INTERFACE WITH.

I'M A SOAP SALESPERSON AND I SAY NOTHING COMPARES WITH WZZZ'S BRIGHTER SOUND.

Specialist IDs with Sound Effects

Anncr: I'M A HUMAN CANNONBALL. I GET SHOT OUT OF A CANNON EVERY HOUR. BETWEEN BLASTS, I LISTEN TO . . .

Sound: (cannon blast)

Anncr: (Voice trailing off) W-Z-Z-Z.

* * * *

Sound: (lion's roar)

Anncr: I'M A PROFESSIONAL LION TAMER—AND I SIMPLY LOSE MY HEAD FOR . . . (barrel voice effect) WZZZ.

* * * *

Anncr: I'M A ROOSTER INSPECTOR AND, BELIEVE ME, WZZZ IS SOME-THING TO CROW ABOUT.

Sound: (rooster crow)

Anncr: SEE?

* * * *

Sound: (surf)
Anncr: I'M A PROFESSIONAL BEACHCOMBER—AND THE BEST THING I'VE FOUND ALL YEAR IS WZZZ.

* * * *

Sound: (train and train whistle)
Anncr: I'M A RAILROAD ENGINEER AND, TAKE IT FROM ME, YOU'RE ON THE RIGHT TRACK WITH WZZZ.

* * * *

Anncr: I'M A PEPPER INSPECTOR AT A SPICE FACTORY. YOU AIN'T JUST A SNEEZING WHEN YOU SAY WZZZ IS ALWAYS IN SEASON.
Sound: (sneeze)

* * * *

Sound: (motorcycle siren and motorcycle coming to a stop)
Anncr: I'M A MOTORCYCLE POLICEMAN—AND I SAY THAT WZZZ IS JUST THE TICKET FOR RADIO.

* * * *

Anncr: HOLD IT NOW. SMILE.
Sound: (click)
Anncr: I'M A PROFESSIONAL PHOTOGRAPHER—AND IF YOU HOLD IT RIGHT WHERE YOU ARE AT WZZZ, YOU'LL ALWAYS HAVE A SMILE.

* * * *

Sound: (horn honking)
Anncr: I'M A TRUCK DRIVER—AND THE BEST RIDE I TAKE IS THE ONE I TAKE WITH WZZZ ON MY RADIO.

11.5   QUOTES AND SLOGANS

"None but the brave deserve the fair."
>   —Not true on WZZZ. Everyone enjoys the fare on this entertainment station.

"To be or not to be—that is the question."
>   —Wrong. The question is: What station is this? The answer: WZZZ.

"Don't count your chickens before they're hatched."
>   —Good advice. Better to count the hours of listening pleasure on WZZZ.

"All the world's a stage."
>   —Right. And in Centerville WZZZ is the star performer.

"I have not yet begun to fight."
>   —Relax. Why fight when you can enjoy WZZZ?

"Put your shoulder to the wheel."
>   —Better to put your finger to the dial and tune WZZZ.

"You may fire when ready, Gridley."
>   —What? And make a lot of noise when WZZZ is on the air?

"Early to bed, early to rise, makes a man healthy, wealthy, and wise."
>   —Also, he'll be up in time for another great broadcast day on WZZZ.

"Mum's the word."
>   —Now, how could you run a popular radio station like that?

"Rome wasn't built in a day."
>   —Neither was WZZZ's great listening audience.

"The fog comes on little cat feet."
>   —But, nevertheless, Centerville folks roar with delight when WZZZ comes on.

"A bird in the hand is worth two in the bush."
>   —Why think about hunting when you can listen to WZZZ?

11.6   WORD DEFINITIONS

The station IDs here are all built around the definitions of slightly unusual words. The words themselves will catch the ear. The definition in each case then involves our station. Dozens more can and should be developed.

insatiable—is the state of seeking more and more of something good—like the way listeners seek good listening on WZZZ.

symposium—is a word for a conference on one subject—like the way neighbors discuss the happy sound of WZZZ.

voracious—describes the entertainment appetite of people for the sound of WZZZ.

grandiose—is a word that only begins to describe the impressive loyalty of WZZZ listeners.

copious—means abundant and ample, as in the pleasant sounds of WZZZ.

veracity—is the quality of truthfulness, like the quality of WZZZ news.

heterogeneous—describes the many different kinds of good listening from late news to relaxing music heard right here on WZZZ.

meliorate—is the rare ability to make good things better—such as the ever-better sound of WZZZ.

kinetic—pertains to motion and action. And WZZZ is where the action is.

esoteric—is a private pleasure, like that belonging to WZZZ listeners.

HUMOROUS SHOW OPENERS 11.7

These show openers should be assigned to just one of your DJs—probably your late-morning one. These should be taped, the first ones by a raspy, ill-tempered voice. The DJ should come out of the opener directly into music.

THIS IS THE TOM JOHNSON SHOW—BECAUSE VIC AND SADE COULDN'T MAKE IT. PLAY THE MUSIC, BLUE EYES.

* * * *

THIS IS THE JOHNSON TOM SHOW. IT USED TO BE THE TOM JOHNSON SHOW— BUT THINGS GOT TURNED AROUND. PLAY THE MUSIC—FROM THE OUTSIDE, BIG BOY.

* * * *

DUE TO CIRCUMSTANCES BEYOND OUR CONTROL—THIS IS THE TOM JOHNSON SHOW. READY FOR THE DOWN-BEAT? ALL RIGHT, HERE WE GO—AND A ONE AND A TWO.

* * * *

THIS IS THE TOM JOHNSON SHOW—AND NO MATTER WHAT YOU'VE HEARD—TOM WILL NOT GIVE A RECIPE FOR SHOO-FLY PIE TODAY. ALL RIGHT, YOU'RE ON, SWATTER—FLY RIGHT INTO IT.

* * * *

THIS IS THE TOM JOHNSON SHOW—AND NO MATTER WHAT YOU'VE HEARD—IF YOU HEARD IT HERE, IT'S WRONG. IF YOU'LL PUT DOWN THE BATON AND PUT ON THE RECORD, WE'LL GET ON WITH IT.

* * * *

THIS IS THE TOM JOHNSON SHOW. WE WANTED TO CALL IT THE BO DEREK SHOW, BUT TOM REFUSED TO CHANGE HIS NAME. ALL RIGHT, SOREHEAD, PLAY THE MUSIC.

* * * *

THIS IS THE TOM JOHNSON SHOW—RADIO'S ANSWER TO BEDLAM. BUT YOU'LL LIKE THE MUSIC. OKAY, BLUE EYES, YOU'RE ON. NO TALK, NOW. JUST MUSIC.

* * * *

THIS IS THE TOM JOHNSON SHOW—AND NO MATTER WHAT YOU'VE HEARD TOM DID NOT WRESTLE AN ALLIGATOR IN A FLORIDA SWAMP. HE CAN'T EVEN WRESTLE WITH HIS CONSCIENCE. PLAY THE MUSIC.

* * * *

THIS IS THE TOM JOHNSON SHOW—AND NO MATTER WHAT YOU'VE HEARD TOM IS NOT A HUMAN FLY. A FLY, YES, HUMAN, NO. AS SOON AS HE GETS OUT OF THE SPIDERWEB, HE'LL PLAY THE MUSIC.

* * * *

THIS IS THE TOM JOHNSON SHOW. NOTHING HAS BEEN CHANGED TO PROTECT THE INNOCENT. THEY'LL HAVE TO LOOK OUT FOR THEMSELVES. DON'T WAIT FOR THE FANFARE, BLUE EYES. JUST PLAY THE MUSIC.

* * * *

THIS IS THE TOM JOHNSON SHOW. OKAY, BOYS, UNLOCK THE CAGE AND LET HIM OUT. TURN ON THE MUSIC FIRST, THOUGH.

* * * *

THIS IS THE TOM JOHNSON SHOW—AND IF YOU CAN FIGURE OUT WHAT TO DO ABOUT THAT, YOU'RE SMARTER THAN WE ARE. OKAY, DREAMBOAT, PLAY THE MUSIC.

* * * *

THIS IS THE TOM JOHNSON SHOW. HE'S A TIGER—BUT WE CLIPPED HIS CLAWS SO HE WOULDN'T SCRATCH THE RECORDS. STOP GROWLING, BLUE EYES, AND PLAY THE MUSIC.

* * * *

THIS IS THE TOM JOHNSON SHOW—AND NO MATTER WHAT YOU'VE HEARD TOM WILL NOT PLAY A SOLO ON THE BAGPIPES TODAY. WHO SAYS THERE'S NO GOOD NEWS? PLAY THE PRETTY MUSIC, BLUE EYES.

* * * *

THIS IS THE TOM JOHNSON SHOW. MR. JOHNSON HAS JUST RETURNED FROM A TRIUMPHANT ENGAGEMENT AT THE MUSIC STORE WHERE HE PURCHASED THE RECORDS YOU'LL HEAR TODAY. IT'S NOW OR NEVER, BLUE EYES. PLAY THE MUSIC.

* * * *

THIS IS THE TOM JOHNSON SHOW. THE MANAGEMENT OF THIS STATION HAS SPARED NO EXPENSE TO TRY TO PREVENT THIS, BUT HE'S GOT A CONTRACT. ALL RIGHT, BLUE EYES, PLAY THE MUSIC.

* * * *

THIS IS THE TOM JOHNSON SHOW—WITH THE ONLY DISC JOCKEY IN THE WORLD WITH TWO BLUE EYES—AND ONE GREEN ONE. DON'T JUST STAND THERE, BLUE EYES, PLAY THE MUSIC.

* * * *

THIS IS THE TOM JOHNSON SHOW—AND NO MATTER WHAT YOU'VE HEARD TOM WILL NOT SING THE TOREADOR SONG FROM CARMEN. AS A MATTER OF FACT, HE WON'T SING AT ALL. AND ON THAT CHEERY NOTE—HERE HE IS. PLAY THE MUSIC, BLUE EYES.

* * * *

Woman: HEY, ARE YOU TOM JOHNSON?

Tom: YUP.

Woman: FROM KEOKUK, IOWA

Tom: NOPE.

Woman: WELL, YOU SURE DO LOOK LIKE HIM. PLAY THE MUSIC.

* * * *

Woman: HEY, WHERE'S TOM JOHNSON?

Tom: RIGHT HERE.

Woman: NO, I MEAN THE ONE WITH THE BLONDE CURLY HAIR.

Tom: THAT'S ME. I HAD IT CUT.

Woman: WITH WHAT—A LAWNMOWER? COME ON—PLAY THE MUSIC.

* * * *

Tom: THIS IS TOM JOHNSON.

Woman: WHAT HAPPENED TO YOUR VOICE, KID?

Tom: I LOST IT.

Woman: YOU SOUND BETTER.

Tom: THANKS.

Woman: SO, IF YOU CAN'T TALK—PLAY THE MUSIC.

* * * *

Woman: TOM JOHNSON?

Tom: THAT'S ME.

Woman: WELL, IT WON'T BE YOU IF YOU DON'T START PLAYING THE MUSIC.

* * * *

Woman: HEY, ARE YOU DON CORNELL?

Tom: NO, I'M TOM JOHNSON.

Woman: YOU DON'T SING.

Tom: NO, I PLAY MUSIC.

Woman: WELL, LET'S HEAR IT BOY. GIVE 'EM A DOWNBEAT.

* * * *

Tom: GIVE ME LIBERTY OR GIVE ME DEATH.

Woman: WHO DO YOU THINK YOU ARE, PATRICK HENRY?

Tom: NO, TOM JOHNSON.

Woman: LOOK, JOHNSON, PLAY THE MUSIC OR YOUR NAME WILL BE MUD.

Tom: HOW ABOUT THAT? MUD JOHNSON.

* * * *

Woman: SAY, ISN'T IT ABOUT TIME FOR THE TOM JOHNSON SHOW?

Tom: ISN'T THIS SUNDAY?

Woman: NO. SO, LET'S HEAR SOME MUSIC.

Tom: I THOUGHT YOU'D NEVER ASK.

* * * *

Woman: HAVEN'T I SEEN YOU SOMEWHERE BEFORE?

Tom: NOPE—I'VE NEVER BEEN ANYWHERE BEFORE.

Woman: THAT'S FUNNY. YOU LOOK JUST LIKE TOM JOHNSON.

Tom: MOST PEOPLE SAY HE LOOKS LIKE ME.

* * * *

Woman:	TOM JOHNSON?
Tom:	YES?
Woman:	WHY DOES THE CHICKEN CROSS THE ROAD?
Tom:	I DON'T KNOW. WHY DOES THE CHICKEN CROSS THE ROAD?
Woman:	I DON'T KNOW EITHER. PLAY SOME MUSIC, TOM.

* * * *

Woman:	HEY, ARE YOU TOM JOHNSON?
Tom:	YUP.
Woman:	TOM JOHNSON THE CIRCUS CLOWN?
Tom:	NOPE.
Woman:	WELL, THEN STOP LOOKING FUNNY AND PLAY SOME MUSIC.

* * * *

Woman:	HEY, ARE YOU TOM JOHNSON?
Tom:	YUP.
Woman:	TOM JOHNSON, THE RAILROAD ENGINEER?
Tom:	NOPE.
Woman:	WELL, GET ON THE TRACK ANYWAY, BOY, AND PLAY SOME MUSIC.

* * * *

Woman:	HEY, ARE YOU TOM JOHNSON?
Tom:	YUP.
Woman:	TOM JOHNSON, THE BOXER?
Tom:	NOPE.
Woman:	WELL THEN DON'T FIGHT IT, BOY. PLAY SOME MUSIC.

* * * *

Woman:	HEY, ARE YOU TOM JOHNSON?
Tom:	YUP.
Woman:	TOM JOHNSON, THE WRESTLER?
Tom:	NOPE.
Woman:	WELL, THEN GET OFF YOUR BACK AND PLAY SOME MUSIC, BOY.

* * * *

Woman:	HEY, ARE YOU TOM JOHNSON?
Tom:	YUP.
Woman:	WELL, WHY ARE YOU WEARING THAT RACCOON SKIN COAT?
Tom:	I WORE MY BEAR SKIN YESTERDAY—BUT THEY OBJECTED.
Woman:	THIS IS NOT THE TIME FOR HUMOR, BOY—JUST PLAY THE MUSIC.

* * * *

Woman:	TOM JOHNSON, I WISH—JUST ONCE—YOU'D GET THE MUSIC STARTED ON TIME.
Tom:	I WOULD IF YOU WOULDN'T INTERRUPT.
Woman:	DON'T GET SMART, BOY. YOU CAN BE REPLACED.
Tom:	BY YOU?
Woman:	NO, BY MUSIC. PLAY IT, BOY.

* * * *

Woman:	HEY, ARE YOU CHARLIE SUMMERS?
Tom:	NO. I'M TOM JOHNSON.
Woman:	YOU LOOK JUST LIKE CHARLIE SUMMERS.
Tom:	THAT WAS MY MAIDEN NAME.
Woman:	THEY DON'T PAY YOU TO BE FUNNY, BOY. THEY PAY YOU TO PLAY THE MUSIC.

* * * *

Woman:	HEY, ARE YOU TOM JOHNSON?
Tom:	YUP.
Woman:	WELL, IF YOU'RE TOM JOHNSON, PROVE IT.
Tom:	HOW CAN I PROVE IT?
Woman:	BY PLAYING SOME MUSIC, BOY. BY PLAYING SOME MUSIC.

* * * *

Woman:	HEY, ARE YOU ROY ROGERS?
Tom:	NO. I'M TOM JOHNSON.
Woman:	WELL, YOU SURE DO LOOK LIKE ROY ROGERS IN THAT COWBOY OUTFIT.
Tom:	SORRY. I'M TOM JOHNSON.
Woman:	THEN STOP HORSING AROUND AND PLAY SOME MUSIC, BOY.

* * * *

Woman:	HEY, ARE YOU FIDEL CASTRO?
Tom:	NO. I'M TOM JOHNSON.
Woman:	YOU CAN'T FOOL ME. YOU'RE FIDEL CASTRO.
Tom:	I TOLD YOU, I'M TOM JOHNSON.
Woman:	WELL, IF YOU'RE TOM JOHNSON, HOW COME YOU'RE NOT PLAYING ANY MUSIC?
Tom:	YOU'RE PRETTY HARD TO CONVINCE, AREN'T YOU.

* * * *

Woman:	HEY, TOM JOHNSON.
Tom:	YUP.
Woman:	WHY DO YOU HAVE ON SHORT PANTS?
Tom:	I DON'T HAVE ON SHORT PANTS. I HAVE ON LONG LEGS.

Woman: ALL RIGHT—CUT THE COMEDY AND START THE MUSIC, BOY.

* * * *

Woman: HEY, ARE YOU TOM JOHNSON?

Tom: YUP.

Woman: FROM CHITTLING SWITCH, ARKANSAS?

Tom: YUP AND YOU MUST BE . . .

Woman: NEVER SAW YOU BEFORE IN MY LIFE. PLAY THE MUSIC, BOY.

* * * *

Tom: PARDON ME. WILL YOU DIRECT ME TO THE MICROPHONE?

Woman: IT'S RIGHT THERE IN FRONT OF YOU. ARE YOU CRAZY OR SOMETHING?

Tom: NO, I'M TOM JOHNSON.

Woman: WELL, THAT EXPLAINS IT. PLAY THE MUSIC, BOY.

SECTION

12

Station Promos

HERE ARE SOME IDEA-STARTERS FOR DIFFERENT WAYS TO PROMOTE YOUR station.

12.1   MOBILE NEWS PROMOS

THE WZZZ MOBILE NEWS UNIT PUTS ITS SPOTLIGHT ON THE FAST-BREAKING NEWS STORIES THROUGHOUT THE CENTERVILLE AREA . . . TAKES YOU THERE—LETS YOU HEAR THE NEWS WHILE IT'S HAPPENING.

* * * *

THE WZZZ MOBILE NEWS UNIT—REPORTING FROM WHERE IT HAPPENS, AS IT HAPPENS. WZZZ MOBILE NEWS—PUTS YOU ON THE SCENE OF THE BIG NEWS STORIES.

* * * *

THE FAST-BREAKING LOCAL NEWS STORY—FROM WHERE IT'S HAPPENING, AS IT'S HAPPENING—VIA DIRECT REPORTS FROM THE WZZZ MOBILE NEWS UNIT.

* * * *

THE BIG LOCAL NEWS STORIES—HEAR THEM AS THEY HAPPEN THROUGH THE REMOTE FACILITIES OF THE WZZZ MOBILE NEWS UNIT. ON-THE-SPOT COVERAGE AROUND THE CLOCK. IF IT'S NEWS—WZZZ TAKES YOU THERE.

* * * *

THE WZZZ MOBILE NEWS UNIT COVERS THE CENTERVILLE BEAT . . . BRINGS YOU THE BIG LOCAL NEWS STORIES DIRECT FROM THE SCENE OF ACTION. THE NEWS IN ACTION—TWENTY-FOUR HOURS A DAY.

12.2   WEATHER PROMOS

WILL IT BE RAINCOAT AND UMBRELLA WEATHER? OR WILL THE SUN BE BEAMING DOWN? YOU STAY UPDATED ON THE WEATHER WHEN YOU STAY TUNED TO WZZZ.

* * * *

MARK TWAIN ONCE SAID: "EVERYBODY TALKS ABOUT THE WEATHER, BUT NOBODY DOES ANYTHING ABOUT IT." HE WAS WRONG. WZZZ DOES SOME-THING ABOUT THE WEATHER: BRINGS YOU THE FULL REPORT THREE TIMES EACH HOUR.

* * * *

NEVER A GUESS ON WEATHER WHEN YOU KEEP YOUR DIAL ON WZZZ. OR THE TIME. YOU <u>KNOW.</u> YOU <u>KNOW</u>—TWENTY-FOUR HOURS A DAY! NEXT WEATHER REPORT, _____ FUN-FILLED MINUTES FROM NOW. NEXT TIME CHECK, RIGHT NOW:_____.

* * * *

SUNGLASSES OR RAIN BOOTS? STRAW HAT OR UMBRELLA? NO CONFUSION WHEN YOU LET WZZZ WEATHER REPORTS GUIDE YOUR DAY. THREE EVERY HOUR—TWENTY-FOUR HOURS A DAY. FREQUENT TIME CHECKS, TOO. ALL DESIGNED TO MAKE WZZZ AN IMPORTANT PART OF YOUR DAY—EVERY DAY.

* * * *

THE TIME:_____. THE TEMPERATURE:_____. YOU'RE IN THE KNOW WITH WZZZ WEATHER AND TIME REPORTS. ADD THESE TO GOOD MUSIC AND THE LATEST NEWS AND YOU'RE ON TOP OF THE DAY—THE WZZZ WAY.

* * * *

NOW, LET'S TURN TO THE WZZZ WEATHER/CLOCK. THE TIME:_____. THE PRESENT DOWNTOWN CENTERVILLE TEMPERATURE:_____. KEEP UP WITH WEATHER CONDITIONS THROUGHOUT THE AREA WITH THE WZZZ WEATHER/CLOCK AND ACCURATE REPORTS _____ TIMES EACH BROAD-CAST DAY.

* * * *

FUN, MUSIC, GOOD COMPANY RIGHT THROUGH THE DAY. THAT'S WZZZ—YOUR BEST ALL-WEATHER FRIEND IN CENTERVILLE. AND, RIGHT NOW, THE WZZZ WEATHER/CLOCK READS _____ DEGREES AT _____P.M. (A.M.).

* * * *

WHAT'S YOUR GUESS AT THE TEMPERATURE? WELL, NO NEED IN THE WORLD TO WONDER. THE BIG WZZZ WEATHER/CLOCK KEEPS YOU POSTED TWENTY-FOUR HOURS A DAY—AT JUST THE TIMES WHEN YOU'D REALLY LIKE TO KNOW. LIKE RIGHT NOW, FOR INSTANCE. THE TEMPERA-TURE:_____. THE TIME:_____.

* * * *

WZZZ—THE STATION THAT MAKES WEATHER NEWS A BASIC FEATURE OF ITS ENTERTAINMENT FORMAT. THE WEATHER NOW—THE LONG-RANGE FORECAST . . . HEAR THEM BOTH RIGHT HERE AT THE 460 SPOT THREE TIMES EACH HOUR. WZZZ WEATHER UPDATES COMING OUR WAY AGAIN IN JUST NINE HAPPY-LISTENING MINUTES.

* * * *

HERE'S A WEATHER QUIZ: WHAT'S THE TEMPERATURE RIGHT NOW? WHAT WILL IT BE LIKE TONIGHT? TOMORROW? IN THE DAYS AHEAD? YOU'LL GET A PERFECT SCORE ON THIS WEATHER QUIZ IF YOU STAY TUNED TO WZZZ— THE STATION THAT MAKES WEATHER AN IMPORTANT PART OF ITS SERVICE— THREE TIMES EACH HOUR. NEXT WZZZ WEATHER REPORT—JUST ELEVEN MINUTES OF GOOD MUSIC AWAY.

12.3 CLOCK RADIO PROMOS

BEFORE YOU GO TO BED TONIGHT—GET READY TO WAKE UP TO MUSIC TOMORROW. SET YOUR CLOCK RADIO AT THE 460 SPOT ON THE DIAL. THAT'S WZZZ—AND YOU'RE TUNED THERE RIGHT NOW.

* * * *

SACK TIME, OLD CHUM? REMEMBER, YOU'LL BE GETTING OUT OF BED ON THE BRIGHT SIDE TOMORROW IF YOU SET YOUR CLOCK RADIO AT THE 460 SPOT. IT'S WZZZ—THE BRIGHTEST THING IN ANYBODY'S MORNING.

* * * *

HEADING FOR BED? YOU'LL HAVE A BRIGHTER TOMORROW IF YOU SET YOUR CLOCK RADIO DIAL AT THE 460 SPOT. RADIO 460—THAT'S WZZZ— WHERE YOU WAKE UP TO MUSIC.

* * * *

IF YOU WOKE UP TIRED, NERVOUS, TENSE THIS MORNING, WHY NOT ROLL OUT THE HAPPY WAY TOMORROW? SET YOUR CLOCK RADIO DIAL AT THE 460 SPOT. THAT'S WZZZ—WHERE CENTERVILLE TUNES FOR MUSIC.

* * * *

MORNING CAN BE A PRETTY GROUCHY TIME. HERE'S HOW YOU CAN MAKE THINGS A LITTLE BETTER. SET YOUR CLOCK RADIO DIAL FOR WZZZ—AT THE 460 SPOT WHERE YOU'RE TUNED RIGHT NOW. TRY IT AND SEE IF WAKING UP TO WZZZ MUSIC DOESN'T MAKE THOSE EARLY HOURS A LITTLE EASIER TO TAKE.

* * * *

LADIES, IF YOUR HUSBAND IS LIKE I AM—KIND OF MEAN AND NASTY IN THE MORNING—WHY NOT EASE HIM OUT OF BED WITH MUSIC? SET YOUR CLOCK RADIO FOR WZZZ—THE 460 SPOT. AND, IF THAT DOESN'T WORK— LET HIM SLEEP. IT'S BETTER THAN FIGHTING.

NEWS PROMOS   12.4

GET THE FULL SCOPE OF THE NEWS—REPORTED TO THE WZZZ NEWSROOM BY REPORTERS FROM EVERY CORNER OF THE WORLD. YOU'RE NEVER MORE THAN MINUTES AWAY FROM THE FAST-BREAKING NEWS WHEN YOU STAY TUNED TO WZZZ. WZZZ—THE 460 SPOT FOR NEWS.

* * * *

THE FAST, ACCURATE REPORTS THAT KEEP YOU ON TOP OF THE BIG NEWS EVENTS . . . THEY'RE YOURS EVERY HOUR, EVERY DAY WHEN YOU KEEP YOUR RADIO DIAL SET AT THE 460 SPOT. THAT'S WZZZ—WHERE CENTER-VILLE TUNES FOR NEWS.

* * * *

HUNDREDS OF CORRESPONDENTS IN EVERY CORNER OF THE GLOBE ARE AT WORK GATHERING AND EVALUATING THE NEWS YOU HEAR ON WZZZ. NO NEWS EVENT IN THE WORLD IS MORE THAN MINUTES AWAY WHEN YOU STAY TUNED TO WZZZ.

* * * *

IF IT'S NEWS, YOU'LL HEAR IT RIGHT HERE AT THE 460 SPOT ON YOUR RADIO DIAL. GET THE LAST WORD FIRST ON WZZZ.

* * * *

WHERE THERE'S NEWS—THERE'S WZZZ. WHATEVER IT IS, WHEREVER IT HAPPENS—YOU'LL KNOW ABOUT IT WHEN IT HAPPENS IF YOU KEEP YOUR RADIO DIAL SET AT 460 . . . THAT'S WZZZ—THE SPOT FOR NEWS.

* * * *

GET THE WZZZ NEWS HABIT—AND GET THE NEWS.

* * * *

WZZZ—WHERE THE NEWS BREAKS FIRST.

* * * *

LIKE HAVING A DIRECT LINE TO THE BIG NEWS EVENTS OF THE WORLD— THAT'S THE NEWS YOU ENJOY WHEN YOU STAY TUNED TO 460. WHEREVER IT HAPPENS, AND WHENEVER, 24 HOURS A DAY—YOU'LL HEAR IT FAST, YOU'LL HEAR IT ACCURATELY—BY EXPERIENCED WZZZ REPORTERS. FROM NEWS BREAK TO YOUR LIVING ROOM—INSTANTANEOUSLY!

* * * *

WHAT BIG NEWS STORIES WILL BREAK TODAY? WILL YOU BE FIRST TO HEAR THEM? YOU WILL WHEN YOU STAY TUNED TO 460. BIG NATIONAL EVENTS AND IMPORTANT LOCAL STORIES—ALL YOURS WITHIN SECONDS OF THEIR HAPPENING! YOU'LL BE FIRST IN THE KNOW WITH WZZZ!

12.5   CHARACTER PROMOS

These promos need a bouncy opening employing funny music, and should have a close using your softest musical jingle ending. These will give you an opportunity to use a great many of the people on your staff, since they require a large variety of character voices. Above each spot we have indicated the type of voice we think is required for the greatest effectiveness.

(Squeaky old maid)

Woman: MY NAME IS MYRTLE WEDEKIND. I'M A SCHOOLTEACHER—AND I LISTEN TO WZZZ RADIO. AFTER SPENDING ALL DAY WITH THOSE LITTLE MONSTERS THAT THE SCHOOL BOARD LIKES TO REFER TO AS STUDENTS . . . WELL, A GIRL HAS TO DO SOMETHING. AND WZZZ IS THE HAPPIEST SOMETHING I KNOW. BESIDES, THERE'S NO ONE AROUND TO PLAY MAH JONG WITH ANYMORE.

* * * *

(Big, phoney cultured voice)

Man: MY NAME IS CHARLES EMERSON FAIRWORTHY. I'M A BANK PRESIDENT—AND I LISTEN TO WZZZ. PURE GOLD THAT STATION. IT'S GOT A SOUND THAT'S ALMOST AS HAPPY AS HARD CASH. YES, SIR, YOU CAN BANK ON WZZZ . . . I SAID, YOU CAN BANK ON WZZZ . . . WELL, THEY THOUGHT THAT WAS QUITE UPROARIOUS AT THE LAST BOARD MEETING.

* * * *

(High-pitched, excited voice)

Man: MY NAME IS BOOT 'EM HOME BILLY BROOKS. I'M A JOCKEY—AND I LISTEN TO WZZZ. LIKE I TELL THE FELLOWS AT THE RACETRACK, YOU'RE ALWAYS RIDING A WINNER WHEN YOU STAY ON WZZZ. THERE'S JUST ONE THING THOUGH . . . I KNOW THEY DON'T HAVE A LICENSE TO OPERATE A RACETRACK—SO HOW COME THOSE WZZZ DISC JOCKEYS ARE ALL THE TIME HORSING AROUND?

* * * *

(Typical gushing movie starlet)

Woman: MY NAME IS MEGAN BRITTANY-MORGAN—AND I AM A MOVIE ACTRESS. WE'RE HERE IN (town) MAKING A SUPER-EPIC OF LIFE IN THE BIG APPLE CALLED "HOW THE WEST SIDE WAS LOST." IT'S GOING TO BE JUST GREAT—AND I WANT ALL OF YOU TO COME AND SEE IT. BUT, IN THE MEANTIME, WHILE I HAVE BEEN HERE IN (town), I'VE BEEN LISTENING TO WZZZ. IT'S JUST A DARLING RADIO STATION. DON'T YOU THINK SO? JUST SOOOOO

PRECIOUS. AND, NOT ONLY THAT—BUT THAT CUTE (program director) SAID HE WAS GOING TO MAKE ME A STAR.

* * * *

(Ivy league accent)

Man: THIS IS LUCIUS CARLSON—AND I'M A PROFESSIONAL WINE-TAS-TER. JUST TASTE, TASTE, TASTE—ALL DAY LONG. BUT IT'S A FUN JOB. I JUST WANT TO TELL ALL YOU OTHER CONNOISSEURS OF THE FINER THINGS IN LIFE THAT I, TOO, LISTEN TO WZZZ. IT'S AS DELIGHTFUL TO THE EAR AS A WONDERFUL BOTTLE OF CHATEAU NEUF '47 IS TO THE PALATE. AND NOW—(popping sound)—AS WE SAY IN THE TRADE . . . BOTTOMS UP.

* * * *

(Tough, with a hint of Brooklynese)

Man: THIS IS DAN MUSCLEBOUND. I'M A WEIGHT LIFTER—AND I LIS-TEN TO WZZZ. YES, SIR, LISTENING TO WZZZ JUST GIVES YOU A GOOD FEELING ALL OVER—LIKE DOING A MILITARY PRESS WITH A FIVE HUNDRED POUND WEIGHT. AND I'VE HAD A LOT OF TIME TO LISTEN LATELY, TOO—EVER SINCE I'VE BEEN IN BED HERE WITH THIS STRAINED BACK.

* * * *

(Drawling, California)

Man: MY NAME IS MARVIN SIMPSON. I'M A BEACHBUM—AND I DON'T DO MUCH OF ANYTHING EXCEPT SIT AROUND AND LISTEN TO WZZZ. THERE AREN'T MANY OF US BEACHBUMS AROUND HERE BECAUSE—WELL, YOU KNOW, THE WEATHER AND ROCKY BEACHES AND THINGS LIKE THAT. I'VE BEEN TRYING TO TALK THE WZZZ PEOPLE INTO MOVING THE WHOLE OPERATION TO TAHITI. BUT, UNTIL THEY DO, I'LL JUST STICK AROUND AND LISTEN.

* * * *

(Gruff, weary voice)

Man: THIS IS SAM STURGEON. I'M A BUS DRIVER. YOU PROBABLY READ ABOUT ME IN THE PAPERS. I'M THE GUY WHO FINALLY SOLVED THE PROBLEM OF HOW TO GET PEOPLE TO MOVE BACK

IN THE BUS. IT WAS EASY. I JUST PUT A RADIO IN THE BACK END AND TURN ON WZZZ. NOW, I'M TRYING TO FIGURE OUT HOW I CAN GET BACK THERE WITH THEM SO I CAN LISTEN TO WZZZ, TOO.

* * * *

(Affected English accent)

Man: MY NAME IS LANCE STERLING—AND I'M A PLAYBOY. I DON'T DO ANYTHING—BUT, BOY, DO I PLAY . . . BOY, DO I PLAY . . . THAT'S A LITTLE JOKE WE USE DOWN AT THE CLUB. ANYWAY, I LISTEN TO WZZZ—BECAUSE I'M RICH, AND I CARE ENOUGH TO HEAR THE VERY BEST. INCIDENTALLY, I WANT TO REMIND ALL OF YOU OTHER PLAYBOYS ABOUT THE BIG GOING-IN PARTY WE ARE HAVING NEXT WEEK. IT'S SORT OF A MATURE VERSION OF A COMING-OUT PARTY.

* * * *

(German accent)

Man: THIS IS ERIC VON SAUER-CRULLER—AND I AM AN ANIMAL-TRAINER. THOSE FEROCIOUS CREATURES—I JUST SNAP MY WHIP AND THEY DO THEIR TRICKS RIGHT NOW, BY GOLLY. HOO—I'M A MEAN ONE. BUT WHAT I WANTED TO SAY IS THAT I LISTEN TO WZZZ. IT SOOTHES MY NERVES AND KEEPS ME HAPPY AFTER A PERFORMANCE. TO TELL THE TRUTH, IT KEEPS ALL THOSE SNARLING ANIMALS HAPPY, TOO. OH YES,—JUST A LITTLE PLUG. COME AND SEE MY ACT. WE PERFORM EVERY NIGHT. IT'S THE WORLD FAMOUS ERIC VON SAUER-CRULLER FLEA CIRCUS.

* * * *

(Tough, gruff)

Woman: MY NAME IS ELSIE ARBUCKLE. I'M A METER MAID AND I LISTEN TO WZZZ. IN MY BOOK, WZZZ'S JUST THE TICKET. WHY LISTENING TO WZZZ IS MORE FUN THAN FINDING A CAR PARKED OVER-TIME HEADED THE WRONG WAY ON A ONE-WAY STREET WITH LAST YEAR'S LICENSE PLATES. AND, BELIEVE ME, THAT'S A LOT OF FUN.

* * * *

(Soft, little voice)

Man: MY NAME IS ELMER BOTTONLY. I'M A CRINKLER IN A CHOCO-
LATE FACTORY—SORT OF A FORGOTTEN MAN IN THE CANDY
BUSINESS. YOU SEE, NO ONE EVER STOPS TO THINK THAT SOME-
ONE HAS TO CRINKLE THOSE LITTLE BROWN PAPERS WE PUT
THE CHOCOLATES IN. ANYWAY, I LISTEN TO WZZZ. BUT THEN, I
GUESS EVERYBODY ELSE LISTENS TO WZZZ, TOO. THAT'S A
SWEET-SOUNDING STATION.

* * * *

(Bronx accent)

Man: THIS IS CARL FILBERT. I'M A TRUCK DRIVER, AND I LISTEN TO
WZZZ. THERE'S JUST NOTHING THAT MAKES THOSE MILES ON
THE HIGHWAY GO BY AS FAST AS HAVING WZZZ ON THE DIAL.
NOTHING, THAT IS, EXCEPT MAYBE HAVING YOUR BRAKES GO
OUT ON A HILL.

* * * *

(French accent)

Man: MY NAME IS JEAN PIERRE VALLON. SO EET IS NOT NECESSARY
TO TELL—BUT I AM A FRENCHMAN. AND I LISTEN TO WZZZ.
NOT MANY OF US FRENCHMEN LISTEN TO WZZZ. THEY ARE
TOO BUSY LOOKING AT BRIDGITTE BARDOT. AND WHO CAN
BLAME THEM?

* * * *

(Hillbilly accent)

Man: MA NAME IS JEETER WILLIAMS. AH'M THE MASH MAN ON A
STILL WE OPERATE UP HERE IN THE MOUNTAINS. AND AH LIS-
TEN TO WZZZ. LIKE WE SAY UP HERE IN THE MOUNTAINS—
WZZZ STILL IS THE GREATEST THING ON THE AIR. IT <u>STILL</u>
IS—GET IT? "STILL" IS . . . FORGET IT.

* * * *

(Broad, affected voice)

Woman: MY NAME IS DELILA. THAT'S ALL. JUST DELILA. I'M A NIGHT-CLUB ENTERTAINER . . . A SORT OF CHAN-TOOSY. THAT'S FRENCH FOR A SINGER. AND I LISTEN TO WZZZ. WZZZ IS THE MOST ENTERTAINING THING I KNOW. AND, BELIEVE ME, I KNOW.

* * * *

(Droolingly southern)

Woman: MA NAME IS HONEY CHILE MILDER. AH'M A SOUTHERN BELLE—AND LISTEN TO WZZZ. AH DON'T CARE WHAT THE REL-ATIVES SAY . . . EVEN IF IT IS YANKEE—AH LOOOOOOOOVE THAT WZZZ. SURE 'NUFF, AH DO, Y'ALL.

* * * *

(Stilted, automatic voice, with an electronic sound behind)

Man: THIS IS XZ 43 72 19 87. I'M A MARTIAN—AND I LISTEN TO WZZZ. ALL OF US MARTIANS DO. WZZZ IS THE GREATEST THING IN ANYBODY'S WORLD.

* * * *

(Deep voice)

Woman: THIS IS ALICE FLUMPF. I'M A BACHELOR GIRL. I THINK THAT'S SO MUCH NICER THAN SAYING "OLD MAID," DON'T YOU? WELL, ANYWAY, I LISTEN TO WZZZ. I'VE NEVER GOTTEN MARRIED BECAUSE I'VE ALWAYS BEEN TOO BUSY GOING STEADY WITH WZZZ. LOVE THAT STATION.

* * * *

(Midwestern twang)

Man: THIS IS PROFESSOR I.Q. HIGHDOME. I'M A PHYSISI . . . I'M A PHY-SISISIS . . . I DO SCIENTIFIC WORK. AND I LISTEN TO WZZZ. ALL OF US PHYSISIS . . . ALL OF US PHYSISISI . . . EVERYONE LISTENS TO WZZZ.

* * * *

(Veddy, veddy British)

Man: THIS IS LORD PERCIVAL KNOTTINGHAM. I'M A MEMBER OF BRIT-
ISH NOBILITY. MY BLOOD IS REALLY QUITE BLUE, YOU KNOW.
I'M A FORMER MEMBER OF THE PEERAGE. BUT I'VE GIVEN UP
PEERING—AND THESE DAYS I SPEND MY TIME LISTENING TO
WZZZ. I DON'T THINK WZZZ WILL EVER REALLY REPLACE
JOUSTING AND SLAYING DRAGONS—BUT, THEN, WE HAVEN'T
BEEN DOING MUCH OF THAT SORT OF THING LATELY, YOU
KNOW.

****

(Punchy fighter)

Man: THIS IS PUNCHY O'TOOLE. I'M A PUGEL-LETIST. THAT'S KIND OF
A FANCY WORD FOR A PRIZE-FIGHTER. I USED TO BE A CON-
TENDER. I AIN'T CONTENDERED IN QUITE A WHILE NOW. THESE
DAYS I JUST SPEND MY TIME LISTENING TO WZZZ. LIKE WE
USED TO SAY DOWN AT THE GYM—THAT WZZZ'S A LOT BET-
TER'N A KNOCK IN THE HEAD.

****

(Southern)

MAN: THIS IS BRECKENRIDGE B. BRECKENRIDGE. THAT MIDDLE "B"
STANDS FOR BOURBON—ON THE ROCKS, PLEASE. I'M A SENA-
TOR. AND I'M PROUD—YES, PROUD—TO BE ABLE TO TELL ALL
YOU WONDERFUL PEOPLE OUT THERE THAT I LISTEN TO WZZZ.
IN MY LINE OF BUSINESS, A MAN HAS TO DO A LOT OF TALKING.
BUT WHEN IT COMES TO LISTENING—WELL, SIR, WZZZ IS MY
KIND OF STATION.

12.6 NATIONAL RADIO MONTH

These "National Radio Month" on-air promos are a little different. They make
their point through humor and use your personalities effectively.

How It Works

All of these promos follow the same general pattern:

(musical opening)

Anncr: (Name) HERE. AND, FRIENDS, YOU KNOW THIS IS NATIONAL RADIO
MONTH. THEY'RE PUTTING RADIOS IN DARK GLASSES, HATS, AND

EVEN CHILDREN'S TOYS. SO BE SURE TO TURN OFF EVERYTHING—
EVEN YOUR HAT—BEFORE YOU GO TO SLEEP OR YOU MAY BE LIS-
TENING TO US ALL NIGHT.

(musical close)

* * * *

THIS IS (name)—AND SINCE MAY IS NATIONAL RADIO MONTH, ON BEHALF OF
MY SHOW I'D LIKE TO EXTEND MY THANKS TO MAXWELL SANGBORN, THE
INVENTOR OF THE CAT'S WHISKER CRYSTAL DETECTOR FOR HIS GREAT
CONTRIBUTION TO RADIO. THANKS, MAX. I'D ALSO LIKE TO THANK CATS
WHO LIVED IN THE EARLY PART OF THE TWENTIETH CENTURY—THEY
WEREN'T TOO CRAZY ABOUT SUPPLYING PARTS FOR EARLY RADIOS.

* * * *

THIS IS (name)—REMINDING YOU THAT MAY IS NATIONAL RADIO MONTH. IN
HONOR OF THE OCCASION, I'D LIKE TO ANSWER A QUESTION THAT WE IN
THE BROADCASTING BUSINESS ARE OFTEN ASKED. A GREAT MANY PEOPLE
WANT TO KNOW HOW THEY, TOO, CAN GET INTO RADIO. WELL—YOU JUST
TAKE OFF THE BACK OF THE SET AND CRAWL INSIDE . . .

* * * *

THIS IS (name)—DURING NATIONAL RADIO MONTH WITH MY ABBREVIATED
COURSE IN ELECTRONICS. DO YOU REALLY KNOW WHAT GOES ON INSIDE
YOUR RADIO? WELL, FIRST, THERE'S THIS LITTLE LIGHT, SEE? (fading off . . .)
AND, THEN THERE'S SOME GIZMOS AND THING-A-MA-BOBS. . .

* * * *

(high, squeaky-voiced character) HI, THIS IS (name)—HOPING THAT ALL OF YOU
OUT THERE REMEMBER THAT MAY IS NATIONAL RADIO MONTH. MANY OF
YOU HAVE WONDERED WHAT ATTRIBUTES IT TAKES TO BECOME A RADIO
PERFORMER. WELL, THE FIRST THING IS A GOOD VOICE. WHEN I FIRST
STARTED OUT, FOR INSTANCE, I USED TO HAVE A HIGH, FUNNY-SOUNDING
VOICE. BUT I KEPT WORKING AT IT AND FINALLY DEVELOPED THE BEAUTI-
FUL SPEAKING VOICE THAT YOU NOW HEAR. THANK YOU.

* * * *

HI, THIS IS (name)—WITH A REMINDER THAT MAY IS NATIONAL RADIO
MONTH. I'M ON THE RADIO, OF COURSE, ON STATION WZZZ EVERY DAY

FROM TEN A.M. TO THREE IN THE AFTERNOON . . . AND IF YOU DON'T LIS-TEN TO MY PROGRAM, I WON'T VALIDATE YOUR PARKING TICKET.

* * * *

THIS IS (name)—REMINDING YOU THAT MAY IS NATIONAL RADIO MONTH . . . TIME TO GIVE PAUSE AND THINK ABOUT WHAT A WONDERFUL MEDIUM RADIO REALLY IS. ONE OF THE GREATEST THINGS ABOUT RADIO IS THAT, IF YOU DON'T LIKE WHAT YOU ARE HEARING, YOU CAN JUST TWIST THAT KNOB AND (SFX: tuning across the radio dial)

* * * *

THIS IS (name)—WITH A MAY NATIONAL RADIO MONTH REMINDER. IT'S ONLY THROUGH THE MAGIC OF RADIO THAT I'M BROUGHT TO YOU EACH DAY. SO, WHAT ARE YOU GOING TO DO ABOUT IT?

* * * *

THIS IS (name)—REMINDING YOU WHEN YOU KISS YOUR RADIO TODAY, GIVE IT A LITTLE EXTRA PAT BECAUSE MAY IS NATIONAL RADIO MONTH. AND I'M INSIDE HERE. SEE ME? OVER HERE, NEXT TO THE FILTER CAPACITOR!

* * * *

HELLO OUT THERE IN RADIO-LAND—THAT'S THE WAY THEY USED TO SAY IT IN OUR BUSINESS. THIS IS (name) WITH A REMINDER THAT MAY IS NATIONAL RADIO MONTH. IT SEEMS A PROPER TIME TO STOP FOR A MOMENT TO SAY THANKS TO MARCONI WHO STARTED THE WHOLE THING. THANKS, MARK.

* * * *

HEY, DID YOU KNOW THAT MAY IS NATIONAL RADIO MONTH? THIS IS (name)—AND, SURE, A LOT OF YOU ARE PROBABLY SMARTIES AND KNOW THAT . . . BUT I'LL BET NOT MANY OF YOU KNOW THAT EVERY DAY IN THE UNITED STATES, MORE THAN 200 MILLION PEOPLE LISTEN TO THE RADIO. ISN'T THAT WONDERFUL? WELL, THEN, ISN'T IT KIND OF NICE, ANYWAY? . . . WELL, SAME TO YOU, BUD!

* * * *

HI THERE. THIS IS (name) OF WZZZ RADIO. THIS IS NATIONAL RADIO MONTH.

SURVEYS SHOW THAT FOUR OUT OF EVERY FIVE AMERICANS ARE LISTEN-ING TO A RADIO EACH DAY. THAT'S AMAZING, ISN'T IT? I KNOW TODAY'S RADIO CAN GET PRETTY LOUD, BUT I DIDN'T KNOW THAT MANY PEOPLE COULD GET CLOSE ENOUGH TO HEAR A RADIO ALL AT ONCE.

Index

Other Bestsellers of Related Interest

HOME-BASED MAIL ORDER: A Successful Guide for Entrepreneurs—William J. Bond

Start a profitable mail order business at home—no experience necessary! This motivational guide shows you how to select a marketable product or service, identify your target market and advertising medium, create a dynamic offer, handle advertising and promoting, and get the most from your printing budget—without taking unnecessary financial risks. 224 pages. Book No. 3045, $29.95 hardcover only

THE BUSINESSPERSON'S LEGAL ADVISOR —Cliff Roberson

Avoid legal problems and find out how to get the best legal advice when needed at the least possible cost. This handy legal survival guide covers all the major legal questions that can affect today's small- or medium-sized businesses. 236 pages. Book No. 3547, $19.95 paperback only

SMALL BUSINESS TAX ADVISOR: Understanding the New Tax Law—Cliff Roberson

Practical, easy-to-follow advice to help you plan how to minimize your taxes is right here in this must-have guide. Roberson gives you strategies for tax liability deductions . . . shows you how to rearrange your financial affairs to discover maximum new tax advantages . . . and deals with amortization of property, capital gains and losses, modified depreciation rules, tax credits, and more. 175 pages. Book No. 30024, $12.95 paperback only

CREDIT AND COLLECTIONS FOR YOUR SMALL BUSINESS—Cecil J. Bond

Gain the credit managing skills you need to reduce losses and increase cash flow for a successful business. You can • set up or overhaul an operational credit department • monitor acounts, collections, and bad debt • recognize problem situations • establish a sound credit policy • monitor bankruptcy proceedings • and more. 192 pages. Book No. 30035, $28.95 hardcover only

SUCCESSFUL BUSINESS FORECASTING —Joan Callahan Compton and Stephen B. Compton

Use forecasting techniques successfully—without having to memorize equations or perform tedious calculations. This plain-English guide shows you how to apply proven statistical techniques to any forecasting problem . . . gauge where best to allocate your company's resources . . . and more. Plus it shows you how to turn your PC into an accurate forecasting machine, test your forecast, make adjustments, and how and when to figure in outside factors. Includes practical sample situations, examples, and methods to help you successfully control your company's future. 214 pages. Book No. 30059, $21.95 hardcover only

SITE SELECTION: Finding and Developing Your Best Location—Kay Whitehouse, CCIM

"I highly recommend it . . . should be required reading and used as a guide to make sure the Realtor is showing the best sites."

—**Roger B. Baumgartner, Realtor**
CCIM, the Baumgartner/Bennett Co.

This time-saving guide can help you spot location pitfalls—visibility, pollution, inadequate utilities, and more—before it's too late. Avoid headaches with Whitehouse's "50 red flags" to watch out for. Use them to analyze a property . . . select the best sites in tourist areas . . . and steer clear of problems with impact fees and future assessments, deed restrictions, traffic jammers, signage problems, and more. 192 pages, 21 illustrations. Book No. 30053, $21.95 hardcover only

GETTING OUT: A Step-by-Step Guide to Selling Business or a Professional Practice
—Lawrence W. Tuller

" . . . this book should be in every business owner's (or would-be business owner's) library and should be read often."

—**Roman P. Fedirka**
Vice President and Chief Financial Officer
ANALYTICS

Selling your business or practice can be a tough decision—both professionally and emotionally. Now you can get top dollar for your business, cope with letting go and move on to new ventures. This thorough guide eases you step-by-step through the selling process from planning the sale to preparing closing documents. Use it to calculate the right asking price, assess the best timing for the sale, locate the right buyer, assist buyer financing and more. 320 pages. Book No. 30063, $24.95 hardcover only

Prices Subject to Change Without Notice.

Look for These and Other TAB Books at Your Local Bookstore

To Order Call Toll Free 1-800-822-8158
(in PA, AK, and Canada call 717-794-2191)

or write to TAB BOOKS, Blue Ridge Summit, PA 17294-0840.

Title	Product No.	Quantity	Price

☐ Check or money order made payable to TAB BOOKS

Charge my ☐ VISA ☐ MasterCard ☐ American Express

Acct. No. _____ Exp. _____

Signature: _____

Name: _____

Address: _____

City: _____

State: _____ Zip: _____

Subtotal $ _____

Postage and Handling
($3.00 in U.S., $5.00 outside U.S.) $ _____

Add applicable state and local
sales tax $ _____

TOTAL $ _____

TAB BOOKS catalog free with purchase; otherwise send $1.00 in check or money order and receive $1.00 credit on your next purchase.

Orders outside U.S. must pay with international money order in U.S. dollars

TAB Guarantee: If for any reason you are not satisfied with the book you order, simply return it (them) within 15 days and receive a full refund.